EDUCATION AND PSYCHOLOGY OF THE GIFTED SERIES

James H. Borland, Editor

*Planning and Implementing Programs
for the Gifted*
James H. Borland

*Patterns of Influence on Gifted Learners:
The Home, the Self, and the School*
Joyce L. VanTassel-Baska
Paula Olszewski-Kubilius
EDITORS

*Reaching the Gifted Underachiever:
Program Strategy and Design*
Patricia L. Supplee

The Academic Acceleration of Gifted Children
W. Thomas Southern
Eric D. Jones
EDITORS

*Understanding the Gifted Adolescent:
Educational, Developmental, and Multicultural Issues*
Marlene Bireley
Judy Genshaft
EDITORS

*Conducting Research and Evaluation in Gifted Education:
A Handbook of Methods and Applications*
Nina K. Buchanan
John F. Feldhusen
EDITORS

Conducting
Research and Evaluation
in Gifted Education

A Handbook of
Methods and Applications

Edited by
Nina K. Buchanan
John F. Feldhusen

Teachers College, Columbia University
New York and London

Published by Teachers College Press, 1234 Amsterdam Avenue
New York, NY 10027

Library of Congress Cataloging-in-Publication Data

Conducting research and evaluation in gifted education : a handbook of
  methods and applications / edited by Nina K. Buchanan and John F.
  Feldhusen.
      p.   cm.—(Education and psychology of the gifted series ; 6)
  Includes bibliographical references and index.
  ISBN 0-8077-3083-1.—ISBN 0-8077-3082-3 (pbk.)
  1. Gifted children—Education—Research—United States.
  2. Special education—Research—United States.   3. Educational
  evaluation—United States.   I. Buchanan, Nina K.   II. Feldhusen,
  John Frederick, 1926-   .   III. Series.
  LC3993.9.C67   1991
  371.95'0973—dc20   91-11269

Printed on acid-free paper

Manufactured in the United States of America

98 97 96 95 94 93 92 91   8 7 6 5 4 3 2 1

CONTENTS

Foreword, *by James H. Borland* vii
Introduction 1
    Nina K. Buchanan and John F. Feldhusen

Part I The Research Process 7

1 In Pursuit of a Problem 9
    Nina K. Buchanan and M. Elizabeth Nielsen

2 Beyond Summary: Constructing a Review
of the Literature 33
    Pamela R. Clinkenbeard

3 Experimental Research 51
    Paula M. Olszewski-Kubilius and Rena F. Subotnik

4 Making Sense of Your Data 69
    Paula M. Olszewski-Kubilius and Marilynn J. Kulieke

**Part II Specific Applications of Research Methodologies
to Gifted Education** 93

5 Developmental and Longitudinal Research 95
    Frances S. O'Tuel

6 Ethnographic Perspective: From Beginning
to Final Product 114
    Sara W. Lundsteen

7 Single-Subject Research with Gifted and Talented
Students 137
    R. H. Swassing and Susan R. Amidon

8 Case Study Research in Gifted Education 157
    Sidney M. Moon

9 Using Prediction Methods: A Better Magic Mirror 179
    *Douglas L. Murphy and Reva C. Friedman
(Jenkins)*

v

10   Multivariate Techniques for Gifted Education   201
     Michael C. Pyryt and Ronald H. Heck

11   Meta-Analysis   220
     J. William Asher

Part III   Program Evaluation   **243**

12   Evaluation of Gifted Programs   245
     Kyle R. Carter

13   Evaluating Gifted Programs with Locally
     Constructed Instruments   275
     M. Elizabeth Nielsen and Nina K. Buchanan

14   Tests in Perspective: The Role and Selection of
     Standardized Instruments in the Evaluation of
     Programs for the Gifted   311
     Ann Robinson

     About the Contributors   333

     Index   337

FOREWORD

The frequently noted paucity of research on the nature and nurture of gifted children is much like the weather; many complain about it, few do anything about it. Nina Buchanan and John Feldhusen are a happy exception to this rule. While the rest of us complained, they took steps to do something about the problem, the result being the book you now hold in your hands.

This volume, the sixth in the *Education and Psychology of the Gifted Series* from Teachers College Press, is a much needed, long overdue, and very welcome addition to the scholarship of the field. Its publication should be good news to all producers and consumers of research on the gifted. It fills not a niche in the literature, but a gaping hole.

I must confess that my interest in this collection is somewhat selfish. I conduct a dissertation seminar for doctoral students in the Program in the Education of the Gifted at Teachers College. For some time, I have wished for a comprehensive volume that not only would address issues relating to research design, measurement, statistics, and evaluation, but would do so in a manner that reflects an awareness of the unique problems faced by those conducting inquiry into the education and psychology of the gifted. This book answers that need, both to my delight and to that of my long-suffering students.

The appeal of this book should, however, extend well beyond the relatively small circle described above. The information contained between these covers should inform the thinking and practice of anyone who conducts, uses, or reads evaluations, literature reviews, and research. That is to say, it should be of use to all of us in the field of the gifted.

The strengths of this collection are too many to enumerate here without serious omission. However, I am particularly pleased to see fine chapters on such neglected topics as conducting literature reviews, longitudinal research, ethnography, single-subject research, case studies, multivariate techniques, and meta-analysis. The remaining chapters, which treat more familiar issues, are notable for the cogency of their presentation and the skillful manner in which their authors relate methodological concerns to the peculiarities of the field of the gifted.

vii

As a field, we owe a collective debt of thanks to Nina Buchanan, John Feldhusen, and the contributors to this valuable collection. The publication of this book will not, in and of itself, remedy the problems attributable to our exiguous data base. It will, however, invalidate many of our excuses for not doing something about them.

JAMES H. BORLAND, EDITOR
Education and Psychology
of the Gifted Series

Conducting Research and Evaluation in Gifted Education

A Handbook of Methods and Applications

INTRODUCTION

Nina K. Buchanan and John F. Feldhusen

In the field of gifted education our past research and evaluation efforts, like Terman's seminal study (1925), have broken new ground by providing sound information about gifted persons and enlarging our perspective of issues related to gifted and talented students. However, the effort has been inconsistent. It has "waxed and waned for many decades" (Feldhusen, 1989, p. 3). We have moved forward slowly through unsympathetic political and economic times and more rapidly during times of financial and philosophical support.

Our knowledge base derived from research and evaluation is available through journals that specialize in gifted education, such as the *Gifted Child Quarterly, Journal for the Education of the Gifted, Roeper Review*, and *Gifted Child International*, and through general educational psychology or psychology publications, such as *Child Development* or the *Journal of Educational Psychology*. In order to better understand "the nature of the research enterprise in gifted education," Pyryt (1988, p. 2) examined articles that appeared in the *Gifted Child Quarterly* from 1980 through 1988. He found that 39.7% of the articles during that eight-year period were research articles and 4% were evaluation reports. Although research was well represented in this sample, upon closer inspection, Pyryt found that less sophisticated designs were more predominant than expected. Even though multivariate techniques seem appropriate for use in gifted education in order to deal with the complex, multifaceted phenomena of giftedness, most of the articles limited their analyses to univariate statistics.

In a similar effort to understand the nature of prominent journal articles, Carter and Swanson (1989) analyzed 600 articles related to gifted education that had appeared in the literature since the Marland Report in 1972. They identified the 25 most frequently cited articles and further compared them to a random sample of 25 other articles in gifted education. The prominent gifted journal articles were less often cited than articles in other special education areas. Only 29% of the prominent and

1

24% of the comparison articles reported original research. These percentages, when compared to other disciplines, are also low. Seventy-nine percent of the prominent and 92 percent of the randomly selected articles received no support from external funding sources. Our efforts in gifted education might well be spent locating, or even creating, new sources of research funds through professional and political action.

Carter and Swanson also found that issues related to identification, such as general identification, definitions, and concepts of giftedness, and tests and testing overshadow (49.5%) important issues such as teaching strategies and techniques (4.2%), social/emotional adjustment (8%), and research methodology/program evaluation (4.2%). Clearly, researchers and practitioners have focused on issues related to identification and neglected equally important areas such as program evaluation, teaching strategies, and counseling. These areas are now in need of exploration and development through new avenues of research and evaluation.

Has this work in the area of identification affected our definitions of giftedness and conceptions of intelligence? Our definitions of giftedness have responded to changes in philosophies and theories of intelligence. Initially, we relied on intelligence as defined by the Stanford-Binet Intelligence Scale (Terman & Merrill, 1973) and the Wechsler Intelligence Scale for Children–Revised (Wechsler, 1974). Many school districts identified students to participate in gifted programs by IQ scores of 130 and above on these measures. Recently, however, these standards are being challenged by competing definitions of intelligence from researchers and theorists such as Guilford (1967), Gardner (1983), and Sternberg (1985). They are also being challenged by practitioners who are exploring alternative methods of assessment. However, it remains to be seen how the new theories and approaches affect programs for gifted students.

Researchers and evaluators in gifted education need to systematically attend to the political, economic, social, and technological changes that have moved us closer to becoming a global village. This means addressing issues such as cultural diversity. For example, in California, Caucasians or Euro-Americans, once a majority, are now one of several minorities. Research samples need to become representative of the population, not limited to traditional, middle- to upper-SES, white students. At the same time, we will need to design programs that meet the needs of a more diverse array of gifts and talents. For example, the Center for Native Hawaiian Gifted and Talented Children (Nā Pua No'eau) incorporates native Hawaiian values, language, arts and crafts, and traditional activities in the curriculum for gifted and talented students. This, we believe, will enhance native Hawaiian students' images of themselves as well as enrich other gifted students and help them to appreciate and value the Hawaiian culture. Evaluation and carefully designed research studies of such programs will contribute to our understanding of gifted students and the ideal of a global community.

Along with changes in our views of intelligence and the blurring of majority/minority cultures, challenges such as pollution, overpopulation, energy shortages, and the greenhouse effect threaten our existence. We may now begin to see that all talents and abilities should be nurtured in order to address these problems, not just traditional verbal and quantitative performance on achievement or intelligence tests. In addition, we may begin to value and nurture creativity, innovation, and invention to a greater degree than we do at present.

Several years ago a group of concerned educators of the gifted met and assessed the current status of research and evaluation in gifted education. From this and subsequent meetings we raised important questions related to our knowledge of gifted and talented children. Although we did not agree on all of the issues, we did agree that the field of gifted education needed more timely, high-quality research and evaluation specific to gifted and talented students and programs. One of the outcomes of our discussions was a special issue of the *Gifted Child Quarterly* on research and evaluation (Feldhusen, 1986). Another outcome of our discussions was the facilitation of research and evaluation sessions at the National Association for Gifted Children (NAGC) annual meetings. Currently, the NAGC annual meeting features a strand on research and evaluation, recognizes excellence in research through several special awards, and supports sessions that translate research into practice for school personnel. The third major outcome of our meetings was this volume.

This text provides teachers, administrators, graduate students, and others who have an interest in gifted education with a practical guide that will enable them to critically read and interpret research in gifted education. Further, it is a handbook of methods and applications to assist them in conducting research related to gifted students and programs for the gifted.

In Part I, "The Research Process," the four chapters are designed to help novice researchers or evaluators get started. The first chapter explains how to use a creative problem-solving process in identifying and stating problems and research questions in gifted education. The second discusses how to write a review of the literature that will form the foundation for a research question or be an end in itself. Reviews of the research help teachers and administrators make sound, research-supported decisions about gifted and talented programs. The next chapter describes the application of experimental and quasi-experimental designs to questions in gifted education. Chapter 4 introduces methods for organizing and analyzing data.

Part II consists of seven chapters, each of which examines a specific research methodology: developmental/longitudinal research, ethnography, single-subject research, case studies, classification and prediction, multivariate techniques, and meta-analysis. These include qualitative as well as quantitative methods and univariate as well as multivariate techniques. Each chapter illustrates the method discussed with examples from research in gifted education.

Part III focuses on special issues related to evaluating gifted programs. Chapter 12 provides an overview of program evaluation, while Chapters 13 and 14 deal with measurement of program outcomes through informal and formal assessment.

This book would not have been possible without the assistance of many experts in the field of gifted education. We thank members of the Research and Evaluation Division of NAGC for providing impetus and reviewing manuscripts. In particular we thank Susan Amidon, Dorothy Armstrong, John O. Cooper, Dewey Cornell, Bonnie Cramond, Rita Culross, Deborah Dillon, Francoys Gagne, Carole Harris, Susan Johnsen, Lannie Kanevsky, Peggy Lazarus, Susan Linnemeyer, Sidney Moon, Kathy Peckron, Ruth Robison, Karen Rogers, Michael Saylor, Gina Schack, Saundra Sparling, Ray Swassing, and Carol Wolfe for providing critical feedback on the chapters and checking them for technical accuracy.

As the need for gifted education grows in the United States and throughout the world, we must continually update, revise, and add to our knowledge base in gifted education. Research and evaluation, with their accompanying methodologies and tools, should provide a foundation for our efforts. Overall our goal in writing this text is to provide clear, simple, and complete explanations of the processes, methods, and tools that are most appropriate for use in studying gifted students and evaluating programs.

REFERENCES

Carter, K. R., & Swanson, H. L. (1989, March). *An analysis of the most prominent gifted journal articles since the Marland Report: Implications for research.* Paper presented at the annual meeting of the American Educational Research Association, San Francisco, CA.

Feldhusen, J. F. (Ed.) (1986). Special focus on research. *Gifted Child Quarterly, 30,* 1–48.

Feldhusen, J. (1989). Introduction. In J. Feldhusen, J. VanTassel-Baska, & K. Seeley (Eds.), *Excellence in educating the gifted* (pp. 1–10). Denver, CO: Love Publishing Company.

Gardner, H. (1983). *Frames of mind.* New York: Basic Books.

Guilford, J. P. (1967). *The nature of human intelligence.* New York: McGraw-Hill.

Marland, S. P. (1972). *Education of the gifted and talented* (Report to the Subcommittee on Education, Committee on Labor and Public Welfare, U.S. Senate). Washington, DC: U.S. Government Printing Office.

Pyryt, M. C. (1988, November). *The* Gifted Child Quarterly *as a database.* Paper presented at the annual meeting of the National Association for Gifted Children, Orlando, FL.

Sternberg, R. J. (1985). *Beyond IQ: A triarchic theory of human intelligence.* Cambridge, MA: Cambridge University Press.

Terman, L. (1925). *Genetic studies of genius* (Vol. 1). Stanford, CA: Stanford University Press.

Terman, L., & Merrill, M. (1973). *Stanford-Binet intelligence scale.* Boston: Houghton Mifflin.

Wechsler, D. (1974). *Wechsler scale for children–revised.* New York: Psychological Corporation.

PART I

THE RESEARCH PROCESS

CHAPTER 1

IN PURSUIT OF A PROBLEM

Nina K. Buchanan and M. Elizabeth Nielsen

Contrary to some misconceptions of the nature of identification of problems in gifted education, the researcher or evaluator often has "only a
rather general, diffuse, even confused notion of the problem" (Kerlinger,
1986, p. 15). In this chapter we present a creative problem-solving framework to aid you in identifying and stating research and evaluation questions. We begin by suggesting ways you can build a broad background in
gifted education that will enable you to identify researchable problems
and meaningful evaluation questions. Next, we present a creative problem-solving approach that can be used as a guide in gathering facts,
posing clear, well-stated problems, and gaining acceptance of your ideas.
Finally, as a synthesis of this chapter, we provide a hypothetical example.

A BROAD VIEW

A sage once observed if you do not know where you are going, it is highly
unlikely that you will get there. Well-stated research problems and evaluation questions are necessary to clearly define the goal of a study and
provide within them the seeds of a solution. The foundation of problem
identification, however, is a knowledge of past and present projects,
connections with current researchers/evaluators and their work in progress, and the ability to flexibly view the field from a variety of perspectives.

Building a Knowledge Base

In gifted education becoming acquainted with the field means reading
early studies, reviews of literature, and model evaluation projects in a
systematic manner, being alert for patterns and trends from year to year
and recognizing forces outside the field that helped influence the direction of investigations. Some important reviews of research in gifted

education are Newland (1953), Goldberg (1958), Fliegler and Bish (1959), Barbe and Stephens (1961), and Gallagher (1966). In addition, there are several annotated bibliographies, such as Gowan (1961), Laubenfels (1976), Gallagher and Courtright (1986), and Anthony and Anthony (1981). These resources, along with general texts such as Witty (1951) and Barbe (1965), provide an historical perspective necessary for an understanding of the broad patterns of development of the field. At the same time you will be exposed to well-stated and not-so-well-stated research and evaluation problems.

Another valuable source of developmental information is publications such as the *Encyclopedia of Educational Research* (Ebel & Noll, 1969; Harris, 1960; Mitzel, 1982; Monroe, 1950). You might compare the entries for gifted education in each of the four volumes. To illustrate, we compared the 1950 and 1982 entries. In 1950, Norris, Hayslip, and Noonan in the entry entitled "Gifted Children" addressed the following areas:

> Characteristics of gifted children
>> Constancy of intelligence quotient
>> Physical traits
>> Social traits
>> Emotional traits
> Adapting the school to gifted children
> Needed research

By 1982 Renzulli and Delisle, writing about "Gifted Persons," explored the following:

> The role of the home/school in developing task commitment
> Learning styles of the gifted
> The identification of specific academic talent
> The development and refining of alternative identification instruments for very young and culturally different students
> The identification of a greater variety of sources of information about the gifted child
> Investigation of nontraditional/nonconventional systems of identification
> Development of evaluation instruments
> Assessment of effective programs
> Exploration of a wide range of program options

Identification, programming, and evaluation appear to be continuing concerns. As stated in 1950 (Norris, Hayslip, & Noonan), there are no infallible identification measures or perfect programs. By 1982, studies in gifted education investigated the role of the home and attempted to recognize a wider range of abilities and talents. Consistent with trends in other fields, gifted education began to consider development from birth to death, not just 5 to 18 years of age. Research on learning styles, information processing, and the total environment were also mentioned. From this brief example, it is apparent that comparisons of the past to the present can be excellent sources of ideas. Such comparisons assist the researcher/evaluator in building schema for gifted education.

Other valuable sources of information are journals that specialize in gifted education and *Dissertation Abstracts*. A systematic perusal of these will help you identify leading researchers and provide examples of problems, designs, and methodologies. For example, one might compare research and evaluation articles in different volumes of the *Gifted Child Quarterly*. (Of the 37 articles published in Volume 28, 15 were reports of research or evaluation; of the 32 published in Volume 31, 19 were studies.) Table 1.1 lists research categories, the number of studies in Volume 28, the number in Volume 31, and some sample research questions. From such a survey, you can begin to detect gaps in our knowledge and, what Gallagher (1966) refers to as redundant research, which you wisely may choose to eliminate from consideration.

Such a systematic but informal approach may identify research and evaluation currently being accepted for publication. It may also enable you to begin identifying gaps in the published literature that you might be interested in pursuing. This, along with knowledge from published reviews, *Encyclopedia* entries (such as Gallagher, 1969), and *Dissertation Abstracts*, will provide part of your essential background information.

Identifying Work in Progress

Most publications, however, lag behind current research and seldom report work in progress. One of the best sources of information in any field is the researcher/evaluator. There are many forums available that provide opportunities for interested scholars to meet and discuss current projects. Some of the most productive in gifted education are conferences sponsored by major organizations. These include the National Association of Gifted Children (NAGC), the Council for Exceptional Children, Talented and Gifted (CEC-TAG), and the American Educational Research Association Special Interest Group on the Intellectually Talented (AERA-SIG). At such conferences participants may attend for-

TABLE 1.1   Research reported in the *Gifted Child Quarterly*, Vols. 28 & 31

Category	Volume 28	31	Sample Problem Statements
Identification	1	2	
Characteristics	1		"The major question addressed by this study was: What learner personality characteristics are valued by teachers of the gifted" (Murphy, Jenkins-Friedman, & Tollefson, 1984, p. 31).
Self-concept		1	
Attitudes		1	
Learning Styles	2	1	
Achievement		1	
Adjustment	1		"The purpose of the present study was to examine the personal and social adjustment of elementary school pupils and compare it with that of their non-gifted peers" (Ludwig & Cullinan, 1984, p. 37).
Creativity		2	
Labeling		1	
Families/Parents	1	2	"The specific purpose of this study is to determine characteristics of the family environment which are correlated with personality adjustment among children who qualify for gifted programs" (Cornell & Grossberg, 1987, p. 59).
Program Evaluation	5	3	"The purpose of this study was to determine the effects of an enrichment program on the self-concept and creative thinking abilities of gifted elementary students" (Kolloff & Feldhusen, 1984, p. 53).
Teachers	1	1	
Special Populations	3	2	

mal research presentations and, equally as valuable, meet informally with others who share their interest in research or program evaluation. Since many experts make special presentations or serve in various leadership roles during these conferences, attendance makes it possible to become acquainted with them and their work. As you begin narrowing your problem for study, you may need to correspond with the authority who is

FIGURE 1.1   Possible perspectives from which to identify problems in gifted
education

HOME	COMMUNITY
•Parents	•School board members
•Siblings	•Business persons
•Significant others	•Local leaders
SCHOOL	•The media
•Peers	**LOCAL COLLEGE OR UNIVERSITY**
•Other gifted students	•Education professors
•Teachers of the gifted	•Professors in other disciplines
•Regular classroom teachers	•Graduate students
•Administrators	•Gifted students
•Other district personnel	•Administrators

known for work in that area. If you have previously met this person,
correspondence is often easier.

Considering Multiple Perspectives

Humans are bound by their roles. In order to see major patterns in the
fabric of gifted education, one must view the issues, questions and
concerns from a variety of perspectives. Figure 1.1 illustrates some possible vantage points. If the role of research, defined through a well-
stated problem, is to suggest solutions to a problem, to identify an
orderly system of relationships in order to explain occurrences not yet
verified, or to relate the known to intelligent guesses about the unknown
(Van Dalen, 1956), then a multifaceted view is preferable. One example
of this is a Ballering and Koch (1984) study that "compared the perceived relationships with all other family members from the perspective
of gifted and non gifted siblings of both sexes" (p. 40). Until this study,
this facet of family relations had not been addressed. By viewing the
unsolved problem through the siblings, one point of view, the researchers gained new insights and filled a gap in existing knowledge.
Another example is a study by Cramond and Martin (1987). They investigated the attitudes of experienced teachers and teachers in training
toward academically brilliant students in order to better understand the
forces within the school that shape the behavior of gifted students.
Through the perspective of teachers, Cramond and Martin learned
about students.

  In addition to knowing the literature and the published experts, researchers need to be in touch with those on the frontlines, teachers of the gifted, coordinators of gifted programs, administrators who are responsible for gifted programs, and parents. Through interaction with these groups, you gain insight from their perspectives. That might mean volunteering time in a gifted classroom to help with a special project, attending or speaking to a group of parents of gifted students, or arranging for an informal meeting of coordinators or administrators of gifted programs in your area. It may also mean assisting your local parent advocacy group or organization of gifted educators. In addition, you may have access to university courses in gifted and talented education that could enable you to examine class members' perceptions of problems in gifted education. We recently asked a group of graduate students (elementary and secondary teachers, some of whom were also parents of gifted children) in a gifted education class to identify problems that researchers/evaluators in gifted education should address. The following are some of their responses:

1. What are the most effective and efficient identifiers of culturally diverse gifted children?
2. What indicators of giftedness are most reliable in identifying young gifted children?
3. What long-term effect does teaching critical thinking through controversial topics have on gifted students' ability to critically analyze local, state, national, and international events?
4. Are students who attend special schools for the gifted more or less likely to be intellectual elitist as adults?
5. Which teaching technique, direct instruction/mastery learning or individualized educational plan, results in greater knowledge acquisition for gifted students?
6. What effect does teacher training in gifted education have on the classroom environment in fostering creativity, encouraging autonomous learning, and meeting the needs of a diverse gifted population?

It is clear that this group was a good source of possible problems.

In summary, the first step toward identifying a research problem is gaining a broad picture of the field of gifted education. Although reading past and present research is a necessary element, other important sources of knowledge include experts who are currently conducting studies and practitioners such as parents, teachers, administrators, and so on. Finally, your vision will be enlarged by considering many vantage points or perspectives of any potential problem. In the next section, the creative problem-solving process is presented as a framework for identifying and stating research problems, questions, and hypotheses.

A CREATIVE PROBLEM-SOLVING APPROACH

Creative problem solving is a recognized thinking tool valued by many in gifted education. Parnes (1967) elaborated and expanded Osborn's (1957) *Applied Imagination* into a flexible system that has been used in industrial think-tanks as well as educational settings as an aid to creative thinking and divergent production. As a researcher or evaluator this process will help you consider many possibilities, avoid premature closure, systematically select research topics, formulate questions and hypotheses, and propose methods for accomplishing the study or evaluation project. Figure 1.2 diagrams the process. First, the investigator encounters a *fuzzy mess*, or ill-defined problem. Then, he or she engages in *fact finding*, where known facts and additional data are gathered about the fuzzy mess. Next, during *problem finding*, the searcher begins formulating a problem and subproblems. Problem statements focus and direct *idea finding*, where more specific ideas related to the newly defined problem are considered. At the conclusion of idea finding, hypotheses are formulated in *solution finding*. The best ideas are combined, extended, and synthesized. The process is complete only after the *acceptance finding* step, during which an action plan is formulated. This plan might take a variety of forms depending on the likely audience and desired outcome. Each phase is detailed below.

FIGURE 1.2   An adaptation of the creative problem-solving process to problem identification in research and evaluation in gifted education

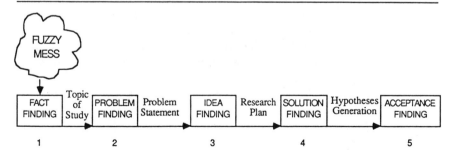

Fact Finding

Fact finding for a researcher or evaluator begins with the broad knowledge base discussed earlier. In the process of steeping yourself in the field of gifted education, you may have begun to identify a fuzzy mess that you would like to pursue. For a graduate student the mess may be to choose a topic for a thesis or dissertation; for a researcher or evaluator it may be to select a new area of study or a new direction within a given area. That mess may be related to identification, characteristics of gifted students, teachers of the gifted, families of the gifted, the highly creative but underachieving gifted, administrative options, program effectiveness, and so on. In fact finding you ask: What do I know about _____? This will involve a specific search of the literature and might include any and all of the sources listed above. It will also mean keeping notes or a journal with a record of all the possibilities. It might also mean brainstorming with a colleague or interested friend. This first phase of fact finding is divergent and should produce a great deal of information about a broad area or topic of study, such as key words and descriptors, definitions, past research results, and current research activity. It should also lead you to new questions.

During the second phase of fact finding, you establish and apply criteria to narrow the search. These criteria should be based on your reason for conducting the research or evaluation and generally accepted goals of experiments and evaluations.

Several authors provide reasons for engaging in the pursuit of a problem (Good, 1942; Sugden, 1973; Van Dalen, 1979; & Webb, 1961). Van Dalen (1979), for example, suggests that researchers consider both personal and social reasons for exploring a topic. Table 1.2 shows these reasons, along with guiding questions. All of these reasons can easily be applied to gifted education. For example, we have often been curious about how to identify gifted students who demonstrate their giftedness in areas unrecognized in the normal public school curriculum, such as mechanical ability or interpersonal communication skills. There are several reasons why we have not yet pursued this fuzzy mess. It may be congruent with our long-term goal of being specialists in giftedness, but, at this point, we do not have the necessary resources and therefore may not be able to generate the necessary data to even partially address the problem. In addition, society as defined in the school does not yet value these abilities to the extent that special programming might be possible. Given these limitations, we have chosen to examine other problems of personal and social significance.

TABLE 1.2   Reasons for exploring a topic

Reasons	Guiding Questions
Personal	
Interest	Am I curious about _____?
Goal Congruency	Do I want to be associated with this area in the future? How does this relate to my future career?
Competence	Is this something I can realistically study?
Resources	Are the necessary hardware and software available? Do I have the energy, time and money to invest in this study?
Access	Can I get to what I need in order to conduct this research or evaluation?
Data	Are the necessary data available or can they be generated given the time, cost, etc.?
Social	
Potential contribution	Will knowledge of _____contribute to our understanding of _____?
Uniqueness	Is this a relatively unexplored topic?
Specificity	Is this narrow enough to lead to conclusions that will get something accomplished?
Generalizability	Will this apply to other samples?

Webb (1961) organized a similar set of reasons for doing experiments into the following six, easy to remember *C*s:

Curiosity
Confirmability (Can the question asked be answered?)
Compassion (Will the results make things better?)
Cost
Cupidity (What's in it for me?)
Conformability (Is this currently an active area of inquiry?)

In general, you should consider how this area of study compares with previous studies, fills a gap in our knowledge, or corrects some errors of past studies. The topic should be generated by dissatisfaction with what we already know. You should avoid subjective topics that rest mainly on intuition, such as gender or racial differences in personality traits (e.g., compassion, warmth, or empathy), and studies that are really only clerical exercises, such as calculating the number of gifted programs in one geographic region compared to the number in another. At the conclusion of fact finding you should have an appropriate topic that meets the applied criteria, although you may not have a clearly stated problem. For example, you may have chosen underachievement as your fuzzy mess. At the conclusion of fact finding, you may have decided that what you really want to investigate are the crucial elements in the development of underachievement. You do not have a problem statement or any hypotheses, but you do have a topic. The next creative problem-solving step is problem finding.

Problem Finding

The first phase of problem finding is elaboration of the selected topic. Again, you would generate as many aspects of the topic and methods for exploring it as possible. Sidman (1960) provided four possible frames of reference for experiments. The first is testing hypotheses derived from theories. In gifted education that might mean exploring Sternberg's (1981) componential theory of intellectual giftedness. You might consider designing a study to verify a metacomponent, performance component, or an acquisition, retention, and transfer component. The second frame of reference is trying out a new method or technique. This might lead to an evaluation of different teaching techniques, grouping plans, or course content. Another frame of reference is the investigator's curiosity. Is this a topic that personally engages you, something you have always wanted to know? Finally, you might explore the conditions under which a phenomenon occurs. In gifted education that might mean trying and assessing different interventions for gifted underachievers.

From another point of view, Gephart and Ingle (1969) see problems as anomalies, uncharted areas, unverified facts of situations involving conflicting evidence. Your chosen topic might also be pursued through more than one frame or point of view.

After you have explored and recorded many possible problems related to your topic, restated and narrowed the problem, you will be prepared to evaluate the options, apply criteria similar to those applied after fact finding, and write a problem statement. According to Kerlinger

(1986), good problem statements should be instruments for supporting or refuting theory, testing the probability of relationships, not isolated facts, and enabling the researcher or evaluator sufficient objectivity to get outside his or her own opinions and values. Problem statements should express a relationship between two or more variables, be stated clearly in question form, and imply possible methods of testing the relationship (Kerlinger, 1986). For example, the topic of interest might be the effectiveness of a mathematics program for gifted high school students. The problem statement might be: What is the relationship between amount of time in the gifted mathematics program and achievement in college mathematics of graduates of _____ high school, 1985–1989? Notice that the problem statement expresses a relationship between variables, is stated as a question, and implies a method of measuring that relationship. It is not a hypothesis. The following are sample problem statements:

1. "Do teachers view the characteristics that define a creative personality as undesirable?" (Dettmer, 1981, p. 12)
2. "Would teachers of pupils of mixed abilities be able to differentiate between the gifted achiever and gifted underachiever in terms of the frequency with which each is likely to demonstrate behaviors indicative of superiority in basic skills, creative thinking, favorable self-concept, and leadership qualities?" (Sauernman & Michael, 1980, pp. 81–82)

Although problem statements are broad, good statements imply a method of investigation. For example, one researcher states: "The investigator will examine locus of control, goal setting and career maturity of gifted college women." This is not well stated because there is no question, it does not express relationships between the variables of locus of control, goal setting, and career maturity, and it does not imply a means of testing a relationship. It would be better to ask: What is the relationship among locus of control, goal setting, and career maturity of gifted college women in the sciences?

During this phase of problem finding you also identify and state subproblems. A good example of a problem and related subproblems is found in a study by Murphy, Jenkins-Friedman, and Tollefson (1984):

The major question addressed by this study was: What learner personality characteristics are valued by teachers of the gifted? Related questions were: Do teachers of the gifted agree with experts more or less than classroom teachers in 1963? Do teachers of the gifted differ from past and current experts in their conception of the ideal child, and if so, on what specific traits do they differ? Do past and current experts in gifted child education agree regarding which traits of the gifted and creative personality should be encouraged or discouraged in gifted students? (p. 31)

At the conclusion of problem finding, you should have a clearly stated problem and, if necessary, subproblems. You are then ready to engage in idea finding.

Idea Finding

During idea finding you will first generate ways of answering the questions you have posed. Remember to take advantage of local experts or those researchers or evaluators you have become acquainted with through readings and conference attendance. You might ask and answer questions such as the following:

1. What different ways might the experiment or evaluation be designed?
2. What instruments might be used to collect the data?
3. Who will be in the sample and from what geographic area might it come?
4. Will there be a control group and how will it be chosen?

In fact, several chapters in this text provide information about specific study and evaluation designs that will be helpful for you during idea finding. All possibilities should be explored.

Next, you will decide upon criteria to use in judging your ideas. They might include the availability of resources, both personnel and supplies, access to the sample and a comparison group, time to devote to the study, funds to pay for all aspects of the study, and other important considerations. At the conclusion of idea finding you should have a feasible design and be ready to continue the process through solution finding.

Solution Finding

During solution finding you will identify alternative hypotheses you might pose. These are extensions of the problem statement that are built on decisions made in idea finding regarding the design of the study. Many published studies in gifted education do not directly state a hypothesis but move from the problem to the procedures and results. For clarity and conformance to accepted research standards, experimental research studies should include one or more hypotheses. Surveys, however, generally state objectives rather than predictions, while evaluation studies may or may not have hypotheses.

According to Van Dalen (1956), hypotheses should express elements in an orderly system of relationships that seek to explain a condition that has not yet been verified by facts or to relate known facts to a theory or an intellectual guess about unknown conditions. They should state the underlying assumptions of the study.

Following are two sample hypotheses:

- H_1: "The self-concept scores in grades five and six will be significantly higher for all gifted children, regardless of program, than in the fifth- and sixth-grade population at large" (Maddux, Scheiber, & Bass, 1982, p. 78).
- H_2: "It was hypothesized that the group of pupils designated gifted high achievers in comparison to the group of pupils defined as gifted low achievers would exhibit higher mean scores on measures of constructs representing field independence, creativity and self-concept" (Sauernman & Michael, 1980, p. 82).

The first assumes that we can identify gifted students and differentiate them from regular students and that the type of program does not affect the self-concept of gifted students. It indicates a relationship between the self-concept of gifted and other fifth- and sixth-graders. In this hypothesis the authors, given their knowledge of past research and their own intuition, guess that the self-concept scores of the gifted students will be higher. It is unclear whether the study was designed to test a broader theory of giftedness.

The second hypothesis assumes that we can differentiate between gifted high and low achievers and measure constructs such as field independence, creativity, and self-concept. It clearly states the expected relationship and implies a method for testing it. Hypotheses clarify and operationalize the problem of the study.

After you have explored many alternatives, you formulate the ones to be investigated in the study. At this point you should have a topic, problem with subproblems, and in some cases hypotheses. The last phase of the creative problem-solving process applied to identifying problems in gifted education is acceptance finding.

Acceptance Finding

The best idea is of little value until it is used. During acceptance finding, a researcher or evaluator creates an action plan to move the idea into reality. A researcher might begin with an exploration of strategies for gaining approval from a dissertation committee, a grant agency, colleagues, or the school districts or agencies from which the sample will come. An evaluator, on the other hand, might explore strategies for gaining the approval of the school board, administration, teachers, and parents. This involves the following:

Identifying the people whose support and assistance you need to gain

Informally discussing your idea with appropriate persons (testing the waters)

Informally providing appropriate background information that will pave the way for acceptance

Identifying the optimum forum for your project

Formally presenting your idea to the most important or key person in authority

Formally presenting the project to secondary groups

For example, let us suppose you are a teacher of gifted students in a pullout program. After five years experience teaching in this program and a master's degree in gifted education, you decide that an experiment to determine whether the current pullout program (grades 3–8), when compared to a full-time gifted class program, is more or less effective in building positive self-concepts in the participating students. In order to make this determination, you decide that it would be possible to randomly place third-grade gifted students in either the pull-out program or a full-time class, provide similar academic content for both groups, and pre- and posttest for self-concept. How would you go about getting your idea accepted so that you could actually perform the experiment? First, you would identify the people whose support you would have to gain in order to proceed. Most likely you would begin by enlisting the support of your immediate supervisor (or in the case of a graduate student, the dissertation chair).

Next, broaden your support by meeting informally with key people such as the district gifted and talented coordinator, the principals whose students might be affected, the central administration, and a school board member who is sympathetic to issues related to gifted education. Discuss your ideas, beginning a dialogue that will hopefully lead them to accept the idea when it is formally presented later. This is the time when you listen at least as much as you talk. After each informal meeting, review the specific points made in favor of or in opposition to your idea.

When you have touched base with all the appropriate people, you will be able to decide what kind of background information each key person will need in order to support your project. This may mean preparing a select review of the literature to address areas of concern, or it may mean identifying a similar project that was successfully conducted in a similar district. These will prepare you for the formal steps to follow.

With the groundwork in place, you will need to decide what formal channel to pursue. Since it is important that your supervisor and colleagues support your idea to experiment with a full-time class for gifted students, you may decide that the most appropriate place to start is at the school level. In that case you would request time during a faculty meeting to provide background information about why the study would be important and what benefits it might have for the students and teachers. Next, you might make your presentation to the central administration or district office. If you have gained the support of your supervisor, the teachers and principals who will be affected, and the central administration, the school board presentation should introduce them to your idea and provide evidence of support from those who will be affected. On the other hand, in your informal approach you may have discovered that the most resistance came from the faculty and the most support from a school board member or administrator. In that case you may decide the forum is the central administration. You would then enlist their support to "sell" the idea. After you have gotten support from the key people, you will turn your attention to other affected groups, such as parents and students.

Do not assume everyone will think your idea is terrific. Instead, assume that you will need to sell the project through your knowledge and expertise, and through informal and formal communication, to gain support from those whose assistance you will need.

A BRIEF EXAMPLE

The creative problem-solving process can be a valuable tool in identifying and stating research and evaluation questions in gifted education. In order for you to better see how this might work in practice, we have included an abbreviated example. The fuzzy mess is attributions made by gifted students.

The first step is to identify what we know about attribution and, more specifically, what we know about attributions that gifted students make. A partial fact-finding list might include the following:

Locus of control

Controllability

Adult pattern

Experimental versus natural setting

Hypothetical versus personal self-report

Gifted students more internal

Development*

Specific attributions in mathematics*

Relationship to behavior

Stability

Dimensions

Instruments for measuring*

Global versus situation specific

In content areas

Effect of significant adults on*

Adaptive versus non adaptive

Achiever versus underachiever*

These 17 ideas are just a start. But for purposes of this example, we will continue to the next stage, fact finding. After reviewing the list, we decide that the starred items are of most interest and promise for further consideration. Then, we choose to use all ten criteria suggested in Table 1.3 to evaluate these ideas. In order to facilitate comparison of the chosen ideas, we decide to organize the information on a matrix, as shown in Table 1.3. The criteria are listed down the left-hand side and the ideas are arranged across the top. In each box created by the intersection of the criteria and the idea we have placed our estimate of how high or low each idea rates. In this example, we have decided to weight all criteria equally. So to find the total for each idea, we have simply added the ratings. Totals are shown in the last row. At this point, the top two ideas are the attributions made by gifted achievers and gifted underachievers and attributions made by gifted students in mathematics. Since our area of interest in is mathematics and there is a great deal of interest nationwide in improving the instruction of mathematics, we select this topic and proceed to problem finding.

During the first stage of problem finding we produce the following list of ideas:

Develop instrument

Relationship to achievement in mathematics

Relationship to attitude about math

Relationship to teacher judgment of student attribution

Develop and test a theory of attribution

Long-term effect on achievement in mathematics*

Effects of attribution retraining

Group counseling—parents, child, and teacher

Classroom program to stimulate adaptive attributions*

Test situational versus global

TABLE 1.3   Evaluation of fact-finding ideas

| | IDEAS | | | | |
CRITERIA	Instrument for Measuring	Effect of Significant Others	Achiever vs. Underachiever	Attribution in Math	Development
Interest	3*	3	5	4	4
Goal Congruency	2	3	4	5	4
Competence	2	5	4	5	3
Resources	3	3	5	5	4
Access	2	·3	3	4	4
Data	2	3	3	4	2
Potential Contribution	5	4	3	4	4
Uniqueness	1	3	5	3	3
Specificity	3	2	5	3	2
General-izability	3	3	4	3	3
Total	26	32	41	40	33

*Note : 5 is high, 3 is average, and 1 is low.

Different teachers produce different attribution patterns in students
Different types of gifted programs*
Different attributions of students in gifted programs versus no gifted
    program
Effect on later mathematics course selection (high school/college)

Each of these ideas might lead to different problem statements. Instead of applying the ten criteria suggested in fact finding (Table 1.3), we have decided to narrow them to resources defined as time, money, and computers and access defined as gifted population, school records, teacher, and parents. The selection matrix is shown in Table 1.4. To illustrate a nonquantitative evaluation method, we will make descriptive comparisons instead of assigning numerical values. The long-term study of the effect of attributions on achievement in mathematics appears to be the most difficult in terms of the criteria applied. Testing a program to stimulate adaptive attributions in mathematics appears to be the next most difficult in terms of the money needed to pay teachers to receive training and to spend extra time preparing and teaching a new program. After consideration of the three topics, we select the third, attributions made in the context of mathematics by students in different kinds of gifted programs. Although there may be some difficulty locating a sample for the study, we will need less resources and minimal access.

TABLE 1.4   Decision matrix for problem finding

		Long-term effect on achievement.	Classroom program	Type of gifted program
RESOURCES	Time	Requires a great deal	Startup, maintenance, and communication are time consuming	May be time consuming to locate different, comparable programs
	Money	Need consistent funds over time	May need to pay teachers to participate	Need funds for testing, travel, and data analysis
	Computer	Crucial for analysis	Not as necessary unless used in treatment	Not as necessary unless used in treatment
ACCESS	Gifted population	Important to have largest possible	Not as important	Finding samples from each program type may be difficult
	School records	Most important	Not as important	Not as important
	Teacher	Not as important	Extremely important	Not as important
	Parents	Very important to have stable, cooperative parents	Not as important	Not as important

The second phase of problem finding is stating the problem in the form of a question about the relationship of two or more variables. It also means implying a method for answering the question and identifying subproblems that might also be answered. Some possible questions follow:

1. What is the relationship between attribution patterns in mathematics and type of program attended by third- through sixth-grade gifted students?
2. Is there a relationship between patterns of attribution in mathematics and type of gifted program attended by third- through sixth-grade gifted students?
3. What is the relationship between the three dimensions of attributions identified by Weiner specific to mathematics and type of gifted program attended by middle school and junior high school (or third-through sixth-grade) gifted students?
4. Is one dimension of attribution in mathematics more strongly related to type of gifted program attended than the others?
5. To what degree could one predict the type of gifted program a student would select by the pattern of attribution he or she demonstrates in mathematics?
6. To what degree would the knowledge of a gifted student's pattern of attibution in mathematics assist program coordinators in selecting the best type of gifted program for that student?

There are many other possible problem statements for this idea. Although problems 1 and 3–6 have potential for future exploration, given our fact-finding information, we decided that these were premature. We know that there is a relationship between attribution and program type; we do not have the information to test one or three dimensions of a theory; and we are not ready to predict behavior based on attribution. We decided that the second problem is appropriate at this time. A modification of the problem will clarify the statement and give more direction to the study as follows: Is there a relationship between patterns of attribution in mathematics and type of gifted program attended by third-through sixth-grade gifted students in large urban school districts where parents are given a choice in program placement? We then might explore subproblems such as the following:

1. If there are differences, are they the same at each grade level or is there a pattern of development?
2. Are there differences in the relationship between attribution and program choice between girls and boys?

Now the problem statement will be used to guide a research plan and determine how the question will be answered in idea finding. A list of possibilities might include the following:

Types of programs	Definition of giftedness
Number of districts	Number in each program type
Control group	Administration time (of school year)
Measure of attribution	Dimensions of attribution
Context of measurement	Administering measure(s)
Coding and entering data	Analyses
Report (audience, deadline)	Timeline

At the conclusion of idea finding, we have decided to examine only two program types, pull-out and self-contained gifted classrooms. The sample for the study will come from two urban school districts that provide both of these program types, allow parental choice between them, and identify gifted students similarly. A control group of identified gifted students who are not participating in either program type will be located in each district. If there are too few identified gifted who are not being served, then a comparably sized district with a similar school population will be located and their gifted students used as a control group. An adapation of Lefcourt, VonBaeyer, Ware, and Cox's (1979) Multidimensional-Multiattributional Causality Scale will be used to gather self-report data on attributions specific to mathematics. We will train two assistants to administer the measure, and they will be randomly assigned to groups of students in both districts. Data collection will begin the first week in January and will be completed by the third week in January. Analysis and report writing will be accomplished by June 15. From this information, we could write a complete research plan.

Next, during solution finding, we would write hypotheses. In this example, it may not be appropriate to "guess" what differences might emerge because there is little research to guide the guesses. Nevertheless, for the sake of illustration, we might consider the following:

- The students in the pull-out program will report more internal locus of control for both their successes and failures in mathematics, while those in self-contained programs will report more internal locus for successes and external locus for failures.
- The girls in both program types will report more internal locus of control for mathematics than the boys.
- The younger the student, the more often he or she will attribute success to effort and failure to lack of effort in mathematics. The

older the student, the more he or she will attribute success to ability and failure to lack of ability.
- Both groups who are attending gifted programs will more often attribute their successes in mathematics to ability than the control group.

At the conclusion of solution finding, we would have one or more hypotheses to test. Acceptance finding is next. It is the most difficult stage of the process to explain hypothetically because it is the most personal and immediate.

In acceptance finding we identify the informal and formal routes available for presenting our project. In this case it will be important to locate two urban school districts that meet the research design specifications. One of the school districts happens to be within our college service area. The informal channel will be communication with the gifted and talented coordinator of the neighboring district. We will sit down together over lunch and in the course of our conversation present our ideas. At this stage, it will be important for the coordinator to see some benefits to our plan and begin to identify with it. We will also enlist the coordinator's help in identifying a similar district to take part in the project. Before a formal presentation is made to the superintendent or the school board, the coordinator will have discussed the project informally and paved the way for its acceptance. The formal presentation can take a variety of forms. Most likely, we will be asked to submit a written plan in advance of a formal meeting. At the meeting, we will present a short oral summary of the project and be available to answer any questions relating to the project. In both, we will clearly state the purpose of the investigation, the expected participation of students, the amount of time required of students away from their normal academic schedule, and the value of the information obtained to the district. The problem-solving process is complete when the idea for a study or evaluation is accepted and begun.

CONCLUSION

In order to advance our knowledge of gifted persons, you as a researcher or program evaluator may find it profitable to invest more creative energies identifying and stating problems. First, take a broad view of the field of gifted education and explore the important studies and reviews of research over a wide range of topics before you begin to narrow your focus. Then, examine the field from a variety of perspectives, including those of the teacher, student, parent, community, and college or university. Be open and sensitive to the concerns and problems of each perspective. After you have built a foundation for understanding the gifted, then you are ready to consider how you will contribute to the knowledge base.

In this chapter, we advocate the use of a creative problem-solving process to assist you in pursuit of a problem. The process is based on divergent thinking designed to produce many ideas and convergent thinking in which you set criteria, judge quality, and select the best ideas. The five steps in the process help prevent premature selection of topics, problems, and hypotheses for research or evaluation studies. The fuzzy mess you identify is examined from all perspectives through fact finding and is refined to become the topic of the study. Problem finding allows you to explore many problem statements that you can evaluate and eventually state as the question and subquestions of your research or evaluation study. Idea finding helps you identify various designs that will become your research or evaluation plan. During solution finding, you consider different hypotheses and decide which will focus the study. Finally, you generate possible ways to gain acceptance of your ideas, which leads to an action plan and propels you toward actually conducting the study. At first, this may appear to be too much work. But as Einstein said:

> The mere formulation of a problem is far more often essential than its solution, which may be merely a matter of mathematical or experimental skill. To raise new questions, new possibilities, to regard old problems from a new angle requires creative imagination and marks real advances in science. (Parnes, 1967, p. 122)

REFERENCES

Anthony, J. B., & Anthony, M. M. (1981). *The gifted and talented: A bibliography and resource guide*. Pittsfield, MA: Berkshire Community Press.

Ballering, L. D., & Koch, A. (1984). Family relations when a child is gifted. *Gifted Child Quarterly, 28*, 140–143.

Barbe, W. B. (1965). *Psychology and education of the gifted*. New York: Appleton-Century-Crofts.

Barbe, W. B., & Stephens, T. M. (Eds.). (1961). *Educating tomorrow's leaders*. Columbus, OH: Superintendent of Public Instruction.

Cornell, D. G., & Grossberg, I. W. (1987). Family environments and personality adjustment in gifted program children. *Gifted Child Quarterly, 31*, 59–64.

Cramond, B., & Martin, C. E. (1987). Inservice and preservice teachers' attitudes toward the academically brilliant. *Gifted Child Quarterly, 31*, 15–19.

Dettmer, P. (1981). Improving teacher attitudes toward characteristics of the creatively gifted. *Gifted Child Quarterly, 25*, 11–16.

Dissertation Abstracts International. (1938–, v. 1–, monthly). Ann Arbor, MI: University Microfilms.

Ebel, R. L., & Noll, V. H. (Eds.). (1969). *Encyclopedia of educational research* (4th ed.). New York: Macmillan.

Fliegler, L. A., & Bish, C. E. (1959). Summary of research on the academically talented student. *Review of Educational Research, 29*(5), 408–450.

Gallagher, J. J. (1966). *Research summary on gifted child education.* Springfield, IL: Department of Exceptional Children Gifted Program.

Gallagher, J. J. (1969). Gifted children. In R. L. Ebel & V. H. Noll (Eds.), *Encyclopedia of Educational Research* (4th ed.) (pp. 537–544). Toronto, Ontario: Macmillan.

Gallagher, J. J., & Courtright, R. D. (1986). *The World Council's annotated bibliography of gifted education.* New York: Trillium.

Gephart, W. J., & Ingle, R. B. (Eds.). (1969). *Educational research: Selected readings.* Columbus, OH: Merrill.

Goldberg, M. L. (1958). Recent research on the talented. *Teachers College Record, 60,* 150–63.

Good, C. V. (1942). Criteria for the selection of the research problem. *Peabody Journal of Education, 19,* 242–256.

Gowan, J. C. (1961). *An annotated bibliography on the academically talented.* Washington, DC: Center for Applied Research in Education.

Harris, C. W. (Ed.). (1960). *Encyclopedia of educational research* (3rd ed.). New York: Macmillan.

Kerlinger, F. N. (1986). *Foundations of behavioral research* (3rd ed.). New York: Holt, Rinehart & Winston.

Kolloff, M. B., & Feldhusen, J. F. (1984). The effects of enrichment on self-concept and creative thinking. *Gifted Child Quarterly, 28,* 53–57.

Laubenfels, J. (1976). *The gifted student: An annotated bibliography.* Westport, CT: Greenwood.

Lefcourt, H. M., VonBaeyer, C. L., Ware, E. E., & Cox, D. J. (1979). The Multidimensional-Multiattributional Causality Scale: The development of a goal specific locus of control scale. *Canadian Journal of Behavioral Science, 11,* 286–304.

Ludwig, G., & Cullinan, D. (1984). Behavior problems of gifted and nongifted elementary school girls and boys. *Gifted Child Quarterly, 28,* 37–39.

Maddux, C. D., Scheiber, L. M., & Bass, J. E. (1982). Self-concept and social distance in gifted children. *Gifted Child Quarterly, 26,* 77–81.

Mitzel, H. (Ed.). (1982). *Encyclopedia of educational research* (5th ed.). New York: Macmillan.

Monroe, W. S. (1950). *Encyclopedia of educational research* (rev. ed.). New York: Macmillan.

Murphy, D., Jenkins-Friedman, R., & Tollefson, N. (1984). A new criterion for the "ideal" gifted child? *Gifted Child Quarterly, 28,* 31–36.

Newland, T. E. (1953). The gifted. *Review of Educational Research, 23,* 417–431.

Norris, D. E., Hayslip, M., & Noonan, N. (1950). Gifted children. In W. S. Monroe

(Ed.), *Encyclopedia of Educational Research* (rev. ed.; pp. 505-510). New York: Macmillan.

Osborn, A. (1957). *Applied imagination.* New York: Scribner.

Parnes, S. (1967). *Creative behavior guidebook.* New York: Scribner.

Renzulli, J. S., & Delisle, J. R. (1982). Gifted persons. In H. E. Mitzel (Ed.), *Encyclopedia of Educational Research* (5th ed.; Vol. 2, pp. 728-730). New York: Free Press.

Sauernman, D. A., & Michael, W. B. (1980). Differential placement of high-achieving and low-achieving gifted pupils in grades four, five and six on measures of field dependence, creativity, and self-concept. *Gifted Child Quarterly, 24,* 81-86.

Sidman, M. (1960). *Tactics of scientific research: Evaluating experimental data in psychology.* New York: Basic Books.

Sternberg, R. J. (1981). A componential theory of intellectual giftedness. *Gifted Child Quarterly, 25,* 86-93.

Sugden, V. M. (1973). *The graduate thesis: A complete guide to planning and preparation.* New York: Pitman.

Van Dalen, D. B. (1956). The role of hypotheses in educational research. *Educational Administration and Supervision, 42,* 457-460.

Van Dalen, D. B. (1979). *Understanding educational research: An introduction* (4th ed.). New York: McGraw-Hill.

Webb, W. B. (1961). The choice of the problem. *American Psychologist, 16,* 223-227.

Witty, P. (Ed.). (1951). *The gifted child.* Boston, MA: Heath & Company.

CHAPTER 2

BEYOND SUMMARY: CONSTRUCTING A REVIEW OF THE LITERATURE

Pamela R. Clinkenbeard

What are the effects of acceleration on gifted students' social/emotional development and adjustment? Is ability grouping best for gifted students? Does instruction in creative problem solving during the gifted program in elementary school affect creativity in high school? Questions such as these may be answered in part through reviews of existing research. If the answers cannot be found in the knowledge available, then you might consider designing a study to address them. In either case you will need to start with a thorough search that will culminate in the construction of a review of the literature.

In this chapter I will refer to *constructing* a literature review to emphasize that the review is a conceptual framework built to support and give evidence to the decision made or to the study conducted. The purposes of this chapter are to present information from methodological sources on how to review literature effectively and to provide examples of effective reviews from psychological and educational literature on the gifted. This information can be valuable at every stage of a research project, from selecting a topic to writing the final report. As Long, Convey, and Chwalek (1985, p. 79) point out, "[The literature review] contains the formal description of the theoretical framework of your study. In this chapter you establish the foundation for the study by providing complete documentation for the study's context, problem, hypotheses, significance, and (in many cases) methodology."

DEFINING REVIEWS OF THE LITERATURE

What Reviews Are

The review "finds, evaluates, and integrates past research" (Cooper, 1984, p. 9). In the process you answer three major questions: where the information was found, what was done with the information, and how the information was interpreted (Wiersma, 1986).

Literature reviews can be categorized by their theoretical purpose or by their methodology. Cooper (1984) defines three kinds of literature reviews based on their purpose. The *integrative* review presents the current state of knowledge in an area and highlights important unresolved questions. (His book, and this chapter, focus on writing integrative reviews.) The *theoretical* review compares major theories on a particular topic on breadth, internal consistency, and predictions. The *methodological* review is a critical review of the way previous studies were designed or analyzed.

Reviews of the literature as categorized by methodology can be *narrative*, *quantitative*, or some *combination* of the two. (This chapter refers primarily to narrative and combination reviews. For information on meta-analysis, see Chapter 11, this volume.) Slavin (1986, 1987b) and Joyce (1987) debated Slavin's proposal for a type of literature review called *best-evidence synthesis*. Slavin suggests incorporating the best of the rigorous quantitative aspects of meta-analysis with the insightful interpretation and discussion of narrative review. He presents his own criteria for *best evidence* and suggests other researchers present their criteria in their own reviews.

The length of a literature review varies depending on whether it is a complete article or part of an article, and whether it is published in a journal or otherwise distributed. A review of the literature can be a chapter or background section of a study involving new data collection, or it can be a study in itself. When it is background information, it is preparatory to gathering data; it allows the new study to be placed in context.

In a review article, the review *is* the data. Accepting or refuting your hypothesis depends on the selection of the material you review and the interpretation you provide (Cohen & Manion, 1985). Review articles are common products of historical research in education. A meta-analysis is also considered a review article. The APA *Publication Manual* (American Psychological Association, 1983) discusses review articles at some length, noting their usefulness for clarifying problems and suggesting solutions.

Because of space limitations, the literature reviews prepared for journal articles are usually much shorter than those prepared for theses or dissertations. APA (1983) suggests describing just enough of the most pertinent literature to show the continuity between previous work and your work; it is assumed that journal readers have some background in the area. For a thesis or dissertation and also for technical reports, the object is to demonstrate your command of the literature in the field. The review is usually comprehensive and will vary in length according to the number of studies available.

What Reviews Are Not

A review of the literature is not an annotated bibliography or just a collection of research summaries. It is a critical synthesis. You demonstrate how previous studies are related to one another and to your study by noting similarities and differences in the studies, discriminating between relevant and irrelevant information, and indicating weaknesses in previous work (Long et al., 1985).

A review of the literature is not the same as the search used to locate a tentative research topic. The purpose of that search is general knowledge, enough to recognize the major research questions in a field, and it usually involves secondary sources such as textbooks and other reviews of the literature. Constructing a review of the literature involves obtaining detailed knowledge, mostly from primary sources (Borg & Gall, 1989).

What Literature Reviews Help You Do

A literature review helps you create the rationale for doing a study. In an experimental study, the review is the foundation for specific hypotheses. While hypotheses are usually explicitly stated at the end of the introduction section or chapter (often as part of the problem statement), the review that follows should build an argument that leads logically to them. In fact, someone reading your review chapter should be able to predict, just from the logical flow of the review, what hypotheses you are going to test.

For educational decision making, a thorough review of the literature can answer several important questions. What is known about the magnitude of the problem? What efforts have been made in the past to solve it? Were they successful? Does existing research suggest any promising new directions? (Light & Pillemer, 1984). The answers to these questions build the rationale for the decision you make.

Borg and Gall (1989) list six additional purposes of the literature review. Reviewing the literature:

1. Delimits a research problem
2. Shows new approaches to research problems
3. Helps avoid sterile approaches
4. Gives insight into the methods of other researchers
5. Reveals recommendations for further research
6. Samples current opinions about a problem (if you search newspaper and opinion articles and other nontechnical pieces, in addition to the technical journal literature)

Reviewing the Literature on the Gifted

There are special concerns that arise when you begin to construct a review of the literature in the area of gifted children or gifted education. One concern is the wide variety of definitions of the main variable under consideration. From IQ score to creative products to teacher recommendations, the criteria for defining who is a gifted child vary considerably from study to study. Another concern is what constitutes the actual *treatment* in a gifted program. If you want to review the literature on pull-out programs versus homogeneously grouped classrooms versus acceleration, you must be aware of the differences within each of those types of program structures. Finally, there is the inclusion/exclusion issue. In this field as well as others, there are many nonexperimental or poorly controlled studies; there are also increasing numbers of good studies that employ qualitative methods. The dilemma is whether to review as many studies as possible on a particular topic, or to make some judgments about the type and quality of methods, leaving out studies that do not meet your criteria.

The next section should provide some assistance in resolving these dilemmas. For each of the steps of the literature review, there are illustrative examples from the literature on the gifted. In general, whatever choices you make, a good review of the literature provides precise definitions of the main variables and explains the criteria used to include and exclude studies.

In summary, a literature review can be defined as both a process and a product that finds, evaluates, and integrates past literature. A review can be a section of an article or an article in itself. It can be narrative, quantitative, or a combination of both. It is not an annotated bibliography, a collection of summaries, or an initial search of secondary sources in order to get research ideas. A review helps clarify what has been done, shows what other authors have recommended for future research, puts the study in context and gives it a rationale, and directs the interpretation of our data or the decision made. There are unique concerns in reviewing literature in gifted education, including the many definitions of gifted-ness and the variety of program treatments.

CONSTRUCTING A LITERATURE REVIEW

For guidelines on the steps involved in constructing a review of literature, I consulted several sources: textbooks on educational research methodology, books on writing proposals and publications in the social sciences, and the *Publications Manual of the American Psychological Association* (APA, 1983). In addition to these sources, I recommend two excellent books that specifically address reviewing literature: *The Integrative Research Review* (Cooper, 1984) and *Summing Up: The Science of Reviewing Research* (Light & Pillemer, 1984). Cooper takes a more quantitative approach to synthesizing the results of studies, while Light and Pillemer give useful suggestions for synthesizing qualitative information. Both are strong presentations of the major issues in reviewing literature.

Many educational research methods books, especially those at the introductory level, devote only a page or two to the topic of reviewing the literature, although most also note the critical importance of the review for shaping the entire study. Two exceptions to this rule are Wiersma (1986) and Borg and Gall (1989). Wiersma (1986) is appropriate for beginning researchers. His presentation assumes little knowledge of the process and concentrates on the logistics of the literature review. On page 49 he provides a helpful flowchart of the entire process. Borg and Gall (1989) is an excellent resource for more sophisticated researchers. This most detailed and advanced of the methodology textbooks mentioned here provides a number of annotated references and complex methods, such as the use of program evaluation and review technique (PERT) charts in planning research projects.

General Advice on the Process

Asher (1976), in discussing how to proceed with the research report, suggests *searching* the literature first, but *writing* the literature review last, so that it is easier to organize around the study's research questions. Asher (1976) and Gall and Borg (1989) provide sample proposals so you can see how the parts of a research report relate to each other.

Borg and Gall (1989) list mistakes often made in reviewing literature:

1. Conducting a hurried review
2. Consulting too many secondary sources

3. Concentrating on findings to the exclusion of useful information on methods and measures
4. Overlooking sources other than journals
5. Defining the topic of the search too narrowly or broadly
6. Copying bibliographic information incorrectly and then being unable to locate the source
7. Recording too much information on each notecard describing a study
8. Not using all relevant narrow descriptors in a computer search

The information in the remainder of this chapter should help you avoid these mistakes.

The following seven sections are in the order you would normally follow to construct a literature review. The number of steps is somewhat arbitrary; some writers refer to as few as three steps in the literature review process. However, almost every source discusses all the activities presented below. I will discuss examples from literature related to the gifted in each of the sections.

Step 1: Finding the Literature

This section indicates sources to use in beginning a search, what to exclude from your search, and how to conduct a computerized search of the literature. The assumption is that you already have identified a general research problem, although in the process of searching the literature you will further define and clarify the problem. For more information on problem finding, see Chapter 1 in this volume.

"Perhaps the greatest frustration encountered by graduate students carrying out their first review of literature is generated by their attempt to determine what they should and should not read" (Borg & Gall, 1989, p. 119). Unfortunately, the authors note that there is no simple solution to this problem. They suggest that in reviewing established areas of research, you should begin with secondary sources such as textbooks and other reviews. For newer areas of research, there are fewer secondary sources, so you need to read widely for background.

Asher (1976) suggests starting with sources that include a general discussion of your topic and using their reference lists to go to more specific sources. Resources he recommends for beginning a review include:

Encyclopedia of Educational Research
National Society for the Study of Education (NSSE) yearbooks

Handbook of Research on Teaching
Review of Research on Education (RRE; annual)
Review of Educational Research (RER; quarterly)

Slavin (1984) and Travers (1978) disagree on the *quality control* issue in finding literature. Slavin suggests looking for major reviews in the RER and RRE for the last five years, and using their references as a place to start. He strongly suggests a focus on high-quality research journals because he believes that "the proportion of useful to useless information in articles that have not been subjected to rigorous review is low" (p. 127). Additionally, you should investigate unpublished or obscure articles only after you have a thorough understanding of the published literature.

Traver, unlike Slavin, cautions against restricting a search to first-rate journals because they are published by the scientific establishment and often include only *safe* research. He feels one must sift through so-called second-rate journals in order to find truly innovative published research, which is less likely to be accepted in more prestigious journals. Getting an idea accepted when it contradicts currently espoused paradigms may be difficult, and an article presenting such an idea is less likely to be published in established journals.

Borg and Gall (1989) provide detailed, lengthy suggestions on listing key words, checking sources (including detailed examples of computer literature searchers), and reading and taking notes on selected references. They suggest reading the most recent literature first, since that will help you gain a better understanding of past literature and will narrow the list of studies you will incorporate into the review. Wiersma (1986) also gives examples of specific indexes and sources for ideas, examines the use of the Educational Resources Information Center (ERIC) system and *Dissertation Abstracts International*, and discusses selecting descriptors for computerized literature searches.

Abstracts and indexes that you will probably find most useful include:

Resources in Education (RIE)
Current Index to Journals in Education (CIJE)
Psychological Abstracts
Education Index
Child Development Abstracts and Bibliography
Dissertation Abstracts International (DAI)
Social Science Citation Index (SSCI).

The SSCI is unique because you can locate citations of a particular article. For example, you may find a classic study that is 12 years old; through using the SSCI, you can find who has cited that study since its publication, thereby gaining access to more recent research on the same topic or theory.

Two good examples of locating sources for a literature review include Rogers (1986) and Slavin (1987a). Rogers (1986), in a review article on cognition and the gifted, provides clear information on how and why she chose her sources. She used a manual search of the *Gifted Child Quarterly, Child Development, Journal of Genetic Psychology, G/C/T,* and the *Review of Educational Research.* In addition, she conducted computer searches of ERIC, Exceptional Child Educational Resource (ECER), and Psychological Abstracts Information Service (PSY-INFO). Slavin (1987a), in a review of research on ability grouping and student achievement, presents a detailed discussion of how and why he selected particular studies based on a priori criteria of both germaneness and methodological adequacy.

Finding the literature involves locating sources and deciding what to include. Should you restrict your search to first-rate journals? There is no consensus on this question. Suggestions from various methodology authors, however, include: start your reading with the most recent literature and that which covers the field broadly; examine the reference lists of those broad sources; and make use of existing indexes and computer search systems.

Step 2: Collecting the Literature

Two important skills of reviewing the literature are keeping track of your sources and taking notes on studies. While several of the authors discuss the use of notecards, many researchers with access to laptop computers use them in the library to take notes on books and journal articles. This means less typing when you write a first draft, since your notes are already in the word processor. However, the clicking sound of the keyboard may disturb other library patrons, and you may be frequently interrupted by those who want to ask about your computer!

Sternberg (1988) recommends using 3-by-5-inch author cards and 4-by-6- or 5-by-8-inch topic notecards. The author card is simply the full bibliographic citation of the source (in APA style). Topic cards have a topic, information about it, the sources of the information (name and year), and your evaluative comments about it. (Be sure to record page numbers for information from books.) Sternberg points out this notecard system should save you from going back to original sources, and the paper is half written when you are finished. He recommends listing all the topics on a sheet of paper, cutting it into strips, and rearranging the strips into an outline of the paper. Wiersma (1986) also lists formats and procedures that you may find helpful for recording information about sources and provides several sample abstracts that summarized studies.

What type of information should you record? Best (1981) lists seven points to note when collecting information on studies:

1. Reports of closely related studies
2. Design of the study, including procedures and instruments used
3. Populations that were sampled and the sampling methods employed
4. Variables that were defined
5. Extraneous variables that could have affected the study's findings
6. Faults that could have been avoided
7. Recommendations for further research

The method of collecting literature is not usually obvious in the final written literature review, so I do not provide examples from the gifted education literature here. However, you can see some evidence of Sternberg's methods (mentioned above) in his review article on conceptions of intelligence (Wagner & Sternberg, 1984).

Collecting the literature carefully can result in the skeleton of your written review. The various authors mentioned above provide suggestions on notecard systems and on the specific kinds of information that should be recorded.

Step 3: Evaluating the Literature

Again, the review of the literature is not just a collection of study summaries. One of its main purposes is to critique previous research. This section addresses the question of evaluating the individual studies in a review. How should you judge quality?

Borg and Gall (1989) present an overview of the critical evaluation process. They note that an evaluation of the literature should be based on a thorough knowledge of research methods. The findings of similar studies may be contradictory, but these can be resolved by discussing the strengths and weaknesses of each study. The purpose is to evaluate others' work and to decide, in view of their limitations, how the findings fit into the overall research related to your problem. They list eight mistakes that are commonly made in evaluating research studies:

1. Giving equal weight to good and poor studies
2. Failing to pull studies together for an overall understanding
3. Not determining overall effect size
4. Failing to weigh sampling bias
5. Overestimating the usefulness of statistically significant results that have no practical significance
6. Missing errors and repeating them in one's own work
7. Doing the critical evaluation too late to apply the resultsw to one's own study
8. Overlooking observer bias

Two authors discuss the evaluation of other reviews of research. Travers (1978) cautions students to beware of both extremely critical and extremely positive reviews of the literature and to judge the reviewed articles individually. The review authors may not have been making a fair presentation of all the available knowledge in a field.

Olszewski-Kubilius, Kulieke, and Krasney (1988), in a review of research on personality dimensions of gifted adolescents, provide thoughtful methodological critiques of the literature. They discuss problems with definitions, sampling, design, and analysis and then incorporate those findings into their summary to help explain the inconsistencies in the literature.

Evaluating the literature involves making quality judgments about the content and methodology of studies and of other literature reviews. These judgments can help resolve contradictions in the literature. Methodologists present a number of suggestions for evaluating literature that will help you avoid common mistakes in this process, such as simply reporting and summarizing the studies without critically evaluating the research methods used and conclusions reached or relating them to the methodologies and content in other studies.

Step 4: Analyzing the Literature

Many textbooks on research methods give advice on the logistics of organizing studies for a review of the literature but are less helpful when it comes to suggestions for conceptual organization. On what basis should you decide which studies belong together? This section deals with questions of grouping and categorizing studies and with the use of charts as tools for organizing and presenting data.

The APA manual (APA, 1983) suggests organizing a review article by relationship. If, however, the review provides background information for an empirical study, it may be presented in chronological order. Borg and

Gall (1989) remind you to read the literature with your research question clearly in mind and to be alert for natural subdivisions into which articles might be classified. As you develop a coding system of these subdivisions for literature notecards, label each card with the appropriate code.

Long and colleagues (1985) recommend making an outline of the aspects of your problem. The main points in the outline (the Roman numerals) can become subheadings for your review. Sort the studies according to these subheadings, then list the pertinent issues for each section. They suggest beginning each subhead with an overview, including definitions. This is followed by general theories, then a review of pertinent studies. Another technique, *idea webbing*, might be a helpful way to experiment with different ways of relating the studies (see Figure 2.1).

Constructing a summary chart or table of your reviewed studies is extremely useful when similar aspects of studies can be compared. Charts make it easier to compare and contrast past literature, to look for contradictions, and to explain study outcomes. They provide information that leads to synthesis and interpretation of the literature. Features you might include in such a chart are:

The nature of the sample
Independent and dependent variables
Procedures or treatments
Statistical analysis
Results
Other special feature of interest

For example, a review of studies evaluating programs for gifted learning disabled (LD) students might require a column to indicate, for each study, whether students received LD programming only (L), gifted programming only (G), both (B), or neither (N). A capsule description of each feature for each study would then be written and placed in table form. You should not stop with the completed chart; the accompanying text should further summarize and integrate the findings.

As an example of one grouping method, see Hollinger (1988), who groups her studies on career development in gifted female adolescents by two major theoretical perspectives. She uses these groups to discuss different predictions the two perspectives would make regarding her research question, then tests the hypotheses generated by one of the perspectives. Proctor, Black, and Feldhusen (1986) developed a clear, comprehensive summary chart of studies on early admission to elementary school. They compared studies on such features as population, sample, admission criteria, outcome measures, and findings.

FIGURE 2.1   Sample idea web for writing reviews of the literature

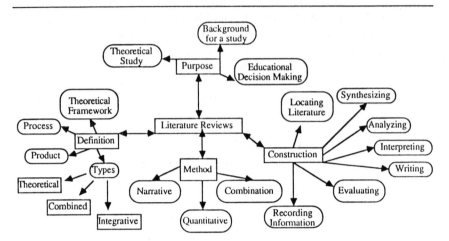

Analyzing the literature involves grouping and categorizing the studies you review. There are several ways studies can be categorized, but any grouping should be based on your research question. Summary charts are an excellent way to compare and contrast various aspects of studies.

Step 5: Synthesizing the Literature

This section refers to generalizing, making inferences, and summarizing the literature review as a whole. Slavin (1984) says that the literature review is not just a catalogue of "so and so found this." He suggests reading articles in the RER and RRE for good examples and also provides an example format of his own:

> Smith (1970) and Wilson (1972) both found A in studies of urban tenth graders, but Jones (1971) found B in a study involving suburban fifth graders. Since Wilson's (1972) study failed to replicate B, it might be assumed that differences in settings and grade levels could account for the different findings. Support for this is also provided by Gonzales (1974), who found. . . . (p. 261)

It is perfectly all right to refer to a study more than once, in the interest of comparing it to other studies and showing how it fits into the literature. It may seem repetitive to you because of your familiarity with the material, but (speaking as a frequent doctoral committee member) it makes the review much easier to read.

A healthy debate is occurring in the world of educational research over how to combine or synthesize the results of research (see Gage, 1989). Borg and Gall (1989) compare traditional (or narrative) reviews with quantitative methods, including vote counting and meta-analysis. Traditional reviews generally are narratives limited to studies with significant results that emphasize the *better* studies. Borg and Gall (1989) note that traditional reviews have been criticized for "being subjective, not using specific inclusion criteria, . . . and placing too much emphasis on statistical significance as the sole criterion of evaluating results" (p. 171). In addition, traditional reviews often omit an overall estimate of treatment effect.

Vote counting is the easiest quantitative method of synthesizing literature. Studies can be placed into one of four categories:

1. Significant and positive (that is, in the direction hypothesized)
2. Significant and negative
3. Nonsignificant but positive
4. Nonsignificant but negative

The category with the most studies "wins." The main problem with this approach is that it considers only the direction of results, not their magnitude.

Meta-analysis, according to Borg and Gall (1989), has its limits but is the best available method for integrating the results of data from several studies. Their main criticism is that some meta-analyses include data from poor studies. They note, however, that including all studies regardless of quality is probably acceptable if the researcher looks at the results in depth, beyond the quantitative procedure.

For a discussion of one compromise method of reviewing the literature (that is, a compromise between narrative and quantitative methods), see the debate between Slavin (1986, 1987b) and Joyce (1987) regarding Slavin's proposal for a best-evidence synthesis (described above).

In organizing the synthesis, Borg and Gall (1989) state that you can interpret results within each topic section, or in a separate section of the review. You may agree or disagree with the interpretations given by authors of their own research. They note that the interpretive sections are the most difficult to write, because they require a very thorough understanding of the research you have reviewed.

Long and colleagues (1985) suggest closing the synthesis of the literature with a brief summary that reemphasizes the salient points and provides the rationale for your study and hypotheses. This summary will be helpful during the discussion of the problem in your introductory chapter and discussion of the rationale for each of your hypotheses.

Two examples illustrate the interpretive aspect of synthesis. Wagner and Sternberg (1984) synthesize their literature on conceptions of intelligence by *telling us what they told us*. Their conclusion section is an interpretive summary of previous sections and implications for future research. Slavin (1987a) provides summary/discussion sections for each major heading of his review of ability grouping, then provides a major synthesis at the end of the article.

Synthesizing the literature involves generalizing and making inferences about the literature as a whole. There are narrative and quantitative methods of synthesis; both have advantages and disadvantages. It is, however, possible to synthesize using a combination of the methods. Synthesis of the literature can be done at the end of each section of your review or in a separate section.

Step 6: Contextualizing the Literature

There is some overlap between synthesizing the literature and contextualizing it. This section deals with how to interpret the review in the context of the other parts of the research report or proposal, as well as in the context of current debates in the field.

Each section (or chapter) of your paper should flow logically to the next (Krathwohl, 1988). An examination of the literature allows you to advance knowledge by profiting from others' successes and mistakes. It permits either the generation of a hypothesis or the creation of a focused research question (if specific hypotheses are not stated in your study). Krathwohl recommends that you show how your study will take its place in this flow of literature and move it forward. He argues that writers need to point out the technical flaws of previous research as well as describe how they will avoid these flaws. In addition, writers should state whether they believe the authors of the studies reviewed interpreted results accurately and described their theoretical bases clearly. Krathwohl also cautions against including too many references and doing too little with them.

Placing your review in the context of current debate shows that you are familiar with how the topic is being interpreted and applied in educational and/or psychological practice today. This will mean including sources such as the *Phi Delta Kappan, Educational Leadership, Psychology Today,* and more general magazines and newspapers when they address your topic. These sources are useful because they provide current, applied discussions of the issues. They should not, however, be used as primary research references.

Southern, Jones, and Fiscus (1989) interpret the literature on acceleration of the gifted by focusing on a contradiction between research and practice. They point out that despite the abundant research in favor of acceleration, educators are reluctant to employ it as an option for gifted children. They resolve this contradiciton by placing it in the context of school-readiness studies, showing how the two bodies of literature relate and demonstrating how the application of school-readiness study results to gifted children is often inappropriate. Reis and Callahan (1989) place their review of research on gifted females clearly in the context of both popular and scholarly debates on the subject. In interpreting the literature, they take note of both the probable biases of previous researchers and their own biases.

Contextualizing the literature means making connections between the review of the literature and the other parts of a study, and between the review and current debate on the topic. There should be a logical flow from one section of a paper to the next. You can show how the research question takes its place in the literature, how you will avoid past mistakes, and how you will contribute to the literature. There should also be a clear relationship between the review and current debates on your topic.

Step 7: Writing the Literature Review

While many of the previous steps include good advice about the written presentation of the literature review, some general comments on writing quality (making the review easy to read) are in order. The main issues here are how to make the point of the review clear, how to organize and present the sections of the review, and how much detail to include.

In writing about publishing in the *Gifted Child Quarterly,* two members of the editorial review board describe what they look for when reviewing manuscripts. VanTassel-Baska (1988) notes that in preparing a manuscript, one of the most important factors is having a strong central focus and developing it through data, argument, and selective example. Robinson (1988) asks "What's the point?" when evaluating a manuscript. A literature review helps explain "what's the point" of conducting a particular piece of research and, if done well, draws the reader toward the central focus, or research question.

Cooper (1984) suggests organizing the sections in the review as you would for a full research report. It would include sections labeled "Introduction" (placing the review in context), "Methods" (of including studies in the review), "Results" (analysis and synthesis of the literature), and "Discussion" (interpretation and implications of the literature).

Several authors discuss how much of the literature to include in the written review. Borg and Gall (1989) suggest discussing in detail only the two or three most important studies for each topic and grouping others with a summary statement of their relevance. Long and colleagues (1985) note that individual studies should be described in more or less detail according to their importance and relevance to your study. Further, Sternberg (1988) states that a lengthy review is inappropriate *except* for theses and dissertations and suggests citing a previous review if voluminous literature exists. You should assume the reader is familiar with the general literature and is primarily interested in your contribution to it.

Finally, Borg and Gall (1989) urge literature reviewers to avoid three common practices: stringing together short descriptions of studies with no attempt at logical organization; giving each study the same format and the same length description (after all, some studies are more important than others and should be emphasized more); and using quotations excessively. Use of these practices indicates that the author needs to synthesize the material better. To help faculty members and manuscript reviewers read your final report, have a colleague proof and evaluate the manuscript to make sure it is not tiresome, overlong, or poorly organized and written.

The presentation of the literature, then, should have a clear point, a central focus, and be organized around the research question or hypotheses. The sections of the written literature review can reflect the sections of a total manuscript: introduction, methods, results, and discussion. Finally, the report should be appropriate to the audience, with the length and detail of the review depending on the research purpose.

CONCLUSION

The purpose of this chapter was to present information from a variety of sources on how to review literature effectively in education and the social sciences and to provide examples from the literature on the gifted. After a discussion of the definition and importance of literature reviews, I presented information from a number of methodology sources about the steps of constructing a literature review. These steps include

1. Locating
2. Collecting
3. Evaluating
4. Analyzing
5. Synthesizing
6. Interpreting
7. Writing the review

In general, a good literature review is driven by your research question and is more than a collection of summaries. It is a thoughtful synthesis and interpretation of previously conducted research. The review is the framework on which the other parts of a study depend.

One way to learn to write a review of the literature is to follow good examples. You may find it valuable to read the articles from the gifted education literature that were mentioned here. Analyze their reviews of literature based on the information presented in this chapter, and also critique your future reading in terms of what you have learned about constructing a good literature review. Another way to learn is to teach. You may gain insight into the process in the context of teaching research skills to students (see Torrance & Myers, 1979). If we want gifted students to be able to employ higher-level thinking skills, then they too should learn to review research and go beyond simply summarizing the research and opinions of others.

REFERENCES

American Psychological Association. (1983). *Publication manual of the American Psychological Association* (3rd ed.). Washington, DC: Author.

Asher, J. W. (1976). *Educational research and evaluation methods*. Boston: Little, Brown.

Best, J. W. (1981). *Research in education* (4th ed.). Englewood Cliffs, NJ: Prentice-Hall.

Borg, W. R., & Gall, M. D. (1989). *Educational research: An introduction* (5th ed.). New York: Longman.

Cohen, L., & Manion, L. (1985). *Research methods in education* (2nd ed.). London: Croom Helm.

Cooper, H. M. (1984). *The integrative research review: A systematic approach.* Beverly Hills, CA: Sage.

Gage, N. L. (1989). The paradigm wars and their aftermath: A "historical" sketch of research on teaching since 1989. *Educational Research, 18*(7), 4–10.

Gall, M. D., & Borg, W. R. (1989). *Educational research: A guide for preparing a thesis or dissertation proposal in education* (5th ed.). White Plains, NY: Longman.

Hollinger, C. L. (1988). Toward an understanding of career development among G/T female adolescents. *Journal for the Education of the Gifted, 12*, 62–79.

Joyce, B. (1987). A rigorous yet delicate touch: A response to Slavin's proposal for "best-evidence" reviews. *Educational Researcher, 16*(4), 12–14.

Kerlinger, F. N. (1973). *Foundations of behavioral research* (2nd ed.). New York: Holt, Rinehart & Winston.

Krathwohl, D. R. (1988). *How to prepare a research proposal.* Syracuse, NY: Syracuse University Press.

Light, R. J., & Pillemer, D. B. (1984). *Summing up: The science of reviewing research*. Cambridge, MA: Harvard University Press.

Long, T. J., Convey, J. J., & Chwalek, A. R. (1985). *Completing dissertations in the behavioral sciences and education*. San Francisco: Jossey-Bass.

Olszewski-Kubilius, P. M., Kulieke, M. J., & Krasney, N. (1988). Personality dimensions of gifted adolescents: A review of the empirical literature. *Gifted Child Quarterly, 32*, 347–352.

Proctor, T. B., Black, K. N., & Feldhusen, J. F. (1986). Early admission of selected children to elementary school: A review of the research literature. *Journal of Educational Research, 80*(2), 70–76.

Reis, S. M., & Callahan, C. M. (1989). Gifted females: They've come a long way— or have they? *Journal for the Education of the Gifted, 12*, 99–117.

Robinson, A. (1988). Thinking straight and writing that way: Publishing in the *Gifted Child Quarterly*. *Gifted Child Quarterly, 32*, 367–369.

Rogers, K. B. (1986). Do the gifted think and learn differently? A review of recent research and its implications for instruction. *Journal for the Education of the Gifted, 10*, 17–39.

Slavin, R. E. (1984). *Research methods in education: A practical guide*. Englewood Cliffs, NJ: Prentice-Hall.

Slavin, R. E. (1986). Best-evidence synthesis: An alternative to meta-analytic and traditional reviews. *Educational Researcher, 15*(9), 5–11.

Slavin, R. E. (1987a). Ability grouping and student achievement in elementary schools: A best-evidence synthesis. *Review of Educational Research, 57*, 293–336.

Slavin, R. E. (1987b). Best-evidence synthesis: Why less is more. *Educational Researcher, 16*(4), 15–16.

Southern, W. T., Jones, E. D., & Fiscus, E. D. (1989). Practitioner objections to the academic acceleration of gifted children. *Gifted Child Quarterly, 33*, 29–35.

Sternberg, R. J. (1988). *The psychologist's companion: A guide to scientific writing for students and researchers* (2nd ed.). New York: Cambridge University Press.

Torrance, E. P., & Myers, R. E. (1979). Teaching gifted elementary pupils research concepts and skills. In J. C. Gowan, J. Khatena, & E. P. Torrance (Eds.), *Educating the ablest* (2nd ed., pp. 131–138). Itasca, IL: Peacock.

Travers, R. M. W. (1978). *An introduction to educational research* (4th ed.). New York: Macmillan.

VanTassel-Baska, J. (1988). The preparation of manuscripts: Some reflections. *Gifted Child Quarterly, 32*, 366.

Wagner, R. K., & Sternberg, R. J. (1984). Alternative conceptions of intelligence and their implications for education. *Review of Educational Research, 54*, 179–223.

Wiersma, W. (1986). *Research methods in education: An introduction* (4th ed.). Boston: Allyn & Bacon.

CHAPTER 3

EXPERIMENTAL RESEARCH

Paula M. Olszewski-Kubilius and Rena F. Subotnik

The purpose of this chapter is to help you learn about experimental and quasi-experimental designs as applied to questions about gifted children and their education. The first segment of the chapter includes illustrations of basic design formats and sample problems from published research studies. The second segment of the chapter demonstrates the application of these research designs to a sample research question. A final segment delineates common design problems in research on the gifted that, if addressed, will result in more rigorous and generalizable research studies.

AN INTRODUCTION TO EXPERIMENTAL RESEARCH DESIGN

Let us begin by considering a published research study. We will refer back to this study throughout the chapter to illustrate basic points.

Ebmeier, Dyche, Taylor, and Hall (1985) were interested in determining whether trained regular classroom teachers would be as effective with gifted students (i.e., producing gains on cognitive tests) as teachers specifically prepared to teach gifted students. The authors reasoned that if a viable program could be developed, then "gifted students could potentially receive the same quality of instruction from regular classroom teachers as from teachers who specialized in gifted education—a realistic alternative to the employment of a 'gifted' specialist in each attendance center" (p. 15).

The study took place in two parts, and each part took one school year to complete. Part 1 involved "the development and testing of a prototype resource room gifted curriculum model." Part 2 involved comparing two groups of gifted students who received the curriculum: those taught by the gifted specialists, and those instructed by the regular classroom teacher.

For part 1, all of the 166 gifted students (Otis-Lennon Ability Index scores above 125) in grades 3–6 were randomly assigned to either a treatment or control group. The treatment in part 1 consisted of the eight-week prototype curriculum followed immediately by a posttest, the Ross Test of Higher Cognitive Processes. The control group received the regular curriculum.

After the first eight-week period the control and treatment groups were switched. That is, the control group received the treatment and the treatment group acted as the controls during the second eight-week period. In this way the effect of the prototype curriculum could be observed twice. The results indicated that the treatment group had higher scores on the posttest compared to the controls and after the second eight-week period the new treatment group had Ross posttest scores that were equivalent to those of the original treatment group. Thus the curriculum was deemed effective in increasing thinking skills.

For the second part of the study, the researchers compared the achievement of students who received instruction by gifted specialists versus trained regular classroom teachers. Logistical and resource limitations precluded random assignment of students to groups. The authors instead randomly assigned 11 district elementary schools to the two conditions; gifted students who were taught the prototype curriculum by a gifted specialist, and gifted students who were taught the prototype curriculum by trained regular classroom teachers. The higher-level thinking skills curriculum that was tested in part 1 was expanded and given to both groups. A pretest was administered and used as a covariate in the analysis to control for preexisting skill differences in thinking skills between the groups. The final data analysis revealed no difference in achievement levels between the two groups. In this study, the specially trained teachers and the regular teachers were equally effective with the gifted students.

The Purpose of Research

Research is conducted for the purpose of understanding natural phenomena and human behavior. Research design helps us determine the existence of relationships between important variables. In part 1 of Ebmeier and colleagues' study, the researchers were interested in whether the curriculum would result in higher levels of thinking for students who received it. The relationship of interest was between the variables of curriculum type and thinking skills. In part 2, the researchers were interested in whether the teacher and his or her training would affect students' learning. The variables were type of teacher training and thinking skills. All research involves the investigation of the relationship between two or more variables.

Experiments

According to Ary, Jacobs, and Razavieh (1985), an experiment has certain characteristics: (1) Independent variables are manipulated; (2) all other variables are held constant; and (3) the effects of the independent variables on the dependent variable(s) are observed. These three essential features—manipulation, control, and observation—are the basis of experimental research.

In addition, the experimental method rests on two assumptions regarding the control of variables. They are:

1. If two situations are equal in every respect except for a variable that is added to or deleted from one of the situations, any difference appearing between the two situations can be attributed to that variable. This statement is called the *law of the single variable*.
2. If two situations are not equal but it can be demonstrated that none of the variables is significant in producing the phenomenon under investigation, or if significant variables are made equal [by matching or by some other means], any difference occurring between the two situations after the introduction of a new variable . . . can be attributed to the new independent variable. This statement is called the *law of the only significant variable*. (Ary et al., 1985, pp. 250–251, citing Mill, 1846, p. 224)

Establishing conditions to test the law of the single variable is rare in educational research. Through judicious research design, however, conditions can be arranged to come as close as possible to the application of the law of the significant variable. Research designs attempt to control variables whose effects are not of interest to the researcher, so that the effect of the independent variable on the dependent variable can be maximized and determined. When extraneous variables have not been adequately controlled, we refer to a research design as *confounded*. For example, suppose you want to study the effects of IQ on performance on a memory task. The independent variable is ability and is operationalized as scores on an IQ test. The dependent variable is performance on the memory task, or the number of words correctly recalled. You choose two groups of subjects, one with IQs above 130 and one with IQs between 90 and 115, and give both groups the memory task. If you find that the majority of the high-IQ subjects are female or are from upper-income families, the variables of gender and income are confounded with the variable of ability (IQ). In this situation, you cannot conclude with any certainty that ability alone has had an effect on performance on the memory task. The results may be due to the variables of gender or socioeconomic status (SES).

Ebmeier and colleagues employed random assignment of subjects to conditions to achieve control of extraneous variables in part 1. Random assignment, we will see later, ensures that extraneous subject variables such as sex, age, SES, and so on are not influencing the outcomes of the study. Part 1 of Ebmeier and colleagues' study attempts, through random assignment, to produce the conditions of the law of the single variable.

Part 2, on the other hand, tries to produce the conditions of the law of the only significant variable. In part 2, the authors were not able to randomly assign subjects to groups, but they could randomly assign schools to groups. The authors were also able to use a thinking skills test as both a pretest and posttest and employ a data analytic technique, analysis of covariance (ANCOVA), to take into account any preexisting differences between the treatment groups. In these ways, Ebmeier and colleagues attempted to control extraneous subject variables.

Manipulation in experimental research refers to the active and deliberate creation of conditions to which subjects are exposed. This set of conditions is the independent variable and is also referred to as the treatment or experimental variable. In Ebmeier and colleagues' study, the independent variable manipulated in part 1 was treatment versus no treatment. In part 2, the manipulated (independent) variable was the type of teacher: a trained teacher of the gifted versus a regular classroom teacher.

In experimentation, you look for the effect of the independent variable on some kind of outcome or dependent variable. *Observations* are made on subjects' responses to the independent variable. These observed responses define the dependent variable(s). In the simplest experiment there must be at least two groups of subjects involved, so that a comparison can be made in terms of the effect of the independent variable on the dependent variable. Typically, one group receives the treatment (treatment group), and one group does not (control group). In Ebmeier and colleagues' study, observations of students' thinking skills were obtained via the Ross Test of Higher Cognitive Processes, and this defined the dependent variable.

The Maxmincon Principle

Another useful perspective on the purpose of research design is that of Kerlinger (1973). According to Kerlinger, research design is "the plan, structure and strategy of investigation conceived so as to obtain answers to research questions and to control variance" (p. 300). The statistical principle embodied in this definition is the *maxmincon* principle.

Maximize the Variance. Suppose you are interested in comparing the effects of two reading programs on gifted childrens' reading achievement. In order to increase the chances of finding statistically significant treatment effects, you must make sure the two reading programs are as different as possible from each other, thus maximizing the experimental variance and the influence of the independent variable on the dependent variable.

In part 1 of Ebmeier and colleagues' study, the authors were interested in the effect of the prepared curriculum on students' thinking skills. One group, the treatment group, received the special curriculum and one group, the control group, received the regular school curriculum. The authors were able to observe the effect of the curriculum quite clearly. This would not have been the case if the regular school curriculum also emphasized thinking skills and thus was not very different from the special curriculum. Other ways in which the effect of the independent variable could have been diluted would have been if the control group were inadvertently receiving exposure to thinking skills either because a particular teacher was emphasizing them or because a new social studies curriculum with a strong emphasis on higher forms of thinking had been implemented.

Control Extraneous Variance. Kerlinger (1973) suggests several ways of controlling extraneous variables. The most effective method is to randomly assign subjects to experimental conditions, as Ebmeier and colleagues did in part 1, because this process randomly distributes the effects of extraneous variables across groups.

Another way of controlling an extraneous variable is to limit the study to subjects who are homogeneous, or alike, with respect to the extraneous variable. For example, if SES is a possible confounding extraneous variable, study only high-SES subjects. This method restricts the generalizability of your findings, however.

A third means of controlling extraneous variables is to build the variable into the research design. If you cannot control the confounding effects of SES by selecting only high-SES subjects, and cannot randomly assign high- and low-SES subjects to treatment groups, deliberately include the variable of SES in the design. You would do this by including groups of both high- and low-SES gifted children in the study and expose one group from each income level to one of the two reading programs. Thus SES becomes an independent variable of the study.

The final way to control extraneous variables is to match subjects in the experimental and nonexperimental groups on the extraneous variables. For example, you could match pairs of students on SES and randomly assign the subjects of each pair to each of two reading programs.

Control of extraneous variables distinguishes a good research design from a poor one. The strength of a research design is calibrated by its internal and external validity. Internal validity refers to how confident we can be that control of extraneous variables was accomplished, so that alternative interpretations of the results of the study (other than a treatment effect) can be ruled out. External validity refers to the generalizability, or representativeness, of the results of the study to other populations and other situations. (See Campbell & Stanley, 1966, for a more thorough examination of specific design formats and their concomitant threats to internal and external validity.)

Minimize Error Variance. Error variance is variance due to either unreliable measures or subjects' fatigue, memory lapses, and so forth (Kerlinger, 1973). For example, if you are interested in subjects' ability to remember words as a function of IQ, presenting the words via computer rather than by a series of flash cards turned by hand would eliminate the variance in the dependent measure that is due to fluctuations in human timing.

Experimental Design

The goal of research is to be able to infer causal relationships between variables under study. This can be accomplished if the effects of all other possible contributing variables, or confounding variables, are controlled or eliminated. The most effective control method is, of course, random assignment of subjects to groups or treatment conditions. Random assignment is the hallmark of a true experiment. With random assignment and a true experiment, a high degree of internal validity can be established.

The process of random assignment involves identifying a pool of subjects by random selection from a larger sample or entire population of subjects (e.g., a sample of second graders from the whole population of second grades). These subjects are then assigned to the groups or treatment conditions via some random process (e.g., by use of a table of random numbers). Random assignment ensures that the treatment and control groups are statistically equivalent with respect to all subject variables. Statistical equivalence does not mean that the groups are really equal but rather increases the probability that they are and that the differences between them are due to chance and not to any systematic bias. With random assignment, any differences obtained between the groups on the dependent variable can be attributed more confidently to the independent variable. However, in reality, random assignment to conditions is often not possible, particularly when applied research questions, such as the effect of school programs on students, are of primary interest.

Experimental research employs a variety of different types of designs, depending on the nature of the research question and the constraints of the research situation. Part 1 of Ebmeier and colleagues' study is an example of a posttest-only control group design. This design involves two groups, a treatment and control group, random assignment to groups, and the administration of a postest. In this design, since a pretest is not given, change over time, from pretest to posttest, cannot be assessed. Such a design is often used when there is concern that a pretest will unduly sensitize the subjects to the nature of the study and influence their performance.

A second example of a true experiment that utilized a slightly different design is a study by Lowery (1982). The investigator was interested in studying the "effects of three creativity instructional methods on the creative thinking of gifted elementary children" (p. 133). The subjects consisted of 36 gifted students from grades 3–5 who had IQ scores above 120. Within grades, students were randomly assigned to one of three instructional groups: one group received a packaged creativity program, the second group received a packaged program enhanced by teacher instruction, and the third group participated in a creativity program that used music and guided imagery as the major techniques. The treatments lasted for six weeks, 60 minutes per week. The Torrance Test of Creative Thinking was administered as a posttest only. The results of the study suggested that the music and imagery instruction had the greatest effect on creativity as measured by the Torrance test.

The Lowery study is an example of the multigroup posttest-only design, a slight variation on the posttest-only control group design. It is a powerful design because it uses random assignment to control extraneous variables. Its main disadvantage is that it lacks a pretest and therefore cannot assess change over time. Some other experimental designs are described below.

The Pretest-Posttest Control Group Design. In this design, subjects are randomly assigned to either a treatment or control group. Both groups are given the pretest and the posttest. This design is more sophisticated than the posttest-only control group design because it can assess changes in the dependent variable over time (i.e., from pretest to post-test). If Ebmeier and colleagues had used the Ross test both as a pretest and posttest in part 1, their design would have been a pretest-posttest control group design.

The Pretest-Posttest Multigroup Design. This design includes a pretest and a posttest given to three or more groups, each receiving a different kind of treatment, or two treatment groups and one control group. If Lowery had employed the Torrance test as a pretest and a posttest, her design would have been a pretest-posttest, multigroup design.

The Solomon Four-Group Design. This is a very sophisticated experimental design that is infrequently used. It is actually a combination of the pretest-posttest control group design and the posttest-only control group design. The Solomon design includes four groups of subjects, two treatment groups and two control groups. Of the two treatment groups, one receives both a pretest and a posttest, and the second receives only a posttest. Similarly with the two control groups, one receives the pretest and the posttest, and one receives only the posttest (Ary et al., 1985, citing Solomon, 1949).

This design is used when the researcher is concerned about pretest sensitization, but unlike designs described above, it actually helps to ascertain whether the pretest affects the treatment. The Solomon four-group design really involves conducting the same experiment twice, once with a pretest and once without. If the results of "both" experiments are similar, the researcher can be fairly confident about the effect of the treatment. The design is illustrated in Figure 3.1.

Let us go back to Ebmeier and colleagues' study to illustrate this design. These authors could have randomly assigned subjects to four groups instead of two. Two of those groups would receive the special gifted curriculum. Treatment group 1 would receive the Ross test as a pretest and a posttest, while treatment group 2 would receive it only as a posttest. Two groups of control subjects would receive only the regular curriculum. Control group 1 would take the Ross test both pre and post, while control group 2 would take it only as a posttest. In part 1, Ebmeier and colleagues actually made the comparison indicated by the broken lines shown in Figure 3.1. By including the other two groups (smooth lines), the experiment is replicated and the effect of the pretest is assessed. If the effect of the curriculum is the same for the comparison indicated by the broken line as for that indicated by the smooth line, the

FIGURE 3.1   Illustration of a Solomon four-group design

	Pretest	Posttest
Treatment Group 1	Yes	Yes
Treatment Group 2	No	Yes
Control Group 1	Yes	Yes
Control Group 2	No	Yes

pretest-posttest control group design

posttest-only control group design

pretest is not unduly sensitizing subjects and influencing posttest performance.

The Factorial Design. Factorial designs are ones in which two or more variables are manipulated simultaneously in order to determine the independent effect of the variables as well as their interaction on the dependent variable. Suppose that you are interested in exploring two or more independent variables, each with at least two levels. The variables can be active (those that are manipulated by the experimenter) or assigned (aspects or characteristics of the subject). In order for a factorial design to qualify as a true experiment, at least one of the variables must be active. You can randomly assign subjects to the active variable within levels of the assigned variable. For example, if you believe that students of varying levels of intellectual ability will differentially respond to and experience success with different counseling methods, you can manipulate the type of counseling, an active factor, but not the intellectual abilities (IQ) of the students. If there are three levels of IQ (below average, average, and above average) and three types of counseling (individual only, group only, individual and group combined), you can randomly assign students within each ability group to the three counseling conditions. In the Lowery study, the author might have wanted to assess the effectiveness of the three creativity programs for males versus females. The author may have had some ideas about differential male and female success with the creativity programs. Such a research study would call for a factorial design.

A factorial design is used primarily when (1) the researcher believes that the effect of treatment varies with a subject trait or characteristic and/or (2) the researcher is specifically interested in studying the effect of the interaction of the independent variables (treatment and the subject characteristic) on the dependent variable.

Nonexperimental Designs

In the best of all worlds, you want to use designs that provide adequate control of extraneous variables. True experimental designs accomplish this through the process of random assignment. However, when working in school settings this kind of control is frequently impossible. Also, it may be that the research question of interest simply does not lend itself to an experimental design.

Quasi-Experimental Design. Many research studies within the field of the education of the gifted employ quasi-experimental designs, or designs in which random assignment is not employed (see Cook & Campbell, 1979, for a fuller discussion). The most typical quasi-experimental design is the nonequivalent control groups design. This design is similar to the experimental pretest-posttest control group design, except that subjects are not assigned randomly to conditions or treatments. Because of this, you cannot assume that the treatment and control groups are equivalent on all variables at the onset of the experiment. A pretest and specific data analytic techniques can be used to assess and control for some of the preexisting differences between the groups (as in Ebmeier et al., part 2). Pretests, however, can only measure and control for differences in whatever the pretest measures and will not control for differences (such as interest or motivation) on other variables.

In many situations, the groups that are available to the researcher for study are intact and naturally assembled, such as two classrooms, or those students who are in a gifted program and those who are not. In other cases the treatment group consists of volunteers, while the control group may consist of subjects who do not seek treatment (Huck, Cormier, & Bounds, 1974). In these situations, random assignment is not possible and a quasi-experimental design must be used. A quasi-experimental design, although not as internally valid as a true experiment, may be more externally and ecologically valid because it is representative of the real environments within which learning takes place and/or subjects are found.

An example of the use of a quasi-experimental design, the nonequivalent control groups design, is a study by Parke (1983). This researcher was interested in the effects of self-instructional materials on the mathematics achievement of gifted elementary school students. Three groups of subjects were involved in the study. One group was the experimental, or treatment, group, which consisted of high-achieving kindergarten, first-, and second-grade children. There were two comparison, or control, groups, one group of same-aged high-achieving children and a randomly chosen group of same-aged children. The groups were assumed to be nonequivalent because they were naturally occurring, intact groups, and random assignment to conditions was not employed.

In the Parke study, only the treatment group received the 10-week intervention of the self-instructional materials. All groups received a skill-based test both as a pretest and posttest. Analysis of covariance (with the pretest as a covariate) was used to determine treatment effects and to statistically control for preexisting skill differences between the groups. The results showed greater growth by the treatment group in comparison to the two control groups. Although Parke concludes that the treatment was effective, she could not be as confident in that assertion as she could have been with results of an experimental design with random assignment.

There are other types of quasi-experimental designs, such as counterbalanced designs or time-series designs. For more information see Ary and colleagues (1985) and Huck, Cormier, and Bounds (1974). In summary, quasi-experimental designs do not control extraneous variables as well as experimental designs because they do not involve random assignment. However, quasi-experimental designs can be more ecologically valid and the results more widely generalizable than the better-controlled experimental designs.

Ex Post Facto Design. Sometimes a researcher's question simply does not lend itself to an experimental or quasi-experimental design. An investigator may be dealing with attribute-independent variables, or aspects of subjects over which he or she has no control. This is frequently the case in gifted education, where we are often interested in studying the differences between subjects who are high, low, or average on some aspect of intellectual ability. This type of research is called *ex post facto* research to emphasize that the research is conducted after variations in the independent variable have already occurred, without intervention or active manipulation by the researcher.

An example of *ex post facto* research is a study by Green, Fine, and Tollefson (1988). These authors were interested in the differences in the quality of family functioning and family environment between gifted achievers and gifted underachievers. Two groups of subjects were identified, high-IQ adolescents who had school performances indicative of underachievement and a second group of high-IQ students who did not show evidence of underachievement. Both groups of students completed measures of family functioning and satisfaction with family functioning. In this study, the independent variable of interest was the achievement level of the gifted students. This is a preexisting attribute of the subjects over which the researcher had no control. It cannot be manipulated. It simply exists in variation among subjects.

In some situations, an independent variable of interest can be actively manipulated and studied with an experimental approach or studied in an *ex post facto* approach. Suppose you are interested in the effects of anxiety on the performance of gifted students in an accelerated class. You could measure students' anxiety levels and form two groups of students— those with high levels of anxiety and those with low levels. This would embody an *ex post facto* research design. Suppose, instead, you manipulate anxiety level by creating a situation in which you increase anxiety for a group of students. You might induce anxiety by telling students that their performance on a test will determine whether you will write a favorable or unfavorable college recommendation for them or that some students need to be weeded out of the class and that this will be done using their exam scores. In this way you have manipulated the independent variable.

You may find in both cases that the more anxious students perform better in the class. With the experimental approach you would have more confidence in concluding that there is a relationship between anxiety and performance and that the results are not due to another variable (e.g., the more anxious students are also the more motivated students). Creating experimentally induced anxiety is marginally ethical and may not pass a human subjects review committee. Therefore, in this case, an *ex post facto* design would be more suitable.

USING RESEARCH DESIGNS

In this section, we will explore various research designs applied to the same research question. Let us suppose that a teacher/researcher in a public school has observed that her sixth-grade female students are doing well and achieving in mathematics as compared to the sixth-grade male students. By eighth grade, however, female students' math achievement is lower than that of the males. These differences continue and increase throughout high school and are most prominent among the most able students at the highest level of mathematics. She wonders why this is the case and hypothesizes that an environmental factor might be important. Specifically, she wonders if females might persist in their interest and participation in mathematics if they were in mathematics classes only with other females. She hypothesizes that a single-sex versus a coed environment is an important factor contributing to the mathematics achievement of high-ability females.

The teacher/researcher has an opportunity to test her hypothesis. She decides to investigate the effect of a single-sex versus coed environment at the highest level of mathematics; in this case, students intending to study Advanced Placement (AP) calculus. She has access to a sample of female high school juniors who intend to enroll in an AP calculus class for their senior year and randomly assigns the females in this sample to a single-sex or coed AP calculus class. The females in the study are equivalent with respect to previous coursework in mathematics. The dependent measures in the study are performance on a teacher-made calculus test, given pretest and posttest, and performance on the AP calculus exam, given as a posttest only. Both classes use the same text and materials and are taught by the same teacher. With this design, she can be reasonably sure that the females in the single-sex class are equivalent to females in the coed class and is more sure that differences in achievement between the groups can logically and causally be attributed to the environmental factor. Therefore, this study has a high degree of internal validity.

As an alternative to this design, let us suppose the teacher/researcher cannot randomly assign subjects to classes. She must allow the eligible female students to volunteer to participate in the single-sex versus the coed class. The same text and materials will be used, and the same teacher will teach both classes. With this design, she will be concerned about the possible preexisting differences between the females who volunteer for the single-sex class and those who choose the coed class. These differences may be substantial and influence the results—for example, the females who choose the single-sex class may be more able or more serious about mathematics study than the other females. This design is less internally valid than the one above, despite being more ecologically valid.

Suppose the teacher/researcher is unable to implement the study in one school. She could arrange to carry out her study in two comparable schools within the district, one a coed parochial school, and the other a single-sex parochial school. If this is all that is available, she would have to be very concerned about preexisting differences between the classes. She would want to try to demonstrate equivalence between the groups on as many variables as possible, such as family income, parental education, math ability, and math achievement. This could be accomplished via some matching process or by including these variables as covariates in the statistical analysis. No amount of manipulation, however, can eliminate a basic difference, which is that the females in the single-sex school have accumulated the advantages (or disadvantages) of that environment for a number of years. This design, though the most likely from a practical point of view, has the most serious drawbacks with respect to inferring a relationship between the independent and dependent variable.

COMMON PROBLEMS RELATED
TO RESEARCH ON THE GIFTED

If you are interested in studying an exceptional population, you must be aware of certain constraints or limitations peculiar to research designs involving atypical learners.

Problems with the Use of Standardized Tests

Educational research is rife with norm-referenced tests used to measure achievement. Certainly standardization allows for generalizability across populations. However, using norm-referenced test results to measure achievement gains with intellectually and academically gifted students can lead to some serious distortions for three related reasons:

1. *Low test ceiling.* Students starting with pretest scores at, for example, the 98th percentile have little room to demonstrate academic growth (the test ceiling is too low).
2. *Inequality of units of measure.* Many standardized tests are designed to discriminate most clearly within the wide average range. The upper ranges of the test often include a smaller number of more difficult items, each weighted more heavily than items in the midrange of difficulty. In other words, a wrong answer in the upper range counts for more and tells us less about how the individual reasons intellectually.
3. *Regression toward the mean.* When large numbers of individuals take both pre- and posttests as part of an experimental or quasi-experimental design, subjects who are at the upper ranges of the pretest tend to score lower on the posttest due to a statistical phenomenon called regression toward the mean. The underlying principle of this phenomenon is that extremely high scores on the pretest can be explained by chance factors that are unlikely to occur on the posttest. An experimental treatment may therefore appear to have *lowered* scores on the study outcome measures!

You will therefore need to exercise caution when analyzing standardized outcome measures, particularly when comparing gifted and nongifted groups. Selection of instruments with a high ceiling ensures a more revealing profile of gifted students' tested achievement. For this reason, Julian Stanley (Stanley & Benbow, 1986) promoted the use of the SAT-M to give a more accurate picture of the mathematical reasoning powers of young adolescents.

Another solution to this dilemma is to determine beforehand whether standardized tests include gifted students as part of the norming population. Check the technical manual to answer this question and find out what criteria the testmakers use to define the gifted classification.

Finally, you can tailor an instrument to meet specific study needs. Creating a truly valid test, however, requires special expertise. Researchers using a criterion-referenced test need to report their efforts in detail to ensure internal validity and reliability. In addition, replication and the study's generalizability become that much more difficult when the instrument is neither commercially available nor in the public domain.

Problems with Generalizability

Researchers describing a study they have conducted will refer the reader to a body of literature from which the methodological or theoretical arguments have been drawn. Unless the review of the literature is extensive and detailed, it is often difficult for you to decipher the operational definition applied to the label "gifted" in each study cited. That is, how were the gifted subjects identified? Gifted students are described by some researchers as individuals scoring in the 99th percentile on an individual IQ test at age 9, by others as scoring 500+ on the SAT-M at age 13, and by still others as having a profile defined by achievement tests, tests of creativity, and teacher and parent nomination. Each definition may be appropriate to each circumstance, but the result may also lead to contradictory outcomes when one looks for consistencies across studies. Noncomparable operational definitions may be the cause. In order to avoid the problem, carefully select studies to support your research hypotheses on the basis of the comparability of the samples and caution readers where noncomparability may be an issue.

In addition to properly describing a gifted subject group, the researcher must find a control or additional experimental group that is comparable across many variables. For example, two researchers in New York City (Subotnik & Strauss, in press) wanted to compare achievement in advanced placement calculus classes between two groups of girls, one from a selective all-female private school and one from an experimental all-female section at a lab school for gifted students. The subjects were all high school seniors. The private school students were admitted on the basis of teacher recommendation, high report card grades and achievement test scores, an interview, and whether or not one of their relatives was an alumna. The lab school students were selected on the basis of achievement test scores and a competitive examination. The researchers wanted to know whether studying calculus in an all-female school is different from in an all-female class in a coed school.

The researchers gave both groups a Mathematics Association of America calculus readiness test at the beginning of the experiment. This test was used to measure mathematical reasoning ability and prior exposure to mathematical content. If the groups had been more comparable at the outset, the researchers would not have needed to be concerned about exposure to mathematics content and reasoning ability. It turned out that there were significant differences between the two groups' scores on the readiness test; therefore the researchers had to employ statistical procedures to take into account or compensate for readiness test score differences.

Unfortunately, you may be hard pressed to find subjects to use as controls in an intervention or evaluation study. If you use a convenient heterogeneous group (i.e., with respect to ability) as a nongifted comparison group, you must deal with the noncomparability of the groups on several other variables. For example, you would need to control for whatever criteria were used for identification, the effects of labeling, and the cumulative effects of special programming up until the point of experiment (history). However, taking the time and expending the resources to obtain an appropriate control or comparison group will increase both the internal and external validity of the study.

SUMMARY

Research design is a tool to assist researchers in studying the nature of relationships among important variables. Key features of experimental research are the control of extraneous variables, manipulation of independent variables, and observations of the effects of independent variables on dependent variables. Research designs vary in the degree to which they allow for the determination or assessment of causal relationships. A true experiment is characterized by the random assignment of subjects to treatment conditions, resulting in a high degree of control over extraneous variables and a high degree of internal validity. With true experiments, causal relationships can be assessed.

In practice, true experiments are difficult to implement and quasi-experimental designs or *ex post facto* research designs are employed to answer research questions. While less internally valid, these designs are typically more ecologically or externally valid, since they mimic the real-world conditions in which students are found and variables interact.

Working with an exceptional population such as gifted students presents some special problems with respect to conducting research. These include problems with standardized tests that have inadequate ceilings for gifted learners and/or are not normed on gifted populations, problems with the generalizability of research findings due to the non-comparability of research samples, and the difficulty of finding an appropriate control group. Research designs can be significantly improved by the careful selection of assessment instruments and by consideration of the careful definition of *gifted* by researchers and practitioners. In addition, the careful selection of control or comparison groups will increase the confidence that you can have in research results.

REFERENCES

Ary, D., Jacobs, L. C., & Razavieh, A. (1985). *Introduction to research in education* (3rd ed., rev.). New York: CBS College Publishing.

Campbell, D. T., & Stanley, J. C. (1966). *Experimental and quasi-experimental designs for research*. Chicago: Rand McNally.

Cook, T. D., & Campbell, D. T. (1979). *Quasi-experimentation: Design and analysis issues for field settings*. Chicago: Rand McNally.

Ebmeier, H., Dyche, B., Taylor, P., & Hall, M. (1985). An empirical comparison of two program models for elementary gifted education. *Gifted Child Quarterly, 29*(1), 15–19.

Green, K., Fine, M. J., & Tollefson, N. (1988). *Gifted Child Quarterly, 32,* 267–272.

Huck, S. W., Cormier, W. H., & Bounds Jr., W. G. (1974). *Reading statistics and research*. New York: Harper & Row.

Kerlinger, F. N. (1973). *Foundations of behavioral research*. New York: Holt, Rinehart & Winston.

Lowery, J. (1982). Developing creativity in gifted children. *Gifted Child Quarterly, 26*(3), 133–139.

Mill, J. S. (1846). *A system of logic*. New York: Harper & Brothers.

Parke, B. W. (1983). Use of self-instructional materials with gifted primary aged students. *Gifted Child Quarterly, 27*(1), 29–34.

Solomon, R. L. (1949). On extension of control group design. *Psychological Bulletin, 46,* 137–150.

Stanley, J. C., & Benbow, C. P. (1986). Youth who reason exceptionally well in mathematics. In R. J. Sternberg & J. E. Davidson (Eds.), *Conceptions of giftedness* (pp. 361–387). New York: Cambridge University Press.

Subotnik, R. S., & Strauss, S. M. (in press). Gender differences in classroom participation and achievement: Experiment involving Advanced Placement calculus classes. *Gifted Child Quarterly*.

Wood, G. (1981). *Fundamentals of psychological research* (3rd ed., rev.). Boston: Little, Brown.

CHAPTER 4

MAKING SENSE OF YOUR DATA

Paula M. Olszewski-Kubilius and Marilynn J. Kulieke

The purpose of this chapter is to assist you, the researcher or evaluator, in making decisions about the appropriate descriptive and inferential statistics for use with quantitative data. We will begin by considering levels of measurement of dependent measures and how this determines the use of various statistics. We will then go on to describe some common statistics and the research questions with which they are most appropriately used.

Let us consider a common situation that you may face as a teacher of the gifted or novice researcher. Suppose you have been recently assigned the task of conducting and evaluating a summer program for gifted students. You find in the files left to you that a great deal of information has been collected about the students in the program. Specifically, you have students' scores on qualifying tests, such as ability tests and standardized achievement tests used as pre- and posttests. You have information about demographic characteristics of the students, such as the employment and educational status of their parents, family income, and their previous participation in special summer programs. Also, data are available about the students' perceptions of the benefits of the program, ratings of aspects of the program, and evaluations of their teachers and classes. Students also completed several inventories that assess their self-concept and motivation. In addition, observational data are available from the summer classes. You want to learn as much as possible about the students who attend the program and you are interested in determining the effectiveness and impact of the program. You have a wealth of data with which to examine these and other issues.

AN INTRODUCTION TO QUANTITATIVE ANALYSIS

Attributes of people or objects and observations such as those in our hypothetical example are often best represented through numbers, rather than words. *Quantitative data* will, by definition, consist of numbers—

numbers that have been assigned meanings. The meanings that can be given to numbers vary and include the following types:

1. Categories such as giftedness categories (general intellectual, specific aptitude, creative, psychomotor), occupational categories (managerial, professional), educational categories (high school, B.A., M.A.), or gender (male, female)
2. Positions or rankings, such as the position of student projects in a rank order of creativeness (1 for the least creative project and 10 for the most creative) or rankings of the quality or effectiveness of instruction on a scale from 1 (very) to 5 (least)
3. Scores on an IQ test, achievement test, aptitude test, or measure of self-concept
4. A frequency count of the number of times a gifted student seeks the aid of the teacher on a learning task or the number of times boys versus girls answer questions in a mathematics class

Purpose of Statistics

Statistics and statistical procedures are ways of handling numerical information and of making that information meaningful. These procedures and methods help you in two important ways. First, they enable you to organize, summarize, and describe sets of observations. Statistics that are used for this purpose are called *descriptive statistics* and include measures of central tendency, such as a mean, median, or mode; measures of variability, such as a range or standard deviation; indices of location, such as a percentile score or *z*-score; and correlation coefficients.

Second, statistics help you determine whether or not what was observed with a small sample of individuals would also be observed in the larger population from which the sample is drawn. These are inferential statistics. With *inferential statistics*, you hope to infer the similarity of a sample to a population (Ary, Jacobs, & Razavieh, 1985). Inferential statistics depend and build on descriptive statistics and include the *t* test, analysis of variance, and chi-square tests. The choice of statistics to use in your study or evaluation depends on two factors—the measurement scale of the variable(s) and the purpose(s) of the research or evaluation.

DESCRIPTIVE STATISTICS

Descriptive statistics are the most basic way to summarize data and are usually the first step in organizing a set of data. We will discuss measurement scales and their relationship to statistics, frequency distributions, measures of central tendency, and several other important concepts in the following sections.

Measurement Scales

Through the process of measurement, you quantify observations into numbers that can then be subjected to various analyses. The nature of the measurement process and the level of measurement of the observations determine the interpretations that can be made from them and the statistical procedures that can be used.

Nominal Scales. Researchers typically employ a taxonomy of measurement that ranges from the most primitive scale to the most sophisticated. The most primitive scale of measurement is the *nominal* scale. With nominal measurement, objects or individuals are placed into categories that differ from one another qualitatively but not on a quantitative dimension. These categories do not imply possession of more or less of an attribute. The only relationship among categories is that they are different from one another (Ary et al., 1985). It is presumed that all the individuals or objects within the category are the same with respect to the attribute. Some of the most common nominal categories used in research include:

Gender (male versus female)
Occupation (managerial, professional)
Religious preference (Catholic, Jewish, Protestant, other)
Race (black, Hispanic, Asian, Caucasian)
Type of giftedness (creative, intellectual, psychomotor)
Program type (pull-out, self-contained)

Because of the categorical nature of this level of measurement, one can only use those statistical procedures that are based on simple frequency counts, such as the number of individuals who fall into a particular category (i.e., the number of males in the sample or the number of students who are intellectually gifted).

Ordinal Scales. The next higher level of measurement is the *ordinal* level. With ordinal measurement, objects or individuals or events are ranked or ordered with respect to their possession of some attribute from highest to lowest.

For example, a group of students can be rank ordered from the most creative to the least creative. Student projects could be similarly ranked on this dimension. Also, students could evaluate the effectiveness of their teacher or their compatibility with the teacher's style of instruction on a 4-point scale, from very effective or very compatible to very ineffective or very incompatible.

With ordinal-level measurement, the only information available about the objects or individuals is the extent to which they possess a characteristic or attribute in comparison to the other ordered objects or events. You cannot talk about their possession of the attribute in any absolute sense. The only meaningful aspect of the numbers assigned to objects or individuals is order. There is no basis for interpreting the difference between the numbers. For example, if you rank a class of gifted students on the characteristic of sociability from the most sociable to the least sociable student, you can speak of one student as being more sociable in comparison to another, but you cannot meaningfully talk about the size of the differences between the students who have been rank ordered. You *cannot say*, for example, that the difference between the most and next most sociable student is the same as that between the least sociable and next least sociable student. The size of intervals between the ranked, or ordered, objects is simply unknown. Because of this, the statistics available to use with ordinal-level data are limited.

Ordinal scales are frequently used in research and evaluation. They are easy to construct and are often all that is required for answering many research questions. For example, the following questions would be satisfied by ordinal-level data:

1. Which group, the gifted or nongifted students, have more or less positive attitudes toward school?
2. Which group of gifted students, those enrolled in an accelerated class or those enrolled in an enrichment program, have higher or lower confidence in their academic abilities?
3. Which group of gifted students, males or females, have higher or lower anxiety about an accelerated class?

Another reason for the frequent use of ordinal scales is that many variables do not lend themselves to a higher level of measurement. For example, you might be interested in assessing students', teachers', and parents' attitudes toward the gifted program, or their perceptions of the success of a gifted program. To answer these questions you might devise your own questionnaire or survey instrument containing questions that involve the ordinal level of measurement (e.g., "How would you rate the teacher of your course: very effective, quite effective, effective, somewhat ineffective, very ineffective?" or "How has your son's or daughter's study habits (motivation) changed as a result of participation in the summer program: greatly improved, improved, stayed the same, declined, greatly declined?").

Interval Scales. The next and more sophisticated level of measurement is the interval scale. An interval level not only orders objects or individuals according to some attribute but also establishes equal intervals between the ordered objects or individuals. When numbers are assigned to objects or individuals on an interval scale, both the order and distance relationships between the numbers are meaningful (Ary et al., 1985). For example, suppose you gave students a mathematics test with a 50-point scale. The student who earns a 45 on the test has done better than the student who earns a score of 40. The difference between the two students who earned a 40 and 45 respectively is the same as the difference between the two students who earned a 30 and 35 respectively. With interval-level data, it is appropriate to talk about and compare the intervals between numbers. In addition, many statistics are available for data analysis.

A property that an interval scale does not possess is that of a true zero. In the example above, if a student obtained a score of zero on the mathematics test, we cannot reasonably talk about the student as having no knowledge of mathematics. In an interval scale, the zero point is arbitrary. Other examples of interval scales are the Fahrenheit and Centigrade temperature scales, most standardized achievement tests, ability tests, and IQ tests.

Ratio Scales. The highest level of measurement is the ratio scale. Ratio scales have ordinal and interval properties and, in addition, possess a true zero (McMillan & Schumacher, 1984). For example, on a yardstick, the zero is a true zero and corresponds to "zero length." A yardstick, therefore, embodies a ratio-level scale. There are very few variables in education that are measurable at the ratio level. Those that are, such as reaction times, tend to be physiological measures.

It is not always easy to determine the level of measurement of the independent and dependent variable(s) in a research study (the dependent variable is the outcome variable, or the variable that we expect to be affected by the independent variable). However, this is necessary because the type of statistical procedures you can use depends on the level of measurement of the variables. Let us recall the example above of the newly hired summer program director. Some of the variables in this data set are nominal in nature, such as parental occupation, or ordinal, such as grades or attitudes toward the program. Other variables are interval in scale, such as achievement test scores and ability test scores. The type of descriptive and inferential statistics that can be employed with each of these variables will depend on their level of measurement.

Frequency Distributions

One of the first steps in organizing a data set would be to look at the distribution of scores via a frequency distribution, or a *histogram* or *polygon*. A frequency distribution involves arranging the scores in a systematic way, from highest to lowest score, and tallying the number of individuals who obtain each score (or the number of times that the score appears in a data set). This is done for each dependent variable.

A frequency distribution allows you to ascertain several important characteristics about the distribution of scores relatively quickly. It will reveal the general shape of the distribution, whether it is symmetrical or skewed (scores are concentrated at either the low or the high end). It will also reveal where clusters of scores tend to be and how many clusters there are. In addition, it will reveal the general range of scores and whether there are any unusually low or high scores (extreme scores) in the distribution. You can graphically depict the frequency distribution in the form of a histogram or polygon.

Suppose our new summer program director wishes to examine the distribution for posttest scores for 25 students who participated in an algebra class. The students took a standardized achievement test with a range of 0 to 35 points. A frequency distribution and polygon are given in Figure 4.1. As can be seen, in this distribution, there is one cluster of scores, at 30. The distribution is fairly symmetrical, and scores range from 25 to 35.

Measures of Central Tendency

One of the first statistics you compute to summarize a set of data is a measure of central tendency. Very simply, a measure of central tendency attempts to reduce a set of individual scores to a single index. Three measures of central tendency are generally used: mode, median, and mean.

The *mode* is defined as the score that occurs most frequently within a distribution of scores. A mode can be reported for any scale of measurement, but it is the only measure of central tendency that can be used with nominal data. For example, if you have measured the college majors of a group of gifted students and wish to characterize the group with respect to that variable, all you can compute and report is the number of

FIGURE 4.1 Sample frequency distribution

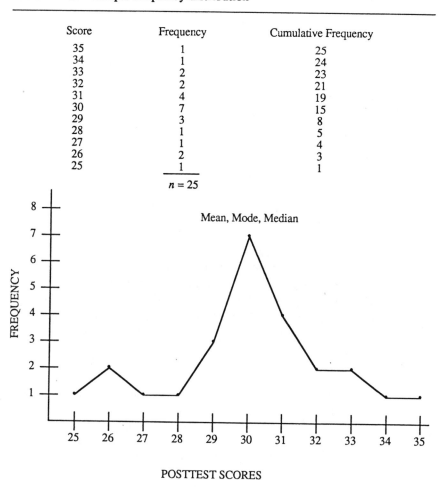

Score	Frequency	Cumulative Frequency
35	1	25
34	1	24
33	2	23
32	2	21
31	4	19
30	7	15
29	3	8
28	1	5
27	1	4
26	2	3
25	1	1
	$n = 25$	

students who have reported each college major and the college major that was chosen the most often. The mode does not take into consideration the size of individual scores or any order information. The mode statistic answers questions such as: What is the course of study most often selected by gifted males and females? What is the most frequent problem encountered by students enrolled in gifted programs? The mode should be employed when you are interested in describing the most frequent score, category, or characteristic.

The *median* is the point (score) in a rank-ordered distribution of scores below which 50% of the scores lie and above which 50% of the scores lie. The median also does not take into consideration the size of individual scores, although it does take into consideration rank-order information. It divides a distribution of scores into two halves, an upper and lower half. The median is the measure of central tendency that is appropriate for ordinal-level data, since it is based on rank order only. For example, you administer an attitude survey to your gifted classes. The most appropriate measure of central tendency would be the median.

The measure of central tendency most frequently used by researchers is the *mean*. The mean is simply the arithmetic average of a group of scores. Because it is an arithmetic average, the mean is an interval-level statistic and should, strictly speaking, be used with interval- or ratio-level data. The mean is employed when you are interested in knowing the average performance or attitude or score of a group of individuals.

Each of the three measures of central tendency corresponds to a particular level of measurement. In addition, there are other factors to consider when choosing a measure of central tendency for your data. The mean is a more precise statistic than either the mode or the median, because it is computed by utilizing every score in the distribution. It is also the most stable of the central tendency statistics "in that if a number of samples are randomly drawn from a parent population, the means of these samples will vary less from one another than will their medians and modes" (Ary et al., 1985, p. 107).

On the other hand, the mean, because it does utilize every score, will be sensitive to the presence of extreme scores in the distribution. In contrast, the median, which does not take into account the size of individual scores, will not be influenced by extreme scores. The median may therefore be the statistic of choice if extreme values are a problem in a data set.

Finally, it is important to remember that the mean "is the best indicator of a combined performance of an entire group," while the "median is the best indicator of a typical performance" (Ary et al., 1985, p. 108). You may choose to use the median statistic because you are interested in describing a typical gifted student or a typical gifted program. You may choose to use the mean when your goal is to describe the average performance of a group of gifted students or the average cost of a gifted program.

In the example depicted in Figure 4.1, the mean of the scores is 30. The median is also 30, as is the mode of the distribution. For these data, the mean is an appropriate measure of central tendency since the data are interval in level and the distribution neither contains extreme scores nor has more than one cluster of scores.

For the newly hired summer program director, dependent variables such as parental occupation or education are categorical in nature and require a mode statistic. Variables such as student attitudes or ratings of teachers are ordinal in nature and can employ the median statistic. And variables such as achievement test scores or scores on motivation and self-concept measures are interval in nature and can employ a mean.

Measures of Variability

Another descriptive statistic that researchers typically report is some measure of the variability or dispersion of scores within a distribution. Variability can be used to characterize a group of scores on a hypothetical dimension of homogeneous to heterogeneous. If the scores are similar, they are relatively homogeneous and have low variability. If the scores are very different from one another, they are heterogeneous and have high variability. Alone, measures of central tendency do not give us the total picture of a distribution. Two distributions may have the same mean, but the variability of the scores can be very different. A measure of variability lets us know how representative of the distribution the central tendency measure is. As with measures of central tendency, measures of variability correspond to levels of measurement.

Variation Ratio. The relevant measure of variability for nominal data is a statistic that is infrequently used, called the variation ratio. The variation ratio gives you the percentage of nonmodal scores, or the percentage of scores that do not fall into the modal (most frequent) category. For example, suppose our summer program administrator was interested in the occupations of the parents of the students in the program. The administrator determines that 60% of the fathers check the category of professional (dentist, physician, nurse, teacher, lawyer). The other 40% of fathers were distributed across the other occupational categories. For this variable, "professional" is the mode and the variation ratio is .40.

Quartile Deviation. For ordinal-level data, a corresponding measure of variability would be the quartile deviation. The quartile deviation is half the difference between the upper and lower quartiles in a distribution (see Ary et al., 1985, for a description). The upper quartile is the point in a distribution below which 75% of the cases fall, and the lower quartile is that point in a distribution below which 25% of the cases lie.

This statistic takes into consideration the rank ordering of scores in a distribution but not the value of each individual score. In the example shown in Figure 4.1, the upper quartile is 31.697 and the lower quartile is 28.656. The quartile deviation is thus 1.521.

Variance and Standard Deviation. For interval- and ratio-level data, measures of variability that are commonly used are the variance and standard deviation statistics. These statistics take into consideration the size and location of each score within the distribution of scores and use the mean of a group of scores as a point of reference (Ary et al., 1985).

Indices of Location within a Distribution

Sometimes you are concerned with finding the location of an individual or object within a distribution of individuals or objects. The kind of index that you can use depends on the level of the measurement scale of the dependent variable. For nominal data, you simply report the category within which the individual falls (e.g., gifted or nongifted).

Percentile Rank. For ordinal-level data, to locate an individual within a distribution, you can compute a percentile. The percentile rank of a score is obtained by finding the percentage of scores that are smaller than that score value. For example, a percentile rank of 75 for a raw score of 50 means that 75% of the scores in the distribution are smaller than 50 and 25% are larger. A percentile rank takes into consideration only the rank ordering of scores, not their values.

The z-Score. For interval- or ratio-level data, the index of location to use is the z-score, which conveys the relative standing of a score within a distribution of scores. A z-score is defined as the distance of the raw score from the mean measured in *standard deviation units*. The z-score helps to locate an individual score within a distribution and can also be used when you wish to make a comparison between the relative standing of the same individual on two tests with different scales.

For example, suppose you want to compare a gifted student's math achievement test score to his or her English test score. If the student obtains a score of 50 on the math test and 75 on the English test, it is impossible to say on which test he or she did better. These raw scores can be converted to z-scores (based on the means and standard deviations of each distribution). In this way the two performances can be compared on the basis of how far above or below their respective mean each score falls.

Another reason to use *z*-scores would be if you want to add student scores obtained on different tests (in the same course for example) to obtain a total score on which to base grades or conduct analyses, especially when the tests yield different ranges and different distributions (e.g., a chapter test that ranges from 0 to 50 points and a midterm that ranges from 0 to 100). Each individual test score can be converted to a *z*-score and then added or averaged to yield a single *z*-score for each student.

You can also employ *z*-scores when you wish to combine two groups of students into one group for purposes of data analysis. For example, suppose you are interested in determining what variables correlate with a successful performance in an accelerated calculus course. Two teachers teach the course, and each has 30 students. In order to combine the two classes for data analysis, you convert scores on a standardized calculus posttest to *z*-scores. Now you have a measure of how a student performed relative to the other students in his or her class, and on a common metric.

Similarly, suppose you want to combine two classes of students, those taking Latin I and those taking Latin II, for purposes of data analysis. Latin I and Latin II students take different posttests. If the posttest scores are converted into *z*-scores, the two classes can be combined for data analysis.

Measures of Association

Measures of central tendency and dispersion describe a group on a single variable. But often you are interested in describing the way two variables are related to one another for a group of individuals. These are called *bivariate relationships*.

Statistical techniques that are used to describe the relationship between two variables are called correlational procedures, and the indices they yield are called *correlation coefficients*. Correlation coefficients provide several types of information, such as the direction and magnitude of the relationship between variables. The direction can be either positive or negative. A positive relationship means that high scores on one variable are associated with high scores on the other variable (e.g., brighter children are more socially mature). A negative relationship means that high scores on one variable are associated with low scores on the other (e.g., brighter students tend to exhibit fewer disciplinary problems).

Correlation coefficients can vary in magnitude from +1 to −1. The closer the correlation is to either +1 or −1, the stronger the relationship is between the two variables. A strong relationship means that one set of scores is highly predictable from the other, or knowing an individual's score on one variable allows you to predict that individual's score on the other variable with a high degree of accuracy. Correlations in the range of .85 and above are high correlations, whereas correlations in the range of .50 to .80 are moderate in size. Correlations below .5 are low in magnitude and indicate a weak relationship between the variables.

Pearson Product-Moment. There are many types of correlation statistics, and the choice of one depends in part on the level of measurement of the variables. The Pearson product-moment correlation (Pearson *r*) is the most used correlation index and is appropriate for either interval- or ratio-level data. An appropriate research question for the Pearson coefficient would be: Do measures of mathematical reasoning ability (SAT-M scores) predict or relate to achievement (a standardized test in algebra) in accelerated mathematics classes among gifted students? This question involves a bivariate relationship between two interval-level variables.

One of the assumptions underlying the Pearson *r* is that the relationship between the two variables is linear (i.e., a straight line represents the relationship rather than a curved line). One way to check whether this assumption is true is to produce a scattergram of the data by simply plotting the scores for one variable on the horizontal axis and the scores for the other variable on the vertical axis (see Figure 4.2). If the dots generally fall in a straight line, one can assume linearity and proceed with the computation of the correlation coefficient. If visual inspection reveals a curvilinear relationship, another index, such as the correlation ratio (eta) should be used.

Spearman Rho. For ordinal-level data, the appropriate index of correlation is the Spearman rho coefficient. The Spearman rho is derived from the Pearson coefficient, and like the Pearson *r*, ranges in size from +1 to −1. The Spearman rho falls into the same category as the median and is computed by first assigning ranks to raw scores. An appropriate research question for the Spearman rho coefficient, especially when both variables are at the ordinal-level of measurement, would be: Do the gifted students who express more positive attitudes towards nongifted students receive more positive ratings from those nongifted students?

Contingency Coefficient. For nominal-level data, a measure of association is the contingency coefficient. According to Silverman (1977), "it is an index of the degree of relationship, or association, between two attributes of events that have been assigned on the basis of these attributes to the cells of a contingency table" (pp. 185–186). A contingency table crosses one set of categories with another set of categories. For

FIGURE 4.2   Scattergram of posttest scores and SAT–M scores

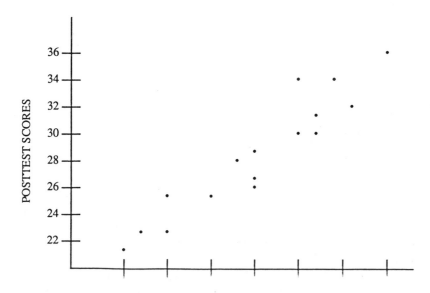

example, you might be interested in the numbers of male versus female students who are classified into different types of giftedness (creative, psychomotor, general intellectual, specific academic aptitude). You cross gender categories with categories of giftedness to get eight different combinations (see Figure 4.3) or cells. A cell is created by the combination of one category or level of an attribute with one category or level of the other attribute (e.g., creative girls). The number of cells in a table can vary but is determined by the number of categories into which the scale for each attribute is divided. The contingency coefficient computed from the contingency table ranges in value from 0 (no relationship exists) to 1 (a strong relationship exists). (See Figure 4.3.) The contingency coefficient is the only measure of association that can be used with nominal-level data.

In addition to the Pearson *r*, the Spearman rho, and the contingency coefficient, there are other correlation coefficients that are appropriate for ascertaining relationships between different types of variables. These indices, however, are less frequently used (see Ary et al., 1985, for a description). They include the *biserial* and *point-biserial correlation coefficients*, which are used when one variable is at the ratio- or interval-

FIGURE 4.3   Contingency table of gender by types of giftedness

	Creative	Psychomotor	General Intellectual	Specific Academic	Total
Males	12	12	8	8	40
Females	10	10	10	10	40
	22	22	18	18	80

level of measurement and the other is a nominal variable with only two levels (dichotomous).

Whenever correlations are used, it should be remembered that they indicate associations and relationships between variables but not necessarily causal relationships. Correlations indicate that changes in one variable are associated with changes in another, but these changes cannot be attributed causally to the other variable.

In addition, the size of a correlation coefficient is in part dependent on the variability of the two distributions that are being related. If the range of one of those distributions is limited or truncated, the size of the correlation will be lowered. This is especially a problem with research on gifted individuals. For example, a strong correlation between intelligence and achievement may exist in the general population, where there is wide variation on both intelligence and achievement. However, if we are looking only at a group of gifted individuals, or the upper end of the distribution on IQ, this correlation may be minimal due to the restriction of range on the IQ variable.

Partial Correlation Coefficients. Measures of association are not limited to describing relationships between pairs of variables but can also be used to describe relationships among three or more variables. Suppose you are interested in the effects of mathematical reasoning ability on success in an accelerated algebra class. However, you want to control for students' socioeconomic status because you believe that it may affect success in the program. You can use a partial correlation coefficient for this purpose. In this case, the measure of mathematical ability (SAT scores) would be correlated with the measure of success (scores on a standardized algebra posttest), controlling for the correlation between socioeconomic status and success. Partial correlation is used to determine the correlation between two variables when a third variable needs to be controlled or taken into account.

Multiple Correlation, or Multiple Regression. Another correlational technique—multiple correlation, or multiple regression—is used when you are interested in which weighting of two or more variables best predicts a third (dependent variable). In the example above, suppose you are interested in what variables (ability, previous experience in the content area, or personality dimensions such as achievement motivation) best predict performance in an accelerated class. You would use the technique of multiple correlation to determine which of these is the best predictor and/or which weighted composite of ability measures, previous experience, and personality measures predicts success. With multiple regression you could also learn whether one variable (e.g., personality measure) provides any additional predictive utility beyond the other independent variables (e.g., ability and previous experience) and just how much of the variability in success can be predicted from the combination of these particular independent variables. Multiple regression is a useful technique when you are interested in asking research questions about prediction and have multiple independent variables. See Table 4.1 for a summary of the descriptive statistics described above.

INFERENTIAL STATISTICS

Descriptive statistics are used to organize, summarize, and describe data. Usually, however, this is only the first step in the process. Most re-

TABLE 4.1 Summary of descriptive statistics

Levels of Measurement	Central Tendency	Indices of Variability	Indices of Location	Correlation Coefficient
Nominal	Mode	Variation ratio	Category	
Ordinal	Median	Quartile deviation	Spearman rank	Rho
Interval/ratio	Mean	Variance and standard deviation	z - score	Pearson r

searchers are interested in being able to generalize their findings from the sample of individuals on which they have collected data to a larger population. This is the essence of inferential statistics.

Population Parameters

Ary and colleagues (1985) observe that inferential statistics involve going from the part to the whole. The part is the small group that is actually observed, or the sample. The whole is the larger group from which the sample is drawn—or the population. According to them:

> Statistical inference is a procedure by means of which one estimates population parameters, based on the characteristics of samples. Such estimations are based on the laws of probability and are best estimates rather than absolute facts. In any such inferences a certain degree of error is involved. (p. 138)

When samples are used to estimate population parameters, a certain amount of error is expected because random samples will vary from one to another. Sampling errors, however, behave in lawful and predictable ways. You use the information gained from observing samples and knowledge of sampling error to make reasonable decisions about populations based on the study of samples.

When you compare the attitudes (say, toward oneself) of two groups of subjects, a group of high-IQ subjects who are enrolled in a gifted program and a group of high-IQ subjects who are not enrolled in a gifted program, you are concerned about determining whether any differences observed are a function of the program participation or are due to chance differences (i.e., sampling error) between the groups. You cannot really or ultimately know which explanation is correct, but you can estimate the *likelihood* of chance alone being responsible for the observed differences. This estimate of likelihood can be used to make a decision about which explanation (the program participation or chance) you can accept. The chance explanation (known as the null hypothesis) states that there is no relationship between the variables of program participation and attitudes. The alternative, or research hypothesis, states that the differences between the groups are due to the independent variable, in this case, enrollment in the gifted program.

In practice, for the research question above, you would create two random samples and estimate their respective population means. You would then compare these and use an inferential statistical test to estimate the probability that the chance explanation is not true. If there is a high probability that the chance explanation is not true (or a low probability that it is true), the research hypothesis can be accepted and mean differences can be attributed to participation in the gifted program.

Levels of Significance

Researchers generally agree to use a predetermined level at which the null or chance hypothesis would be rejected. This is called the level of significance and usually is .05 to .01. These levels of significance mean, in effect, that the estimated probability that the null hypothesis is true and that differences are due to chance is about 5 out of 100 (or 1 out of 100).

There are numerous inferential statistics available to test a null hypothesis, and you make choices based both on the nature of the research question and characteristics of the data. Two broad categories of inferential statistics are parametric and nonparametric. Parametric statistics make three assumptions about the nature of the quantitative data that nonparametric statistics do not. These assumptions are that:

1. The data are normally distributed within each group
2. There are equivalent variances within comparison groups for a given dependent measure (i.e., homogeneity of variance)
3. The data are ordinal or interval in scale

If these assumptions cannot be met, the researcher should use a nonparametric statistic instead. Nonparametric statistics are appropriate for ordinal- or nominal-level data.

Comparing the Means of Two Samples

The *t* Test. The *t* test is a parametric test that can be used to compare the means of two groups. For example, suppose a researcher were interested in whether gifted students had higher average scores on a self-concept measure compared to nongifted age mates. If these two groups (gifted and nongifted) are drawn independently from a population without any matching or other relationship between them, the *t* statistic for independent samples can be used. Basically, the *t* statistic is a ratio. The numerator of this ratio is the numerical difference between the means of the two groups. The denominator is a numerical estimate of how much these two groups would be expected to differ by chance alone and is based on the sample sizes and the variation within each of the two groups. Many research questions can be addressed using the *t* test. All that is required is two different groups of subjects and ordinal- or interval-level measurement of the dependent variable.

When you are interested in comparing the scores of the same individuals who have been measured on two different occasions (e.g., a pretest and a posttest) and/or exposed to two different experimental conditions, use the *t* test for nonindependent samples. This statistic is computed similarly to the *t* test for independent samples, except one uses the average difference between pairs of scores rather than the actual score values in the numerator. (Other names for the *t* test for nonindependent samples are the paired, dependent, correlated or matched *t* test.) A correlated *t* statistic would be appropriate if you were interested in whether gifted students' self-concepts improved or declined as a result of participation in a special program and you measured self-concept twice, at the start and at the end of the program.

The Median Test. One nonparametric analogue to the *t* test for independent samples is the median test, which is used to test whether two groups or samples have the same median or are drawn from the same population. To calculate the value for the median test, you actually use the chi square formula. You would use the median test if your question was whether the typical gifted student was rated as more physically attractive than the typical nongifted student.

The Mann-Whitney *U* Test. The Mann-Whitney *U* test is a more powerful nonparametric test than the median test and a better alternative to the parametric independent *t*-test. The Mann-Whitney *U* actually tests for the difference between the rankings of scores in two different samples. (You actually utilize the rankings to compute a *U* statistic and use a table of critical values of *U* at various levels of significance to determine whether the difference in rankings is statistically significant.) You might use a Mann-Whitney *U* to determine whether gifted students receive more positive ratings from gifted and nongifted classmates compared to nongifted students, especially if these ratings are at the ordinal level of measurement and/or do not meet the other assumptions for a parametric test.

The Sign Test. A nonparametric equivalent for the correlated *t*-test is the sign test, which uses data on the direction (+ or −) of the differences between pairs of scores rather than their numerical values. The sign test is used "in ascertaining whether two conditions are different for related samples when the data for each pair can be ranked but quantitative measurement is not possible" (Huck, Cormier, & Bounds, 1974, p. 201). For example, you might employ the sign test if you are interested in whether a group of gifted children engaged in imaginative play more than their nongifted matched (on age and sex) controls. All you know is which member of each pair plays more, as estimated by teachers, but not to what degree or how much more. The sign test computes the number of + and − signs and uses these numbers to obtain a critical value.

The Wilcoxin Matched Pair Test. The Wilcoxin test, unlike the sign test, takes into consideration the magnitude and the direction of the difference between each paired score. It is a more powerful test than the sign test. To use the example above, if you knew how many hours each child spent in imaginative play during the past week, you could compute the difference in hours for each matched pair of children and use the Wilcoxin test instead of the sign test. This would be especially appropriate if the data are not normally distributed and/or the variances for the gifted and nongifted groups are very different.

The above tests would also be appropriate if you have more than one measurement on the same group of individuals. For example, suppose you are interested in whether young gifted children engage in more high-level kinds of play, such as imaginative play compared to manipulative play. If the only information you have is parents' estimates of which type of play the child produced more of, the sign test is appropriate. If you know the number of hours spent in each type of play in the past two weeks, the Wilcoxin test is appropriate.

Comparing Two or More Means

When you are interested in comparing the sample means of two or more groups on one independent variable, the parametric statistic of choice is the analysis of variance (ANOVA). This extension of the *t* test allows a researcher to test the differences between all groups more accurately than by conducting many *t* tests between pairs of groups. It is called ANOVA because "the statistical formula uses the variances of the groups and not the means to calculate a value that reflects the degree of differences in the means" (Ary et al., 1985, p. 257). The ANOVA computes an *F*-ratio instead of a *t*. ANOVA addresses the question of whether there exists a significant difference between any two means.

For example, you might ask: Do high-IQ students resemble chronological age mates or students who are equivalent in mental age on measures of interpersonal effectiveness? You would identify three groups of subjects: (1) a sample of 14-year-old gifted children, (2) a sample of 14-

year-old nongifted children, and (3) a sample of 16-year-old nongifted children. You would then compare their mean scores on a test of interpersonal effectiveness with ANOVA. Another example would be the assessment of the effects of three different types of creativity training programs on gifted students' divergent production. Students would be randomly assigned to one of three treatment groups: (1) guided imagery, (2) imagery plus music, or (3) music and creative movement. ANOVA would be used to determine if the means for any of the groups are significantly different from one another.

A significant *F*-ratio on an ANOVA will tell you only that some combination or pair of means is different. To determine which pairs of means are statistically different, you must conduct multiple comparison tests, or post-hoc comparisons.

An ANOVA can and should be used when there are multiple independent variables as well as multiple groups of subjects. This situation calls for a *factorial* ANOVA. Suppose, in the last example, you were interested in the effects of gender. The study now has two independent variables (gender and type of creativity program) and a single dependent measure (divergent production). A factorial design and ANOVA allow you to examine the effects of the interaction of the two (or more) independent variables. In the example above, you are interested in determining whether the effect of the type of creativity training on divergent production varies for males and females, or whether males and females are differentially responsive to, or successful with, a particular type of creativity training program.

The nonparametric equivalent to the ANOVA is the Kruskal-Wallis test. This test is computed using rankings rather than the actual score values and helps you determine whether three or more samples come from the same population. The Kruskal-Wallis could be used to determine, for example, whether gifted children of different ages (e.g., ages 7, 9, and 11 years) differ in their subjective feelings of acceptance by their classmates. Feelings of acceptance may be determined by a teacher-devised questionnaire with ordinal scaling. Each child in the study sample would be given a rank based on his or her acceptance score. The Kruskal-Wallis would determine if these rankings differ for the three age groups.

An ANOVA is also used when you have repeated measures for one or more groups of individuals on the same variable. For example, suppose you have given a group of gifted students a series of lists of words to memorize. These word lists differ in difficulty. You then would have, as a dependent measure, the number of words correctly recalled for each word list. A *repeated measures* ANOVA could be used to assess mean differences in the memorability of the different word lists for the same group of subjects.

Also, suppose you have measured the same group of individuals on three different occasions on the same instrument or task. For example, you are interested in the effects of a gifted program on students' perceptions of support from key groups (e.g., friends, classmates, family, and teachers). You might give students the same questionnaire at three different times: (1) before the program, (2) at the start of the program, and (3) at the end of the program. The repeated measures ANOVA can help ascertain whether there are significant changes in students' perceptions of support over time.

The nonparametric analogue to the repeated measures ANOVA is the Friedman Two-Way Analysis of Variance. It is used when the same group of individuals is measured repeatedly. The Friedman test is conducted on rankings of the data rather than the actual scores. A research question that could be addressed with a Friedman test is: Do gifted childrens' ratings of popularity (by classmates) change during or after they participate in a gifted pull-out program?

Analysis of covariance, or ANCOVA, is a statistical procedure used in situations similar to ANOVA. ANCOVA, however, attempts to adjust statistically for initial differences between groups on variables that are related to the dependent variable but uncontrolled (e.g., control for preexisting differences in knowledge of a subject matter by covarying on pretest scores). In the example above on interpersonal effectiveness, you might want to control for family variables, such as the number of siblings, presuming that the presence of brothers and sisters enhances the development of interpersonal skills. The independent variables would be gender and age, while the covariate would be the number of siblings and the dependent variable, interpersonal effectiveness. In the second example above, you might want to control for preexisting differences in the groups on divergent production by using the test of divergent production as a pretest. In this case, the independent variables would be gender and type of creativity program; the covariate, a pretest for divergent production; and the dependent measure, a posttest of divergent production.

Comparing Proportions

Finally, you might be interested in determining whether the proportions of individuals that fall into certain categories are different (e.g., gifted achiever, gifted underachiever). The chi-square statistic is appropriate for this type of research question. It compares actual or observed frequencies or proportions to those expected on the basis of chance alone.

The chi-square test also can be used when you are interested in the proportions of individuals who fall into more than two categories (e.g., the number of mathematically talented students who are left- versus right-handed versus ambidexterous) and to compare proportions for two different groups of subjects (e.g., the proportion of gifted and nongifted students who are left- versus right-handed versus ambidexterous). In this latter case, the chi-square test assesses whether the two variables, giftedness and handedness, are independent or related. Unlike the ANOVA or the *t* test, which use the actual scores, the chi-square test examines the number of individuals who fall into a particular category. There is no parametric analogue to the chi-square test.

SUMMARY

In summary, there are many types of inferential statistical tests to use to test hypotheses. To assist you in identifying the appropriate test, the following pieces of information about the data are useful:

1. The level of measurement of the independent and dependent variables
2. Whether you have a number of (two or more) measures on the same group of individuals or the same measures on several groups (samples) of individuals (in other words, whether you have related samples or independent samples)
3. The number of groups you wish to test the differences between
4. Whether the dependent measures satisfy the assumptions of parametric tests such as homogeneity of variance and normality

Inferential tests are summarized in Table 4.2.

It is often difficult to know where to begin to organize your data once it has been collected. The following checklist of steps may help you organize and make decisions about your data.

1. Make sure data are clean and free from coding and data entry errors.
2. Decide on the level of measurement for each dependent and independent variable.
3. Produce frequency distributions and/or histograms for each dependent variable.
4. Examine distributions for skewness, bimodality, and extreme scores.
5. Compute the appropriate measure of central tendency and variation

TABLE 4.2 Tests of significance

Test Name	Levels of Measurement	Related or Independent Sample	Number of Samples
t-test for independent samples	interval/ratio	independent	two
Paired *t*-test	interval/ratio	related	two
Median test	ordinal	independent	two
Mann-Whitney *U*	ordinal	independent	two
Wilcoxin matched pair test	ordinal	related	two
Sign test	ordinal	related	two
ANOVA	interval/ratio	independent	two or more
ANCOVA	interval/ratio	independent	two or more
Repeated measures ANOVA	interval/ratio	related	two or more
Kruskal-Wallis one-way ANOVA of ranks	ordinal	independent	two or more
Friedman two-way ANOVA of ranks	ordinal	related	two or more
Chi-square	ordinal	independent	two or more

for each variable, taking into consideration the level of measurement, the research questions, and the nature of the distributions.

6. Determine which bivariate relationships you are interested in examining.
7. Product scatterplots for bivariate relationships to check for linearity.
8. Decide on an appropriate descriptive statistic (correlation coefficient) for bivariate relationships.
9. Determine appropriate inferential tests based on level of measurement, whether data satisfy the assumptions of parametric analysis (homogeneity of variance within groups and normality of distributions within groups), number of sample means (medians) to be compared, and the independence of groups or samples.

In summary, when conducting research on gifted individuals that involves quantitative data, statistics will most likely be employed. There are two types of statistics, descriptive statistics and inferential statistics. Descriptive statistics include measures of central tendency, variation, and association. They are used to initially characterize the group(s) of individuals under study and to ascertain the relationships between variables. Inferential statistics are used to determine whether findings on a sample of individuals can be generalized to a larger population. They answer the question: Can the finding for this particular group of gifted children be expected with other groups of gifted children? Parametric statistics such as the independent *t* test, the correlated *t* test, and the ANOVA, as well as nonparametric tests such as the sign test, the Wilcoxin test, and the Kruskal-Wallis test, are examples of inferential statistics.

Decisions about which statistic to employ rest on the nature of the research question, the level of measurement of the variables under study, the number of groups being studied, and the number of variables involved. One of the most important steps that a researcher in gifted education can take is to thoughtfully consider the types of data he or she will collect and the kinds of statistical procedures that can be employed on them prior to any actual data collection.

REFERENCES

Ary, D., Jacobs, L. C., & Razavieh, A. (1985). *Introduction to research in education* (3rd ed., rev.). New York: CBS College Publishing.

Huck, S. W., Cormier, W. H., & Bounds, W. G., Jr. (1974). *Reading statistics and research*. New York: Harper & Row.

McMillan, J. H., & Schumacher, S. (1984). *Research in education*. Boston: Little, Brown.

Silverman, F. H. (1977). *Research design in speech pathology and audiology*. Englewood Cliffs, NJ: Prentice-Hall.

Wood, G. (1981). *Fundamentals of psychological research* (3rd ed., rev.). Boston: Little, Brown.

PART II

SPECIFIC APPLICATIONS OF RESEARCH METHODOLOGIES TO GIFTED EDUCATION

CHAPTER 5

DEVELOPMENTAL AND LONGITUDINAL RESEARCH

Frances S. O'Tuel

Developmental research refers to the study of the development of some trait or characteristic over time. The methodology recommended for collecting data in such research is a longitudinal design. Longitudinal research is used to answer questions related to changes over time, individual differences, and patterns of behavior of groups or individuals. In contrast, cross-sectional research is used when decisions must be made immediately, when relationships or predictions need to be established, and when funds as well as time are limited. The major difference between them is in the design and selection of subjects. In most longitudinal research the investigator collects data on the same sample of individuals at intervals over time; in cross-sectional studies the data are collected on several different age groups at the same instant in time. For example, if creativity is the characteristic to be investigated in a longitudinal study, a sample would be identified at a particular age by some measures (tests, juried products, performance, etc.). Then repeated measures would be collected over a period of years from the same individuals on these same dimensions. A record of any related experiences, such as training in creative problem solving or experiences related to creativity, would also be accumulated. Collecting cross-sectional data on different age groups at the same time does not yield developmental information about how subjects change (or do not change) over time because they are not the same subjects and the data are not collected over time.

LONGITUDINAL RESEARCH AND THE GIFTED

Longitudinal research has been sparse in the literature of gifted education because it is costly, requires a stable staff of investigators, suffers from the loss of subjects who move or drop out of programs, and takes a long time to complete. Terman's study of gifted students is probably the best-known effort to collect repeated information on the same group of gifted individuals (Terman, 1925). Funded by the Commonwealth Fund of New York City, Terman identified more than 1,500 students who were approximately 11 years of age and had IQ scores above 140 on the Stanford-Binet. He initially collected information on the personal, social, and scholastic aspects of their lives. For more than 30 years Terman and his colleagues continued to collect follow-up data. Although he experienced many of the problems common to longitudinal studies, Terman was successful because of consistent funding, support from Stanford University, and cooperation of the subjects in the sample. Other longitudinal studies on the gifted are Benbow and Stanley (1982), Smilansky and Nero (1975), and Wolf and Shigaki (1983).

You may have a limited knowledge base and/or lack experience reading and interpreting research studies. In reading this chapter, do not become discouraged if a section seems difficult to follow or overly technical. When you are ready to conduct your own study, there are statisticians who can assist you in both the design and analysis. It is most important that you understand when longitudinal studies are appropriate and what information they might add to our knowledge of gifted persons.

The first step in any research study is posing the question (see Chapter 1, this volume). Here are some questions for which a longitudinal design would be particularly appropriate:

1. Is one type of gifted program more appropriate for one grade level than others?
2. Do gifted children become more reflective as they grow older?
3. What effect does change or lack of it have on problem solving at different ages?
4. As children progress through stages of cognitive development, what changes take place in their "gifted behaviors"?
5. What is the relationship between gifted students' present performance and previous events, training, experiences, family characteristics, and so on?
6. When does a particular behavior or characteristic appear? Does a behavior or characteristic develop gradually or appear suddenly at a certain time?
7. What chain of events precedes the appearance of a behavior? What training experiences precede a behavior or are necessary for its appearance?
8. What increases or decreases a certain behavior?

9. What individual differences are observed between students in a gifted program and those not enrolled?

Appropriateness of Longitudinal Research

The next step after posing broad questions in any research study is the clear delineation of the question to be answered. Four types of questions are particularly well suited for longitudinal studies (Wohlwill, 1973).

Preserving Developmental Information. In art, for example, Lowenfeld (1957), Kellogg (1969), Goodnow (1977), and Piaget (1954) supported the view that a child's production in art goes through developmental stages that are observable. You might be interested in a longitudinal study of such developmental changes in a sample of gifted students that could document the rate and types of changes that occur.

Amount and/or Pattern of Change. Students in academically gifted programs increase their knowledge over time. You might ask how gifted students acquire this knowledge, how they organize it in long-term memory, and what differences in rates of acquisition and patterns of responding develop. The research on expert and novice individuals, for example, indicates a difference in the structure of long-term memory between these two groups. Unfortunately, short-term studies have designs that limit the information they can contribute to what is known about these issues. Longitudinal research is ideal for studying amount and pattern of change.

Early Behavior and Later Behavior. Relationships between early and later behavior are well suited to longitudinal investigation. One question might be, does performance of some kind at age 5 predict performance at age 12? This type of question examines the stability of behavior and the ability of the earlier measures to predict what will happen later.

Antecedent Events and Later Behaviors. Examining the relationships between antecedent events and later events is also best done with longitudinal research. For example, research has shown that the best predictor of next year's achievement is this year's achievement. Such antecedents may be related to a later behavior or they may not. Bloom and Sosniak (1981) looked for antecedent events in their recent study of exceptionally talented young people. They found antecedents such as parental valuing of the talent and shifting of home responsibilities to other members of the family so the *talented* could receive training and practice no matter what talent was being investigated. Cause and effect may not be clear in such studies, but relationships can shed much information about which variables were present in the past when some behavior is exhibited in the present. Baseline data and continued collection of additional data are necessary for confirming relationships between antecedent events and later behaviors.

Advantages of Longitudinal Research

The major advantage of longitudinal research for the above types of inquiry is stated succinctly by Wohlwill (1973):

> Data involving repeated measures of the same subjects provide a more powerful test of the significance of the time related differences than those based on the comparison of independent samples drawn to represent points on a time dimension. (p. 124)

Longitudinal research can rule out the cohort difference effect of cross-sectional studies. Cohort difference means that different subjects at different ages may not be comparable to one another due to (1) different experiences that happened to one age group but did not occur for another age group and/or (2) the different backgrounds and characteristics of each group. If you collected data on gifted students in the fourth, seventh, and tenth grades of a school district and you made the assumption that the tenth-grade gifted students were like the seventh-grade students would be in three years, you might have a cohort difference. You would need to be sure that the tenth-graders had experiences in the gifted program similar to those the seventh-graders would have in the next three years. However, if the district program has only identified tenth-graders this year for the first time, they would have had no previous experience in a gifted program, but the seventh-graders would be experiencing that program for the next three years. Any differences or similarities could be the result of different experiences, not change over time. In cross-sectional studies the assumption is made that the next oldest age group is performing like a younger age group will perform when they reach that age. Such assumptions can lead to poor decisions and erroneous conclusions.

Another advantage of collecting data on the same individuals at different points in time is the opportunity to make predictions based on actual experiential results. For instance, if you wanted to predict who would do well in a program for gifted and the pool of students was identified at the end of the first grade, you could collect data on their performances in subsequent years. You could then see how valid the identification process was in relation to student performance in the program and compute correlation coefficients between identification measures and one or more later performances to determine which identification measures best predict student performance.

Disadvantages of Longitudinal Research

Longitudinal studies are rare in gifted education. In this section, I will discuss the disadvantages that lead researchers to consider other designs.

Time. To collect repeated observations over periods of time requires a long overall time span and a number of blocks of time for data collection. These may not be realistic for many researchers.

Attrition. Students move away, change schools, and drop out of programs. Therefore, your sample may no longer be composed of the same proportions of different subgroups that was true when the study began. Changes that occur at later points may be attributable to a lack of proportionate representation of the target population rather than to the variable(s) under investigation.

Cost. Because funding looms so large in carrying out research, cost is a major issue. It may be costly to follow up on the original sample. You need personnel and resources to keep track and collect additional measures. You can reduce costs by selecting your sample from a school district composed of a stable student population, identifying them early, and continuing to locate them within that district. Maintaining physical facilities, equipment, alternate forms of measures, secretarial help, and so on may also require continued funding.

Personnel. In order for you to successfully maintain the focus of longitudinal research, you will need stable staff members who will still be there when data collection, analyses, and results are done in subsequent years.

Measures. You must consider test-retest effects. If the same instrument is administered to the same group at several different times, there is always the possibility that any improvement in scores is the result of practice rather than treatment. If alternate, equivalent forms of the instrument are available, this problem is somewhat diminished. You must also determine the appropriateness of the instrument for subjects of different ages. Different instruments for different age groups may introduce the problem of whether they measure the same characteristics.

VALIDITY ISSUES

In designing a longitudinal study, you need to guard against threats to internal and external validity. *Internal validity* exists if alternative explanations can be ruled out as causes of the findings. It is concerned with controlling for extraneous variables that might influence the outcomes or prevent the drawing of cause-and-effect relationships. *External validity* refers to the appropriateness of generalizing the findings to other subjects and situations where the circumstances appear to be similar. Without addressing these validity issues in the planning stage, you may be left with uninterpretable garbage.

Internal Validity

The threats to internal and external validity are discussed in detail in Cook and Campbell (1979). These must be key concerns in the design of any study. In this section I briefly describe the problems and suggest solutions to them.

History. Events that may occur during the span of the study and influence the results, but were not part of the treatment, must be recorded and considered in interpreting results. If your sample is not somewhat homogeneous and if you have no control group, you may not be able to interpret the results. You must also ask whether the individuals were so different at the beginning on some influencing variable such as prior knowledge that the causes of change are confounded.

Maturation. Obviously, in longitudinal results you expect maturation of subjects to occur. If treatment rather than maturation is the variable of interest, you may consider controlling for maturation. The easiest way is to have an equivalent group serve as a control group. If, however, other experiences, except perhaps the treatment (such as a gifted program), are roughly the same, changes in the control group due to maturation can be ruled out of the results of the experimental group.

An interaction between selection and maturation may also be a problem where there is a differential growth pattern for one group. This might occur if you have no "comparable" control group. A comparable control group is one of approximately the same ability/achievement level as the treatment group, as well as one having a proportionate representation by age, gender, race, and socioeconomic status. In studies of gifted programs, this is a problem because most school districts will not withhold services from one-half of the students who meet the criteria for the program in order for these students to serve as a control group. If there is no comparable ability group, you may identify the group closest in level to the treatment group and use them as a control group. This near, but not comparable, group may not have the same rate of learning as the gifted group. Thus the experimental group may appear to have made greater gains that will be attributed to the treatment than actually occurred; the experimental group's rate of learning may appear to be faster than the control group's rate. If you select a control group like this, you might measure their growth on the variables of interest and measure that of the treatment group over several previous years to establish that the rate of learning is not significantly different for the two groups. If the two groups have different rates but the rates are linear and predictable, you could make a statistical adjustment when you compare the data.

Another possibility is to take the pool of students identified as gifted and divide them into two groups. Provide one group with the treatment during the first half of the study and the other group during the second half. This may be more acceptable to administrators, since each group is treated; at the same time it will provide you with a control group.

Instrumentation. Several considerations are important in the area of measurement. Changing levels of a test instrument may well change the objectives a test measures; the scores on different levels of tests are not always continuous. If this is the case, you cannot compare across the levels. Second, the practice effect mentioned earlier must be addressed. Third, and probably most relevant to gifted research, is the effect of having an instrument on which all the members of the sample score at or near the top of the potential range of scores. Using out-of-level testing (one or two levels above the particular grade level) may be one of the best ways to combat this. For example, the Johns Hopkins programs for mathematically and verbally precocious youth have used the Scholastic Aptitude Test (SAT), normally taken by 11th- and 12th-grade students as a college admission criterion, as an aptitude test for 7th graders.

Statistical Regression. It is critical that a ceiling effect on a test does not distort the performance of students who do so well that they

have nowhere to go but down. Regression toward the mean is the predicted result when tests bunch all subjects at an extreme of the range of
scores. It is also a predicted result on repeated measures.

Selection. A sample must be representative of the population from
which it is drawn. If the population is all gifted middle school students in
a school district, then the sample would be best obtained by randomly
selecting from that population. Practically speaking, this is not usually
possible; students may be available because they are in a particular
school or grade or taught by certain teachers. When you cannot randomly
select participants for your study, try to select as representative a group
as possible. For example, you might be interested in the effect of a
particular gifted program over an extended period of time. The experimental sample would consist of those students who participate in the
program. You would then need to select a control group that is similar to
the experimental group but will not receive the treatment.

Mortality. Under attrition in the above section on the disadvantages
of longitudinal research, I made the point that the type of person who
drops out may change the composition of the group on the posttest. The
remaining sample may not be representative of the population from
which the original sample was drawn. If this occurs where you have
experimental and control groups, you might take the pretest results and
match pairs, one from the treatment group and one from the control
group, instead of aborting the study. This will reduce the sample size and
limit the generalizability to groups that possess the same characteristic as
the matched groups.

Direction of Causal Influence. Because longitudinal research is
designed on an extended timeline, determining the direction of causal
influence is not likely to be a problem. You will assume that what came
first on the timeline would be the causal influence of the variables that
come after.

Diffusion or Imitation of Treatment. Sometimes when a particular
program is implemented in a place where the control groups may also be
located, parts of the program may be carried out in groups other than the
experimental group. Teachers or students may talk to others about what
they are doing, and other classes or groups may decide they will also try
it. Even if the location is not the same, there may be cross-communica-
tion, with some of the elements of the treatment bleeding to other groups,
such as the control group. The solution to this threat to internal validity,

of course, is to locate a control group at a site where the persons involved have little communication with individuals in the experimental group. You may be able to locate such a control group in another district that has similar demographic characteristics. The danger in this is that over the extended period of time that a longitudinal study is ongoing, the other district may institute some treatment of its own over which you have no control. Finding a site within the same district, similar in characteristics but removed geographically, is probably more feasible.

Compensatory Equalization. Some administrators may be concerned that the identified experimental group is receiving a special program and therefore offer another special program to other students. Such a program may address some of the same outcomes as those of the treatment and thus reduce the differences between the experimental and control groups. In addition, other teachers may implement some intervention to show that their students can do as well as the experimental group. Again, you might need to find different sites within the district for the experimental and control groups.

Resentful Demoralization. When one group receives a special program, as occurs with almost all gifted programs, and another group (e.g., not identified as gifted) does not, there may be resentment, and sometimes even sabotage, of the special program. This is a particular problem of programs for the gifted and should be taken seriously as a threat to the outcomes and/or success of the treatment. Pull-out gifted programs may have this problem with the regular classroom teachers. The teachers whose students go to a gifted class daily or weekly may assign them extra work or require them to do every exercise they missed. The director, coordinator, teacher of the gifted, and you, the researcher, must constantly address problems of public relations in the schools, the district, and the community. As a researcher, you may facilitate one-on-one interaction between teachers in the regular classroom and the teachers in the gifted program in order to reduce resentful demoralization. You should address this issue before you begin the research and monitor it during the study.

External Validity

External validity is central to the generalizability of the findings to the population and to other similar populations. The more restricted the range of performance by samples (the more homogeneous the sample), the more limited is the generalizability. This is particularly an issue in gifted research. Because there is no agreement on procedures for the identification of gifted between states and/or school districts, samples drawn from a "gifted" group in one district may not be representative of other populations of "gifted." Such differences are obvious when one examines the criteria in the performing arts and in the academic programs for the gifted. Less obvious among programs with similar purposes, such as the academic programs, is the fact that different instruments, different cut-offs, different matrices for selection, and different program objectives limit the generalizability of one study of "gifted" students to another setting.

Interaction effects among selection, setting, and/or history, and the treatment may also affect the generalizability of results. These, to some extent, can be addressed in the types of statistical analyses used and will be addressed in a later section.

METHODOLOGY

In Chapter 3 of this volume, you were introduced to several basic experimental and nonexperimental designs. Longitudinal research presents special challenges that should be considered when you plan your study or evaluation.

Design Issues

The question drives the design. In most longitudinal/developmental research you will want to examine intraindividual results; that is, repeated measures of the same individuals on the variables. At the same time you may also examine interindividual differences. These are calculated by averaging the intraindividual observations of members of a group at each point in time and then studying group differences and similarities. If you are only interested in intraindividual patterns, a control group is not a must. This would be descriptive research, in which the patterns of change over time are studied and described. If, on the other hand, your focus is on interindividual differences, you will need a control group. This comparison group will enable you to generalize about how the findings are alike or different from some other group. Even if change in individuals on some variable(s) from one point in time to other points in time is the issue, a comparison group may be wise. Changes in a comparison group as a result of maturation can be taken into account so that you can attribute changes in the experimental group to causes other than maturation. You can do this by using the pretest data on two groups as covariates in the comparison of posttest results of the two or more groups that will be discussed below in the section on statistical analysis.

Time-Series Design. The most frequently recommended design for longitudinal/developmental research is a time-series design (Achenbach, 1978; Baltes, Reese, & Nesselroade, 1977; Bergquist & Graham, 1980; Borg & Gall, 1983; Cook & Campbell, 1979). In general this design calls for repeated measures, usually on the same subjects, over time. When it was developed and used in agriculture and science, 50 or more measures for each subject on each variable of interest were collected. In spite of this impractical number of repeated measures, the time series has been usable where fewer than 50 observations are available. In its simplest form, where only one group of individuals is being observed (measured) at multiple points in time, the design would be represented as follows:

$$O_1 \ O_2 \ O_3 \ O_4 \ O_5 \ O_6 \ O_7 \ O_8 \ O_9 \ O_{10}$$

This represents observation (O) 1 at time 1, observation 2 at time 2, and so on. In the above design there is no treatment. Usually, the results will be reported as descriptive information. You should collect data about events surrounding the observation points in order to rule out or explain variations from outside sources.

The same design in which a treatment has been inserted would appear as follows:

$$O_1 \ O_2 \ O_3 \ O_4 \ O_5 \ X \ O_6 \ O_7 \ O_8 \ O_9 \ O_{10}$$

The X represents the treatment, and the observations are the same as in the previous design.

In designs without control groups there may be several threats to internal validity. Differences may be a result of history or maturation, for instance, instead of treatment. To rule out or control for these you might use the following design:

$$O_1 \ O_2 \ O_3 \ O_4 \ O_5 \ X \ O_6 \ O_7 \ O_8 \ O_9 \ O_{10} \text{ (experimental group)}$$

$$O_1 \ O_2 \ O_3 \ O_4 \ O_5 \ O_6 \ O_7 \ O_8 \ O_9 \ O_{10} \text{ (control group)}$$

If you select samples from the same population, the above design would provide valid results if no unusual outside event occurred with one group and not the other. It might, however, raise an ethical issue. Suppose the treatment (X) is a gifted program; if the groups are comparable, both have been identified as gifted, yet only one group has received service. Does this violate one group's right to an appropriate education? To overcome this problem you might use an interrupted time series with switching. Both groups would receive the treatment but at different times. The following is an example:

$$O_1 \ O_2 \ O_3 \ X \ O_4 \ O_5 \ O_6 \ O_7 \ O_8 \ O_9 \ O_{10}$$

$$O_1 \ O_2 \ O_3 \ O_4 \ O_5 \ O_6 \ O_7 \ X \ O_8 \ O_9 \ O_{10}$$

In any case of time series, changes in the slope of values, the level of intercept, and/or the move toward greater homogeneity around means are indicators of effect. Change in slope refers to how much the variable changes between the observation times before treatment and after treatment. If each time you measure the variable before treatment, the mean value has risen 2 points over the time before and the mean value has risen 4 points between observation after the treatment, the slope has changed from a ratio of 2:1 where the number one is the time interval to 4:1 (see Figure 5.1). Change in level or intercept refers to the pattern of mean values for observations before and observations after the treatment. If the mean value is gradually increasing until the point of treatment and then increases sharply immediately after the treatment and then continues its pattern of gradual increase, the level or intercept has changed; the slope of pretreatment mean values would have a different intercept from the slope of the posttreatment mean values if extrapolated to a common origin (see Figure 5.2). If on the variance of values at each posttreatment observation the subjects have become significantly more homogenous in their repsonses, the results of the treatment are notable. Any of these changes—slope, level, or homogeneity of response—can be significant findings.

Time series allows maturation effect or trend to be observed before treatment. Cyclic and seasonal effects that may appear to be treatment effects also can be observed. Since this design allows for the assessment of trends prior to treatment, you can check for the plausibility of regression toward the mean as an explanation. Without the repeated measures, you may find a linear relationship when there is not one or find no correlation when the relationship is really curvilinear. By plotting the mean values on repeated observations, you can more accurately determine the relationship.

FIGURE 5.1   Example of change in slope

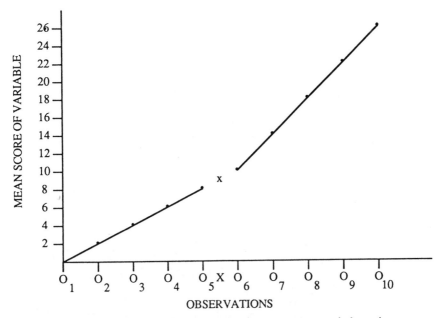

Change of Slope: Pretreatment 2:1—Pretreatment mean rises 2 points between each observation
Posttreatment 4:1—Posttreatment mean rises 4 points between each observation

Longitudinal Cross-Sectional Design. The longitudinal cross-sectional design has proved to be both a time saver and a manageable way to look at issues of development and changes over time. It controls for cohort differences, maturation effects, and other threats to validity; it also can be done in fewer years. An example of the design appears in Figure 5.3. The left column shows the year of birth for each cohort group; the bottom line shows the data collection years for the longitudinal group; the diagonal shows the cross-sectional data collection points. You could translate this design into fewer years by changing the data collection points. The spacing between observations would depend on the question that is being asked. In the sample in Figure 5.3, however, there is an eight-year span from the initial collection and the final data collection (1996). The cross-sectional data would be available in 1988 and their results could be confirmed, disconfirmed, and/or expanded with longitudinal data beginning in 1990.

FIGURE 5.2   Example of change in intercept

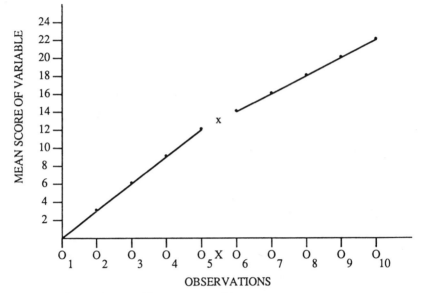

Expected mean without treatment--12
Expected mean with treatment--14
Result: Level of intercept changed due to increase after treatment

FIGURE 5.3   A longitudinal cross-sectional design

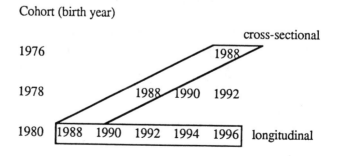

In summary, there are many suitable longitudinal designs to consider. You could simply identify one group of gifted students and observe them at several points in time in order to describe their development. If, however, you are interested in assessing the effects of some treatment, such as a gifted program, a creative problem-solving unit, or performance in a self-contained versus a pull-out program, you might identify one group of gifted students at several points before treatment, apply the treatment, and then make additional posttreatment observations. To combat the threats to the internal validity of your study, you might include a control group and/or conduct an interrupted time series. Finally, you might choose a longitudinal, cross-sectional design to compress the amount of time for the study. More elaborate designs are also available. Because longitudinal studies require investing a great deal of time, effort, and funds, and must overcome a number of problems associated with long-term research, shortcuts in design are unwise.

Sampling

Sampling is closely related to design issues. The major concern in sampling is that the sample be representative of the population to which you will generalize the findings. Of course, random sampling from that population is preferred. By assigning a number to each person in the population of interest, you can select your sample with a computer-generated list of random numbers or by manually using a table of random numbers. Most schools, however, have systems of assigning students to classes that are not random and that reflect some type of grouping criteria. This often makes random selection difficult to achieve in field settings. Another important consideration is the representativeness of subpopulations within the sample. For instance, in a district where gifted programs include both academic and performing arts students, it would be important to examine the two groups separately as well as together. However, there are usually more students in academic programs than in the programs for performing arts. In a stratified random sample, this proportion should be reflected.

Another important consideration in sampling is the stability of the sample. Longitudinal research requires repeated observations. If stability is a serious problem, then longitudinal research will probably not be feasible.

Measurement

An observation is not a measurement unless it has certain characteristics. A measurement must be objective, reliable and valid.

Objectivity. A measurement is objective when the resulting values will be the same even when different individuals collect the data or when different scorers assign values to the data. If a scoring key furnished by the publishers is used to score the instrument, the resulting scores should be the same (objective) no matter who uses the key.

Reliability. Reliable measures are those that yield the same score when an individual takes the test on several occasions. Some variation in performance is expected because humans are not perfectly consistent; therefore the scores will not be identical. Reliability for a standardized instrument is usually reported in the manual, although, in some cases, the technical manual must be ordered to obtain reliability coefficients. Other sources of reliability information are *Mental Measurement Yearbook* (Buros, 1982) or articles in research journals where the instrument has been used in research. If the reliability is not high (.85 for cognitive instruments and .70 for affective measures), you should not use it in lognitudinal research. Since time will elapse between measurement points, it is critical that the instrument consistently measure the variable(s) in question.

Validity. The third characteristic of a measurement is that it is valid. Validity refers to the appropriateness of the instrument to measure the variable in question. An intelligence test, for example, might be valid for measuring intelligence but not valid for measuring achievement.

When an instrument is used at different points in the development of the individuals, reliability and validity should be addressed each time it is used. What is valid for 10-year-olds may not be valid for 17-year-olds. Another major concern is whether continual testing with the same instrument results in gains that are no more than practice effects. If you change instruments, then you must ask if the new measurement is equivalent and if it is a comparable measure of the same variable. One way to address some of these concerns is to use a latent trait model such as Rasch measurement (Wright & Stone, 1979) to construct equivalent forms that measure the same unidimensional trait. For further explanation of this model, see Wright and Stone (1979).

Statistical Analysis

There are several ways to analyze longitudinal data. The most often recommended way is repeated measures analysis of variance (ANOVA). ANOVAs report between- and within-group differences. If you find that differences within each group are small and differences between groups are large, you will report significant statistical results. However, your analysis will assume that any sources of error are independent and not correlated.

I recommend using multiple regression when several predictors are beileved to influence a single outcome. This analysis requires interval or ratio measurements (see Chapter 4, this volume). For example, if your district is attempting to validate its identification criteria for student entrance to the gifted program, you might use multiple regression or an extension of this procedure called discriminant analysis (see Buchanan, 1987, for an example of this procedure).

Multivariate analysis using structural equation models is another method of analysis. The model assumes that you have a theoretical model to test. The model is translated into mathematical equations that show the relationship of the variables. This approach is particularly useful in long-term developmental phenomena where experimental or manipulative procedures are not available. For more complete description of this analysis see Joreskog and Sorbom (1979), Lomax (1982), and Wolfle (1980).

If your data do not meet the requirements of interval or ratio measurements, you may consider using nonparametric analyses such as chi-square. In longitudinal studies these might help you explore the data but probably would not be used to answer the major questions.

Statistical programs are available to calculate all of the above analyses on mainframe or microcomputers. The *Statistical Analysis System* (SAS) and the *Statistical Packages for the Social Sciences* (SPSS or SPSS-X) are two commonly used applications for data analyses.

SUMMARY OF MAJOR PRINCIPLES

At the beginning of this chapter I discussed several types of questions for which longitudinal/developmental research is most appropriate. Particularly where threats to internal validity are difficult to control and where cohort differences in cross-sectional data may mask relationships and effects, you should consider conducting longitudinal/developmental studies. The following principles apply to longitudinal research:

1. Longitudinal/developmental research is recommended when your questions involve changes over time, individual differences, and patterns of behavior of groups or individuals.
2. The design of your study must be carefully selected and implemented. With the exception of correlational studies, most of the recommended analyses require some type of repeated measures design.

3. The use of a control group(s) is generally necessary in order to explain outcomes that might be affected by confounding variables, for example, maturation.
4. Samples that are used must be representative of the population and stable enough to be present at subsequent observation points.
5. Carefully selected measurements that will give valid results over time and repeated administration are essential.
6. Because longitudinal research requires large expenditures of time, effort, and funds, formulate questions that are critical concerns and likely to add significantly to our knowledge and understanding of gifted and talented persons.
7. Select the method of statistical analyses best suited to the form of the results and the questions of the study. Analysis should help you view the data in meaningful ways. Remember that statistical significance does not always mean or imply educational significance.

As you weigh the advantages and disadvantages of longitudinal research, one important consideration should be whether the studies you conduct will add significantly to our knowledge and understanding of the gifted. Perhaps we have been guilty of overreliance on Terman's (1925) study, which began in 1921, and need more detailed, extended knowledge of gifted persons for the year 2000.

REFERENCES

Achenbach, T. M. (1978). *Research in developmental psychology: Concepts, strategies, methods.* New York: Free Press.

Baltes, P. B., Reese, H. W., & Nesselroade, J. R. (1977). *Life-span developmental psychology: Introduction to research methods.* Monterey, CA: Brooks/Cole.

Benbow, C. P., & Stanley, J. C. (1982). Consequences in high school and college of sex differences in mathematical reasoning ability: A longitudinal perspective. *American Educational Research Journal, 19*(4), 598–622.

Bergquist, C. C., & Graham, D. L. (1980). Developing models for special education using multiple time-series/multiple baseline design in the ESEA IV-C project. *Evaluation Review, 4*(3), 307–321.

Bloom, B. S., & Sosniak, L. A. (1981). Talent development vs schooling. *Educational Leadership, 39*(3), 86–94.

Borg, W. R., & Gall, M. D. (1983). *Educational research: An introduction.* New York: Longman.

Buros, O. K. (1982). *Eighth mental measurement yearbook.* Highland Park, NJ: College Board Publications.

Buchanan, N. (1987). Evaluating the identification process of a program for the gifted: A case study. *Roeper Review, 9,* 231–235.

Cook, T. D., & Campbell, D. T. (1979). *Quasi-experimentation: Designs and analysis issues for field settings.* Boston: Houghton Mifflin.

Glass, G. V., & Stanley, J. C. (1970). *Statistical methods in education and psychology.* Englewood Cliffs, NJ: Prentice Hall.

Goodnow, J. J. (1977). *Children drawing.* Cambridge, MA: Harvard University Press.

Joreskog, K. G., & Sorbom, D. (1979). *Advances in factor analysis and structural equation models.* Cambridge, MA: Abt Associates.

Kellogg, R. (1969). *Analyzing children's art.* Palo Alto, CA: National Press Books.

Lomax, R. G. (1982). A guide to LISREL-type structural equation modelling. *Behavior Research Methods and Instrumentation, 14,* 1–8.

Lowenfeld, V. (1957). *Creative and mental growth* (3rd ed.). New York: Macmillan.

Piaget, J. (1954). *The construction of reality in the child.* New York: Basic Books.

Smilansky, M., & Nero, D. (1975, March). A longitudinal study of the gifted disadvantaged. *Educational Forum* (Kappa Delta Phi), 272–294.

Terman, L. M. (1925). *Genetic studies of genius* (Vol. 1). Stanford, CA: Stanford University Press.

Wohlwill, J. F. (1973). *The study of behavioral development.* New York: Academic Press.

Wolf, W., & Shigaki, I. (1983). A developmental study of young children's conditional reasoning ability. *Gifted Child Quarterly, 27,* 173–179.

Wolfle, L. (1980). Strategies of path analysis. *American Educational Research Journal, 17,* 183–209.

Wright, B. D., & Stone, M. H. (1979). *Best test design: Rasch measurement.* Chicago: MESA Press.

CHAPTER 6

ETHNOGRAPHIC PERSPECTIVE: FROM BEGINNING TO FINAL PRODUCT

Sara W. Lundsteen

The discipline of ethnographic research has a special orientation that distinguishes it from quantitative research. This subset of qualitative methodologies focuses on human culture in the manner of an anthropologist. Some have a preference for using the term *qualitative* rather than *ethnographic*, as the umbrella term, particularly when observation of behavior departs in any way and at any time from a natural context (e.g., Goetz & LeCompte, 1984). I, however, prefer the term *ethnographic perspective* to describe the contrasts with quantitative research and the six steps of methodology outlined in this chapter.

AN ETHNOGRAPHIC PERSPECTIVE IN GIFTED EDUCATION

The process of observing and analyzing in ethnographic methodology is a rigorous and demanding one that can be well worth the time and effort for those interested in the complexities of gifted education.

The value of an ethnographic perspective derives in large measure from the explanatory power of the inherently holistic and humanistic point of view it embodies. In gifted education, a study of *highly gifted* children using the ethnographic perspective is worth the time and effort because we don't currently understand how to help these students realize their potential. Among the questions in gifted education that might best be answered by using the ethnographic perspective are:

1. What social roles do gifted children play during school?
2. What are the rules children and teachers in gifted classrooms have to know in order to participate?

3. How do participants in gifted programs hold one another accountable in relationship to tasks?
4. What processes and materials are available for gifted students to
   choose from? How do these interact with gifted abilities and learning?
5. What are the social interactional consequences of innovations in
   gifted education? (Innovations might refer to, for example, pullout
   programs, mentors, special projects.)
6. How do teachers of gifted children orchestrate different participation levels? (For example, consider competitive, cooperative, and
   individual activities.)
7. Why are materials in gifted programs placed and used as they are?
8. In what contexts do gifted abilities flourish?
9. What other cases and contexts support, contradict, or expand present
   findings?
10. In general—"What's going on here?"

A Comparison to Quantitative Methods

To begin, consider some clarifying contrasts between an ethnographic
perspective and a quantitative one.

Setting and Time Frame. Ethnographers observe human behavior
in its natural setting and over a substantial period of time. Moreover, an
ethnographic perspective deems the inquirer and the objects of inquiry as
inseparable and interactive. In contrast, quantitative research may use a
laboratory and a relatively short time span for better control of the
variables under study.

Sampling, Exceptions, and Transferability of Contexts. An ethnographic perspective claims that classes of events (e.g., operations of
gifted programs) are better understood through intensive examination of
carefully selected particular cases and significant exceptions, not randomly selected cases. An ethnographer's interest is in transferability from
one specific and fully described context to another (Lincoln & Guba,
1985). Quantitative researchers, however, more frequently prefer large,
randomly selected samples so that generalizations concerning the total
population may be made.

The Nature of Reality. Ethnographic research with qualitative
methods tends to incorporate as many of the complexities and variables
in the setting as possible and use as many tools as appropriate for

credibility. The objective is to extract patterns and explain the behaviors observed. The ethnographer views reality as multiple and constructed by each individual. For example, in the field of gifted education there are many meanings (realities) assigned to the term *gifted*. The definition depends on the context—the who, where, what, and when of those involved in a particular school, district, or university. For the ethnographer, reality is context bound, probabilistic, and contingent.

Quantitative research, however, tends to define the study with predetermined hypotheses about the key variables and to use a few predetermined standardized measures that have established reliability and validity. Ethnographic research, on the other hand, tends to examine participants' point of view in field settings which result in the formulation and reformulation of questions and field-based hypotheses. Quantitative research begins with a theory and a research question or hypothesis already formulated and ready to test.

In the remainder of this chapter, I will develop further the central concepts of an ethnographic perspective. The chart in Figure 6.1 is a guide for the information to follow. To illustrate the ethnographic perspective, I will use two of my own studies, an ethnographic study at the kindergarten level (referred to as the Gooch Center study) and a quantitative study of fifth graders. These studies focus on creative problem solving—a process of interest to educators of the gifted (Lundsteen, 1970, 1983, 1985). My purposes are to: (1) indicate a research gap in gifted education that ethnographic studies could fill; and (2) offer a step-by-step approach for conducting work from an ethnographic perspective.

STEPS IN THE ETHNOGRAPHIC CYCLE

Ethnographic studies are systematic investigations conducted in natural settings. They begin with the selection of a project site and continue through the formulation of questions, data collection and management, data analysis, and report writing. The steps in conducting ethnographic studies are presented in detail below, with particular emphasis on data collection and management.

Step 1: Project Selection

In selecting a gifted program or a problem related to gifted students for an ethnographic study, consider how what you will find in that setting is representative of what occurs in *other* settings. Also consider how the results of your study can explain the relationship of this program or

FIGURE 6.1   Ethnographic research—A compendium of concepts

Origin of methods: *anthropology*

Behavior studied: *real-life human processes* as they occur

Setting: *natural environment of subjects* under study

Time: *extended* time span for observation of full cycle of events; study of historical, evolutionary processes

Theory: well grounded, but *flexible;* adapt to emerging data

Qualifications of researcher:
  Knowledgeable about unit of study, ethnographic research
  Able to *relate to people* with understanding and respect
  Not ethnocentric
  Aware of personal biases
  Willing to be flexible

Process of research: *rigorous;* equal time given to data collection and data analysis

  Data collection: *multiplicity of methods* to permit corroboration
  • Key means of obtaining data: *observation*
    —*interactive:* researcher participates, interacts with subjects (participant observation, questions, interviews, surveys, life histories, etc.)
    —*non-interactive:* researcher examines records (videotapes, written records, artifacts, etc.)
  • *Field notes* recorded: observations, personal reactions, methodology, hypotheses, and mapping
  • Key instrument: *researcher*—using trained, prepared human beings to understand human behavior
  • Data elicited beyond what is already known or would obviously be expected—provide new *understandings*

  Data analysis: *inductive* (patterns emerge from data)
  • Data analysis done both *during and after data collection,* analysis influencing new collection of data
  • *Content* analysis
  • Data *reduction*
  • *Triangulation*—corroboration through multiple sources
  • *Coding* categories—quantifying chosen patterns

Product of research: *descriptive*
  Thick description conveying a feel of what people said, did, or indicated they were feeling
  Meaning conveyed, from subject's viewpoints
  Definition of units (topics and/or people) studied, so that *comparison and synthesis* may be made with studies of other groups
  Particulars described so that *generic* may be understood

(Ideas gathered from Bogden & Biklen, 1982; Guba, 1978; Heath, 1982; Wolcott, 1980)

problem to other settings. Avoid simply collecting a mass of mere concrete detail.

In the Gooch Center study, my research assistant and I were interested in creative problem solving in young students, a general, broad area
at an age level for which we found little previous research. It is, however,
an area of considerable interest to those in gifted education. Is the
development of creative problem solving in young children influenced
by varied learning styles, and if so, when and how? Our goals, appropriate to an ethnographic perspective, were to explore and to raise new
research questions.

Step 2: Access, Entry, and Rapport

The second step in this ethnographic research is to gain entry and access
and establish rapport. This process begins with visits to likely sites.
Stainback and Stainback (1988) declare:

> There are no hard and fast rules to follow when entering a research site or
> gaining permission to conduct research. Each situation is unique. However,
> in most situations, it is beneficial to be as straightforward, honest, relaxed,
> and friendly as possible. (p. 29)

In order to establish rapport, accommodate yourself to the setting, get to
know the participants (discover commonalities), be helpful when appropriate and possible, show enthusiasm and interest for the participants,
and, finally, be yourself (Taylor & Bogdan, 1984).

In our case, we knew we might be somewhat obtrusive. The nature
of the study required us to be in the classroom 3 hours per day for the first
3 weeks and at least 3 hours per week thereafter for an entire school year.
In conducting such a study, we considered how it might benefit the
participants, and what roles we, as experimenters, would play. Access
was facilitated because I had previously been a teacher in the district.
Access and entry were also made easier by a supportive principal who
wanted her school (Gooch Early Childhood Center, Dallas Independent
School District) to benefit from the stimulation provided by researchers.
The principal introduced us to the selected teacher, and we began establishing rapport. In addition, we spoke to parents during the school's open
house. Initially, we were identified as *volunteers* in the school who stayed
after school to help clean off tables in the room and assisted the teacher in
other ways.

As we worked with the teacher, we assured her that we weren't there
to judge but, instead, to learn about creative problem solving in young

children in the school setting. We considered her a *research collaborator*, not demanding too much of her time, but inviting her to learn, explore, and gather information with us. In addition, she would help us verify and interpret what we thought we saw. Our efforts must have been successful, for at the end of the year the teacher told us she thought it would be fine if every classroom had researchers in residence. Being an ethnographer is not a rude business; persistent, yes, but sensitive to the needs and feelings of all participants (Wolcott, 1980).

Gaining access and entry is also important in some quantitative studies. For example, my early, carefully designed experimental study to test varied programs for teaching creative problem solving was almost rejected because the public school system had felt misused by previous university researchers (Lundsteen, 1970). However, because of the intimate, almost live-in, nature of the researcher's role in ethnographic work, this step assumes even greater importance.

Step 3: Question Formulation

Ethnographic researchers generally begin a study with a broad question or problem, much like the *fuzzy mess* discussed in chapter 1 of this volume. Only after the researcher has observed can more definite questions or hypotheses be posed and tested. Denzin (1978) advocates the use of an analytic inductive strategy, while Bogdan and Biklen (1982) prefer a constant comparative strategy. In either case, questions are generated as the study progresses.

The Gooch School study provides a good example of how questions are formulated. We started out with a background that included both previous research and theoretical understandings. We knew quite a lot about child development in general, and the literature on creative problem solving and learning styles in particular. We understood qualitative methodology and were familiar with general as well as specific theories of creativity and learning styles. For example, we were interested in the Rosenberg (1968) constructs of learning styles (Rigid-Inhibited, Undisciplined, Acceptance-Anxious, and Creative), especially with regard to how they might relate to gifted students. We wondered if we could recognize these patterns in young gifted children and if the patterns would be related to individual differences in problem solving. Although we had ideas about the relationship of creative style to problem solving, at this point, we felt it was premature to formulate hypotheses, devise training programs to promote the creative style, or test for improvement, as might be done in a quantitative study.

Rather than being predetermined before entry, research questions and hypotheses evolved as we learned and described what we saw happening to these young children, their teacher, and their parents in this setting. Any vague initial questions that we had were reformulated as we discovered and then verified patterns of behavior with various data collection methods. This wave-like mode or cycle of inquiry—question, observe, organize, verify, and reformulate—recurred repeatedly.

Step 4: Data Collection and Management

The ethnographic perspective incorporates a variety of data collection and management techniques. In this section I will discuss a continuum of participant observation, types of evidence, including documents, artifacts, products, physical traces, interviews, and the management of data through different types of field notes.

Although participant observation has typically been thought of as the primary tool used in ethnographic work, an ethnographer might use almost any type of data gathering tool, even a standardized test but possibly in a highly unstandardized way (Wolcott, 1980). *Triangulation* is defined by Denzin (1978, p. 291) as "the combination of methodologies in the study of the same phenomenon." With triangulation, different kinds of data are examined for evidence of corroboration (or just as likely, puzzling differences). For example, in gifted education we often examine different evidence that might indicate that a student is gifted. We use a variety of data—such as standardized tests, teacher, peer, self-, and parent nomination, and student products—in search of corroboration of high ability or potential. In general, ethnographers attempt to construct meaningful descriptions or explanations of the whole from the observed parts. Using several measures instead of one does not necessarily guarantee validity and reliability. We will return to this point later in the chapter.

Reactive Ethnographic Methods. The researcher may be *reactive* or *nonreactive* while collecting data (Heath, 1985). Reactive means the researcher participates and interacts with the subjects. Reactive data collection techniques include: participant observation, interviewing, surveying, and examining life histories. These tools interact with the researcher's presence, and they have many advantages. They enable us to examine a few subjects in depth and to follow up on actions or statements they make. Information from such varied sources helps us better understand the setting from the subjects' point of view, and, over time, enables us to see growth and change.

For example, in our kindergarten study, we were able to build trust with the students and teacher. The use of reactive measures demonstrated our interest in them and allowed us to examine a variety of activities and aspects of the young children's lives—from social problems encountered on the playground or at home to motor problems in designing paper circle collages and cognitive problems in discovering principles of balance, force, and gravity.

A final advantage of reactive measures such as interviews, surveys, and life histories is that they are not strange linguistic phenomena to the individuals involved. In our study the participants became accustomed to being questioned and interviewed. Our activities did not seem like sterile lab games. To ethnographers, this is valuable *context*, though researchers more focused on purely quantitative means view it as *contamination*.

On the minus side, when we used our reactive measures for data collection, it was like looking for a needle in a haystack at first. What we thought we saw in observation with these measures was difficult to validate. We had to rely on validating the observed patterns by triangulation of data over an extended period of time. For example, as we observed D, we began to suspect that she was gifted. We noted her reactions to problem-solving situations and recorded her use of precise, descriptive vocabulary, higher-level thinking, and creative solutions. Because we had information from standardized mathematics and reading tests and the parental interview, we could triangulate the data. We examined the consistency of her performance across settings and eventually worked with the teacher to enrich the environment for this gifted student. In this process we used what we thought were internally logical arguments, but we realized that our reactive measures were human and fallible—and we admitted it. Tests, other measures, interviews, and observations helped validate what we thought we saw.

To ensure reliability of our methods, we followed three procedures at Gooch Center. First, in my field notes I carefully assessed our particular roles. Since we were part of the context, we had to observe ourselves as closely as we did the children, trying to remain objective while noting our biases in a straightforward way. Second, we triangulated our sources of information: what we saw, what the teacher saw, what the parents saw, what the children saw, and even what one of us saw as opposed to the other. In regard to our context, we realized that at Gooch Center we had a supportive principal, and children from middle- to upper-middle-class families. We also understood that the parents who were most willing to bring us evidence of their children's problem-solving behavior might not present *typical* parents. They might be exceptionally cooperative and/or interested in research related to child development, or, at the other extreme, they might be fringe elements who had nothing to lose in associating with us, the outsiders. Third, to further aid our endeavors for reliability and validity, we had tape recordings and field notes that could be reexamined repeatedly and offered to others for critical appraisal.

Nonreactive Ethnographic Methods. Another division of data collection tools and sources used in ethnographic research, nonreactive observation, is exemplified by documents, artifacts, products, and physical traces.

- *Documents.* A document is any formal written source. At Gooch School we used the readiness test data available for all district students. Although relatively unimportant to us, they tended to confirm the general levels of giftedness in verbal and school-oriented tasks that we observed, and helped describe the sample of children.
- *Artifacts.* In the Gooch Center study, some artifacts were toys that individual children brought to share and art supplies, pencils, and paper seen during our home visits.
- *Products.* Any concrete object or creation made by the subjects can be considered a product. In our study they included: stories the children dictated; works of art such as clay pieces, collages, "portraits of family," and pictures; combined stories with pictures such as how to stop a cat-and-dog fight; taped responses to the problem of telling the story in a wordless picture book; records of the children's responses to our on-the-spot devised "junk test," in which children displayed the abstractness of their perceptions of classification, an important dimension in the Rosenberg (1968) theories of style; and seatwork the children completed each morning.
- *Physical Traces.* These are unobtrusive measures in which the researcher has no opportunity to have an impact. For example, we used such traces as the contents of the children's storage cubbies or work boxes and the children's responses to the teacher's directives, or nondirectives. A field note entry might be, "C simply sat all morning at his desk when the teacher did not tell him explicitly what to do." The fact that he did this for almost all of the morning work period was an initial clue to his Rigid-Inhibited style, which we repeatedly verified.

Examples of Observation. So far I've said that tools for data collection in this ethnographic discipline can be reactive or nonreactive, mentioned some advantages and disadvantages of the reactive ones, and provided some examples from my own work. Reactive or nonreactive, the basic tool of the ethnographer is *observation*. We watched the children in the classroom; we examined the things they made; we listened to the teacher's comments; we looked at school records.

Types of observation can be placed on a continuum from nonreactive to reactive (Heath, 1985):

Nonparticipating observer
Transient observer
Observing participant
Participant observer

At the beginning of our Gooch study we were *nonparticipating* observers who sat delicately on the fringes making maps of the room and school, sketching faces, trying to learn names, testing our tape recorders, and learning to use video equipment. It is difficult, however, to be truly nonparticipating in the classroom with young children. We might ask one student what his name is, another might ask us a question, and a third may be noticing where our attention is directed. This is quite different from a person viewing videotapes of students in a classroom who is unable to participate with them in any way. Next, we became *transient observers*, wandering through the classroom among the tables, and driving through the community where the children lived.

After the first three weeks we became *observing participants*, stopping at children's tables and asking questions (usually open-ended ones, such as, "Tell me about your picture"). We answered requests for help with an interested look and comments like, "What could you do about that?" We even followed a child into the washroom when she complained she was having trouble getting a paper towel out of the dispenser. We had observed her reliance on adult help before and were interested to see what would happen when we persisted in turning the problem back to her. When she realized how "useless" we were, she solved the problem herself by using the bathroom tissue for drying. We were, of course, intruding and changing the children's natural setting, but in this manner we became observing participants in many of the children's natural activities, encouraging their display of problem-solving behavior.

It was not our original intent to stage activities for the children outside of their classroom—we wanted to observe their problem-solving behavior in their natural setting, the classroom. However, this kindergarten classroom was not activity oriented. Most work periods consisted of individuals completing worksheets. We had little opportunity to observe creative problem solving but were curious to know what the children were capable of doing.

With some desperation we moved into the *participant observer* role, altering the learning context with modified forms of task analysis (Safran, Greenberg, & Rice, 1988). We began to plan and devise tasks in which individuals and small groups would participate. During these tasks, which were conducted in a room separate from the classroom, we observed behaviors of creative problem solving in social, aesthetic, cognitive, and motor areas, or mixtures thereof. As the planners, organizers, and presenters responsible for that period of time, we gradually became regular participant observers with children selected as representative of particular learning styles (Rigid-Inhibited, Undisciplined, Acceptance-Anxious, and Creative). Data were gathered both when we were active participants and when we were unobtrusive observers.

It is likely that we had a subtle but definitive impact on the group and the individuals we were studying as the year progressed. An important role of ethnographic research is to realize and attempt to describe this impact. For example, we wondered to what extent we had influenced student behavior when C, who normally showed few signs of autonomy, volunteered in the late spring to bring his own book to show us. We showed him our wordless picture books, and he responded with, "I've got my own book," and bounded away to get it to show us, in a manner that was neither rigid nor inhibited.

Data-Collection Considerations. A variety of additional factors will influence the quality of the ethnographic data gathered in the research. Though they cover a range—from questions of which subjects to focus on to decisions about exactly what measures to utilize—they are all best addressed by a researcher who reflects on them carefully in advance and retains the flexibility to adapt them as new opportunities arise.

Because qualitative research often requires that greater amounts of time be spent with individual subjects, the researcher may not be able to devote equal attention to all members of the population under study. One important technique for dealing with this constraint is *purposeful sampling*, which can be defined as the selection of particular cases for intensive observation and interviewing according to criteria established by the investigator. Some researchers (e.g., LeCompte & Goetz, 1982) believe that one of the criteria should be diversity. Any attribute of the subjects that might influence the problem under study may be used as a criterion.

During the first two months of our Gooch study, we observed all students in order to select some of the students for further intensive observation. We wanted to identify cases that consistently demonstrated behaviors characteristic of the four Rosenberg (1968) learning styles and then study their problem-solving behaviors intensely with the teacher and parents as collaborators.

The measures used for data collection in qualitative research can be quite different from those in quantitative studies, though there is some overlap. In our Gooch study, for example, we devised tasks for the children that provided us with baseline data on their performance. However, the measures we used for assessing problem-solving behavior were not static; they were developed, revised, and re-revised on the spot. Table 6.1 shows the range of measures we used to collect background information, comparison data, and parental and teacher perceptions. The table provides the following: (1) the title of the measure (Measures); (2) the number of subjects who took that measure (N); (3) the manner in which it was administered (Admin.—i.e., individually, in small groups, or to a couple, two parents); (4) who and how many people administered the measure (# Exp.); (5) how often the measure was administered (Freq.); (6) over what period of time the testing took place (Time Period); and (7) comments about the measures (Comments).

Interviews are a primary source of data in qualitative research. Ethnographers define *interview* broadly, allowing it to encompass a variety of strategies. Interviews can be informal, unplanned, and serendipitous, taking advantage of opportunities as they arise; many of our interviews with teachers, parents, and children in our Gooch study fell into this category. On the other hand, interviews can be structured, focusing on a particular set of research concerns; an example of this from our Gooch study is the "Who in the Class" questionnaire we devised for the teacher, incorporating the Rosenberg (1968) behaviors for each learning style: "Who in the class frequently seeks teacher contact and approval?" "Who in the class thinks creatively in new situations?" We structured another questionnaire for a parental interview that examined the Rosenberg theory of learning styles, problem-solving variables, and parenting style. Another questionnaire designed for the children simulated a social problem between animal puppets. The puppets respond differentially, using language that might be attributed to each of the Rosenberg (1968) styles, and we asked each child to indicate the puppet response they preferred, and why they preferred it. These materials were developed as the research showed a need for them. What we observed guided our next move.

In contrast, the data-gathering tools I used in my first experimental study of creative problem solving were: (1) three measures of two variables related to problem solving, as well as a measure of problem solving administered pre-, post-, and follow-up via TV; (2) IQ scores used for covariance in order to account for initial differences in intelligence; and (3) reading scores to describe the sample. The treatment was the presentation of a new problem-solving curriculum. The significant results were developed into a technical report that was accepted for publication; the funding agency, the superintendent, and my dean were pleased. Unfortu-

TABLE 6.1: Measurement Instruments Used in the Gooch Center Study

Measures	N	Admin.	# Exp.	Frequency	Time Period	Comments
A. Baseline Data						
1. Conservation tasks (Piagetian)	22	Indiv	1	1	Sept.-Oct.	4 tasks: (1) number with chips; (2) mass with play-doh; (3) draw-a-diamond; (4) ask child about siblings as child views drawing of family
2. Paper circles (art collage)	22	Sm Gr	1	1	Sept.-Oct.	
3. Dictated story	22 10	Indiv	1	3	Sept.-Oct.	For selected subjects, compare the beginning, middle, and end
4. Sorting task (Junk Test)	22	Indiv	2 Teams	1	Sept.-Oct.	To determine verbal use of abstract, functional, and concrete language, to check approach style
5. The Burr & Meese puppet presentation	10	Indiv	2	2	Sept.-Oct.	Puppets' verbalizations according to varied learning/solving styles
6. DISD Reading & Math Readiness Test	22	Sm Gr	Tchr	1	Sept.-Oct.	Relate scores to observational information
7. "Who in the Classroom"	1	To Tchr	2	1	Sept.-Oct.	Questionnaire administered to teacher re child style

			Tchr &			
B. Comparison Data						
1. Videotapes of discussion, puppet script #1	22	Sm Gr	2	3	Dec., Feb., Apr.	10 subjects in two groups, 5 each (remainder of class in a 3rd group); *Problem Solving Objective Scale of Child* coding scheme applied
2. Tasks to stimulate problem solving in different contexts: social, cognitive, aesthetic	10-22	Indiv/Sm Gr	2	3	Once/mo., Nov.-Apr.	10 subjects (other interested students); examples include Kamii rollers, DeBono tasks, wordless picturebook tasks, child's own puppet scenario, "I Am the Master" movement
C. Parental Data						
1. Parental interviews	10	Indiv/Couple	2	1	Jan.	After formal observation, open house, and conversations in parent-teacher conferences
2. Parent/child problem-solving task	10	Indiv/Couple	2	1	Feb.	Audiotaped
3. Parents teach child task	10	Indiv/Couple	2	1	Apr.	Audiotaped
D. Teacher	1		2	Ea. puppet discussion	During data analysis	Use *Checklist of Teacher Behaviors*; focus on guidance of children's problem-solving behavior

Note: Measures were not all predetermined before the data collection began; most were prompted by observations and created on the spot to meet evolving needs and interests.

nately, I was still wondering what was really going on. Two years later, I conducted follow-up interviews with the experimental teachers and wished I had interviewed them earlier. Their responses convinced me that I should have been in the classrooms observing.

Field Note Management. All of the evidence and observations are meaningless without the ethnographer's prime tool of field notes. I would like to review the possible kinds and provide practical suggestions for data management when using an ethnographic perspective (Heath, 1985).

Consider using a series of notebooks (see Figure 6.2.) Avoid trying to keep everything in the same place. Notebook #1 (loose leaf) is for structured interview data. For example, in the Gooch Center study we kept parent interview data in chronological order in one notebook. The notebooks may be sectioned in many different ways. We divided the Gooch Center notebook by personnel: principal, teacher, primary care givers, children. Children's interviews may be further subdivided by time of year: beginning, middle, end.

Notebook #2 was for field notes. One spiral notebook with side margins and ruled paper for each month works well. If you are using audio tapes, number them and record their number and contents at the front of each month's notebook.

When we began entering field notes in the spiral notebooks, we placed field notes on about one third of the page to the right (leaving three columns on that page for other information (see Figure 6.2, #2.3). Entries were placed about a third of the way down to leave room for a map or diagram of the room plan for the day. (Since we soon learned that the environment of the classroom rarely changed, early maps sufficed for the rest of the year.) The blank page across from the field notes would be used later for conceptual notes—reactions, interpretations, and questions.

We began each field note session by noting the time in one column and resetting the audio tape recorder to "0." Later, playing the tape while we reread our field notes aided our recall of the session. We were able to fill in gaps in the dialogue and listen to the tone of voice, words stressed, and other verbal cues. When we were audiotaping, we could concentrate on the nonverbal behaviors of the children, but we strove for balance between verbal and nonverbal information in our notes.

At the beginning of the year, we recorded field notes on all class members by observing for three hours every day for the first week. Then, we began purposely sampling. In the far right hand column of the field note page we indicated who was being observed (see the sample in

FIGURE 6.2   Field notes management: A suggested series of notebooks

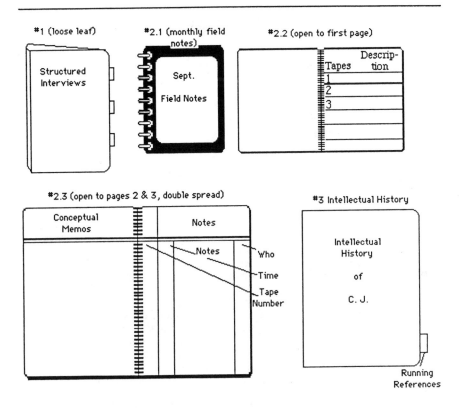

Figure 6.3). Later we tabbed pages of observations of specific children who were of particular interest to us. At this point, we began photocopying observations of these interesting cases and organizing them into file folders.

Instead of rushing to transcribe the tapes, we read our notes while listening to the tapes three or four times and made conceptual notes on the left-hand side. When we knew which portions of the tapes were needed, we selectively transcribed them.

The *conceptual notes* were of several kinds:

1. *Methodological:* "Tomorrow my assistant and I should switch places, she by the door and I near the teacher's desk."
2. *Personal:* "What is it about that mother I don't like? I am not being objective about her, placing a value judgment on her behavior."

FIGURE 6.3   Sample field notes

Room Map

		Board	
Centers		Work table	
Housekeeping			

Blocks with trucks

Books

	Tables		Teacher's desk
Easel		Carpet for circle time	

Tape #	Date/ Time	Notes	Group/ Individual
No tape today	9/15/79	Setting: Classroom, children are going from one assignment to the next, as they complete each one. J. and E. are working on their math papers. Assignment is to copy the numeral 6 and then draw and color the correct number of boats.	
	9:30	J. asks, "Do we color now?" He has completed 2 boats, which occupy about half the page, and has started to use a blue crayon. E. looks at J.'s paper 3 times and looks toward the teacher. J. is using blue crayon to put "water" under the boats. E. tells him, "You will not have enough room to fit all 6 boats on the page." J. answers, "I will too." Then he looks at his paper again and goes to ask the teacher. She tells him to make his boat smaller.	J E
	9:40	I went by his table and saw his work. I asked him how he had solved his problem. He said, "I made them smaller [pointing to latter 4 boats] and I made them submarines." He also told me that the propellers were to make the boats move.	J

Conceptual Notes

9/15/79   Is E. being a "little mother"? Is she criticizing or trying to prevent J.'s getting into trouble? Watch her other behavior--is she trying to please (protect?) (acceptance-anxious) or is she trying to be difficult (undisciplined)?

9/15/79   J.'s solution to the "boats" problem is very exciting. He was able to "correct" his math work very gracefully and "snatch victory from the jaws of defeat." He also spoke quite assertively to E., although he did go to the teacher, so may have been somewhat unsure of what to do. High level of creative problem solving indicated--see how he responds to "junk" test. Is his level of abstraction consistent with a creative style?

130

3. *Inferential:* "J. is looking more and more like a likely candidate for Rosenberg's creative style."
4. *Theoretical:* "I wonder if I couldn't use the family pictures (the ones the teacher had the children draw) to see if they are able to figure out the Piagetian task which asks about siblings. Can the child count himself or herself as a brother or sister of a sibling? Perhaps we could use a little girl who drew herself and her little sister in the family constellation, 'Does your sister have a sister?'"

Any time we had a question about the data, a hunch about a particular student, or felt we saw a pattern evolving, we shifted to the left-hand page. Sometimes we drew arrows toward the raw field note data that matched the statements on the right. Every day after observation, we reread our notes, spotted tape portions corresponding to the field note, and added to our conceptual memos. This review helped us decide what to do next.

Notebook #3, the intellectual history notebook, was created after we had been in the setting long enough to begin reformulating questions. In this looseleaf notebook we organized longer conceptual memos (dated) along with photocopies of material from previous conceptual memos pages. These longer memos synthesized some of interview materials, field notes, reviews of recent related literature, and other insights. They also contributed to long-range planning. For example, in one of these memos in the Gooch study, we evolved the following idea:

Why not team children with different styles together? We could call in a child who had exhibited a more creative style of problem solving, for example, and have that child play with one who had demonstrated one of the less creative styles. Would the more productive problem solver have a beneficial effect on the other child—would some of the more productive approaches "rub off" on the less successful child, or would the very inhibited child just put a damper on the whole play session?

When you gain ideas from readings or lectures, put them in a running reference section within the conceptual memos and separately in a running list of bibliographic entries at the back of the intellectual history notebook. In this history, research hypotheses and reformulated theories can be recorded.

As each new set of tasks for the month contributed data about the kindergarteners' problem-solving abilities, we reviewed our earlier notes to see if patterns of development or change might have been heralded by previously observed behavior. We began writing monthly summaries (taking care not to mark the original field notes). Summaries were stapled to the front page of each month's notebook. Any transcribed tapes or other loose pages were stapled to the back. Copies were also placed in individual student file folders if deemed appropriate. Patterns emerged as we repeatedly reviewed the field notes. These patterns were recorded in dated intellectual history entries. The intellectual history included only copied portions of tapescripts, interviews, and field note pages. The more time available to review the intellectual history notebook, the more insights we experienced. Review also stimulated planning for the next field study. The intellectual history can be helpful in the preparation of papers for professional meetings. These summaries and subsequent presentations usually necessitate refinements through the next step in the six-step ethnographic cycle, data analysis.

Step 5: Data Analysis

The analysis, as can be seen from the previous description, is inductive. You begin by recording specific instances, formulating tentative hypotheses, collecting more instances, and reformulating the hypotheses. Analysis is an on-going process that occurs during and after collection (not just after the posttests, as in my quantitative study). In data analysis, you look for patterns, categories, concepts, or themes and consider units of analysis such as words, phrases, patterns of behavior, or other recurring observations (Stainback & Stainback, 1988). You develop classification schemes and determine similarities and relationships as well as contrasts and comparisons. One challenge of the ethnographic perspective is to consider all data, not just the data that supports your theoretical stance. Some qualitative researchers, such as Strauss (1987), advocate grounded theory analysis, which is a style of qualitative analysis that includes theoretical sampling and guidelines for coding data and making comparisons. Network analysis is another promising method. In any method, the analysis must be conducted in a logical sequence that can be explained and justified when you report your conclusions.

Much of my analysis of the Gooch Center study was captured in the intellectual history notebook. Each month we analyzed the data as we reviewed our notes. Some of our analyses were of the *discourse* related to problem solving, some were of the *content* displayed in the children's products, such as their responses to wordless picture books or their clay pieces. Some of the analyses focused on the *cognitive process* of creative problem solving. We would like to have done life histories of some of the interesting cases, their families, and school contexts, following up for several years, as was done in my Swedish study of older children (Lundsteen, 1983).

Following is an excerpt from the intellectual history in the Gooch Center study which illustrates the nature of on-going analysis:

April. We want to do an activity which has even less guidance than the last one. We plan to take in a Fisher-Price toy that depicts a village with little people, cars, furniture, etc. We'll take children into the room where we work, and already have the toys on the floor (in a predetermined manner, so it will be the same for all the children). We won't give instructions this time, just sit down and observe what they do; they will give even the initial structure to the situation. We are curious to see what pairs of children will do, and now we want to systematically pair the different styles to see if we can observe any trends. This will have to be repeated with different situations, of course, but it seemed to us that while we were watching the work that the creative children had a good effect on the undisciplined ones—they seemed to know how to handle them, and still carry on. The acceptance-anxious children did not seem to try as many different things if they were with other children like themselves, but seemed to enjoy the company of the creative children. Let's see what happens now when we deliberately pair them, one style with another, and they have little recourse but to ignore or interact with the one other child present in the room.

Step 6: Products of Ethnographic Research

This last step in the ethnographic research cycle can take several forms. In general, the product is descriptive—a *thick* description that accurately conveys what the individuals said, did, or indicated they felt. The writing highlights significant meanings held by the participants, from their point of view, and the generic emerges from the particulars.

I recommend that the final written product include:

1. Description of the context of the study so that others can compare their context to yours
2. Explanation of your role in the field study
3. Description of the data gathering methods
4. Reduction of the data by plucking out one fully described situation, happening, theme or focus (i.e., a particular type of behavior or topic studied)
5. Explanation of the relationship of the illustration to your central theme (with confirmations, if any, from the related literature)
6. Exploration of issues and suggestions for other comparative studies (Heath, 1985)

An ethnographic product, whether book or article, is a literary genre with a research discipline of its own, both a process and a product.

These then are the six steps which are descriptive of the ethnographic perspective:

Step 1: Project selection
Step 2: Access, entry, and rapport
Step 3: Question formulation
Step 4: Data collection and management
Step 5: Data analysis
Step 6: Products of ethnographic research

Conducting such qualitative research is a rigorous and demanding task that requires systematic, detailed planning and logical, thorough implementation in natural settings.

ETHNOGRAPHIC RESEARCH IN GIFTED EDUCATION

Lutz and Lutz (1981) investigated patterns of social interaction among gifted children. The researchers noticed, for example, greater voluntary social interaction among the gifted students during the time they were attending the pull-out program. While with their usual classmates, however, they tended to prefer children who were not in the gifted program but were nevertheless bright. Did the gifted children in this study like having a best friend who was a little less gifted than they because they enjoyed the lack of competition in such a relationship, or were there other shared interests? Is this a general pattern among gifted students? Does the level of giftedness make a difference? These hypotheses can be further tested in other settings. Ethnographic studies can produce descriptions so others can formulate and test hypotheses.

Since the Lutz and Lutz study there have been an increasing number of qualitative studies conducted in gifted education. Buchanan (1984), Gross (1986), and Kennedy (1989) have used qualitative methodologies to explore mathematical problem solving, radical acceleration, and classroom interactions of gifted students.

CONCLUSION

In conclusion, I leave you with the following recommendations:

1. Become conversant with a number of qualitative fieldwork tools and techniques, especially interactive and non-interactive observation.

2. Read studies that use an ethnographic perspective; they will illustrate how to apply tools and techniques to actual situations.
3. When you are trying to understand what's going on in a setting, consider examining *more* rather than fewer factors about the concept of interest.
4. Develop a concern for a broad context. Attending to the context may be the most important contribution of this kind of research, making research more natural, true-to-life, and valuable to teachers and administrators.

By analogy, the strength of ethnography is in its background tapestry—busily detailed, seemingly chaotic (Heath, 1982). But upon closer inspection, an ethnography reveals patterns and, with repeated scrutiny, may reveal yet other patterns, as in the studies by Speck (1984), Kitano (1985), and Kramer (1985). Upon this tapestry may be placed the studies of others in an effort to explain as fully as possible the factors that help determine success or failure of gifted programs and gifted children or, more importantly, the principles that explain the processes of stability and change, while at the same time providing vivid details and concreteness that allows a reader to identify with situations described.

REFERENCES

Bogdan, R. C., & Biklen, S. K. (1982). *Qualitative research for education*. Boston: Allyn & Bacon.

Buchanan, N. K. (1984). *Mathematical problem solving performance: A study of cognitive and noncognitive factors*. Unpublished doctoral dissertation, Purdue University, West Lafayette, IN.

Denzin, N. K. (1978). *The research act* (2nd ed.). New York: McGraw-Hill.

Goetz, J. P., & LeCompte, M. D. (1984). *Ethnography and qualitative design in education*. San Diego, CA: Academic Press.

Gross, M. (1986). Radical acceleration in Australia: Terence Tao. *Gifted Child Today, 9*(4), 2–11.

Guba, E. G. (1978). *Toward a methodology of naturalistic inquiry in educational evaluation*. Los Angeles: University of California, Center for the Study of Evaluation.

Heath, S. B. (1982). Ethnography in education: Defining the essentials. In P. Gilmore & A. Glatthorn (Eds.), *Children in and out of schools* (pp. 33–55). Washington, DC: Center for Applied Linguistics.

Heath, S. B. (February, 1985). Workshop presentation for Committee on Reading, Texas Women's University, Denton, TX.

Kennedy, D. M. (1989). *Classroom interaction of gifted and nongifted 5th grad-*

ers: A qualitative perspective. Unpublished doctoral dissertation, Purdue University, West Lafayette, IN.

Kitano, M. K. (1985). Ethnography of a preschool for the gifted: What gifted young children actually do. *Gifted Child Quarterly, 29,* 27–71.

Kramer, L. R. (1985, April). *Social interaction and perceptions of ability: A study of gifted adolescent females.* Paper presented at the meeting of the American Educational Research Association, Chicago.

LeCompte, M. D., & Goetz, J. P. (1982). Problems of reliability and validity in ethnographic research. *Review of Educational Research, 52,* 31–60.

Lincoln, Y. S., & Guba, E. G. (1985). *Naturalistic inquiry.* Beverly Hills, CA: Sage.

Lundsteen, S. W. (1970). Manipulating abstract thinking as a subability to problem solving, in the context of an English curriculum. *American Educational Research Journal, 7,* 373–396.

Lundsteen, S. W. (1983). Problem solving of Swedish and American children. *National Council of Teachers of English International Assembly Newsletter,* 14–19.

Lundsteen, S. W. (1985, May). *The impact of learning/solving styles and development on young children's performance of a prereading task.* Paper presented at the meeting of the International Reading Association, cosponsored by the International Council of Psychologists, New Orleans.

Lutz, F. W., & Lutz, S. B. (1981). Gifted pupils in the elementary school setting. *The Creative Child and Adult Quarterly, 4*(2), 93–102.

Rosenberg, M. (1968). *Diagnostic teaching.* Seattle: Special Child Publications.

Safran, J. D., Greenberg, L. S., & Rice, L. N. (1988). Integrating psychotherapy research and practice: Modeling the change process. *Psychotherapy, 25*(1), 1–17.

Speck, A. M. (1984). *The task commitment of young gifted children: A micro-ethnographic study of the effects of teacher and peer behavior on creative productivity.* Unpublished doctoral dissertation, University of Connecticut, Storrs.

Stainback, S., & Stainback, W. (1988). *Understanding and conducting qualitative research.* Dubuque, IA: Kendall/Hunt.

Strauss, A. L. (1987). *Qualitative analysis for social scientists.* New York: Cambridge University Press.

Taylor, S., & Bogdan, R. (1984). *Introduction to qualitative research methods: The search for meaning.* New York: Wiley.

Wolcott, H. (1980). Ethnographic research in education. In R. M. Jaegar (Ed.), *Alternative methodologies in educational research* (AERA Cassette Tape Series L-2). Washington, DC: AERA Central Office.

CHAPTER 7

SINGLE-SUBJECT RESEARCH WITH GIFTED AND TALENTED STUDENTS

R. H. Swassing and Susan R. Amidon

Single-subject research examines the causal relationship between the treatment and the behavior. It is also frequently known as single-case research (Hersen & Barlow, 1976) and infrequently as single-systems research (Bloom & Fischer, 1982). In the discussions that follow, the main expression we will use is single-subject. In the field of gifted education creativity has been extensively researched using this design alternative (Campbell & Willer, 1978; Glover & Gary, 1976; Goetz, 1982; Goetz & Baer, 1973; Henson, 1974). It is a valuable method for researchers interested in exceptional populations because the focus is an individual student who serves as his or her own control.

Winston and Baker (1985) have presented an important review of creativity studies conducted with single-subject research. Aside from studies of creativity, single-subject strategies have received only minimal attention in gifted education studies (Fichter & Swassing, 1985; Foster, 1986). We believe one of the major reasons for this situation is that the designs are not common knowledge, and they are infrequently taught as part of introductory research courses. In addition, the tactics of this approach to research have been developed with handicapped and low-functioning individuals. There have been few translations of the strategies to gifted persons. Finally, the tactics require that researchers and consumers adopt a mindset acknowledging the value of decisions based on data obtained from individuals rather than decisions based on group data (Hersen & Barlow, 1976) developed in the Fisher (1935) tradition.

Our purposes in this chapter are to discuss the key issues and describe the major tactics for conducting single-subject research. Our discussions will include the following: a brief bit of orthodoxy; the major designs with examples drawn from studies conducted at the Ohio State

University with gifted persons; the principles of single-subject research; issues in the study of behaviors that have limited accessibility; criteria for the studies; and criteria for evaluating the research. We will conclude with a discussion of the implications for future research and the role of research in the total effort to expand the body of knowledge necessary to develop the study of giftedness as a discipline.

PRINCIPLES OF SINGLE-SUBJECT RESEARCH

The emphasis of single-subject research is on observable (operant) behavior that can be shown to be the result of environmental events and that also effects some change in the environment. The environment (environmental events) "refer only to those stimuli that can be linked with the behavior of an individual" (Bijou, 1963, p. 97). Environmental events are of two types: biological and external. The biological environment includes the size, shape, and appearance of the individual; the genetic and prenatal elements of development; and the mental functioning of the individual. The *biological environment* begins with the genetic characteristics of the parents and includes the anatomy, physiology, physiognomy, and psychology (intellectual and emotional status) of the individual (Bijou, 1963). Simply put, the *external environment* is that which is outside of the individual. It includes prenatal, natal, and postnatal conditions as well as later environmental interactions (Bijou, 1963). The environment is longitudinal. It begins at the moment of conception and continues throughout the life of the person. Therefore, giftedness may be considered as the result of the maximizing relationships of the children and their environments, both biological and external.

Single-subject research seeks to identify laws that govern human behavior and to determine the functional relationships between behaviors and their causes. The causes of behavior are not inferred from hypothetical constructs such as intelligence (Bijou, 1963). Such constructs may not, of necessity, be bad. The line of questioning we suggest, however, is: What environmental changes can be made that will result in improved performance? Were the variables controlled in such a way as to empirically demonstrate a relationship between what was presented (the antecedent stimulus), the response, and what happened after the response (the consequence)? Answers to such questions provide guidance for the development of educational strategies to improve performance. The antecedent stimulus, the response, and the consequence are known as the *three-term contingency* to demonstrate the "interdependency of the three components" (Cooper, Heron, & Heward, 1987, p. 30).

Tactics of Single-Subject Research

We strongly believe that the effective use of single-subject research tactics requires:

Training
A scientific attitude
Accurate use of the terminology
Skill in implementing the techniques
Ample reading of the literature

Training involves reading, practice, and feedback from qualified directors of study (Bijou, 1971). The works of Cooper (1981), Cooper et al., (1987), and Johnston and Pennypacker (1981) are primary references.

The skillful conduct of research in this tradition requires a certain mindset. It is, first of all, an attitude of developing a *science* of behavior. "Science is more than the mere description of events as they occur. It is an attempt to discover order, to show that certain events stand in lawful relations to other events" (Skinner, 1953, p. 6). A science of behavior (Hersen & Barlow, 1976; Sidman, 1960; Skinner, 1953) directs us all to empirically determine the relationships between the behavior and its consequences.

Any researcher will find that two basic issues of any science are variability and generality (Hersen & Barlow, 1976). Variability in single-subject research will be discussed in our section below on baselines. A behavior is said to have generality if it "lasts over time, appears in environments other than the one in which the behavioral change techniques were applied, or spreads to other behaviors" (Cooper et al., 1987, p. 6). Instead of the findings of an investigation generalizing to another population, the behavior of interest is said to generalize if it is observed in circumstances other than the actual setting of the study.

Second, there is a set of knowledge and attitudes we find prerequisite for the appropriate interpretation of the research reports. The attitudes are:

1. *Determinism.* Events occur as the result of other events and follow orderly and lawful processes.
2. *Empiricism.* Observations should be precise, objective, and based on thorough descriptions of the events being observed.
3. *Parsimony.* Results should be described in light of the most simple explanations prior to looking for more complex explanations.
4. *Scientific manipulation.* Experiments should be conducted systematically

to examine the effects of events suspected of having an effect on the behaviors under study.

5. *Philosophic doubt.* Hold *truth* open to question at all times. (Cooper et al., 1987, pp. 3–4)

Third, researchers and consumers of research need to become familiar with the differences between experimental and educational (clinical or practical) significance (Hersen & Barlow, 1976). The central issue in this debate rests with "criteria for evaluating change. . . . The [educational] clinical criterion refers to the importance of the change achieved, whereas the experimental criterion refers to the reliability of that change" (Hersen & Barlow, 1976, pp. 265–266). The change found in single-subject research is of practical importance if it improves the functioning of the individual. In group statistical studies, there may be a large and significant difference between the experimental and control conditions, yet there may be no change observed among individual members of the experimental group.

> When a behavior is altered, as evidenced by objective data, *and* when individuals in contact with the client (student) indicate that the original behavioral goal has been achieved, the program has attained a change of clinical (practical or educational) significance. (Hersen & Barlow, 1976, p. 267)

A treatment or experiment may be statistically significant and yet have no practical or educational significance for the individual. Yet a statistically nonsignificant difference may have considerable import for the *individual*. For example, a comparison of group scores on two reading tasks may show no significant differences. If, however, one student scored extremely high on one task and very low on the other, then there was a significant difference for that student. This emphasis on the individual is the strongest case for the use of single-subject research with gifted persons.

BASIC SINGLE-SUBJECT DESIGNS

Beginning in the early 1930s, B. F. Skinner formulated a science of behavior (operant behavior). His pioneering work (leading to *Science and Human Behavior*, 1953), along with that of a small group of like-minded researchers such as Bijou (1955) and Sidman (1960), developed the principles, tactics, and designs of applied research. They began to define and manipulate variables, identify ways to make comparisons, address issues of precision, variability, and generalization, and develop a vocabulary sufficient to express the processes and products of human behavior (Hersen & Barlow, 1976).

Terminology

One suggested prerequisite to conducting single-subject research is an understanding of the terminology used in the analysis of behavior. The terms have precise meanings in the field of behavior analysis. Their purpose is to communicate the behavior, the procedures for data collection and analysis, and the procedures for reporting the results of research. We will define the major terms needed to understand the discussion that follows:

- *Baseline.* The graphic presentation of the natural occurrences of the behavior (dependent variable) prior to starting an independent variable is referred to as baseline.
- *Dependent variables.* Behaviors that are to be studied during the investigation are called dependent variables (the research question is whether or not the behavior is *dependent* on the variables manipulated during the experiment).
- *Independent variables.* Environmental events manipulated during the study are the independent variables.
- *Generality.* If the behavior transfers to other than experimental conditions or if changes occur in behaviors not directly treated, we say that the behavior has generalized. We are interested in whether the behavior change has been maintained over time.
- *Graphs.* Graphs are "relatively simple visual formats for displaying . . . organizing, storing, interpreting, and communicating" data (Cooper et al., 1987, p. 107).
- *Variability.* Whether the behavior changes over time and how much of a change occurs refers to variability.

Criteria

A second suggested prerequisite for the implementation of these research strategies is to understand the criteria by which such research is to be judged. Criteria for studies include:

1. The behavior and the treatment must be clearly defined in such a way that two or more independent observers observe the same behavior.

2. There needs to be systematic measurement throughout the study to closely monitor the effects of the treatment. That means measurement of the behavior(s) under investigation before, during, and after the treatment.

3. Changes in the experimental conditions must be systematic. There must be no more than one change made to an intervention at a time, and the effects of each change must be observed prior to another change.

4. The data need to be recorded consistently and accurately. There must be a design or plan for data collection, and the data must be collected according to the plan.

5. The primary method of data analysis is visual inspection and interpretation of the precise display of the data in graphic form as defined by Cooper (1981).

6. A central issue in the case study approach as critiqued by Campbell and Stanley (1966) is the absence of a means of comparing treatment effects. In research the comparison is made with regard to the baseline. The baseline demonstrates the exact nature of the behavior prior to any treatment or intervention. The comparison then takes place when the effects of the intervention are examined in relation to the nature of the behavior prior to the intervention (Note: the designs that follow will provide ample evidence of the need for, and character of, the baseline (Baer, Wolf, & Risley, 1968).

Four Basic Single-Subject Designs

There are four basic designs (data collection arrangements) in single-subject research, with variations on these designs. They are:

1. Withdrawal and reversal designs
2. Multiple baseline designs, across behaviors, groups, and settings
3. Changing criterion designs
4. Multi-element designs

The baseline, as we mentioned above, is the key point of comparison and the beginning point of any research design. A short discussion of baselines will help you understand the designs. Suppose a teacher wanted to teach a child to write higher-order questions. The teacher then designs a study to investigate the effects of a particular instructional strategy and selects analysis as the questioning level with which to begin. The teacher may first select a series of passages for the child to read, then develop a series of lessons to teach the child the nature and processes of preparing analysis questions. In addition, data collection procedures and definitions of the means for judging whether the child's questions are at the analysis level or not are determined.

During the first, or baseline, phase of the study the teacher chooses, for example, three passages, one for each day. On day 1, the teacher asks the child to read a passage and write three questions that can be answered in the passage. The child writes the questions, reads the passage, and then takes the comprehension quiz. The teacher collects the student's questions and judges whether or not they meet the predetermined criteria for analysis questions. On each of the next two days the teacher and the student repeat the process for a set of three observations. The teacher judges that the student wrote no analysis questions on day 1, one analysis question on day 2, and no analysis questions on day 3 (see Figure 7.1). The teacher concludes that, in the absence of instruction, the child is unlikely to write analysis questions. The teacher also concludes that instruction will help the child prepare such questions.

The baseline in Figure 7.1 contains five data points. This appears to be a rather brief set of data. However, the baseline has been the subject of considerable study, and five data points are adequate to establish a trend (Cooper, 1981). The behavior should be stable and consistent but not necessarily *flat*. It may be flat, or it may show an increase or a decrease, or it may show some consistent variability. Consistency is the important point. Actually, a flat baseline is far less common than increasing, decreasing, or variable baselines, since normal human behavior is more likely to be variable. "Fewer data points suffice when a high degree of stability is evidenced" (Cooper et al., 1987, p. 131). It is also the

FIGURE 7.1 Example baseline showing analysis questions written during the baseline phase

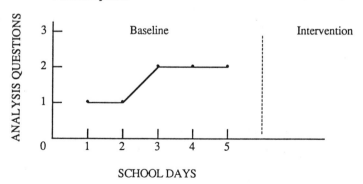

baseline that allows the researcher to make the comparisons that Campbell and Stanley (1966) pointed out as basic to scientific evidence. Obtaining baseline data is the starting point of any design. This discussion
leads us directly to the first two, and most powerful of the designs, the
withdrawal and reversal designs (presented for pedagogical purposes to
clarify the role of the baseline in the process of comparison).

Withdrawal and Reversal Designs. At first glance, the two seem
quite similar. However, there are considerable differences between
them. When implementing the *withdrawal* design the researcher first
takes a baseline (phase A), then initiates the treatment program (phase
B), and continues to observe and record the behavior until a trend is
noted. Then the design calls for returning to the baseline condition (the A
phase) when treatment is *withheld*, that is, there is no intervention. The
treatment, or B phase, is compared to the baseline, or A phase. The
comparison is weak, however, since there is only one comparison. To be
able to place some confidence in the effectiveness of the intervention, the
A and B phases would need to be carried out two or three times. This
design is abbreviated A-B-A-B (A = baseline, B = intervention) (see Figure 7.2).

FIGURE 7.2   An example of A–B–A–B design

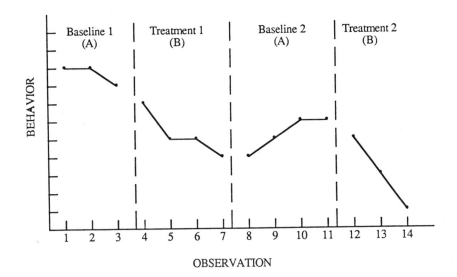

The *reversal* design is also an A-B-A-B design, with one very important difference. During the second B, or intervention phase, instead of withholding the treatment, the teacher would reinforce some behavior other than the target behavior. During the first B phase the researcher withholds some treatment, while during the second B phase, he or she reinforces some behavior other than the target behavior.

The A-B-A-B design demonstrates the effects of treatment or intervention. The effects can be clearly examined by continuing the A and B phases. Other variables can be systematically eliminated, and the effects of extraneous variables can be examined carefully.

While the withdrawal and reversal designs are powerful research strategies, we do not find them to be particularly useful techniques in educational settings for the gifted. First of all, it makes little sense to reinstate an undesirable behavior. Nor does it make any sense to try to eliminate desirable behaviors. Second, most educational behaviors are not likely to return to baseline (Hersen & Barlow, 1976). For example, vocabulary words acquired are not likely to be forgotten by a gifted child during a five- or eight-day baseline period.

Multiple-Baseline Design. Given the limitations of the A-B-A-B design, the *multiple-baseline* design is most commonly used in educational settings. Now, instead of collecting baseline data on only one behavior, the researcher collects baseline data on three or more behaviors at the same time. Following the emergence of a stable baseline, the researcher initiates an intervention on one of the behaviors while continuing to collect baseline data on the other behaviors. With the emergence of a stable baseline for the treated behavior, a second behavior is treated, so now two behaviors are in treatment while the third is still in baseline. Finally, the third behavior is treated in the same way. Angleberger (1978) used the multiple-baseline to study the creative writing behavior of high-achieving children, and Brown (1979) studied gifted children's production of higher-order questions with this design.

In her study, Brown (1979) evaluated the effects of training on the ability of high-achieving fourth graders to write analysis, synthesis, and evaluation questions using the levels of Bloom's taxonomy (Bloom, 1956). Prior to instruction, the children were asked to write four questions at each of the three cognitive levels. The researcher and a trained observer then rated each of the questions the children wrote to determine into which of the three levels the questions would reasonably fit. Following a five-day baseline, Brown began a training program to teach the writing of analysis questions while at the same time baseline data were collected on synthesis and evaluation questions. After five days of instruction in and observation of the analysis questions, instruction was begun on synthesis questions, and baseline was continued on evaluation questions. Five days later, instruction in evaluation questions was initiated. To examine for generalization, observations were taken 11 and 25 days later. Figure 7.3 displays a graph from the Brown (1979) study with the results for one child.

Analysis of the graph clearly indicates that prior to instruction this child wrote no analysis, synthesis, or evaluation questions. Following instruction, the student was able to write four questions at each level. In addition, the checks 11 and 25 days later indicate that the child had retained the skill. We can see a cause-and-effect (functional) relationship between the treatment and the student's ability to write questions meeting the criteria for higher-order thinking skills.

FIGURE 7.3   Multiple baseline design of the effects of instruction, praise, and graphing, with follow-up, for one high-achieving fourth-grade student (Brown, 1979)

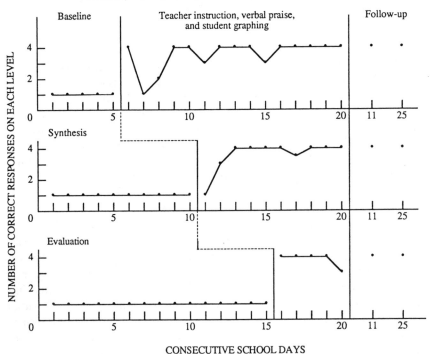

CONSECUTIVE SCHOOL DAYS

One observation we believe is of interest to educators of the gifted is that in the study by Brown (1979) the children had to write four questions each day for many days. This obviously would be boring to able students. To accommodate this design problem, the *multiple-probe technique* is suggested (Horner & Baer, 1978). Instead of continuous recordings as in the multiple-baseline design, the experimenter now only *probes* the behavior on several occasions during the baseline phase—then, during the instruction phase, the observations are again continuous. The probe technique is particularly useful where there is little likelihood of the target behavior's occurring (Cooper, 1981).

The Brown (1979) study represents a multiple-baseline design across behaviors. In this instance students were asked to write three levels of questions. Multiple baselines, with or without probes, may also be employed across groups or settings. Had Brown grouped the children into three groups and provided instruction to each group, one at a time, it would have been a *multiple-baseline across groups* design. If the instruction had been given systematically in three different locations—for example, the regular class, the library, and the resource room—the study would then have been a *multiple-baseline across settings* design. The choice of design depends on which one will most effectively allow the functional relationship to be evaluated.

Changing-Criterion Design. We find this design (Figure 7.4) suitable for basic skill learning and situations where *stepwise* learning is likely. An example of this is learning a foreign language vocabulary. A study would begin, for example, with a baseline reflecting the number of words learned per day over a five-day period. The teacher then calculates an average of words learned per day. To that average the teacher may add two more words so that the child must surpass the average by two words each day to reach criterion. Once a new stable baseline is reached, the teacher may add two more words to the criteria (the size of the increment depends on the performance of the learner during the last phase and on researcher judgment). The phases may continue until some predetermined/expected maximum is reached. The changing-criterion design is particularly useful for new basic skills acquisition by gifted students. By using the previous phase as the baseline for the next phase, the need for returning to baseline or continuing a long baseline is eliminated. Further, it allows for learning that will become progressively involved or more demanding.

Multi-Element Design. The final design, and one considered appropriate for complex behaviors (Sulzer-Azaroff & Mayer, 1977), is the

FIGURE 7.4   Example of the changing-criteria design

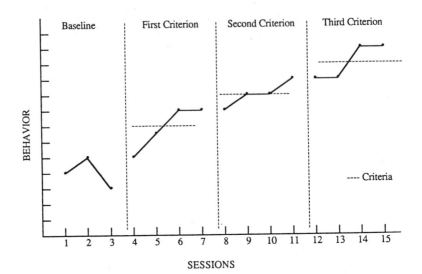

SESSIONS

multi-element design. O'Brien (1978) (Figure 7.5) utilized this design to study the modalities through which five gifted second-graders learned paired associate tasks. Each day the children were given six trials to learn ten paired associates. The tasks were presented in one of three modalities (auditory, visual, or kinesthetic), with the order of presentation randomly varied. The design allows for comparison of more than one independent variable at a time; in this instance the independent variable was the effectiveness of each modality for learning a task. This design is also sensitive to the rapid changes in the learning of gifted students (Sulzer-Azaroff & Mayer, 1977).

In Figure 7.5 each of the lines represents the effects of instruction using a different modality. We make comparisons by noting the stability and directions of the lines for each of the modes of instruction. You can see some overlap between the visual and auditory modes, but neither the auditory nor the visual modes overlapped with the kinesthetic. Yet each of the three lines showed an increase in the number of correct responses. It can be concluded from the graph that the auditory and visual methods of instruction were more effective than the kinesthetic approach. However, with a little overlap the auditory method resulted in more learned paired associates than did the visual approach. A functional relationship

FIGURE 7.5   Multi-element design showing the rate of acquisition by gifted
second-graders of paired associate tasks presented visually,
auditorily, or kinesthetically (O'Brien, 1978)

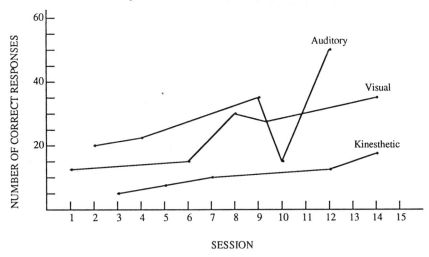

did exist, which was not obvious when examining the results from the
first two methods.

In summary, we find the multiple-probe technique and the multi-
element designs have the most promise for studies involving gifted students. They allow for the study of complex behaviors, do not require
long and often tiresome baselines, and accommodate academic behavior
that neither readily nor reasonably returns to baseline after it has been
acquired. The withdrawal, reversal, and changing-criterion designs serve
the analysis of basic behavior (such as learning paradigms and rates of
acquisition) well, but they are felt to be less applicable in classroom
settings involving complex behaviors of gifted children.

MEASUREMENT AND REPORTING

Regardless of the design chosen, the data are only as good as the precision and detail given to measuring and reporting the behavior under
study. Measurement and reporting are complex issues. Here we can only
briefly discuss these topics (for elaboration, see Cooper, 1981; Cooper
et al., 1987).

Observational Systems

There are basically five measurement, or observational, systems for recording data (Cooper et al., 1987):

1. *Event recording:* direct counts of specific behavior
2. *Duration recording:* recording the amount of time a behavior occurs during a predetermined length of observation
3. *Latency recording:* recording the time between the presentation of the stimulus and the behavior
4. *Interval recording:* counting the presence or absence of the behavior during a time interval
5. *Momentary time sampling:* counting the behavior after some specified time period, whether the intervals are of consistent length or of specified variability.

In the studies by Angleberger (1978), Brown (1979), and O'Brien (1978) the measurements were all event recordings: number of sentences, number of questions written, and number of paired associates learned. These three behaviors are discrete, can be counted easily, and do not occur over long periods of time.

Units of Measurement

Once the data have been collected, they must be reported as precisely as the methods by which they were gathered. Reporting the data impacts directly on the analysis and interpretation of the outcomes of the study. To accomplish this, the "amount of behavior should be converted to other units of measurement to allow for comparison of behavior across time" (Cooper et al., 1987, p. 70). The most frequent units of measurement include:

1. *Frequency:* number of behaviors during some period of time (e.g., number of vocabulary words learned each day)
2. *Rate:* number of responses per period of time (e.g., minute or hour), such as words learned per hour
3. *Percentage:* the units of behavior per 100 responses (percentage of correctly spelled words)

Other units of measurement that are less frequently used include: *trials to criterion,* the number of trials required to reach some stated criteria of mastery (e.g., the number of times a foreign language vocabulary list was presented before the learner could correctly identify 8 out of 10 words); *complexity of task*, breaking the task into subparts and recording the number of parts correctly completed (e.g., the number of operations needed to correctly multiply a 3-digit number by a 2-digit number); pre- and posttest measures, which determine performance before and after some treatment, usually instruction—often reported as gain scores (e.g., testing with the Unusual Uses portion of the Torrance test before and after instruction and comparing the two scores, which are frequently reported as a percentage of the possible score); and *probes*, periodic recordings to see if the learned material generalizes (e.g., if taught in a specific setting, can the learner use the skill in another setting?).

The choices of observational and recording systems are clearly dependent on the research questions being asked and the nature of the behavior under study. The more readily observable behavior is the better starting point for those of you who are undertaking your first study, since observation and recording are skills that you will acquire with practice. We further suggest you read published studies, practice the skills, and conduct sample recording sessions before undertaking more complex studies.

Self-Reporting

Self-reporting is a technique that holds promise for studying *inaccessible* behaviors. For example, students are asked to describe their individual thinking processes as they progress through a specific problem. Students may describe such things as the logic behind their categorization of problem-solving strategies, the strategies behind their grouping of categories and classifications, or the associations they made to remember paired associate tasks. The think aloud problem-solving strategies of Whimby and Lockhead (1986), protocol analysis methods (Ericsson & Simon, 1984), and knowledge engineering in expert systems (Larkin, McDermott, Simon, & Simon, 1980), coupled with the theoretical work of Sternberg and his colleagues (e.g., Detterman & Sternberg, 1982), offer exciting possibilities for the current study of many of these previously inaccessible behaviors.

We must also point out some concern with the use of self-reports. The first problem with self-reporting is that the person reporting the behavior is also the person emitting the behavior. Some individuals may report what they *think* will satisfy the researcher. For those who have worked with gifted and talented students, it is also possible that some will give alternative responses just to see what will happen, or because their alternative just makes more sense to them. Stemming from the *behaver as reporter* situation, Johnston and Pennypacker (1981) state that the "stability, accuracy, and believability" (p. 183) may be difficult to establish. The most economical means of eliminating these problems is to replicate the studies with careful attention to the variability of the data across subjects. In summary, prior to undertaking a single-subject investigation the Johnston and Pennypacker (1981) work must be carefully studied.

Interobservation Agreement

Our final note on observational systems and reporting is concerned with *interobserver agreement*. Baer and colleagues (1968) indicated that one criterion for the research should be that the behavior and the treatment must be clearly defined in such a way that two or more independent observers observe the same behavior. In reporting the studies, the interobserver agreement is of considerable importance. Interobserver agreement, first of all, requires that the behavior be adequately defined so that the same behavior is being observed by all of the observers. The definition of the behavior has to be very carefully drawn. It must allow no fuzziness about the specific target behavior(s) of the study. Some behaviors seem easy enough to define, such as the number of correctly spelled words. More complex behaviors are another question; for example, creativity may be defined in many ways. Is a response creative if it is one of low probability, or must it be both of low probability and original? Will novelty only be counted as a creative response? Must the response show both flexibility and fluency? Since much of the work in gifted education deals with constructs of this nature (e.g., intelligence and leadership), the agreement between observers is even more critical.

We express interobserver agreement as a percentage of agreement between observers. It is computed by dividing the total number of agreements by the total number of observations (agreements and disagreements) and multiplying by 100 to convert to percentage (Cooper, 1981). For example, if I as an observer A tallied 23 different uses for a tin can, and you as observer B tallied 21 uses, there would be 21 agreements and 2 disagreements. We calculate the interobserver agreement by dividing 21 (total number of agreements) by 23 (total number of agreements and disagreements), which is equal to .91. To convert this to a percentage we multiply .91 times 100 and find that we agreed 91% of the time. Generally, agreements should be at or above 80% before continuing the study (Cooper, 1981).

FUTURE POSSIBILITIES

For the field of gifted education, single-subject designs hold exciting research possibilities. New concepts of intelligence, thinking skills, and creativity from the field of cognitive psychology lend themselves to such individual or small-group research tactics. Cognitive instructional strategies used by teachers to help gifted students process information in meaningful ways (Jones, 1986) and direct instructional strategies for teaching thinking skills (Beyer, 1985) can be examined. Student repertoires of specific thinking and study strategies used to interact with instructional materials during problem solving (Anderson, 1980) offer an exciting line of investigation. Methods of protocol analysis (Ericsson & Simon, 1984) or think aloud problem solving (Whimby & Lockhead, 1986) allow the researcher access to the processes utilized by students during times of critical thinking problem solving. The work being done on expert and novice problem solvers (Larkin et al., 1980) is a fruitful area for research. Importantly, such studies may suggest new behavioral strategies for intelligence training programs (Detterman & Sternberg, 1982).

Further, in the Winston and Baker (1985) review of creativity studies, it is suggested that the creative process as defined by cognitive psychology is a potential source of ideas for future behavioral analyses of creativity. For example, in a study by Wisnyai (1988), processes related to the acquisition of scientific insight were taught to gifted high school students. Further single-subject investigations of the specific creative problem-solving strategies used by novice and experts would be of practical interest to educators of the gifted. All of these areas may be studied using single-subject techniques.

There are many exciting questions to be researched. For example:

- Can gifted students be taught to become more effective problem solvers?
- What insight processes are utilized by gifted students when solving science, math, and other types of problems?
- Can the creativity part of the creative writing process be taught and generalized?
- Can verbal mediation help gifted students with attention deficit-hyperactive disorder (ADHD) gain control of their behavior?
- Will total communication (TC) facilitate the socialization of a severely hearing-impaired gifted student?
- Will a program of social skills improve the social risk taking of a gifted female adolescent with cerebral palsy?

We adhere strongly to a belief in the individual nature of gifts and talents. Contemporary researchers must have access to varied research techniques. There are several groups of research strategies, each with their own strengths and limitations; single-subject research is one set of techniques that has merit for questions addressing the individual character of giftedness.

CONCLUSION

In summary, the emphasis of single-subject research is on applied rather than theoretical research. It is considered applied research if the behavior under investigation is of importance to the individual or society. It is applied if (1) it seeks to improve behavior rather than to improve the discussion of the behavior (unless the behavior under study is verbal behavior), (2) the experimenter can demonstrate control of the behavior under investigation, (3) the procedures are precisely and completely described. Finally, the procedures are to be based on behavioral principles, and the behavior studied must show some generality (Baer et al., 1968).

There are four designs for the scientific study of behavior. The cornerstone of the analysis of behavior is the case study, where the means of comparison is the performance of the individual during and after treatment with performance prior to treatment—the baseline. The subject serves as his or her own control. We suggest that before attempting to conduct research with these tactics you must be familiar with the underlying principles, attitudes, and significance of such studies. In addition, you must be skilled in the use of the proper designs, recognizing the importance of the baseline, definition of the behavior, data recording, and data measurement. Interobserver agreement is of paramount concern for the collection, interpretation, and communication of research.

REFERENCES

Anderson, T. H. (1980). Study strategies and adjunct aids. In R. J. Spiro, B. C. Bruce, & W. F. Brewer (Eds.), *Theoretical issues in reading comprehension* (pp. 483–502). Hillsdale, NJ: Erlbaum.

Angleberger, N. W. (1978). *The application of reinforcement techniques to improve the quality of selected aspects of creative writing among high-achieving children.* Unpublished master's thesis, Ohio State University, Columbus.

Baer, D. M., Wolf, M. M., & Risley, T. (1968). Current dimensions of applied behavior analysis. *Journal of Applied Behavior Analysis, 1*, 91–97.

Beyer, B. (1985). Practical strategies for the direct instruction of thinking skills. In A. Costa (Ed.), *Developing minds: A resource book for teaching thinking* (pp. 145–150). Alexandria, VA: Association for Supervision and Curriculum Development.

Bijou, S. W. (1955). A systematic approach to an experimental analysis of young children. *Child Development, 26*, 161–168.

Bijou, S. W. (1963). Theory and research in mental (developmental) retardation. *Psychological Record, 13*, 95–110.

Bijou, S. W. (1971). What psychology has to offer education—now. *Journal of Applied Behavior Analysis, 3*, 65–71.

Bloom, B. S. (Ed.). (1956). *Taxonomy of educational objectives: The cognitive domain*. New York: McKay.

Bloom, M., & Fischer, J. (1982). *Evaluating practice: Guidelines for the accountable professional*. Englewood Cliffs, NJ: Prentice-Hall.

Brown, S. D. (1979). *Effects of teacher instruction and positive reinforcement on the questioning techniques of gifted students*. Unpublished master's thesis, Ohio State University, Columbus.

Campbell, D. T., & Stanley, J. C. (1966). *Experimental and quasi-experimental designs for research*. Chicago: Rand McNally.

Campbell, J., & Willer, J. (1978). Modifying components of "creative behavior" in the natural environment. *Behavior Modification, 2*, 549–561.

Cooper, J. O. (1981). *Measuring behavior* (2nd ed.). Columbus, OH: Merrill.

Cooper, J. O., Heron, T. E., & Heward, W. L. (1987). *Applied behavior analysis*. Columbus, OH: Merrill.

Detterman, D., & Sternberg, R. J. (Eds.). (1982). *How and how much can intelligence be increased?* Norwood, NJ: Ablex.

Ericsson, K. A., & Simon, H. A. (1984). *Protocol analysis*. Cambridge, MA: MIT Press.

Fichter, G., & Swassing, R. H. (1985). Program implementation and evaluation. In R. H. Swassing (Ed.), *Teaching gifted children and adolescents* (pp. 402–430). Columbus, OH: Merrill.

Fisher, R. A. (1935). *The design of experiments*. London: Oliver & Boyd.

Foster, W. (1986). The application of single subject research methods to the study of exceptional ability and extraordinary achievement. *Gifted Child Quarterly, 1*, 33–37.

Glover, J., & Gary, A. L. (1976). Procedures to increase some aspects of creativity. *Journal of Applied Behavior Analysis, 9*, 79–84.

Goetz, E. M. (1982). A review of functional analyses of preschool children's creative behaviors. *Education and Treatment of Children, 5*, 157–177.

Goetz, E. M., & Baer, D. M. (1973). Social control of form diversity and the emergence of new forms in children's blockbuilding. *Journal of Applied Behavior Analysis, 6*, 209–218.

Henson, F. O. (1974). *A preliminary investigation into the effects of token reinforcement on one aspect of creativity.* Unpublished doctoral dissertation, Ohio State University, Columbus.

Hersen, M., & Barlow, D. H. (1976). *Single-case experimental designs: Strategies for studying behavior change.* New York: Pergamon.

Horner, R. D., & Baer, D. M. (1978). Multiple probe technique: A variation on the multiple baseline design. *Journal of Applied Behavior Analysis, 11,* 189–196.

Johnston, J. M., & Pennypacker, H. S. (1981). *Strategies and tactics of human behavioral research.* Hillsdale, NJ: Erlbaum.

Jones, B. F. (1986, April 5). Quality and equality through cognitive instruction. *Educational Leadership,* pp. 5–10.

Larkin, J. H., McDermott, J., Simon, D. P., & Simon, H. A. (1980). Expert and novice performance in solving physics problems. *Science, 208,* 1335–1342.

O'Brien, D. E. (1978). *A functional analysis of the learning modalities of gifted children.* Unpublished master's thesis, Ohio State University, Columbus.

Sidman, M. (1960). *Tactics of scientific research: Evaluating experimental data in psychology.* New York: Basic Books.

Skinner, B. F. (1953). *Science and human behavior.* New York: Free Press.

Sulzer-Azaroff, B., & Mayer, G. R. (1977). *Applying behavior analysis procedures with children and youth.* New York: Holt, Rinehart & Winston.

Whimby, A., & Lockhead, J. (1986). *Problem solving and comprehension.* Hillsdale, NJ: Erlbaum.

Winston, A. S., & Baker, J. E. (1985). Behavior analytic studies of creativity: A critical review. *The Behavior Analyst, 8,* 191–205.

Wisnyai, S. A. (1988). *Effect of insight training on the critical thinking skills of gifted students in biology.* Unpublished doctoral dissertation, Ohio State University, Columbus.

CHAPTER 8

CASE STUDY RESEARCH IN GIFTED EDUCATION

Sidney M. Moon

Imagine for a moment a gifted child you know. See him or her clearly in your mind's eye. How would you describe that child physically? What are that child's unique talents? How did those talents develop? How is that child faring in school? Who might you talk with to find out more about the child, to understand him or her better? What might studying this child contribute to our understanding of the nature and nurture of gifted youth?

These questions can be answered effectively by designing a holistic, single-case study (Yin, 1989). Questions like these often give rise to case study research designs.

Case study methods have been a cornerstone of research on giftedness. Terman and his associates reported numerous case studies of gifted children in their pioneering research on children with IQs above 140 (Burks, Jensen, & Terman, 1930; Terman, 1925). Hollingworth (1942) devoted a major portion of her career to intensive case study research on 12 children whose IQs were above 180. More recently, researchers in gifted education have used case study methods to provide in-depth descriptions of gifted twins (Witty & Coomer, 1955), ten highly gifted Indiana adolescents (Flack, 1983), and the radical acceleration through school of an extraordinarily gifted Australian child (Gross, 1986).

During the 1980s, case study methods were used to explore the characteristics of special populations of gifted youth and to develop theory about these populations. Whitmore and Maker (1985) structured each chapter in their book describing a specific type of handicapped gifted person around a case study. The special populations described by Whitmore and Maker include the hearing impaired, the visually impaired, the physically impaired, adults incurring a specific disability, and the learning disabled.

Feldman and Goldsmith (1986) used case study methodology to conduct a longitudinal study of prodigies, another special population of gifted children. From their intensive study of six highly unusual children, they developed theory about the nature of prodigies and the "coincidence" of events necessary to produce a prodigy. Theory which is developed in this way, by examining concrete instances and looking for general principles that hold true across those instances, is called *grounded theory* by Glaser and Strauss (1967) because the theory is grounded in empirical observations. Grounded theory is developed by inductive methods of data analysis. Feldman and Goldsmith's work demonstrates the power of qualitative, case study research for developing grounded theory about special populations of gifted youth and the talent development process.

Bloom (1985) and his colleagues also used case study methods in their retrospective research into the developmental histories of *world class* performers in six talent areas (piano, sculpture, swimming, tennis, math, research neurology). Their research yielded grounded theory about the talent development process. Across all six talent areas, Bloom and his colleagues identified characteristic stages of talent development. Each stage required a particular type of teacher and developed different abilities in the student. Bloom's research has important implications for the development of gifted programming in school settings and clearly demonstrated the power of case study research to develop theory and enhance practice within the field of gifted education.

WHAT IS CASE STUDY RESEARCH?

Case study research is intensive. It attempts to develop and understand universal principles by a close examination of particular cases. It is a powerful methodology that has given birth to transformational, theoretical advances in the social sciences. Freud, Piaget, and Terman are all examples of researchers whose use of case study methods created new fields of inquiry.

In spite of this proven power to discover new principles, case study research has historically been considered a weak and inferior research method by many social scientists. The historical bias against case study research occurred for two reasons. First, many social scientists in the middle part of this century were so steeped in the quantitative research paradigm that they were unable to see the value of qualitative, nonexperimental, case study research. The recent upsurge of interest in the qualitative research paradigm has revived interest in case study research and given such research renewed respectability.

Second, for a long time scholars incorrectly thought that the case study was identical to one of the weakest types of quasi-experimental designs, the so-called *one-shot case study*, a posttest-only design (Cook & Campbell, 1979; Yin, 1989). The demeaning association of case study research with the one-shot case study design was corrected by Cook and Campbell (1979) in their text on quasi-experiments and by Campbell (1979) in a chapter on the important differences that exist between the assumptions and techniques of statistical research and case study research. The posttest-only design continues to be a weak quasi-experimental design, but scholars now understand that the case study is something altogether different. It is not a weak experimental design; it is a powerful qualitative research strategy.

It is vital to separate case study research from experimental research. Case study research stems from the qualitative, rather than the quantitative, paradigm. It is undergirded by a different epistemology from experimental research—the epistemology of the phenomenological rather than the positivist paradigm. In the phenomenological paradigm, the focus is on holistic perceptions of reality from the perspective of the participants in that reality. Context, meaning, complexity, interactions, and thick descriptions of specific, concrete cases are stressed (Bogdan & Biklen, 1982; Campbell, 1979; Lincoln & Guba, 1985; Moon, Dillon, & Sprenkle, 1990).

Case study research also uses different logic from experimental research, especially in the sampling and data analysis phases (Goetz & LeCompte, 1984; Yin, 1989). For instance, most case studies use the logic of criterion sampling rather than the logic of probabilistic sampling, and the logic of analytic generalization rather than the logic of statistical generalization (Goetz & LeCompte, 1984; Yin, 1989).

The case study is now established as an accepted and rigorous method of social science research (Lauer & Asher, 1988; Lincoln & Guba, 1985; Merriam, 1988; Yin, 1989). The first goal of the case study is a detailed, concrete, and intensive description of particular circumstances of an individual life or event (Foster, 1986). The scientific value of such a detailed understanding of a single case is that such knowledge can inform theory (Stake, 1979). Yin (1989) was one of the first scholars to offer a more technical definition of the case study. He describes the case study as:

> An empirical inquiry that investigates a contemporary phenomenon within its real-life context; when the boundaries between phenomena and context are not clearly evident; and in which multiple sources of evidence are used. (p. 23)

This definition works well for case study research in the field of gifted education with one exception. The restriction to contemporary phenomena excludes the work of a number of scholars who have reported fascinating case studies of eminent historical figures (Cox, 1926; Goertzel & Goertzel, 1962; Montour, 1977). The work of these researchers has traditionally been considered case study research by scholars within the field of gifted education (Foster, 1986). Life history research has made an important contribution to our understanding of the nature and nurture of gifted individuals.

Some authors have characterized all case studies as a form of qualitative research (Foster, 1986). Qualitative research generally involves (1) detailed observation of the natural world by a trained observer and (2) the attempt to avoid prior commitment to any theoretical model as part of a generative, rather than a verificative, purpose (Bogdan & Biklen, 1982; Yin, 1989). However, Yin (1989) believes that, although case studies are usually qualitative, they do not have to be. They can be based partially or entirely on quantitative evidence. For instance, Terman's ambitious longitudinal study of 1,000 gifted persons was a multiple-case study, yet much of the evidence reported was quantitative (Burks et al., 1930; Terman, 1925; Terman & Oden, 1947, 1959). Case studies also do not have to be limited to exploratory research designed to generate hypotheses or theory. They have a distinctive place in evaluation research as well (Cook & Reichardt, 1979; Patton, 1980).

TYPES OF CASE RESEARCH

Recently scholars have begun to develop taxonomies of the different kinds of case study research that have appeared in the social science literature (Bogdan & Biklen, 1982; Borg & Gall, 1989). I have developed the following taxonomy from the work of these scholars. I believe these forms of case study research hold the most promise for answering questions in the field of gifted education:

1. Clinical case studies
2. Developmental case studies
3. Observational case studies
4. Situational analysis case studies
5. Task analysis case studies

I will define and describe each in the sections which follows.

Clinical Case Studies

Clinical case studies are designed to understand a particular type of individual using a variety of data collection techniques, such as clinical interviews, clinical observations, and testing results (Borg & Gall, 1989). For example, one might conduct a clinical case study in order to understand the learning characteristics of a gifted child with a learning disability. This type of case study research has its roots in psychology. Clinical case studies are often conducted to assess an individual in order to determine the best educational or therapeutic interventions for that individual.

Developmental Case Studies

Developmental case studies have been a very prominent research method in the field of gifted education. Developmental case studies attempt to understand the development across time of an individual, an organization, a program component, or a concept. Developmental case studies can be retrospective, as in Bloom's (1985) study of talent development, or they can be prospective, as in Feldman and Goldsmith's (1986) longitudinal study of six child prodigies. They can describe the development of a single individual, as in Moon's (1990) study of a gifted child with multiple handicaps, or a large group of individuals, as in Terman and Oden's (1947, 1959) longitudinal follow-ups of Terman's (1925) original 300 gifted children. Data collection techniques for developmental case studies emphasize structured or unstructured interviews and analysis of extant records, documents, and products.

Developmental case studies can also examine the development of various elements of gifted programs. VanTassel-Baska (1988a, 1988b, 1988c; VanTassel-Baska & Campbell, 1988a, 1988b) has written a series of articles for *Gifted Child Today* that describe a case study of the development of a scope and sequence for a K–12 language arts curriculum in the Gary, Indiana, school system. Moon, Feldhusen, and Kelly (in press) reported a case study of the evolving improvements that took place over a number of years in the identification system for a pull-out enrichment program when staff members were committed to implement the often neglected validation phase of identification. Similarly, Buchanan (1987) has described a case study of the evaluation of an identification process for a specific gifted program.

Observational Case Studies

In this type of case study you gather data by observing an individual or a group of individuals in naturalistic contexts (Borg & Gall, 1989). Observational case studies can focus on a variety of subjects. Such studies can examine a specific group of children, such as fifth-grade gifted students in a self-contained classroom; some activity in a school, such as curriculum planning; or a particular individual, such as a gifted resource teacher. The potential of this kind of case study research has barely begun to be tapped in the field of gifted education.

It is important at this point to understand the similarities and differences between observational case studies and a related qualitative methodology, ethnography (see Chapter 6, this volume, for more information). Both employ many of the same data gathering techniques, such as participant observation, interviewing, and triangulation. Both can be used to develop grounded theory about the meaning of the events and contexts studied (Bogdan & Biklen, 1982; Foster, 1986; Goetz & LeCompte, 1984; Yin, 1989). However, Foster (1986) correctly distinguishes the two by saying that the case study:

> Is interested in developing a portrayal of the unique contextual circumstances and phenomenology of individual experience within a setting whereas ethnography seeks to describe the shared, social phenomenology present in a situation through roles, cultural mores and the like. (p. 34)

Situational Analysis Case Studies

In situational analysis you examine a particular event from the viewpoint of all the major participants (Borg & Gall, 1989). This type of case study research can be an effective way to study the impact of educational change. For example, the implementation of an international baccalaureate program in a large high school might be examined from the perspectives of the participating students, the nonparticipating students, the teachers, the administration, and the community. The goal of such research is to provide an in-depth understanding of the impact of an event on the lives and institutions affected by the event. This type of case study is a useful component of research on the outcomes of educational innovations.

Task Analysis Case Studies

One of the newer forms of case study research is task analysis (Moon & Piery, 1991). In a task analysis the researcher studies the performance of individual subjects intensively and then attempts to generalize to the performance of other subjects through multiple replications (Safran, Greenberg, & Rice, 1988). This type of research has been used to illuminate human problem solving (Newell & Simon, 1972) and the differences between the thinking processes of immature and expert writers (Flower

& Hayes, 1980). It is a useful method of case study research any time human performance on a task is being studied.

While these five types of case study research are not exhaustive, they do represent the most useful types of case study research for the field of gifted education. The methods are not mutually exclusive. They often overlap and can be more powerful in combination than they are alone. For example, in Moon's (1990) case study of a verbally gifted boy with multiple handicaps, three types of case study research (clinical, developmental, and observational) were combined to thoroughly describe and understand the learning characteristics of a unique gifted child.

CASE STUDY RESEARCH DESIGN

Experimental and quasi-experimental research designs have been categorized and described by a number of authors (Cook & Campbell, 1979; Kerlinger, 1986). Case study research designs are not as well defined. Yin's (1989) groundbreaking book on case study research formulates a basic set of four case study designs:

1. Holistic, single-case designs
2. Holistic, multiple-case designs
3. Embedded, single-case designs
4. Embedded, multiple-case designs

Holistic Designs

Holistic designs examine a single unit of analysis using a global approach. Holistic designs are most appropriate when no logical subunits exist and the theory underlying the case is holistic. When the focus of a study is an individual, gifted child, the most logical design choice is a holistic, single-case design. The single unit being examined is the child. A study that aims at analyzing the teaching strategies of six different gifted resource teachers would be a holistic, multiple-case design. The single unit being examined in such a study is the teacher.

Embedded Designs

Embedded designs examine more than one unit of analysis within a single case. They are especially appropriate for examining complex, nested systems. Thus a study interested in the effect of a gifted child on his or her family system would use an embedded design. Units of analysis might include the gifted child, siblings, parents, and the family as a whole. Another case where an embedded design might be appropriate would be in an evaluation of a comprehensive gifted program. Units of analysis could include the various program components, the parents, students, the staff, and the administration.

Single- and Multiple-Case Study Designs

The distinction between single- and multiple-case study designs is crucially important because it illustrates one of the many places where the logic of the case study has been misunderstood in the past. The major insight here is that a single-case study design is analogous to a *single* experiment and a multiple-case study design is analogous to a *series* of experiments. The logic of the multiple-case study is replication logic, not sampling logic (Yin, 1989). The evidence from multiple-case studies is more robust than the evidence from a single-case study, just as the evidence from a meta-analysis of 12 experiments is more robust than the evidence from a single experiment. In conducting a multiple-case study the investigator carefully selects a series of cases so that either (1) each case is expected to produce similar results (a literal replication) or (2) some cases are expected to produce contrary results but for theoretically predictable reasons (a theoretical replication) (Yin, 1989).

As an illustration, suppose that you are interested in studying the learning characteristics of a subpopulation of the learning disabled gifted who have high verbal and low performance scores on the WISC-R (Tannenbaum & Baldwin, 1983). You might design a holistic, multiple-case study that involves two stages of research. In the first stage, you would locate three children who have high verbal and low performance scores on the WISC-R; then you would conduct three separate, single-case studies of these three children. Next these three cases would be compared to one another in order to discover grounded theory about the learning characteristics of verbally gifted, learning disabled students.

In the second phase of the study, you might select three sets of cases to test the newly developed theory. For the first set of cases, you might choose three children who are similar to the first three studied in that they also have *high verbal* and *low performance* scores on the WISC-R. You would then carry out case studies of these children, predicting that the results of these three studies would be similar to the results of the first three (literal replication).

Simultaneously, you would select six children to study who are quite different (theoretical replication). You might look at three children who have *high* scores on both the verbal and performance sections of the

WISC-R and three children who have *low* scores in both areas to see if your predictions of differences between these two groups of children and the children who score high on the verbal section and low on the performance section would be confirmed. If your predictions are confirmed in this phase of the research, then the theory would also be confirmed. Because of the number of replications involved in developing and testing the theory, you can be reasonably confident that the theory is sound if the predictions are confirmed.

In carrying out this complex, multiple-case study, you would need to conduct 12 single-case studies. Again, this is analogous to conducting 12 single experiments. Multiple-case studies are a demanding undertaking, but they have tremendous power to advance knowledge in the field of gifted education. The multiple-case study method of developing and testing theory is particularly powerful in areas where methods based on sampling logic are difficult or impossible to use because of the rarity of the phenomena, as is true in much of the research in gifted education. It is hard to obtain large *n*'s when studying subpopulations of gifted students. Case study methods make large *n*'s unnecessary.

STEPS IN CONDUCTING CASE STUDY RESEARCH

How does an investigator begin a case study research project? What steps are involved? What techniques are used? What decisions must be made? What resources are needed? This section is designed to provide brief answers to these questions. In order to illustrate the steps, two examples will be woven into the theoretical discussion. Both examples are from my own research. The first example will be called the Alec study. It was a holistic, single-case study of an individual child (Moon, 1990). The second study will be referred to as the PACE identification study. It was an embedded, single-case study of the development and validation of an identification procedure that I conducted with a colleague (Moon, Feldhusen, & Kelly, 1991).

There are three phases and seven steps involved in conducting case study research. The phases are: (1) planning, which consists of developing questions, choosing a research design, and selecting the units of analysis and sample cases; (2) implementation, when data collection and analysis occur; and (3) dissemination, where the study is reported and evaluated. Although the steps are in a logical sequence, in actual practice they are often recursive instead of sequential. The investigator may loop backwards frequently to repeat an earlier step. This is especially true during the data collection and data analysis phases of case study research.

In generative research it is quite common for an investigator who has reached step 4 (data collection) to decide that a loop backwards to step 1 (questions) is needed to revise the initial research questions on the basis of new information from the data collection. Similarly, in qualitative case studies, steps 4 (data collection) and 5 (data analysis) usually occur simultaneously and recursively, rather than sequentially as an experimental research. Such recursive data collection and analysis must be undertaken with a clear understanding that both the researcher and the participants have been altered by the earlier observations. A researcher's observational experience has an unalterable effect on the researcher's perspective that changes what he or she *sees* when making future observations.

Phase I: Planning

The planning phase consists of developing questions, choosing an appropriate research design, and selecting the unit of analysis and sample cases. In any kind of research, the first step is the development of research questions. Research questions guide the selection of a research paradigm and the creation of a research design. Case study designs should be selected only when such designs are the most appropriate designs for the questions asked.

Once the research questions are formulated, you must select the case(s) to study (step 2). In case study research, criterion-based selection (Goetz & LeCompte, 1984) usually replaces probabilistic sampling as the primary mode of subject selection. With criterion-based selection, subjects are chosen because they match predetermined criteria generated from the research questions and the theory undergirding the research. Extreme case selection, typical case selection, unique case selection, and reputational case selection are some of the techniques used to ensure that the units of analysis will be relevant to the research questions and help develop sound theory (Goetz & LeCompte, 1984).

The Alec study (Moon, 1990) was an example of unique case selection. Alec was chosen for study precisely because he was unique. Not only was he highly verbally gifted, but he also had a string of handicapping conditions, including severe allergies, which had prevented him from attending school. Alec was 11 years old when the study began. My initial research question was an open-ended, informal, "What's going on here?" This question suggested a qualitative, exploratory, holistic, single-case study design. Alec was one of a kind.

During the course of the study, I developed more formal research questions: (1) How did Alec's giftedness develop? (2) What are Alec's current learning characteristics in the verbal area, his area of greatest giftedness? To answer these questions, I created a research design that combined the clinical, developmental, and observational types of case studies.

In the PACE identification study (Moon et al., 1991), we were concerned with describing and evaluating the development of the PACE identification process over a seven-year period. We wanted to know (1) What revisions had been made and why? (2) Were the changes effective? Since only one identification procedure was being studied, we selected a single-case study design for the research.

The design for this case study needed to be embedded because several units of analysis were of interest. The overarching unit of analysis was the PACE identification procedure. However, this unit of analysis was composed of several subunits because the identification procedures for PACE had changed over time. Thus subunits of analysis included two formative evaluation cycles, one summative evaluation cycle, and three different sets of identification procedures. In addition, a survey was developed for the final phase of the research, creating an additional embedded unit of analysis. This study illustrates the difficulty of defining the units of analysis when the *case* is an entity or event rather than a single individual. It also clearly demonstrates the richness and complexity of embedded case study designs.

The design for this PACE study combined the developmental and situational analysis types of case studies. The situational analysis evolved out of the developmental phase of the research. When the data analysis phase of the developmental study had been completed, we felt a need to evaluate the current effectiveness of the revised identification procedures more comprehensively in order to determine if the validation process had really worked. Therefore we returned to the planning stage and designed a situational analysis case study.

We began by formulating two more specific variations on the initial research questions: (1) How effective is the current match between student needs and PACE program services? (2) Have the PACE identification procedures become more accurate and efficient over the years? Then we designed a survey that contained both forced-choice and open-ended items. In this embedded portion of the study, subunits of analysis were the PACE identification procedures and the perceptions of the PACE teachers, classroom teachers, and administrators who had been involved in implementing those procedures. Because the situational analysis evolved out of the developmental portion of the study, the PACE identification study is an example of a recursive case study design.

The PACE identification study also demonstrates the eclectic nature of case study research. For example, in the embedded survey used for the situation analyzed, probabilistic sampling was used. This in no way negates the criterion-based selection or sampling of the primary subject(s) for the case study itself.

As the final step in the planning phase of case study research (step 3 in the overall process), Yin (1989) recommends codifying the case study design and procedures in a protocol. The creation of a case study protocol enhances the reliability of case study findings and serves as a guide to the investigator throughout the implementation phase of the research. Protocols are essential for multiple-case study designs and designs that involve many investigators. Yin recommends that the protocol include:

1. An overview of the project
2. Field procedures
3. Case study questions
4. Copies of any instruments that will be used
5. Guidelines for how to use the instruments
6. Analysis procedures
7. Guidelines for the writing of the case study report

Phase II: Implementation

The heart of case study research is the implementation phase. It is during this phase that data are collected (step 4) and analyzed (step 5). Case studies are similar to the ethnographic perspective described in Chapter 6. Both involve ongoing interaction between data collection and analysis.

Data Collection. It is important to use *multiple sources of evidence.* A multimodal, eclectic approach to data collection is a hallmark of both qualitative research (Goetz & LeCompte, 1984) and case study research (Yin, 1989). Gathering data from different sources is a form of triangulation that enhances both the reliability and the validity of the findings. Just as a surveyor locates points on a map by triangulating observations from several vantage points, case study researchers check the accuracy of their conclusions by converging on the phenomena under study from various sources. Common sources of data collection in case study research include participant and nonparticipant observation, interviews, questionnaires, documents, archival records, and physical artifacts.

In addition to using multiple sources of evidence, it is important to create and maintain a *case study data base.*

> Every case study project should strive to develop a formal, retrievable data base, so that in principle, other investigators can review the evidence directly and not be limited to formal reports. (Yin, 1989, p. 99)

The case study data base should include copies of all raw data gathered during the study. It should be indexed and filed with clear cross-referencing so that the raw data can be easily retrieved. Establishing a case study data base is a major tactic for enhancing the reliability of case studies.

Another important principle of data collection in case studies is the maintenance of a *chain of evidence* (Yin, 1989). The key idea here is to enable the reader of the final case report to follow your trail from initial research questions through various sources of evidence to the ultimate case study conclusions, much in the same way that Sherlock Holmes might tell Watson how he solved a murder case by explaining how he worked from clue to clue until he could identify the murderer. Making this chain of evidence clear is a challenging task and another growing edge for case study researchers. The task is complicated by the complex and recursive interactions between data collection and data analysis in such research. Citing relevant portions of the data base in the text of the report and including raw data in figures that are referenced within the body of the report are two common methods of documenting the chain of evidence in written reports.

Lincoln and Guba (1985) refer to the chain of evidence as an "audit trail." In Appendix A of their book *Naturalistic Inquiry,* they have compiled an extensive taxonomy of audit trail categories, file types, and evidence. Examining this taxonomy during the planning phase of case study research should help you both to develop a substantial data base and to maintain a chain of evidence throughout your study.

Data Analysis. In case study research it is essential that you have a general analysis strategy in mind before beginning to collect data. Choosing a general strategy helps you identify and employ appropriate analytic techniques. Since data collection and analysis are often simultaneous activities in case study research, it is vital that you decide on a general strategy for conducting the analysis early in your research. Yin (1989) describes two such general strategies: (1) relying on theoretical propositions and (2) developing a case description.

In the Alec study, I collected data from three major sources. First, I examined archival clinical records, which included test scores and a narrative report. Second, I interviewed Alec's parents about his developmental history. Third, I designed and conducted a year-long, participant observation of Alec in a learning situation to collect data on Alec's current learning characteristics. I organized the data from each source into a discrete, formal data base and then analyzed each separately, using techniques appropriate to the source. Then the analyzed data from all three sources were woven into a rich case description that was structured around the initial research questions. The case description frequently referenced sources in the data base in order to maintain a chain of evidence.

In the PACE identification study the implementation phase was more complex. The general analytic strategy we used throughout this study was *reliance on theoretical propositions* (Yin, 1989). The theoretical propositions that led to the study were that (1) it is important to validate the effectiveness of identification procedures subsequent to the implementation of those procedures and (2) identification procedures should be continuously refined to ensure the best possible match between student needs and programming services. The overarching purpose of the study was more than just descriptive. It was theoretical. We wanted to determine if consistent attention to the validation phase of identification could result in improved identification procedures.

The developmental portion of this study was qualitative. It focused on describing and assessing the historical evolution of the PACE identification procedures using the data collection techniques of participant observation, document analysis, and interviewing. The situational analysis relied on a survey instrument that contained both qualitative and quantitative items. The quantitative portion of the survey study was analyzed with traditional statistical techniques, while the qualitative portion was analyzed by analytic induction (Goetz & LeCompte, 1984).

Because the strategies and techniques for data analysis in case study research have not been well defined in the past (Yin, 1989), there is a need for creative development in this area of case study research. Data analysis is undoubtedly the most difficult part of case study research, especially for the novice researcher. A full treatment of the data analysis phase of case study research is beyond the scope of this chapter. You may consult Chapter 5 in Yin's (1989) book for a detailed overview of analytic techniques appropriate for case study research. For a detailed treatment of techniques to use when analyzing data in qualitative case studies, see Chapter 6 in Goetz and LeCompte (1984) and Chapters 2 and 5 in Bogdan and Biklen (1982).

Phase III: Dissemination

Reporting case study research is a demanding task. Voluminous amounts of data must be compressed into a concise and clear report. You must possess above-average creative writing skills, be willing to subject your work to searching criticism, and be intimately familiar with the case (Lincoln & Guba, 1985).

One advantage of qualitative case study research is that it can be easily accessible to the consumer because it is in harmony with the reader's experience (Stake, 1978). Qualitative case study research is concrete. It provides detailed descriptions of specific persons, places, or events. According to Lincoln and Guba (1985), case studies:

> Permit the reader to build on his or her own tacit knowledge in ways that foster empathy and assess intentionality, because they enable the reader to achieve personal understandings . . . and because they enable detailed probing of an instance in question rather than mere surface description of a multitude of cases. (p. 358)

Excellent writing enhances all of these natural advantages of qualitative case study research.

Multiple-case studies are particularly complex to write. They often contain both individual case studies and some cross-case chapters (Yin, 1989). Terman's work illustrates these principles. In Volume 1 (Terman, 1925) a number of family vignettes and individual case studies are described. There are also cross-case chapters on topics such as educational history, play interests, reading interests, school accomplishments, character, and personality traits. Both quantitative and qualitative data are included. In Volume 3 (Burks et al., 1930) there is one chapter, entitled "Three Gifted Girls," that describes three individual cases: Millie, a phenomenally early reader; Dora, a typical gifted child; and Verda, a girl with a superior scholastic record. In the remaining chapters of Volume 3 the emphasis is on concepts. These chapters discuss such topics as school acceleration and social adjustment, deterioration of IQ or achievement, the conquest of obstacles, and so on. Each of the cross-case chapters includes a brief theoretical introduction and then describes several specific children who illustrate the chapter concepts.

In writing a case report (step 6) it is important to select an organizing structure. Yin (1989) has suggested six illustrative structures:

1. Linear-analytic structures
2. Comparative structures
3. Chronological structures
4. Theory-building structures
5. "Suspense" structures
6. Unsequenced structures

The structure of the reporting in Terman's work was theory building and comparative. In contrast, the Alec study used a linear-analytic structure. The linear-analytic structure is the same format as the standard research report. Reports using this structure contain separate sections on the nature of the research problem, a review of relevant literature, the methods and procedures, the results, and a discussion of conclusions and implications.

Nested within the overarching structure of the Alec study were two additional levels of structure. The entire results section was written using a theory-building structure keyed to the initial research questions. Then the results section was divided into two subsections based on those research questions. A chronological structure was used to describe the historical development of Alec's verbal giftedness, and a theory-building structure was selected to report the findings on Alec's current learning characteristics.

The final step (step 7) in case study research is the evaluation of the study. Yin (1989) lists five characteristics of an exemplary case study:

1. The case study must be significant.
2. The case study must be complete.
3. The case study must consider alternative perspectives.
4. The case study must display sufficient evidence.
5. The case study must be composed in an engaging manner.

Issues of reliability and validity are also a critical part of the evaluation stage of case study research, especially when attempting to defend the results to the traditionally oriented scientific community—as when applying for research grants. These issues are discussed in the next section.

ISSUES OF RELIABILITY AND VALIDITY

All research designs are judged by testing their validity and reliability. Case study research is no exception. However, the tactics for ensuring reliability and validity in case study research are different than they are in research based on sampling logic. Reliability and validity in case study research are viewed and handled in much the same way as they are handled in qualitative research.

Construct Validity

The most important kind of validity in case study research is construct validity. Construct validity has two meanings in educational research. In measurement theory construct validity is the degree to which a test measures the hypothetical construct about the nature of human behavior that it purports to measure (Borg & Gall, 1989). When research has this kind of construct validity, the investigator has been able to establish correct operational measures for the constructs being studied (Kidder, 1981).

The second meaning of construct validity is less technical. It refers to the extent to which abstract terms, concepts, and meanings are shared across times, settings, and populations (Cook & Campbell, 1979; Goetz & LeCompte, 1984). This type of construct validity is crucial for case study research that is conducted to generate and develop theory. Construct validity can be enhanced in case study research by using multiple sources of evidence, establishing a chain of evidence, and having key informants review drafts of the case study report (Yin, 1989). Construct validity has been difficult to determine in some published case studies of gifted children because the investigators neglected to detail their methods and sources. When reporting case study research, it is important to make the methods used to collect data as explicit as possible in order to enable the reader to more accurately assess construct validity.

Internal Validity

In experimental research, internal validity refers to the extent to which extraneous variables have been controlled by the researcher. When these variables are not controlled, it is difficult to know whether the changes observed in the experimental group are due to the experimental treatment or to some extraneous variable (Borg & Gall, 1989; Campbell & Stanley, 1963; Cook & Campbell, 1979).

Internal validity is a crucial concern in experimental research where researchers are attempting to develop causal explanations (Asher, 1976; Cook & Campbell, 1979; Kerlinger, 1986). Internal validity is much less of a concern in descriptive and exploratory studies, which are not concerned with making causal statements (Yin, 1989). Internal validity is important in such studies to the extent that inferences are made from events that have not been directly observed. According to Yin (1989), specific tactics for achieving confidence in the inferences made in case study research have not yet been clearly delineated by social scientists.

However, Yin (1989) tentatively identifies three possible tactics based on analytic logic that can enhance internal validity in case study research. These tactics are pattern matching, explanation building, and time-series analysis. While a full explanation of these tactics is beyond the scope of this chapter, details may be found in Yin (1989). The development of tactics for the enhancement of the internal validity of case study research is an area that needs further work. New tactics are waiting to be discovered or invented. Existing tactics need clearer definition and wider application.

External Validity

This refers to the characteristics of a research study that allow generalization to similar populations, settings, and treatments (Asher, 1976). The external validity problem has been considered a major barrier in doing case studies because critics of case study research have incorrectly imposed sampling logic on such research (Yin, 1989). When analytic logic is employed instead, external validity is less of a problem. The goal of analytic logic is to enable you to generalize results to theory. The major tactic for such generalization is the replication logic of multiple-case studies, discussed in the section on case study research design above. This logic is called constant comparison by some authors (Glaser & Strauss, 1967; Goetz & LeCompte, 1984).

A needed future direction in case study research is a technique for using analytic logic to synthesize the results of a number of published, single-case studies in much the same way that meta-analysis now enables researchers to synthesize the results of a number of experimental studies. Such a technique would greatly enhance the external validity of case study research and amplify the power of such research to develop theory.

Reliability

Finally, case study researchers must come to grips with the issue of the reliability of their results. Reliability refers to agreement among observers and the replicability of results (Asher, 1976). Replication is a problem in case studies of unique or naturally occurring events (Goetz & LeCompte, 1984). External reliability can be enhanced in case study research by such techniques as careful documentation of data collection and analysis methods, detailed reporting of research methods, and clear identification of the researcher role and status (Goetz & LeCompte, 1984). Development of a case study data base and the use of case study protocols are additional tactics for enhancing the external reliability of case study research (Yin, 1989). Tactics for improving the internal reliability of case study research include use of multiple researchers, inclusion of low-inference descriptors such as direct quotations, peer examination of drafts of the case report, and reliance on mechanically recorded data (Goetz & LeCompte, 1984).

A VISION FOR THE FUTURE

Case study methods have much to offer the field of gifted education. There are many questions in the field that can be answered most effectively by case study methods and some questions that can be answered only by such methods. Case study researchers in gifted education have exciting frontiers open before them. They can be in the forefront of the movement to develop improved case study methods. They can use case study methods to build the knowledge base of the field, to develop grounded theory, and to bridge research, theory, and practice.

Case study research is a particularly powerful methodology for developing rich descriptions of gifted individuals, gifted family systems, and various aspects of educational interventions on behalf of gifted students. Case study research allows exploration of both horizontal and vertical complexity. It allows researchers to examine phenomena in context and across time. The descriptive virtues of case study research have been powerfully exploited in the past by researchers in gifted education. Similar research should continue to be done in the future, with particular attention to such growing edges of the field as special populations, gifted family systems, patterns of interaction influencing the gifted, the change process in school settings, and articulated programming efforts. A growing literature of such rich descriptions will build the knowledge base of the field and provide a sound foundation of research with which to examine prediction and causation.

In addition, case study methods are a powerful tool for the discovery of grounded theory. The field of gifted education has been characterized by an overreliance on untested, a priori, invented, or borrowed theory (Foster, 1986). If the field is to move forward, more researchers need to focus on discovering grounded theory about the nature and nurture of giftedness. Case studies are an ideal vehicle to propel the development of grounded theory into the twenty-first century.

Finally, case study methods hold great promise for helping to bridge research, theory, and practice within the field of gifted education. Case study research can empower teachers to be both better consumers of and more active participants in research. Case study research is accessible to teachers because it is informally written and describes concrete phenomena in context. Qualitative case study researchers and teachers share similar concerns. Both are "concerned with specifics of local meaning and local action; that is the stuff of life in daily classroom practice" (Erikson, 1986, p. 156).

In addition, teachers are in an ideal position to become case study researchers. They are in daily contact with individuals, groups, and events that are appropriate units of analysis for educational case studies. Teachers are immersed in the raw data of real children in real learning situations. Almost by definition, teachers are participant observers of the educational process. Informal qualitative research is part of every good teacher's day.

Erickson (1986) believes teachers need to move toward becoming formal researchers if the profession of teaching is to advance:

> Teachers in public schools have not been asked, as part of their job description, to reflect on their own practice, to deepen their conceptions of it, and to communicate their insights to others. . . . If classroom teaching is to come of age as a profession—if the role of teacher is not to continue to be institutionally infantilized—then teachers need to take the adult responsibility of investigating their own practice systematically and critically, by methods that are appropriate to their practice. (p. 157)

Case study research is one such method. Case study methods offer promise for building a synergistic unity between research, theory, and practice in education.

The gifted education movement has long been in the forefront of innovation in American education. Case study researchers in the field of gifted education have vast territories to explore. They can refine and develop case study methods. They can answer questions that are important to the field. They can discover grounded theory about the nature and nurture of gifted youth. And they can help bridge the gap between research, theory, and practice in gifted education.

REFERENCES

Asher, J. W. (1976). *Educational research and evaluation methods.* Boston: Little, Brown.

Bloom, B. S. (Ed.). (1985). *Developing talent in young people.* New York: Ballantine.

Bogdan, R. C., & Biklen, S. K. (1982). *Qualitative research for education: An introduction to theory and education.* Boston: Allyn & Bacon.

Borg, W. R., & Gall, M. D. (1989). *Educational research: An introduction* (5th ed.). New York: Longman.

Buchanan, N. K. (1987). Evaluating the identification process of a program for the gifted: A case study. *Roeper Review, 9*(4), 231–235.

Burks, B. S., Jensen, D. W., & Terman, L. M. (1930). *Genetic studies of genius: Vol. 3. The promise of youth.* Stanford, CA: Stanford University Press.

Campbell, D. T. (1979). "Degrees of freedom" and the case study. In T. D. Cook

& C. S. Reichardt (Eds.), *Qualitative and quantitative methods in evaluation research* (pp. 49–67). Beverly Hills, CA: Sage.

Campbell, D. T., & Stanley, J. C. (1963). Experimental and quasi-experimental designs for research on teaching. In N. L. Gage (Ed.), *Handbook of research on teaching* (pp. 171–246). Chicago: Rand McNally.

Cook, T. D., & Campbell, D. T. (1979). *Quasi-experimentation: Design and analysis issues for field settings.* Boston: Houghton Mifflin.

Cook, T. D., & Reichardt, C. S. (1979). *Qualitative and quantitative methods in evaluation research.* Beverly Hills, CA: Sage.

Cox, C. M. (1926). *Genetic studies of genius: Vol. 2. The early mental traits of three hundred geniuses.* Stanford, CA: Stanford University Press.

Erikson, F. (1986). Qualitative methods in research on teaching. In M. Wittrock (Ed.), *Handbook of research on teaching* (Vol. 3) (pp. 119–161). New York: Macmillan.

Feldman, D. H., & Goldsmith, L. T. (1986). *Nature's gambit: Child prodigies and the development of human potential.* New York: Basic Books.

Flack, J. D. (1983). *Profiles of gifted of giftedness: An investigation of development, interests, and attitudes of 10 highly gifted Indiana adolescents.* Unpublished doctoral dissertation, Purdue University, West Lafayette, IN.

Flower, L., & Hayes, J. R. (1980). The dynamics of composing: Making plans and juggling constraints. In L. W. Gregg & E. R. Steinberg (Eds.), *Cognitive processes in writing* (pp. 31–50). Hillsdale, NJ: Erlbaum.

Foster, W. (1986). The application of single subject research methods to the study of exceptional ability and extraordinary achievement. *Gifted Child Quarterly, 30,* 33–37.

Glaser, B. G., & Strauss, A. L. (1967). *The discovery of grounded theory: Strategies for qualitative research.* New York: Aldine.

Goertzel, V., & Goertzel, M. G. (1962). *Cradles of eminence.* Boston: Little, Brown.

Goetz, J. P., & LeCompte, M. D. (1984). *Ethnography and qualitative design in educational research.* San Diego, CA: Academic Press.

Gross, M. (1986). Radical acceleration in Australia: Terence Tao. *Gifted Child Today, 9*(4), 2–11.

Hollingworth, L. S. (1942). *Children over 180 IQ.* Yonkers-on-Hudson, NY: World Book.

Kerlinger, F. N. (1986). *Foundations of behavioral research* (3rd ed.). New York: Holt, Rinehart & Winston.

Kidder, L. (1981). *Research methods in social relations* (4th ed.). New York: Holt, Rinehart & Winston.

Lauer, J. M., & Asher, J. W. (1988). *Composition research: Empirical designs.* New York: Oxford University Press.

Lincoln, Y. S., & Guba, E. G. (1985). *Naturalistic inquiry.* Beverly Hills, CA: Sage.

Merriam, S. B. (1988). *Case study research in education: A qualitative approach.* San Francisco: Jossey-Bass.

Montour, K. (1977). William James Sidis: The broken twig. *American Psychologist, 32,* 265–279.

Moon, S. M. (1991). *Multiple exceptionalities: A case study.* Unpublished manuscript.

Moon, S. M., Dillon, D. R., & Sprenkle, D. H. (1990). Family therapy and qualitative research. *Journal of Marital and Family Therapy, 16,* 357–373.

Moon, S. M., Feldhusen, J. F., & Kelly, K. W. (1991). Identification procedures: Bridging theory and practice. *Gifted Child Today, 14*(1), 30–36.

Moon, S. M., & Piery, F. P. (1991). *Recent developments in task analysis: Applications to the field of gifted studies.* Manuscript submitted for publication.

Newell, A., & Simon, H. A. (1972). *Human problem solving.* Englewood Cliffs, NJ: Prentice-Hall.

Patton, M. Q. (1980). *Qualitative evaluation methods.* Beverly Hills, CA: Sage.

Safran, J. D., Greenberg, L. S., & Rice, L. N. (1988). Integrating psychotherapy research and practice: Modeling the change process. *Psychotherapy, 25*(1), 1–17.

Stake, R. E. (1978). The case-study method in social inquiry. *Educational Researcher, 7,* 5–8.

Stake, R. E. (Speaker). (1979). *Seeking sweet water: Case study methods in educational research* (Tape). Urbana, IL: Center for Instructional Research and Curriculum Evaluation. American Educational Research Association.

Tannenbaum, A. J., & Baldwin, L. J. (1983). Giftedness and learning disability: A paradoxical combination. In L. H. Fox, L. Brody, & D. Tobin (Eds.), *Learning-disabled/gifted children* (pp. 11–36). Baltimore: University Park Press.

Terman, L. M. (1925). *Genetic studies of genius: Vol. 1. Mental and physical traits of a thousand gifted children.* Stanford, CA: Stanford University Press.

Terman, L. M., & Oden, M. H. (1947). *Genetic studies of genius: Vol. 4. The gifted child grows up.* Stanford, CA: Stanford University Press.

Terman, L. M., & Oden, M. H. (1959). *Genetic studies of genius: Vol. 5. The gifted group at mid-life.* Stanford, CA: Stanford University Press.

VanTassel-Baska, J. (1988a). Developing scope and sequence in curriculum: A comprehensive approach. *Gifted Child Today, 11*(3), 29–34.

VanTassel-Baska, J. (1988b). Developing scope and sequence in curriculum: A comprehensive approach. *Gifted Child Today, 11*(4), 58–61.

VanTassel-Baska, J. (1988c). Developing scope and sequence in curriculum: A comprehensive approach. *Gifted Child Today, 11*(5), 42–45.

VanTassel-Baska, J., & Campbell, M. (1988a). Developing scope and sequence in curriculum: A comprehensive approach. *Gifted Child Today, 11*(2), 2–7.

VanTassel-Baska, J., & Campbell, M. (1988b). Developing scope and sequence in curriculum: A comprehensive approach. *Gifted Child Today, 11*(6), 56–61.

Whitmore, J. R., & Maker, C. J. (1985). *Intellectual giftedness in disabled persons.* Rockville, MD: Aspen.

Witty, P., & Coomer, A. (1955). A case study of twin gifted boys. *Exceptional Children, 22,* 104–108.

Yin, R. K. (1989). *Case study research: Design and methods.* Newberry Park, CA: Sage.

CHAPTER 9

USING PREDICTION METHODS: A BETTER MAGIC MIRROR

Douglas L. Murphy and Reva C. Friedman (Jenkins)

> *The Queen asked, "Mirror, Mirror on the wall/Who is the fairest one of all?"*
> *And the Mirror replied: "Skin like snow, hair dark as night/Lips ruby red, her name—Snow White!"*

Unlike the situation facing the Queen, supporting theory and validated, empirical approaches have reduced the *mystical* aspect of selecting students with high potential for gifted education programs. However, central to the gifted education movement are the principles of identifying students who demonstrate exceptional achievement or extraordinarily high potentials and designing qualitatively differentiated educational programs for them (Marland, 1972). Estimating potential always involves using present achievement (or other characteristics) of students to make predictions about how they will probably perform in the future. This activity, whether explicit or implicit, is at the heart of all identification systems.

Anywhere School District 2001 is revising the identification system for its middle school gifted education program. The system currently employed uses a matrix method to weight intelligence and achievement test and checklist scores and combines them into a total *gifted* score. However, program teachers believe that this system is missing students who have the most potential to become creative, higher-level thinkers and motivated producers of ideas. They want to know how to weight identification information more accurately.

Such situations as the one above pose special challenges to gifted child educators and researchers. How do we know that appropriate students are identified for gifted education services? What are the impacts of particular programming approaches? How do we know if we have used the right test scores or combinations of scores in the identification process? Should we use nontest information? How might we use nontest information in a defensible way? All these questions have to do with making predictions about variables and subsequent outcomes.

In this chapter, we will introduce methods for studying the relationships among sets of variables and particular outcomes, ranging from higher-level thinking to self-concept. We will concentrate on correlational and multiple regression analyses as the model for conducting research involving prediction paradigms.

THE PREDICTION PERSPECTIVE

Similar to other quantitative research methods, prediction paradigms are employed to study large samples of individuals and then to generalize findings to the population they represent. Prediction assumes that the researcher is testing hypotheses about the strength and direction of the relationship between several variables (for example, intelligence, creativity, motivation, and achievement) and some outcome (higher-level thinking, self-efficacy, or the likelihood of performing independent work). Thus prediction is a deductive method: we understand the dynamics of many cases, then apply findings to specific instances.

In the situation we described at the beginning of the chapter, school district personnel could analyze identification profiles of students participating in the program relative to their performance on some important program outcome. If they find significant relationships between particular pieces of identification information and certain outcomes, they could use the resulting regression equations to predict how a student being screened for the program would perform on the same outcomes.

Flexibility is a key aspect of the prediction perspective. This quality is manifested in two ways. For instance, researchers are not limited to using test scores; any information that can be quantified is appropriate for inclusion. Imagine that the educators in the Anywhere School District want to include a broader range of data in their identification system than relying on test scores. Among the entry information they could collect are samples of students' work—essays, artwork, tapes of dramatic readings, or science projects. They would need to develop a checklist of key indicators of gifted performance, educate the professionals evaluating the student products, and make periodic checks on the consistency of the ratings made by the evaluators. Although this activity might be time consuming at the outset, it can make an identification system more consonant with a key principle espoused by the field, namely, that in identifying gifted students we should incorporate a mix of objective and subjective data. Using these pieces of information that are more about behaviors than abilities is consonant with the prediction perspective and demonstrates the method's flexibility.

Prediction is flexible also in its applicability to controlled and field settings. Similar to other quantitative methods, prediction is useful in experimental situations. However, the bulk of studies using prediction methods employ the technique in real-life settings. For instance, in a recent review of prediction studies Baird (1985) attempted to answer the question: Do grades and tests predict adult accomplishment? Baird conducted a comprehensive review and analysis of research literature in fields ranging from medicine to art. All of the studies considered in the analysis were conducted in field settings rather than in laboratories, and all used prediction methods to study the relationships between measures of academic ability, achievement, and personality variables and a host of academically and professionally relevant outcomes. For example, in an analysis of studies exploring the predictive power of the ACT, Baird concluded that there were very small relationships between academic ability and accomplishment in the high school or college years.

Prediction is time-sensitive. Unlike many quantitative methods, prediction is not limited to the present. Using prediction methods, we can make the assumption that the outcomes being studied will be valuable at some time in the future. In fact, we use information available now to predict the likelihood that a certain behavior will occur some time in the future. This quality of prediction makes the method especially relevant to studying giftedness: a key rationale for special provisions for gifted students is that these are individuals who, because of their extraordinary potential, require services above and beyond the general school program to meet their needs. We provide additional services to gifted/talented youngsters so that they will be more likely to manifest their talents in the future. In addition, as you will see in the later sections on implementing prediction methods, time can be built into a prediction equation and studied much the same way as we might study the relationship between achievement test scores and a valued program outcome such as higher-level reasoning.

KEY TERMS

To aid your understanding of the vocabulary we will use in the balance of the chapter, we will present, define, and illustrate a few important terms related to prediction and correlational methods used to analyze prediction information. Additional terms are introduced later, in the context of explaining particular aspects of the prediction paradigm.

Correlation

The most common method for analyzing prediction information is correlation. "In statistical analysis . . . correlation refers exclusively to a quantifiable relationship between two variables" (Popham & Sirotnik, 1967). Another way to conceptualize correlation is as the shared variance between two pieces of information.

For instance, knowing that the Pearson correlation coefficient between fifth-grade students' group intelligence and achievement test scores is +.80 tells us that 64% of the factors that make up our measure of intelligence are shared by achievement. In real-world terms, 64% of the differences among students on their group intelligence scores is predictable on the basis of differences on their achievement test scores. Keep in mind that the strength, not the direction, of the relationship is most important. The direction of the relationship merely indicates if the scores increase and decrease together (positive relationship) or if, as one increases, the other decreases (negative relationship).

Imagine for a moment that you are the director of the Anywhere School District's gifted education program. You decide that the quality of students' creative products in the gifted program is a good measure of the effectiveness of the identification program. In other words, you believe that students who are selected for the program will be more likely to produce high-quality, creative products than students who are not selected. Suppose further that you discover that the most readily obtainable information on students is their yearly achievement test scores. Knowing also that there is a relationship between achievement and later accomplishments, you might develop a prediction equation for students currently enrolled in the middle school program for later use with entering sixth graders. You calculate the correlation between the averaged ratings of each student's creative products and the comprehensive achievement test scores from that year. You find that the Pearson correlation coefficient between these two variables is +.60. (In standard regression equation form, the .60 is known as the *regression coefficient* and is denoted by the letter b. The regression coefficient is equivalent to the correlation coefficient when raw scores have been transformed to standard scores. Otherwise, the following can be used to calculate b: $b = r(S_Y/S_X)$, where S_Y and S_X refer to the standard deviations of the criterion and predictor variables.) The equation would look something like this:

$$Y' = .10 + .60X1$$

In this equation the symbol Y' (Y *prime*) stands for the predicted ratings of a student's creative products in the first year of the middle school gifted program (Y' is also referred to as the criterion variable). X, referred to as the independent or predictor variable, represents the student's comprehensive achievement test scores, and .10 is the constant term of the equation. Substituting a student's achievement test score into the equation in place of the X would enable you to estimate the quality of the student's creative products. For example, if a student's comprehensive achievement test score (for example, a t-score) is 85, you could enter it into the equation as follows (.10 + .60 $\times$ 85) for an estimated rating of 51.1 on a 55-point rating scale for creative products.

Studying patterns of relationships between pairs of variables can also be a preliminary step to conducting more complex correlation procedures, described below. Consider the situation of Anywhere School District. In the course of revamping their identification system, they could choose to add more identification information to their system. Imagine that all students already take yearly achievement tests and that students referred to the gifted education program also complete an individually administered intelligence test and a test of creative thinking. As part of determining the value of information currently being collected, school officials could study the correlations among all subtests on the achievement test, the full-scale score on the intelligence test, and the scale scores on the test of creative thinking through examining a matrix of correlation coefficients. Pearson correlation coefficients between pairs of variables are often called zero-order correlations. Low to moderate zero-order correlations among measures of identification information would indicate that the test scores being gathered are relatively unique pieces of data about students' abilities. School district personnel could therefore justify using all the information, as in the context described below.

Multiple Correlation

The term "multiple correlation" refers to an analysis involving two or more predictor variables and one criterion. Relationships are displayed in a multiple regression equation, which follows the same form as a simple prediction equation, but with additional predictors, each represented by a different X symbol. Logically, if a single piece of information cannot allow us to predict future performance with 100% accuracy, additional pieces of information can permit us to reduce errors and make our predictions more accurate.

We were interested in applying scores on intelligence and achievement tests, used in the process of identifying gifted students, to predict how well they would perform on tests of higher-level thinking given a year after the achievement tests were administered (Murphy, 1989). We calculated a regression equation using the following predictors: performance and verbal IQ scores, section scores on the achievement test battery, gender (coded 0 for girls and 1 for boys), and time enrolled in the gifted program. When the IQ scores were used alone in the equation, results were not impressive. However, when the other variables were entered, prediction was somewhat improved. One of the (statistically significant) regression equations produced in our analyses was for the Synthesis section of the Developing Cognitive Abilities Test (DCAT), given to fourth-grade gifted students:

> Predicted DCAT Synthesis Score = 38.4 + .33(Verbal IQ) + .37(Performance IQ) + 4.98(Vocabulary Achievement) + 11.13(Work/Study Skills) + 6.89(Math Achievement) − .97(Language Achievement) − .33(Reading Achievement) − .17(Time in the Gifted Program) − 4.09(Gender).

By multiplying each score included in the equation by its regression coefficient, we were able to compute for each student a predicted score on the DCAT Synthesis subtest.

APPLYING PREDICTION METHODS

Predicting some future performance for gifted students is not an end in itself. Prediction information has several valuable applications in research, practice, and evaluation. In this portion of the chapter we differentiate prediction from difference-oriented designs, discuss key applications, and present examples of prediction in action.

An Alternative to the ANOVA Design in Research

Research designs based on analysis of variance (see Chapters 3 and 4, this volume) were developed primarily as a means to control for the effects of limited numbers of factors (independent variables) and their interactions in experimental research. Furthermore, such designs assume that the independent variables can be ordered, or at least categorized, into levels whose differences are meaningful in some way. Analysis of variance (ANOVA) models can be used for other purposes, even in prediction research. However, their use limits the kinds of studies that we can conduct and the conclusions we can draw from those studies.

Consider this example. You want to study self-concept among identified gifted boys and girls in an affective development program. You hypothesize that the program will have different effects, depending on their gender and how long they had participated in a gifted education program.

First you collect self-concept data on all students and analyze it for initial differences. Finding no significant overall differences, you set aside those data, and then divide boys and girls into two program membership groups—those who have participated for five years or more, and those who have participated for four years or less. The result is a repeated measures 2 × 2 ANOVA design (gender by program participation) to investigate their effects on self-concept.

Contrary to what you anticipated, there is no main effect for length of program participation or for gender, and no interaction effects between the independent variables. Your final report of the study concludes that the program had no differential effects on self-concept of gifted boys and girls who had participated in the program for different amounts of time. Therefore you recommend dropping the affective development program from the curriculum.

Based on the results of the difference-oriented study, the conclusion was probably correct. On the other hand, had you used a correlational model such as multiple regression, the final report might have been different. First, a correlational model would have allowed you to use all the information about program membership in the analysis. The ANOVA model, which forced categorization of this information, resulted in a loss of information such that students who had participated for four years were considered to be equivalent to those who had participated for one year, but different from those who had participated for five years.

Next, you could have included other variables that you believed to be related to self-concept (e.g., self-efficacy, attributions for success and failure, and perfectionism). The difference paradigm would not have allowed including as large a number of independent variables without drastically increasing the number of subjects.

Finally, even if the predicted effects had been found, it would have been difficult to use those results when making recommendations about the program. For instance, if boys in the group that had participated for less than five years had shown the greatest mean difference in posttest scores, should you recommend excluding girls from the affective development program? What about boys who had participated in the program for four and a half years? Correlational models do not offer solutions to all the problems surrounding prediction. However, the approach can assist you in making some accurate and useful recommendations.

Suppose, instead, that you decide to examine the impact of the affective development program through employing prediction methods. As in the previous study, pretest and posttest scores on a self-concept measure are used, but this time the analysis compares the relative effects of several variables of interest hypothesized to be related to differences in self-concept. The predictor variables are:

1. Pretest self-concept scores (Pretest)
2. Grade level in school (Grade)
3. Gender (Sex)
4. Number of years of participation in a gifted education program (Years)
5. Interactions among the above variables—Grade × Sex, Grade × Years, Sex × Years, and Grade × Sex × Years

Thus the posttest self-concept score (criterion variable) is predicted from the pretest score in combination with the main and interaction effects for Sex, Grade, and Years. This model allows you to identify the relative impact of single variables and sets of variables on the criterion.

In our hypothetical results, the pretest score accounts for a large proportion of the variance in posttest scores. However, signficant increments in the explained variance are added by the interaction of the other variables. For example, the Sex × Years interaction is a significant predictor of posttest self-concept $[F(1,199) = 10.62, p < .05]$. The regression equation for the posttest self-concept score is:

Posttest Self-Concept $= 12.20 + .67$(Pretest) $+ 10.68$(Sex) $+ 1.18$(Grade) $+ .59$(Years) $+ .08$(Grade × Years) $- 1.10$(Grade × Sex) $- 2.20$(Years × Sex) $+ .08$(Grade × Years).

Further examination of the Years × Sex interaction reveals that both sexes evidence an initial drop in self-concept in the first two years following placement. Girls' self-concept then rises significantly, drops in the fourth year, then rises again. In contrast, boys' scores remain relatively stable after an initial, slight drop, then plunge an average of 7 points in the fourth year before rising again. You conclude that boys might have had an inflated self-concept and that over time and exposure to the affective development curriculum, they became more realistic in their self-perceptions. You also note the reversal in the downward trend in girls' self-concepts. This leads you to suggest that the program be continued for incoming students and that teachers pay special attention to girls' self-perceptions in the first few months following program participation (Jenkins-Friedman & Murphy, 1987).

Thus, in contrast to the difference-oriented study described earlier, the prediction paradigm offers three advantages. It avoids incorrectly concluding that a treatment makes no difference (a Type II error), yields more finely detailed results, and allows for practical suggestions to improve the gifted program.

USING PREDICTION IN APPLIED SETTINGS

The section above was a discussion of prediction as an alternative to a commonly used research model. To some of you, this might appear to be the stuff of which ivory towers are made. The next three sections pertain to practical uses of prediction methods, many of which can be integrated into existing gifted programs.

Using Prediction for Selection and Placement

As noted at the beginning of the chapter, identifying, selecting, and placing students in gifted programs imply that we can predict, with some degree of certainty, who will excel in some domain. In our opinion, it is not adequate to say that we will select for a gifted program those students who are high achievers and have high measured intelligence. As in any other education plan, we must be able to state what outcomes we wish for our pupils. If measured achievement and intelligence are related to (if they predict) the desired outcomes, we can justify our selection process. However, it is possible that we could find four other results.

First, we might find that our prediction can be improved by including other information. We might decide to include such personality traits as task commitment and sentiment toward school or measures of previous performance to improve the prediction model. If we can improve prediction, our identification system will be more accurate and defensible.

Second, the prediction model including all the information used for identification and placement might have a significant relationship with our outcomes. But it is possible that the accuracy of our prediction might not be compromised if we were to eliminate prediction information that is redundant, or highly related to other predictors. Paring down the prediction model, and thus the identification system, to the essential predictors could result in great savings in testing, data collection, and data analysis.

Third, we might find that the predictors we are using in our identification system have weak or nonexistent relationships with the criteria we select as student outcomes. If so, we might consider developing an informal minitheory about factors that might have a relationship with the criterion. At this point, the process would resemble the theory-testing and exploratory methods mentioned below, but on a smaller scale.

A fourth result might show no predictive relationship between identification information and criteria. We might decide that the criteria were inappropriate for the students we selected. This decision would lead to a reevaluation of our program philosophy and goals and their relevance to our students.

Teachers with whom we worked recently were in the same quandary as teachers in the Anywhere School District 2001. They were concerned that their identification system was missing students who might benefit from their gifted program and was inaccurately identifying students who did not have extraordinary potential for the types of outcomes emphasized in their program. After several discussions about program goals and outcomes, they identified higher-level thinking as the program's key cognitive goal. They agreed to explore the accuracy of their matrix-based identification system for predicting that outcome. We suggested that an empirically tested identification system based on the multiple regression method might be a more relevant identification system than their current procedures.

Program teachers discussed hoped-for program outcomes with us, and we then selected several possible measures. For the purposes of this example, we will focus on one such measure: Analysis of Irrelevant and Relevant Information (a subtest of the Ross Test of Higher Cognitive Processes). In order to avoid the problems of a restricted range of scores, district administrators agreed to place in the program all students meeting the state's minimum criteria (measured intelligence of 130 or above OR any two standardized achievement subtest scores at or above the 90th percentile). Thus IQ scores ranged from 122 to 150, and achievement subtest scores ranged from the 75th to the 99th percentile. A 24-item teacher rating scale was extrapolated from the scales developed by Renzulli, Smith, White, Callahan, and Hartman (1976) to assure congruence between valued student characteristics and program goals (note: the scales were factor analyzed to reveal four highly reliable factors, included in the regression below). The resulting regression equation was as follows:

Predicted Ross Test Score = −17.7 + .07 (Composite Achievement) + .02 (IQ) + .09 (Teacher Rating of Self-Directedness) −.02

(Vocabulary Achievement) + .01 (Teacher Rating of Creativity) −.02 (Language Achievement) + .17 (Work Study Skills Achievement) + .09 (Math Achievement) + .02 (Reading Achievement) −.17 (Teacher Rating of Communication Ability) −.03 (Teacher Rating of Abstract Reasoning Ability).

We tested the accuracy of the prediction equation by randomly pulling cases and calculating students' predicted scores. In each instance, the predicted score was within hundredths of a point of the student's actual score.

Next, we calculated scores of students who were excluded from the program. We found the matrix-based identification system was inaccurate in several instances. Several students who had not qualified for the program scored above the cutpoint, reflecting a high potential for success in the program. In ordinary circumstances, these potentially successful students would have been denied special services. Applying the regression equation enabled teachers to make better predictions of future performance and, thus, to identify more accurately those students who had greater potential and those who did not (Jenkins-Friedman & Murphy, 1988).

Advantages of Using Prediction Methods for Selection and Placement. There are several advantages to using prediction methods as the basis of selection and placement systems. First, relative emphases on various pieces of information used in the selection system are based on experience. Regression equations provide the means for weighting scores so that the most accurate prediction can be made. In contrast, when commonly used matrix identification models are used, weights are assigned intuitively. Compounding this problem, the number of measures relating to a certain type of ability tips the matrix toward that ability. Thus, for example, achievement and intelligence test scores often receive greater emphasis than they should. As a result, the accuracy of prediction is weakened and the usefulness of the selection system is diminished.

Second, selection procedures can be tailor-made for different kinds of program outcomes. If certain sets of information are shown to predict specific outcomes, they can be used for screening, placing, and counseling students for gifted programs with different emphases. This advantage can enable teachers and school psychologists to consider talent pools other than those composed of highly intelligent high achievers.

Third, prediction methods can allow for diversity among students selected for programs. For example, if a hypothetical selection system uses task commitment and achievement as the principal information for identification, usual procedures would require that students exhibit relatively high levels of each. In reality, it is possible that two other types of students might excel. The first might be exceptionally committed to tasks but be underachievers. For these students, task commitment can compensate for deficits in achievement. The second type might be high-achieving students with deficits in task commitment. A prediction equation based on multiple regression would allow for the selection of all three types of students.

Finally, the use of prediction equations enables the cross-validation of identification and selection models. Cross-validation involves applying the regression equation derived from information from a previous year's students to a group of incoming students. This permits us to determine whether the selection system needs to be retained or modified. Most selection systems are static and are not amenable to cross-validation.

Disadvantages of Using Prediction Methods for Selection and Placement. On the other hand, prediction-based selection systems have several disadvantages. First, for most accurate use, they require collecting information for a larger sample of students (perhaps 15%-20%) than just those who meet selection criteria for placement in a program. This assures that there will be sufficient variance in the data. For example, if we wish to use achievement as a predictor of outcomes, we should develop the prediction equation for a sample consisting of students in the top 10%, or even top 20%, of their norm group. While this requirement might not be problematic for readily obtainable information, it does present difficulties when we consider collecting other information—for example, measured intelligence—for larger numbers of students.

Second, prediction-based selection procedures necessitate cross-validation. That is, in addition to demonstrating that an identification system was successful in predicting the performance of one group of gifted students, we should test the system on other samples of students. Alternative identification systems should also be tested. Such processes are ongoing and require some skills in statistical analysis. We are, however, unaware of cases where cross-validation or investigation of alternative identification systems have occurred. Consequently, little is known about the accuracy of other selection systems for identifying students with high potential for attaining desired program outcomes.

Third, in general, these procedures are difficult to *export* for use with gifted students in other school districts. Regression equations developed using prediction methods are applicable to designated outcomes, particular sets of predictors, and specific populations of gifted students. In effect, each program needs to start from scratch with its own system.

Finally, to provide the most accurate estimates of potential for achieving program outcomes, fairly large numbers of students (about 30 students per predictor) are required. This is a disadvantage only for smaller school districts or programs.

Using Prediction Methods for Program Evaluation

A key issue in justifying programs for gifted and talented students is that they make a difference in the lives of these young people. This assertion raises the questions: How do you know if what you are doing makes a difference? What specific types of differences do programs for gifted students make?

Problems of Difference-Oriented Methods in Evaluation. Questions such as those mentioned above lead logically to evaluating programs. Here again, prediction can be a useful method for assessing the impact of gifted education programs. Difference-oriented models emphasize such questions as: Did the gifted education program make a change in student performance on designated student outcomes? Prediction-based methods, however, allow us to ask: What combinations of factors contribute to differences in student performance on particular, valued program outcomes? We believe this is an important distinction.

In addition to the problems of using difference-oriented methods outlined in an earlier section, there is general agreement that gifted education programs yield outcomes that can be subtle and difficult to measure in the limited context of school environments—such programs seek to produce lasting effects on the lives of youngsters with exceptional potential. Earlier we discussed the evaluation of an affective development program that incorrectly concluded that the gifted education program made no difference when, in fact, it did. This unfortunately leads to the common scenario of avoiding questions about student performance on any outcomes and instead focusing on measures of consumer satisfaction (for example, prime interest groups' feelings about the program).

Finally, difference models often use change scores in studying the effect of various interventions, but some research indicates change scores might not be appropriate (Keppel, 1973). In situations where scores on the criterion instrument are likely to be very stable (that is, change very little) the range of possible variance is even more restricted, thus decreasing the likelihood of finding significant results. For instance, knowing that students are selected for gifted education programs because they are outstanding higher-level thinkers would mean they would be less likely to show dramatic gains on a test of higher-level thinking. However, this finding does not mean that the program has failed to enhance students' ability to think on higher levels.

Qualitative Methods in Evaluation. More recently, program evaluators have begun to use qualitative methods to assess the impact of gifted education programs. We believe that this is a promising avenue; however, we urge the reader to consider a comprehensive program evaluation consisting of a blend of qualitative and quantitative methods. By examining the relationships among key student qualities and subsequently their relationships to valued program outcomes, we operate from the perspective that gifted education programs do affect participants. Our task as program evaluators is to discover patterns of relationships, understand them, and apply this information to improving the gifted education program being evaluated.

Regression Discontinuity. Regression discontinuity is a prediction-oriented method that allows testing for the effects of program participation on particular outcomes without using a randomized control group or withholding services (Robinson, Bradley, & Stanley, 1990). The design "statistically controls for prior differences [among students] by using the identification variable, along with program participation (status) as independent variables in a multiple regression model" (Robinson et al., 1990). Robinson and Stanley (1989, p. 259) describe the design as the following linear equation:

$$Y = a + bX + cZ$$

in which Y would be the outcome variable, a is the constant, X is the identification variable, Z is coded to represent program membership, and b and c are regression coefficients. They assert that the method would be used to evaluate a program by testing for a significant separation between students identified and not identified for program participation.

In situations where it is not possible to identify a group of nonparticipants, one could consider students at the grade level of interest prior to program implementation a de facto control group. Alternately, one could use the method to study differential program impact between identifiable groups of students by age, number of years of program participation, gender, or other key variables.

For example, in a recent study, Robinson and colleagues (1990) used regression discontinuity to find answers to these program evaluation questions:

1. Are there differences between white and black students identified as gifted in entry-level mathematics skills and abilities?
2. Do black students benefit by participating in a special program for mathematically talented students?
3. Are there differences in gains made by students due to ethnicity and participation in the gifted education program?
4. Do the identification data used for identifying mathematically talented black students effectively predict later performance?

They discovered that there were no initial differences between black and white students in computational skills and that both groups of students appeared to benefit by participating in an enriched mathematics program. In addition, there was a trend toward higher gains for black students. Most surprisingly, the regression identification coefficient was lower for blacks than the evaluators felt comfortable with (.40), although overall there were no significant differences between the two groups, and the correlation between the identification variable and the program outcome measure was judged "substantial" (.76). They concluded that there was hope that the procedure was effective; however, they cautioned against using the identification procedure in the same way for black and white children, since the identification variables contributed less to predicting mathematics performance for black than for white students.

Using Prediction Methods for Instrument Development

There is much discussion within the field of gifted child education about the usefulness of various psychological and achievement tests, behavior checklists, and rating forms commonly used in assessing students and evaluating programs. Many of us regard such instruments with a mixture of love, hate, and suspicion. We recognize their limits as we use them with gifted learners. But we realize the limits of our own intuition and subjective judgment, so we understand the basic need to have solid measures so that we can make informed, accountable, and professional decisions about and for our students. There is a growing demand for good tests to measure academic achievement, creativity, higher-level thinking, and almost any other behavior we might like to investigate among gifted students.

Incorporating prediction studies into the process of developing new tests, checklists, and rating forms could result in more accurate, more useful measures related to specific program outcomes. There are two primary applications of prediction methods for developing instruments:

(1) to refine the theory used as the basis for instruments and (2) to gather evidence of criterion-related validity.

Refining Theory. We believe that tests, checklists, rating scales, and other instruments used for assessing students' performances should be based on theory or, at least, on a solid conceptual framework. As we develop more clearly delineated theories, we can use our new knowledge as the basis for new ways to measure important traits and behaviors of gifted students. (For a discussion of applications of prediction methods to theory development, see the section below on using prediction in research.

Gathering Evidence of Criterion-Related Validity. When we speak of validity, we are referring to the appropriateness of the interpretations we make of scores on tests or other kinds of measures we use with gifted students. Criterion-related validity pertains to whether we can interpret test scores as good indicators of some other valued behavior or trait. For example, intelligence tests were developed to be and are recognized as good predictors of academic achievement, a widely valued outcome for all students. That is, for the general school population scores on intelligence tests have a moderate to strong relationship with scores on achievement tests. We regard this relationship, inferred from the strength of correlation coefficients, to be evidence of criterion-related validity.

If we wish to use test results to predict some future outcome (criterion), we will be concerned about the predictive validity of our interpretation and we will collect scores on the test and keep them on file until we are able to collect scores on the criterion measure. At that time, we will examine the relationship (correlation) between the sets of scores. If the correlation coefficient is high, we can say that we can use the test to predict accurately how well students are likely to perform in the future. The correlation coefficient can be considered evidence that our interpretation has predictive validity.

In a study mentioned above (Murphy, 1989), we investigated the question of whether intelligence and achievement test scores could be used to predict higher-level thinking skills. The assumption is often made that intellectually gifted students are most capable of thinking at high levels. We used IQ scores and standardized achievement test scores from the previous year, along with gender, to create a (regression) equation to predict scores on two tests of higher-level thinking. The results of the study were hopeful, to some degree, and somewhat sobering. Using multiple regression techniques, we found that a combination of IQ scores, several achievement subtest scores (Math, Reading, Language,

Vocabulary, and Work Study Skills) were, at best, only moderately predictive of scores on tests of higher-level thinking. In most analyses, Math Achievement had the strongest predictive relationship with higher-level thinking, and often it alone accounted for most of the variance. Rarely were IQ scores even moderately predictive. We discovered that students' scores on the outcome tests could be predicted almost as well by using only their Math Achievement scores as by using IQ and all the other achievement test scores.

These results should be viewed with some caution because of the problems of the restricted range of scores and the ceiling effect so common in gifted education research and evaluation. However, they suggest some conclusions that should make us think carefully about the tests we use for identifying gifted learners and about the nature of tests we sometimes use for evaluating program outcomes. For example, it is doubtful that the same combination of scores from the math achievement and other tests could be used to predict creative productivity as well as a combination of scores from other, quite different tests. Yet all too often the very same identification procedure is used for all students in a program, despite very different goals across programs and students. Finally, the recurring predictive relationship of Math Achievement with higher-level thinking test scores suggests that both tests are measuring primarily deductive, rule-governed thinking skills, rather than the inductive and divergent thinking often emphasized in gifted programs.

In another study, similar in intent to ours, the authors studied the validity of identification information to predict actual program outcomes. Postlethwaite and Denton (1983) compared the usefulness of teacher ratings of student potential and general aptitude for predicting gifted program outcomes in English, French, physics, and math with that of earlier subject-area test scores. Zero-order correlations revealed that the earlier tests were considerably better than were teacher ratings and general aptitude scores at predicting which students would excel. Using this procedure enabled the authors to make decisions about the validity of their interpretations of results from commonly used rating scales and tests for identifying students with high potential in specific academic areas. On a practical level, they were able to devise a more accurate system for making predictions about their students' future achievement.

On the other hand, if we wish to interpret results from tests or other measures as indicators of how students might perform at the same time on a measure of another valued behavior or trait, we will require evidence of concurrent validity. Even though the measures are made at about the same time, the independent variable is termed the *predictor*. Aside from the lack of a time lapse between obtaining scores on the predictor and the criterion, the process of assessing the relationship between them is the same as when gathering evidence of predictive validity. A correlation coefficient is used to examine the relationship between predictor and criterion, and the coefficient is used as evidence of validity.

USING PREDICTION IN RESEARCH

Because gifted education in its present form is a relatively new and uncharted discipline, many questions remain unanswered. We need to know more, for example, about the nature of giftedness, effective approaches to encouraging and developing giftedness, and ways to measure giftedness and extraordinary achievement. Many of these questions can be answered by using a prediction paradigm. Two basic applications of prediction in research in gifted child education are in theory testing and exploratory research.

Theory Testing

A classic definition of a theory is "a set of formulations designed to explain and predict facts and events which can be observed" (Mason & Bramble, 1978). Others define a theory as a cluster of "interrelated hypotheses" (Rosenthal & Rosnow, 1984). Both definitions integrate the notion of prediction.

At a general level, common conceptualizations of giftedness can be considered theories. For example, if we define giftedness as the potential for extraordinary achievement in a specific domain, clusters of interrelated hypotheses readily come to mind. From this theory one might surmise that gifted children might show precocious signs of expert-like talent or productivity. In his book *Nature's Gambit*, D. H. Feldman (1986) describes prodigies in creative writing, music, chess, science, and foreign language. Through the use of in-depth case studies compiled over ten years, Feldman develops his theory of giftedness, complete with predictors (early signs of talent and personal and family characteristics) and criteria (adult-level performance and later-life achievements). From the work of Feldman and others (e.g., Baird, 1985; Bloom, 1985; R. Feldman, 1982; Goertzel & Goertzel, 1962; VanTassel-Baska & Olszewski-Kubilius, 1989), we could generate and test hypotheses to assess the fit of the theory with reality.

On the other hand, if we define giftedness as the ability to excel in problem solving, a very different cluster of hypotheses would be produced. In his triarchic theory of intelligence, Sternberg (1985) identifies several processes involved in solving problems and argues that gifted persons process problem information differently from nongifted or retarded individuals. It is conceivable that one could create tasks designed to measure individual differences in information processing and use the tasks (independent or predictor variables) to predict exceptional ability to solve problems in other situations (criterion).

Of course, other classes of theories can be proposed, each with its unique set of explanations and predictions. In each case, the use of a prediction paradigm would be a primary method for testing the theory and would require the translation of hypotheses into research tasks. We must decide first what the theory says about the nature of the criterion, the central element of the theory. Once the criterion is identified, we attempt to define it in such a way that it can be operationalized—so that it can be observed and measured. For example, in the "prodigy" theory, Feldman uses adult-like performance as the criterion for defining and assessing giftedness. Sternberg's criterion is performance in solving novel problems.

Next, we determine which predictors the theory might suggest or specify. As with the criteria, we must adequately define and operationalize predictors. Feldman's key predictor is precocity. For example, one child with exceptional musical talent showed a strong interest in music shortly before his third birthday. A foreign language prodigy first spoke at the age of three months. Sternberg's essential predictor is speed in processing information.

Finally, we analyze relationships between the predictors and criteria, and compare what we find with what the theory hypothesizes. To the extent that our findings support the hypotheses—that is, if there is a significant and meaningful relationship between predictors and criteria—we can say that the theory is a representation of the real world.

Exploratory Research

Unfortunately, no well-defined, comprehensive theories of giftedness have yet been developed, although some show promise of fulfilling this need (Feldman, 1986; Gardner, 1985; Horowitz & O'Brien, 1986; Sternberg, 1985). Before we can propose theories, we must be able to observe patterns of association in phenomena. These patterns stimulate speculation about relationships among events or behaviors. As questions begin to revolve around central issues or variables, hypotheses can emerge.

For instance, in the course of her work with gifted students Bransky (1989) became concerned about the prevalence of disabling perfectionism among high school age students. She noticed, though, that students who allowed themselves to be average in an important activity tended to be less disabled by their perfectionistic tendencies than those who insisted on excelling in everything. Bransky asked: Besides these lessened demands on themselves to be exceptional in all areas, what other behaviors and traits could be used to predict less disabling, more productive reactions to perfectionism among gifted students?

As she observed students and read about perfectionism, she began to notice patterns among students' behaviors and traits. She formed tentative hypotheses about several predictors and the criterion, perfectionism. Ultimately, the field of likely predictors was narrowed to attributions for success and failure on academic tasks, irrational beliefs, and self-concept. Bransky administered "tests" of the predictors and perfectionism to junior high gifted students and analyzed the relationships by use of multiple regression. She found that irrational beliefs about high self-expectations, effort attributions for successful outcomes, and feelings of shame or guilt significantly predicted academic perfectionism. The findings of this exploratory study contributed to our understanding of perfectionism theory, and it provided valuable information that can be incorporated into programs for gifted adolescents.

SUMMARY AND CONCLUSIONS

In this chapter, we introduced the prediction method: flexibility, deductiveness, and time sensitivity are its defining attributes. The bulk of the chapter concentrated on uses of prediction methods in applied settings: as an alternative to the ANOVA design, for selection and placement, for program evaluation, and for instrument development. Last, we discussed briefly two uses of prediction in research: theory testing and exploratory research.

We would like to emphasize that our advocacy of prediction methods for selecting students, evaluating programs, conducting research, constructing theories, and validating tests is a qualified stance. Research methods are merely tools of the researcher, evaluator, or program administrator.

For instance, in the book *Choosing Elites*, its author and former Harvard administrator Klitgaard (1985) makes the point that no predictor or outcome is entirely accurate or reliable. Therefore, he asserts, we must use several predictors and several outcome measures. Finally, he emphasizes, there is much to be gained, for the students, the institution, and society at large, by creating a diverse student body. By implication, one would not expect all students to even qualify on all predictors. We need to consider the best available theory, tests or other instruments, time to develop and check predictions, and characteristics of our target population affecting the use of quantitative techniques when using prediction or any other method.

Thus, in action, prediction should reflect a philosophical stance: we cannot afford to be driven by the numbers alone. We need to begin with the needs and characteristics of gifted students and then consider the best available theory; use the most appropriate tests or other instruments; and take time to develop and check predictions.

In the fairy tale world of the Queen, an instrument designed to heighten perception and judgment became corrupting. We, too, need to keep in mind that even the most powerful statistical tool must have a justifiable foundation on which to rest, or its usefulness will be limited. In closing, we would like to remind you that any quantitative method or combination of qualitative and quantitative research methods is destined to be imperfect; however, we can develop a research/evaluation perspective that is truly defensible—a vast improvement over attempts that resemble the Queen's Magic Mirror more than defensible practice.

REFERENCES

American Psychological Association. (1985). *Standards for educational and psychological testing*. Washington, DC: Author.

Baird, L. L. (1985). Do grades and tests predict adult accomplishment? *Research in Higher Education, 23*(1), 3–85.

Bloom, B. S. (Ed.). (1985). *Devloping talent in young people*. New York: Ballantine.

Braṅsky, P. S. (1989). *Perfectionism in intellectually gifted adolescents: The role of attribution, self-concept, and irrational beliefs*. Unpublished doctoral dissertation, University of Kansas, Lawrence.

Feldman, D. H. (1986). *Nature's gambit; Child prodigies and the development of human potential*. New York: Basic Books.

Feldman, R. D. (1982). *Whatever happened to the Quiz Kids?* Chicago: Chicago Review Press.

Gardner, H. (1985). *Frames of mind: The theory of multiple intelligences*. New York: Basic Books.

Goertzel, V., & Goertzel, M. G. (1962). *Cradles of eminence*. Boston: Little, Brown.

Horowitz, F. D., & O'Brien, M. (Eds.). (1986). *The gifted and talented: Developmental perspectives*. Washington, DC: American Psychological Association.

Jenkins-Friedman, R., & Murphy, D. L. (1987). *Advice from the caterpillar:*

Ameliorating diminished self-concept among newly placed gifted students. Paper presented at the 7th World Conference on Gifted and Talented Children, Salt Lake City, UT.

Jenkins-Friedman, R., & Murphy, D. L. (1988). *How appropriate a placement? Relationships between identification information and important outcomes in gifted programs.* Paper presented at the annual meeting of the National Association for Gifted Children, Orlando, FL.

Keppel, G. (1973). *Design and analysis: A researcher's handbook.* Englewood, NJ: Prentice-Hall.

Klitgaard, R. E. (1985). *Choosing elites.* New York: Basic Books.

Marland, S. (1972). *Education of the gifted and talented.* Report to the Subcommittee on Education, Committee on Labor and Public Welfare, U.S. Senate, Washington, DC: U.S. Government Printing Office.

Mason, E. J., & Bramble, W. J. (1978). *Understanding and conducting research: Applications in education and the behavioral sciences.* New York: McGraw-Hill.

Murphy, D. L. (1989). *Do measured intelligence and achievement predict higher-level thinking processes?: Assessing the criterion-related validity of two measures used to identify intellectually-gifted elementary students.* Unpublished doctoral dissertation, University of Kansas, Lawrence.

Popham, W. J., & Sirotnik, K. A. (1967). *Educational statistics: Use and interpretation* (2nd ed.). New York: Harper & Row.

Postlethwaite, K., & Denton, C. (1983). Identifying more able pupils in secondary schools. *Gifted Education International, 1*(2), 92–96.

Renzulli, J. S., Smith, L. H., White, A. J., Callahan, C. M., & Hartman, R. K. (1976). *Scales for rating the behavioral characteristics of superior students.* Wethersfield, CT: Creative Learning Press.

Robinson, A., Bradley, R. H., & Stanley, T. D. (1990). Opportunity to achieve: Identifying mathematically gifted black students. *Contemporary Educational Psychology, 15*(1), 1–12.

Robinson, A., & Stanley, T. D. (1989). Teaching to talent: Evaluating an enriched and accelerated mathematics program. *Journal for the Education of the Gifted, 12*(4), 253–267.

Rosenthal, R., & Rosnow, R. L. (1984). *Essentials of behavioral research: Methods and data analysis.* New York: McGraw-Hill.

Ross, J. D., & Ross, C. M. (1976). *Ross test of higher cognitive processes.* Novato, CA: Academic Therapy Publications.

Sternberg, R. J. (1985). *Beyond IQ: A triarchic theory of human intelligence.* Cambridge, England: Cambridge University Press.

VanTassel-Baska, J. L., & Olszewski-Kubilius, P. (Eds.). (1989). *Patterns of influence on gifted learners: The home, the self, and the school.* New York: Teachers College Press.

CHAPTER 10

MULTIVARIATE TECHNIQUES FOR GIFTED EDUCATION

Michael C. Pyryt and Ronald H. Heck

The purposes of this chapter are to provide a broad overview of several techniques in multivariate statistics that may be applied to research problems in gifted education and to encourage you, the potential researcher in gifted education, to apply multivariate techniques when appropriate. First we describe exploratory and confirmatory factor analytic procedures that may be used to explore underlying dimensions or constructs of data sets. Then we discuss multivariate tests of group differences that can be used to analyze structural relationships among the underlying constructs. We focus on multivariate analysis of variance and discriminant analysis, extensions of multiple regression analysis (i.e., canonical correlation, path analysis). Because this is an introduction, we will provide you with references that contain additional information on each of the techniques discussed.

USES OF MULTIVARIATE TECHNIQUES IN GIFTED EDUCATION

There are several reasons why you might find multivariate techniques especially appropriate for investigating research problems in gifted education. Typically, problems in educational research involve several causes and several effects; that is, nearly all problems are multivariate in nature because the effect of any one variable, such as age, gender, or attitude toward school, is likely to be small compared to the effects of several variables combined. For example, in attempting to assess the determinants of a student's performance, we know that various sets of variables in an individual's background, such as socioeconomic status, language facility, parental attitudes, and the individual's learning aptitudes, as well as a variety of variables associated with the school, all affect the level of his or her performance.

Additionally, you may want to evaluate the effects of school programs or instructional treatments on groups of students. Careful delineation of the evaluation questions will help you decide what type of information is needed and how this information will be analyzed. As discussed in Chapters 3 and 4 of this volume, some questions call simply for descriptive statistics. Some, however, call for comparisons between groups, possibly across time. Other designs call for more complex methods of analysis, such as a variety of possible multivariate analyses.

Multivariate techniques are also useful in evaluating the effects of school programs where several levels of analysis may be required. For example, programs targeted for gifted students may feature classroom-based interventions, school-level programs, district-level, and, finally, state-level interventions. These programs produce hierarchical multilevel designs having students within classes, within grade levels, within schools, and so forth. This multilevel structure of schooling has often been overlooked by researchers, sometimes with serious consequences (Heck, Larsen, & Marcoulides, 1990; Koepke & Flay, 1989; Sirotnik & Burstein, 1985). Such multilevel analyses simultaneously estimate the effects of a variety of variables at each level on one or more dependent variables at each level. They could also include interactions of variables at different levels (e.g., school characteristics, gifted program characteristics, beliefs and attitudes of gifted students on subsequent performance outcome measures). If you plan to investigate the performance of gifted students, you will need to anticipate the potential effects of these sets of variables in connection with assessments of outcomes.

A final set of conceptual issues for using multivariate techniques in conducting research with gifted students and programs concerns the nature of giftedness. The current conceptualization of giftedness in the United States, as exemplified by Public Law 95-561, is multidimensional in nature. Gifted students can be identified in the areas of general intelligence, special academic aptitude, creative and productive thinking, leadership, visual and performing art, or combinations thereof. In fact, the use of multiple criteria—such as standardized aptitude or achievement tests, student products, and/or teacher, parent, and peer nomination—is often advocated to identify gifted students (Baldwin & Wooster, 1976; Jenkins-Friedman, 1982; Renzulli, 1984). In addition, many of the measures currently used in gifted education, such as the Torrance Tests of Creative Thinking (Torrance, 1974) generate several subtest scores. Whenever our conceptual framework is such that these measures are used as dependent variables—that is, when we wish to explain such subtest scores in terms of other variables (such as student background, school treatments, or multilevel analyses of programs)—multivariate techniques are an appropriate means of data analysis.

MULTIVARIATE ANALYSIS AS AN EXTENSION OF UNIVARIATE ANALYSIS

Multivariate techniques may be thought of as extensions of univariate techniques such as correlation and analysis of variance (ANOVA) (Cohen & Cohen, 1983; Harris, 1975; Kerlinger & Pedhazur, 1973; Rulon & Brooks, 1968). A general understanding of univariate techniques is helpful for comprehending the nature, procedures, and subtleties of multivariate techniques (see Chapters 4 and 9, this volume, for additional information). Primarily, these techniques, which are all extensions of the general multivariate linear model, can be categorized into three areas: factor analysis, analysis of variance between groups, and multiple regression (Amick & Walberg, 1975). The foundation of multivariate techniques, then, is based in analysis of both variance and regression. The reason is partly historical: ANOVA has been associated with experimental designs and the manipulation of variables by an experimenter, whereas regression has been viewed as a technique to examine relationships between variables existing in their *natural* setting, primarily through survey research or observational data (Amick & Walberg, 1975; Ferguson, 1976). In cases involving a single dependent variable, ANOVA is viewed as appropriate for handling qualitative (categorical) independent variables, regression for quantitative independent variables, and analysis of covariance for cases where the independent variables are of both types (Wildt & Ahtola, 1978).

With any of these univariate techniques, or their multivariate counterparts, however, you examine the influence of several independent (or predictor) variables on either one or more dependent variables. For example, in a univariate analysis, you may investigate the effects of a set of independent variables, such as gender, previous mathematics experience (M-EXP), and attitudes toward mathematics (A-M), on a dependent or criterion variable, such as a score on the mathematics section of the Scholastic Aptitude Test (SAT-M). In the regression analysis, the calculation results in the maximum multiple correlation or optimal weighting of the independent or predictor variables for predicting the criterion variable (see Chapter 9, this volume, for details of the use of multiple regression in prediction). In the previous example the equation would look like this:

$$\text{Score on the SAT-M} = (\text{Weight} \times \text{Gender}) +$$
$$(\text{Weight} \times \text{M-EXP}) + (\text{Weight} \times \text{A-M}) + \text{Error}$$

Weights are multiplied by the raw scores to predict outcome or dependent variables for a new sample. These weights are typically referred to as unstandardized regression weights. They can also be derived from the standard scores for each variable, in which case they are called standardized regression weights or *beta* weights. The *error* term represents the unaccounted-for variance in the variable set (e.g., variables not measured in the equation or unreliability of the measurement).

The logic of this analysis may be extended to cases where you are investigating several such equations simultaneously. Multivariate analyses, therefore, differ from multiple regression and analysis of variance and covariance because they involve multiple independent variables and multiple dependent variables. These sets of variables are analyzed to reduce them to a minimum number of factors that have internally consistent characteristics, or are a lot alike within the factor, but are generally unrelated to the other factors. By becoming familiar with multivariate techniques, a researcher with access to computer software packages can easily perform analyses that incorporate as many variables as specified by the research design.

In this chapter we describe three classes of interrelated multivariate techniques that are appropriate in examining a variety of research and evaluation questions in gifted education. To illustrate the techniques we use examples from the research literature in gifted education when they are available. You may, however, notice that the procedures employed by previous researchers in gifted education have often lagged behind recommended practices and have not always been applied appropriately. We hope that this chapter will challenge and encourage you, the potential researcher, to apply multivariate techniques when they are appropriate for the research or evaluation question under investigation.

FACTOR ANALYSIS: ESTABLISHING THE DIMENSIONAL CHARACTERISTICS OF DATA SETS

The first multivariate technique discussed in this chapter, factor analysis, is frequently mentioned in psychology and educational psychology courses in discussions of such constructs as intelligence, attitudes, and test anxiety. In gifted education we often refer to constructs such as creativity, positive attitude, and self-concept and attempt to measure these underlying constructs by using a variety of instruments. For example, a researcher might study gifted students' subtest scores on the California Psychological Inventory, a personality measure. These subtest scores are moderately correlated; that is, they are to some degree related to one another. It is quite likely that there is an underlying construct or factor that could explain the pattern of relationships among these variables. Factor analysis allows us to estimate the number of underlying dimensions or factors and the correlations among them (Cattell, 1988). It would make it possible for a researcher to determine if a test with six subtests really measures six unique abilities, skills, or traits.

Factor analysis assumes that the observed variables are linear combinations of some underlying construct (Kim & Mueller, 1978) that is of theoretical interest but cannot be directly observed (Long, 1983). The purpose of factor analysis, then, is to express a large number of observed variables in terms of a smaller number of hypothesized, or latent (unobserved), constructs called factors. In this manner, you attempt to reduce the number of dimensions in the data set as a means of simplifying its overall structure. Through factor analysis, you attempt to develop a measure for a construct and discover the underlying structure of a phenomenon by studying covariation among sets of observed variables (Long, 1983). The correlation between each observed variable and the factor is referred to as its factor loading.

Exploratory and Confirmatory Approaches to Factor Analysis

There are a wide variety of methods associated with using factor analytic techniques. The discussion of each of these is outside the scope of this introductory chapter on multivariate methods. In broad terms, there are two approaches to factor analysis in current use: exploratory and confirmatory approaches. In an exploratory factor model, you specify only the number of common factors to be retained (or allow the computer program to specify) and the number of observed variables to be included in the analysis. In this sense, the structure of the factor model (and loadings of the observed variables) is driven by the structure of the data. The analysis becomes *exploratory* because you must make certain assumptions about factor loadings regardless of their substantive and theoretical appropriateness. You may assume that all common factors are correlated, or uncorrelated, depending on the rotation scheme; that all observed variables are directly affected by all common factors; or that all factors are uncorrelated with all error terms. Because the exploratory factor model is unable to incorporate theoretical constraints into the development of a final substantive model, it is most appropriately used in new research where little is known about the underlying constructs.

Exploratory factor analysis was used by O'Tuel, Ward, and Rawl (1983) to determine the dimensionality of the Structure-of-Intellect Learning Abilities Test (SOI-LA). Results of this analysis were generally supportive of the operations and content dimensions of Guilford's (1967) structure-of-intellect model. Scholwinski and Reynolds (1985) used factor analysis of the Revised Children's Manifest Anxiety Scale to determine that the same constructs explain anxiety in gifted children and the general population. Becker (1980) factor analyzed SAT, ACT, and selected DAT scores of mathematically gifted students and extracted a three-factor solution, consisting of mathematical reasoning, verbal reasoning, and spatial visualization.

The limitations of exploratory factor analysis, however, have now largely been overcome by the development of the confirmatory factor model (Joreskog & Sorbom, 1984). In contrast to exploratory factor analysis, which uses mathematical criteria to create factor models, confirmatory factor analysis allows you to generate factor models that are theory driven (Heck et al., 1990; Pitner & Hocevar, 1987). In confirmatory factor analysis, you impose theoretically motivated constraints on the specification of the underlying dimensions in the model. These constraints determine before the model is tested with actual data which pairs of factors will be correlated (and which ones may be uncorrelated), which observed variables are affected by which unique factors (the residual error), and whether unique factors (i.e., error terms) are to be correlated. You therefore have tremendous control over the specification of the factor model to be tested.

Statistical tests can then be performed to determine if the sample data *confirm* the hypothesized factor model (Long, 1983). Because a series of constraints are imposed on the model prior to testing, the procedure is thought of as confirmatory, as opposed to exploratory. In practice, you may not have one model in mind, but rather a series of competing models. Each model may be tested to find the one that most closely corresponds to the underlying subtleties in the data. In addition, by relaxing constraints one at a time, you may find the *best-fitting* model to describe the data through a specification search that approximates using this type of analysis in an exploratory fashion. Note that if all the constraints on the parameters in the model were relaxed (i.e., no constraints imposed), an exploratory factor analysis would be performed. Examination of the factor loadings enables you to identify and then label the underlying latent variable(s) that explain(s) the observed correlation among variables in the factor model. The proper labeling of such constructs is important because of the implications for future research. For example, Weiner and Robinson (1986), in their factor analysis of the California Psychological Inventory (CPI) (Megargee, 1972), determined that two weighted dimensions underlie the 18 CPI scales. They labeled these factors *self-confidence and drive* and *general adjustment*. Other researchers, however, have labeled the two factors *extroversion* and *socialization*. Factors should be named with care after a thorough examination of the previous research literature.

MULTIVARIATE ANALYSIS OF VARIANCE: EXPLORING STRUCTURAL CHARACTERISTICS OF DATA SETS

After you have established the dimensionality of a given phenomenon, you may wish to explore functional relationships among the dimensions. As a researcher in gifted education, you would use univariate techniques such as *t* tests, analysis of variance (ANOVA), or analysis of covariance (ANCOVA) to see if students receiving an experimental treatment such as metacognitive skills training differ from students in a control group who received no training. Univariate analysis would be appropriate if you were examining improvement on one dependent variable such as reading achievement. If you were interested in demonstrating multiple effects, such as improvement in reading achievement and self-concept, you would need to perform a multivariate analysis of variance (MANOVA). When questions focus on differences among groups with respect to a set of dependent variables, you may use multivariate analysis of variance (MANOVA) if the dependent variables are continuous, or discriminant analysis if the dependent variables are categorical.

For example, you may wish to study gifted and nongifted students not only in terms of their test scores but also in terms of their attitudes toward school and their career aspirations. Some researchers would conduct separate ANOVA analyses for each dependent variable, which would tend to blur significance levels. A more appropriate technique is multivariate analysis of variance (MANOVA), using all criterion variables together (Tatsuoka & Silver, 1988). The null hypothesis now tested refers to the equality of the number of group population centroids (vectors of means), rather than means, one for each criterion variable (Tatsuoka & Silver, 1988). One statistical test of significance that is reasonably powerful in testing the null hypothesis is Wilks's lambda ratio (Tatsuoka & Silver, 1988).

It is important to note that like other parametric statistical techniques such as ANOVA, there are some assumptions about how the research sample is drawn and how the data are gathered. The major assumptions of MANOVA are random sampling, statistical independence of observations, and multivariate normal distribution of dependent variables for each group (Maxwell, 1988). With MANOVA, therefore, you assume that the shape of the distribution of the set of dependent variables is normal for each group. You also assume that both the variances and correlations among variables are similar for each group. MANOVA appears to be sensitive to violations of the assumptions of random sampling and independence of observations and less sensitive to violations of multivariate normality.

The technique may be illustrated with an example from the literature on gifted students. Tomlinson-Keasey and Smith-Winberry (1983) compared gifted and nongifted college students' responses on the California Psychological Inventory (CPI). Since the CPI has 18 scales, univariate procedures would require 18 separate ANOVAs and greatly inflate the Type I error rate (the probability of calling a nonsignificant difference a statistically significant difference). Instead they used a MANOVA to determine mean differences between gifted and nongifted students, male and female students, and to examine the interaction between gender and ability level on the 18 scales (used as dependent variables in the analysis). The multivariate results indicated a significant gender effect and a significant gender and ability-level interaction.

If the multivariate null hypothesis can be rejected through using one of several possible test statistics, it is desirable to determine which of the criterion variables were most important in contributing to the rejection. In the previous example, Tomlinson-Keasey and Smith-Winberry (1983) used univariate procedures to follow up each significant multivariate effect. Yet this procedure at least partially defeats the purpose of the multivariate analysis because the criterion variables are considered one at a time instead of in conjunction with their combined effects (Tatsuoka & Silver, 1988). Because variables in a multivariate analysis are likely to be intercorrelated, a univariate analysis may not yield accurate interpretation of such interrelationships among criterion variables. For example, the second criterion variable that is responsible for rejecting the null hypothesis may be highly correlated with the first variable, and so on. That is, the differences among groups may simply reflect one difference, such as gender.

Discriminant Analysis

In order to assess the relative importance of several variables in discriminating among groups, a better procedure in the previous example would be to perform another multivariate analysis to explore simultaneously the interrelationships among those variables (Tatsuoka & Silver, 1988). One possible technique is discriminant analysis. The logic of discriminant analysis is to locate a set of variables among the various criterion variables that *discriminates*, or distinguishes, among groups under study (in this case, gifted or nongifted students). Discriminant analysis forms combinations of variables that are uncorrelated among themselves and that discriminate most highly, second most highly, and so forth among several groups under investigation.

Weiner and Robinson (1986) examined gender differences on five dependent variables: (1) mathematical reasoning ability, (2) verbal reasoning, (3) spatial orientation, (4) social confidence and drive, and (5) general adjustment. After reporting a rejection of the null hypothesis, they explored the data further by finding the set of criterion variables most responsible for the rejection. The discriminant analysis revealed a pattern favoring males in math reasoning ability and favoring females on verbal reasoning, with little gender differentiation in spatial orientation, confidence and drive, or adjustment.

Canonical Analysis

Canonical analysis is an analytic technique that encompasses both regression and multivariate analysis of variance as special cases (Darlington, Weinberg, & Walberg, 1973). You may be interested in testing a model that specifies theoretical relationships among sets of variables within a multivariate framework. Canonical analysis can incorporate research studies such as this with multiple predictors and multiple outcomes. Variables may be continuous (interval), categorical (nominal), or mixed (Cohen & Cohen, 1983; Darlington et al., 1973; Knapp, 1978; Thompson, 1988). There are three conditions or types of studies in which canonical analysis is especially appropriate:

1. To correlate multiple ratings from two samples of raters, such as parents and teachers
2. To correlate scores among several variables collected at two points in time
3. To correlate multiple scores from measures of two different constructs, such as personality and achievement

In gifted education you must sometimes deal with multiple predictors, such as fluency, flexibility, and originality scores of gifted and nongifted students five years ago and the same scores collected later. You may want to determine the relationship between the set of predictors (early scores) and the criteria (current scores). Canonical analysis would allow you to do so.

The goal of the analysis is to find two sets of weights for sets of independent variables and dependent variables that maximize the correlation between the composites of the two sets of variables (Darlington et al., 1973). Canonical analysis, therefore, asks the question: Which variables are needed to explain the relationship between sets X and Y? (Darlington et al., 1973). The relative contribution of sets of independent variables on a set of dependent variables can then be assessed through the calculation of a series of mathematical equations. Generally, the number of canonical relations calculated on a sample will equal the number of observed variables in the smaller set (Darlington et al., 1973).

In the process of performing a canonical analysis, canonical variates or weighted composites of the variables in each set are derived. These composites are defined by weighted combinations of the variables, so that they are maximally correlated. The first canonical correlation, then, is the highest correlation that can be found between the weighted composite scores for each set of X and Y variables, or canonical variates (Darlington et al., 1973).

Stanley and McGill (1986) used canonical analysis to determine the relationship among *demographic variables* (age, gender, Study of Mathematically Precocious Youth affiliation, credits at college entrance, attendance at private high schools, Oriental parentage) and *indices of college performance* (age at graduation, number of credits earned, simultaneously earning bachelor's and master's degrees, percentage of time on the dean's list, cumulative grade-point average (GPA), honors at graduation) for 25 students who entered the Johns Hopkins University two to five years earlier than usual. While this is a very small data set, it serves as an illustration of how to use canonical analysis, because there were two sets of variables (demographic and performance related) and the research purpose was to determine the relationship between the variables in the first set and the variables in the second set.

Out of a possible six canonical correlations and six pairs of weighted composites in their analysis (limited by six criterion variables in the Y set), Stanley and McGill (1986) reported two statistically significant canonical correlations of .87 and .73 between composites of the two sets. The first canonical correlation will be the maximum correlation possible between weighted composites of the two sets. The second canonical correlation will be the highest correlation between scores on a second pair of canonical variates, which are independent of the first pair of canonical variates. Notice that the first reported canonical correlation (.87) is higher than the second canonical correlation (.73). Other descending pairs of canonical variates (e.g., the third set, and so on) are defined similarly but were found to be nonsignificant.

To explore the multivariate complexity of the data (i.e., the nature of the variables needed to explain sets X and Y), other analysis may also be needed. Some researchers choose to report the standardized function weights for pairs of statistically significant canonical variates. These weights (similar to beta weights in regression analysis) indicate the relative importance of each variable in the set; that is, the higher the weight, the greater the relative importance of a particular variable. For example, in the Stanley and McGill (1986) study, degree, honors at graduation, credits earned, and cumulative GPA were most highly weighted within the set of performance indices composite variable.

As a product-moment correlation, the squared canonical correlation can be interpreted as the percentage of variance of the weighted composites. The two statistically significant canonical correlations can be squared to find the common variance [76% ($.87^2$) and 53% ($.73^2$)].

Researchers (Darlington, 1968; Darlington et al., 1973; Kerlinger & Pedhazur, 1973) emphasize caution in interpreting these weights, particularly in cases when variables within a set are highly intercorrelated. Additionally, weights will change from sample to sample and as the number of variables within any set changes (Kerlinger & Pedhazur, 1973). One currently preferred alternative is to calculate structure coefficients, or correlations between a variable in the set (e.g., within the set of college performance indices) and the canonical variate (Cooley & Lohnes, 1971; Darlington et al., 1973; Thompson, 1988). For example, the correlation between GPA and the weighted composite of the indices of college performance would give an indication of the relative importance of GPA in the weighted composite. Variables that correlated highly with the canonical variable best define the underlying dimension that the canonical variate represents.

The major limitation of canonical analysis is that only two sets of scores can be simultaneously related. If you wanted to compare the relationship among the attitudes of teachers, parents, and students, you would need to perform three separate analyses: relating teachers' with parents' attitudes; relating parents' with students' attitudes; and relating teachers' with students' attitudes. Another limitation is that the analysis forces all pairs of canonical variates to be independent of any previously derived pair of canonical variates (e.g., the first composite of teachers' attitudes must be separate from the second). In the real world, for example, variables are more likely to be correlated than independent.

Although the application of canonical analysis in gifted education has been limited, canonical analyses have been performed by Stanley and Benbow (1980) to compare student SAT scores and parental educational level and by Torrance (1972) to examine the relationship between divergent thinking scores and indices of creative achievement.

PATH ANALYSIS: TESTING STRUCTURAL RELATIONSHIPS

Another technique that can be used to examine the structural relationships among sets of variables is path analysis. Path analysis enables you to test a causal model in which the assumed relationships among variables under study have been clearly specified. Several related methods may be used to perform path analysis. One is simple multiple regression, another is factor analysis, and still a third is canonical analysis (Spaeth, 1975). Causal models in general, and path analysis in particular, have been developed to examine and test a variety of causal relationships in nonexperimental data (Asher, 1976; Blalock, 1964; Hackett, 1986). The goal of path analysis is to determine the extent to which the data collected from a particular sample fit a hypothesized causal model derived from theory and previous research. It allows you to move beyond simple or multiple correlations to testing the structure of a set (or several sets) of variables.

Because research in gifted education tends to involve *one-shot* approaches to data collection rather than theory-driven longitudinal studies, path analysis has been rarely used in gifted education research. It would be especially useful in long-term studies of the effectiveness of various systems and models in gifted education (Renzulli, 1986) or to determine the effectiveness of various conceptions of giftedness (Sternberg & Davidson, 1986).

In path analysis, one set of variables is referred to as *exogenous*, or variables whose variability is determined by factors outside of the causal model being tested. These correspond to independent variables in an experimental study. The other set of variables is termed *endogenous*, in that their variability is determined by other exogenous and/or endogenous variables in the proposed model. The endogenous variables roughly correspond to dependent variables, except that in some cases an endogenous variable may function as both a dependent variable (e.g., in relation to an exogenous variable) and an independent variable (e.g., in relation to another endogenous variable). A path model allows you one analytical option to conceptualize and test some rather complex models, models that may more closely approximate the real world than simple analyses of relationships between two variables.

Moving from the situation where a set of predictors is tested against a single dependent variable (represented by one regression equation) to path analysis requires the specification of a structural model (represented by several regression equations). In specifying the relationships to be tested in the analysis, you must clarify the conceptual reasons for allowing exogenous and endogenous variables to be related (Heck, Marcoulides, & Glasman, 1989). These relationships should be derived from previous theory and specified before the data are analyzed.

Once the data are collected, the model is tested to see how well the actual data set conforms to the hypothesized model. To test this model from a path analytic view, you assume that errors in the system are uncorrelated and conduct a series of multiple regression analyses between variables. Each endogenous variable in the model is regressed on all causally prior variables (Asher, 1976). The standardized regression coefficients, or beta weights, become path coefficients that specify the size of the direct links of variables in the model. Examination of path coefficients is then used to revise the model if necessary to develop the most accurate and parsimonious model. For example, path coefficients that are negligible (often less than .10) may be dropped out of the model, and the regression analyses performed again on the reduced model.

Simonton (1977, 1984) used path analysis to predict the eminence of 696 classical composers. He found that 60% of the variance in the differential fame of composers as measured by six indices of musical eminence could be explained in terms of productivity, longevity, and birth year. That is, given the composer's birth year, productivity operationalized as works and themes, and longevity divided into 5-year age periods, we could correctly predict 60% of his or her rated eminence. Other variables examined included role model availability, geographic marginality, creative precociousness, and life-span analysis. Simonton began by developing a causal model that identified the variables, specified the causal links of paths in the model, and indicated the time sequence in which the variables occurred (see Figure 10.1). Birth year is the first exogenous variable hypothesized to affect creative productivity, creative longevity, and eminence. Creative productivity is an endogenous variable related to birth year that dirrectly affects creative longevity and eminence. Creative longevity is an endogenous variable related to birth year and creative productivity that directly affects attainment of eminence. Eminence is an endogenous variable explained by birth year,

FIGURE 10.1	Path analysis for Simonton (1977) model for predicting eminence of musical composers

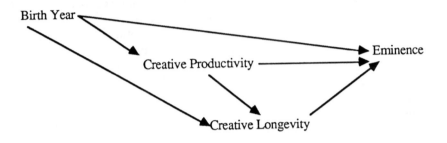

creative productivity, and creative longevity. The model can be formally specified as follows:

$$E = BO + B_1Y + B_2P + B_3L + D$$
$$L = BO + B_1Y + B_2P + D$$
$$P = BO + B_1Y + D$$

where BO = a constant

$B_1 B_2 B_3$ = standardized regression weights

E = an indicator of the endogenous variable—Eminence

L = an indicator of the endogenous variable—Longevity

P = an indicator of the endogenous variable—Creative Productivity

Y = an indicator of the exogenous variable—Birth Year

D = Disturbances (errors in the system/residual)

Given the data presented by Simonton (1977), it is possible to propose a more parsimonious model. This model is shown in Figure 10.2. Eminence is a direct effect of birth year, creative productivity, and creative longevity as originally proposed. Creative longevity, however, is only caused by creative productivity. Birth year does not appear to directly affect creative productivity. For other illustrations of path techniques, see Hackett (1986) and Heck and colleagues (1989).

Path analytic methods are thus useful tools for exploring relationships in a multivariate framework if they are theory driven. The path model must attempt to include the variables thought to be relevant to explaining the social phenomenon. Thus you should always consider the results of a path model as limited to the variables that were specified and tested within the model framework. Of course, sample sizes should

FIGURE 10.2   Path analysis for Simonton (1977) revised model for predicting eminence of musical composers

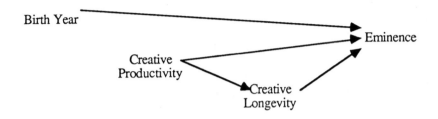

be reasonably large and representative of the population to which you wish to generalize (Spaeth, 1975). The major limitation of path analysis is the requirement that causality be unidirectional. Reciprocal causality is likely to occur in the real world. For example, a poor self-concept might lead to underachievement and underachievement might further diminish self-concept. In order to examine complicated models of causality, a more complicated covariance structure analysis must be performed (Joreskog, 1988). Path coefficients are also susceptible to sampling error, as are any multiple regression coefficients (Darlington, 1968).

SUMMARY

We have described and illustrated several multivariate techniques and discussed some of the methodological considerations involved in performing these techniques. The points we have made are summarized in Table 10.1.

In deciding whether or not a multivariate technique is appropriate for a particular research situation, ask the question: How many dependent or outcome variables are involved? If the answer is two or more, a multivariate technique is appropriate. A multivariate analysis would also be appropriate if one or more of the independent or predictor variables are continuous (interval). Although the mathematical operations underlying multivariate techniques are quite complex, readily available computer programs simplify such analyses. We caution that the sophistication of such programs cannot substitute for solid theoretical groundwork, which must be developed before the application of any of these powerful, but easily misused, techniques. In addition, the collec-

TABLE 10.1: A Summary of Multivariate Techniques

Technique	Purpose	Key Steps	References
Factor analysis	To determine the underlying dimensionality of a set of variables	• Choose method (exploratory or confirmatory) • Calculate via computer program • Interpret factor loadings	Becker, 1980
Multivariate analysis of variance (MANOVA)	To analyze multiple dependent variables simultaneously	• Identify dependent, independent, and control variables • Calculate via computer program • Check statistical significance • Use discriminant analysis to examine significant results	Weiner & Robinson, 1986
Canonical analysis	To correlate multiple predictors with multiple criteria	• Determine set of predictors and set of criteria • Calculate canonical correlation • Check statistical significance • Use structure coefficients and standard weights to find the most important variables	Stanley & McGill, 1966
Path analysis	To test a causal model	• Specify a unidirectional model • Test model through multiple regression • Revise the model and retest	Simonton, 1977

tion of psychometrically sound data must always accompany such an analysis (Bentler, 1987; Heck et al., 1990).

It appears that researchers in gifted education could benefit from further exploration of the methodological literature with respect to testing of theoretical relationships. We hope that this rudimentary chapter will encourage other researchers to utilize multivariate techniques when appropriate.

REFERENCES

Amick, D., & Walberg, H. (1975). *Introductory multivariate analysis for educational, psychological, and social research*. Berkeley: McCutchan.

Asher, H. (1976). *Causal modeling*. Beverly Hills, CA: Sage.

Baldwin, A., & Wooster, J. (1976). *The Baldwin Identification Matrix*. Buffalo, NY: DOK.

Becker, B. J. (1980). Performance of a group of mathematically able youths on the Mathematics Usage and Natural Science Readings Tests of the American

College Testing Battery vs. the Scholastic Aptitude Tests. *Gifted Child Quarterly, 24,* 138–143.

Bentler, P. (1987). Structural modeling and the scientific method: Comments on Friedman's critique. *Journal of Educational Statistics, 12,* 151–157.

Blalock, P. (1964). *Causal inferences in nonexperimental research.* New York: Norton.

Cattell, R. B. (1988). The meaning and strategic use of factor analysis. In J. R. Nesselroade & R. B. Cattell (Eds.), *Handbook of multivariate experimental psychology* (2nd ed.) (pp. 131–203). New York: Plenum.

Cohen, J., & Cohen, P. R. (1983). *Applied multiple regression/correlation analysis in the behavioral sciences.* Hillsdale, NJ: Erlbaum.

Cooley, W. W., & Lohnes, P. R. (1971). *Multivariate data analysis.* New York: Wiley.

Darlington, R. B. (1968). Multiple regression in psychological research and practice. *Psychological Bulletin, 69,* 161–182.

Darlington, R. B., Weinberg, S. L., & Walberg, H. J. (1973). Canonical variate analysis and related techniques. *Review of Educational Research, 43,* 433–454.

Ferguson, G. (1976). *Statistical analysis in psychology and education* (4th ed.). New York: McGraw-Hill.

Guilford, J. P. (1967). *The nature of human intelligence.* New York: McGraw-Hill.

Hackett, G. (1986). Role of mathematics self-sufficiency in the choice of math-related majors in college women and men: A path analysis. *Journal of Counseling Psychology, 32,* 47–56.

Harris, J. J. (1975). *A primer of multivariate statistics.* New York: Academic Press.

Heck, R., Larsen, T., & Marcoulides, G. (1990). Principal instructional leadership and school achievement: Empirical validation of a causal model. *Educational Administrative Quarterly, 26,* 94–125.

Heck, R. Marcoulides, G., & Glasman, N. (1989). The application of causal modeling techniques to administrative decision making: The case of teacher allocation. *Educational Administration Quarterly, 25,* 253–267.

Jenkins-Friedman, R. (1982). Myth: Cosmetic use of multiple criteria. *Gifted Child Quarterly, 26,* 24–26.

Joreskog, K. G. (1988). Analysis of covariance structures. In J. R. Nesselroade & R. B. Cattell (Eds.), *Handbook of multivariate experimental psychology* (2nd ed.) (pp. 207–230). New York: Plenum.

Joreskog, K. G., & Sorbom, D. (1984). *LISREL VI* (Computer Program). Mooreville, IN: Scientific Software.

Kerlinger, F. N., & Pedhazur, E. J. (1973). *Multiple regression in behavioral research.* New York: Holt, Rinehart & Winston.

Kim, J. O., & Mueller, C. (1978). *Factor analysis: Statistical methods and practical issues.* Beverly Hills, CA: Sage.

Knapp, T. R. (1978). Canonical correlation analysis: A general parametric significance testing system. *Psychological Bulletin, 85,* 410–416.

Koepke, D., & Flay, B. (1989). Levels of analysis. *New Directions in Program Analysis, 43*, 75–87.

Long, J. S. (1983). *Confirmatory factor analysis*. Beverly Hills, CA: Sage.

Maxwell, S. E. (1988, April). *Recent developments in MANOVA applications*. Paper presented at the meeting of the American Educational Research Association, New Orleans, LA.

Megargee, E. (1972). *The California Psychological Inventory handbook*. San Francisco: Jossey-Bass.

O'Tuel, F. S., Ward, M., & Rawl, R. K. (1983). The SOI as an identification tool for the gifted: Windfall or washout? *Gifted Child Quarterly, 27*, 126–134.

Pitner, N., & Hocevar, D. (1987). An empirical comparison of two-factor versus multifactor theories of principal leadership: Implications for the evaluation of school principals. *Journal of Personnel Evaluation in Education, 1*, 93–109.

Renzulli, J. S. (1984). The triad/revolving door system: A research-based approach to identification and programming for the gifted and talented. *Gifted Child Quarterly, 28*, 163–171.

Renzulli, J. S. (Ed.). (1986). *Systems and models for developing programs for the gifted and talented*. Mansfield Center, CT: Creative Learning Press.

Rulon, P. J., & Brooks, W. D. (1968). On statistical tests of group differences. In D. K. Whitla (Ed.), *Handbook of measurement and assessment in behavioral sciences* (pp. 60–99). Reading, MA: Addison-Wesley.

Scholwinski, E., & Reynolds, C. R. (1985). Dimensions of anxiety among high IQ children. *Gifted Child Quarterly, 29*, 125–130.

Simonton, D. K. (1977). Eminence, creativity, and geographic marginality: A recursive structural equation model. *Journal of Personality and Social Psychology, 35*, 805–813.

Simonton, D. K. (1984). *Genius, creativity and leadership*. Cambridge, MA: Harvard University Press.

Sirotnik, K., & Burstein, L. (1985). Measurement and statistical issues in multilevel research on schooling. *Educational Administration Quarterly, 21*, 169–186.

Spaeth, J. (1975). Path analysis. In D. Amick & H. Walberg (Eds.), *Introductory multivariate analysis for educational, psychological, and social research* (pp. 53–89). Berkeley: McCutchan.

Stanley, J. C., & Benbow, C. P. (1980). Intellectually talented students: Family profiles. *Gifted Child Quarterly, 24*, 119–122.

Stanley, J. C., & McGill, A. M. (1986). More about "young entrants to college: How do they fare?" *Gifted Child Quarterly, 30*, 70–73.

Sternberg, R. J., & Davidson, J. E. (Eds.). (1986). *Conceptions of giftedness*. New York: Cambridge University Press.

Tatsuoka, M. M., & Silver, P. (1988). Qualitative research methods in educational administration. In N. Boyan (Ed.), *The handbook of research in educational administration* (pp. 677–701). New York: Longman.

Thompson, B. (1988, April). *Canonical correlation analysis: An explanation with comments and correct practice*. Paper presented at the meeting of the American Educational Research Association, New Orleans, LA.

Tomlinson-Keasey, C., & Smith-Winberry, C. (1983). Educational strategies and personality outcomes of gifted and non-gifted college students. *Gifted Child Quarterly, 27,* 35–41.

Torrance, E. P. (1972). Predictive validity of the Torrance Tests of Creative Thinking. *Journal of Creative Behavior, 6,* 236–252.

Torrance, E. P. (1974). *The Torrance Tests of Creative Thinking: Norms-technical manual.* Bensenville, IL: Scholastic Testing Service.

Weiner, N. C., & Robinson, S. E. (1986). Cognitive abilities, personality and gender differences in the math achievement of gifted adolescents. *Gifted Child Quarterly, 30,* 83–87.

Wildt, A., & Ahtola, O. (1978). *Analysis of covariance.* Beverly Hills, CA: Sage.

CHAPTER 11

META-ANALYSIS

J. William Asher

The purpose of meta-analysis is to collate systematically all the prior data that has been gathered about a phenomenon of interest. In gifted and talented education the topic could be early entrance, homogeneous grouping, acceleration, advanced placement, or creativity instruction. The great advantage of meta-analysis is that it allows us to integrate results of research across studies, something the physical and biological sciences have been doing for several hundred years but has been almost impossible in psychology and education (Glass, 1976; Hedges, 1986; Lauer & Asher, 1988). The result of meta-analysis is fourfold:

1. It provides a much clearer view of the relationships among the variables involved.
2. The theory evolved is much more general than is possible from the results of studies assembled qualitatively.
3. The strength of the treatment effect can be calculated, not merely tested for statistical significance. (These treatment effect differences calculated are called effect sizes.)
4. Hypotheses can be tested about variables that differ among studies that generally would be difficult to test within a study, such as differing grade or age levels, inner city versus suburban school effects, or types of schools.

All four of these advantages of assembling data quantitatively via meta-analysis across research studies are major steps forward in our understanding of educational and psychological phenomena in general and gifted education in particular. Data from true and quasi-experiments in gifted education can be analyzed together to examine cause-and-effect relationships. Meta-analysis can also be used to combine correlational data in descriptive research (Hunter, Schmidt, & Jackson, 1982), as in predicting success in gifted and talented programs.

The problem in meta-analysis is how to combine the data from the original studies. Typically the original data for individuals in the research studies are not available. The next best set of data for this purpose are the means, standard deviations, and number of subjects (and possibly the matrix intercorrelations among the variables) for the control group and the various treatment groups in the experiments. With these sets of summary data, properly weighted, we can estimate rather well what the overall mean and standard deviation and distribution of the various experimental and control groups would have been had the original individual subjects' data been available. Why must we be involved in the arithmetic of weighting and estimating these statistics? Why do we simply not find the experimental studies that use gifted educational treatment or condition of interest and qualitatively summarize the literature, or, even more simply, count the number of statistically nonsignificant and significant results and determine the direction of the outcomes?

The answer lies in the nature of research in education and psychology, the number of subjects typically used, the reliability of the observations, and the methods of statistical hypothesis testing. Educational and psychological research in gifted education over the years has not received major funding. Most of the research has been done by faculty in universities and occasionally by the staff of school systems on time available after other duties and with existing resources. The number of students involved is seldom more than 100. Further, because of the nature of gifted programs, except in metropolitan areas such as New York City, Los Angeles, and Chicago, there are not many gifted students in any one place. With relatively small numbers of subjects, somewhat imprecise measurements, and the probabilistic outcomes of standard statistical hypothesis testing, the demonstration of statistical significance is rather unlikely. (In more technical terms, the power of the statistical tests is low. In other words, we are likely to have to declare any seeming differences between means of groups as *not significant*, and this is distinctly *not* the same as saying that the experimental and control group treatments do *not* make a difference. The statistical tests simply are unable to detect any differences because of the small number of students involved and the less than perfect reliability of observations or tests.) The overall statistical conclusion for many studies in gifted education often should be *not proved*. These types of conclusions, known as Type II statistical inference errors, frequently occur. (Type II errors occur when a true difference may indeed exist between the gifted and talented instructional methods, but with the sample sizes and the usual levels of statistical significance, only a statistically nonsignificant difference can be reported.) Thus, as the result of these frequent Type II errors, when the statistical testing results of individual studies are summarized, we are unable to detect many important results. These, in turn, overwhelm the literature review summary. As a result, worthwhile educational treatments are not identified. Thus, there is the great need to summarize original data as much as possible from all the individual experiments rather than the results of the individual statistical tests, in order to gain the statistical power of the larger numbers in the summary.

Where there are many subjects available, the opposite statistical problem can occur; that is, statistical significance can be declared for differences between experimental and control treatments that for practical purposes are unimportant. Again, the meta-analysis methodology is useful because part of the result is an effect size. An effect size (ES) is the difference between the means of the experimental group and the control group divided by the average standard deviation of the two groups:

$$\bar{X}_E - \bar{X}_C/\sigma_w = ES$$

(For readers familiar with measurement systems in education and psychology, an effect size is a standard score. It has a mean of zero when there are no differences between groups and has upper and lower limits of about + 3.00 and −3.00.) For practical purposes, effect sizes much above +1.00 are seldom found, and there are negative effect sizes when the experimental condition is actually worse than a standard method of instruction. For instance, student compositions carefully marked for all mechanical and grammatical errors have been judged to be worse than those not as carefully marked for errors, a negative effect size (Hillocks, 1986). For practical purposes, effect sizes of .20 are considered *small*; .50, *medium*; and .80 or greater, *large* (Hedges & Olkin, 1985, p. 5).

THEORY BUILDING WITH META-ANALYSIS

Meta-analysis can help you, as a researcher in gifted and talented education, begin to build theories. In this section I examine the advantages and disadvantages of meta-analysis in building theories in gifted education.

Advantages of Meta-Analysis

In combining all available true and quasi-experimental research on topics of interest to gifted educators, such as ability grouping, accelerated instruction, or creativity, the variables, such as ability grouping, accelerated instruction, or creativity instruction, are conceptually and operationally defined according to the standards in the area. When all the studies in the area are identified, the conceptual definition may be somewhat expanded because there may be several varieties of ability grouping, accelerated instruction, or creativity. However, each of these varieties can be conceptually defined separately and then operationally defined in the several studies by the kinds of activities by which they are implemented. For instance, it is possible to have several subgroups of gifted educational treatments within the construct *acceleration*. This is advantageous because in a meta-analysis it is readily possible to group the various experimental acceleration studies into their subgroups and calculate within the subgroups the differences between the means of the experimental and control groups. Then, the means of the subgroups' differences can be tested to see if there really are statistically significant differences among them. If not, this is evidence that all the groups are really homogeneous in their effects and that these groups can be combined. This result, in effect, might indicate that what appeared to be conceptual differences between various operational definitions of grouping or acceleration or creativity are unimportant. Thus, the several operational definitions could be combined into one broader, more multifaceted definition, and, in turn, the conceptual definition of the terms *grouping, acceleration,* or *creativity* are broadened and enriched. Better empirically based variables are developed and the theories of gifted instruction and methods are enhanced. The theories are more generalizable because the variables are more broadly defined operationally and conceptually.

Further, rather than just declare results *statistically significant* or *not statistically significant,* the effect sizes ·of the differences among the subgroups are available so that in addition to statistical significance, the strength or degree of the differences among the subgroups can be used to make decisions about which instructional strategy to adopt.

In addition, the Type II errors of statistical decision making (no significant differences) are not nearly as rampant in meta-analysis as they are in individual research studies, because the numbers of subjects in all of the studies in a meta-analysis group are combined, thus making the results of the statistical tests far more representative of the true nature of the phenomenon observed. The probability of an important difference in educational outcome *not* being statistically detected as *significant* (a Type II error of statistical inference) is markedly reduced in doing meta-analyses. In fact, researchers may have to change somewhat in doing and reading meta-analyses. Statistical significance will be achieved far more frequently because of the larger samples involved in the meta-analysis. Instead of the usual spate of nonsignificant differences in a series of studies, now we may find statistically significant results in a meta-analysis that are relatively unimportant because the effect size difference is not of major import.

With meta-analysis we are much more likely to firmly establish facts in gifted research than we have been able to do before. When we examine data via traditional statistical analyses we are viewing the world "through a glass darkly." The smaller the number of subjects (as in gifted programs), the darker the glass, and the more difficult it is to identify important variables and to differentiate among instructional methods. With the combined number of subjects over a series of studies used in the meta-analysis, the picture of the world of the gifted can be clearer. When the facts are more firmly established, important or unimportant differences in operational definitions of variables can be established, and generalizations about the variables and the true strength of their interrelationships can be more readily developed. Constructs are developed from the operational definitions (and vice versa), the various strengths of their interrelationships are established via the effect sizes, and the cause-and-effect relationships among the variables are developed from the true and quasi-experimental nature of the data collection. All of these factors combine to form an excellent base for broader generalizations and theory development than has been possible via other methods in the educational and psychological world.

Another advantage of meta-analysis is that we make a determined attempt to find *all* of the literature in the area under investigation. In addition to bringing larger numbers of subjects to the statistical analysis, a marked advantage has been that the search also shows where there are gaps or a limited number of studies in an area. A meta-analysis, like all research projects, has objectives, states procedures, and proposes hypotheses; but like most research, inevitably some of the important findings are those that are serendipitous. For example, several studies that compare an innovative gifted instructional treatment with regular classroom instruction may conclude that there were no significant differences. However, if the same studies were examined using meta-analysis, they might show significant differences across the studies. It is also possible that standard instructional practices may actually be less effective than alternatives, or even harmful. One typical finding of a meta-analysis study is that few, or even no, experimental studies have been done in an area.

Disadvantages of Meta-Analysis

Two scholars have raised considerable objection to meta-analysis. Eysenck (1978), a distinguished British psychologist, was an early rejector of the method. He doubted the general effectiveness of psychotherapy and reviewed considerable literature to support his thinking. When Smith, Glass, and Miller (1980) published their book on the meta-analysis of the experiments in the area, *The Benefits of Psychotherapy*, strongly verifying the major effect sizes produced by psychotherapy, Eysenck attacked the results and labeled the method "mega silliness." Since the meta-analysis method and further examination of the experimental research in psychotherapy strongly supported Glass and colleagues' results, Eysenck's attacks seem less relevant. Science has progressed, as a general rule, because it tends to reject appeals to authority while accepting appeals to data.

Slavin (1986) also declined to accept the evidence resulting from meta-analysis, opting instead for a procedure from jurisprudence, which is labeled "best evidence." Slavin firmly rejected the collection of all research that meets certain minimum conditions (e.g., is experimental, has a general gifted educational treatment classified as acceleration, and has criterion variables that are academic achievement tests). Instead, Slavin set rather exact, high-quality specifications for research bearing on an area and used only one or a few studies which met his rigorous criteria to draw conclusions about the educational or psychological phenomena involved. His concern for high standards of admission of evidence and specific criteria for treatments, subjects, and methods is admirable, but the small samples and limited number of treatments and measures considerably restrict the generalizability of the results. In education and psychology we frequently define constructs generalized from a common core of variables with related multiple operational definitions. The construct *self-concept*, for example, is defined as what is common among the tests of ego strength, self-concept, academic self-concept, and so on. This triangulation of definitions and methods is considered a scientific strength. In the multiplicity of operational definitions there is the core of the construct, which actually gains generality and suggests added, broader, and also more specific meanings as the result of the multiple definitions. The same is true of definitions of types of subjects as well as research methods, treatments, and conditions. If we restrict scientific evidence in education and psychology to the results of research studies selected for their few, specifically defined conditions, we markedly restrict the generality of the results despite the seeming purity of the studies. Further, given the necessarily probabilistic nature of all research in education and psychology, the more subjects involved in a summary of research, the more precise will be the results of the studies. With only one or a few studies, the number of subjects is necessarily limited and thus Type II errors, being unable to detect differences or relationships that really exist, are far more common.

Slavin (with Karweit, 1984) used meta-analysis to summarize the best-evidence studies. They reviewed 43 studies overall of between- and within-class grouping and found that single-subject-matter groups had more positive effects than did comprehensive groupings, but this result was for a sample of just seven studies.

Another common criticism of meta-analysis is that it attempts to compare "apples and oranges." However, it is interesting that those who reject the method with this objection would use two objects, both of which are biological entities, are fruits, containing vitamin C, are common foods, and having fiber. One of the major goals of science is to organize (pun unintended) the natural world conceptually into classes with common characteristics that may have functions or properties that generalize to other objects in the class. Recognizing, structuring, and organizing these functions or properties is called theory and is one of the major goals of the scientific method. If the objectors had attempted to deride meta-analysis by saying it attempts to compare, say, prayer and iron ore, then they might have had a point. Certainly these two constructs have little in common.

When we do meta-analyses with a number of studies it allows us to test statistically between-study results as well as within-study contrasts. For example, do criteria such as general self-concept tests or academic self-concept tests yield different or similar results? Are there differences between students in Grade 4–6 gifted programs and those in Grade 7–9 gifted programs? Do true experiments and quasi-experiments yield different results? The concerns about intervening variables, such as special research conditions, unusual criteria, research done in different decades, and so on, can be tested empirically. The possible generalizability of the several studies therefore is markedly enhanced.

Meta-analyses, I suggest, attempt to build theory on a far better basis of evidence than is possible in any other way yet devised in education and the behavioral, cognitive, and social sciences. Meta-analysis attempts to build theory on the basis of the broadest assemblage of data collected.

PERFORMING META-ANALYSIS

The first consideration when planning a meta-analysis is to define the problem. Next, you must locate the studies, code them, and calculate the effect sizes. In this section I will discuss each briefly and offer suggestions to facilitate your decision making. The remainder of the chapter will be an extended example detailing how these decisions are made.

Defining the Problem

The most important part of doing a meta-analysis is defining the problem. That means deciding:

1. The phenomenon to be studied
2. The definitions of the treatment construct
3. The subject populations to admit from the studies reported in the literature
4. Whether experimental studies (yielding cause-and-effect relationships between treatment conditions and criteria results) or simple descriptive studies will be acceptable
5. The criteria measures to be used or excluded, and how they will be organized

Each of these decisions may contain other choices. For example, your decisions about which criteria measures to use may depend on other issues, such as whether general achievement measures will be differentiated from intelligence measures and both of these from other measures such as creativity. You may need to consider whether to admit studies where several criterion measures are all used separately (thus perhaps overweighting the particular study from which they are drawn) or studies where several criteria measures in a study are combined.

Locating the Studies

The major constructs and limitations you impose on the meta-analysis in the problem statement will need to be translated into key words for electronic searches of the literature repositories, such as the Educational Resources Information Center (ERIC), *Dissertation Abstracts International,* and *Psychological Abstracts.* You can then use references from the studies found in electronic searches to find still other studies. The objective is to make a valiant attempt to find the entire body of literature extant to summarize all the available data bearing on a problem. If the ERIC search yields 5,000 articles and reports, you will need to reduce the definition of the problem to a more manageable size. Conversely, if only four or five studies are found, you will need to expand the problem definition.

Examining the Studies

Next, you examine the studies found. Here you will consider whether the studies are experimental or nonexperimental and whether they describe the subjects, the treatment conditions, and the criteria variables in sufficient detail that you can include them in the analysis. Perhaps even more important in this era of abbreviated reporting, you will need to know the means, standard deviations, and numbers of subjects in the various groups reported, or be able to calculate them from the analyses reported. Many studies have had to be excluded from a meta-analysis simply because one of these vital facts is not available in the study report or from the investigator. You will also need to find sufficient studies using roughly the same treatment conditions and criteria variables to make their combination in a meta-analysis worthwhile. Finally, you should consider the possibility that while a number of studies with statistically significant results have been published, perhaps there are even more studies with statistically nonsignificant results that sit in investigators' file drawers unpublished. (This is called the *file drawer* problem, which generally has been found not to be a problem.)

Coding the Studies

Having selected the acceptable studies for a problem (or redefined the problem to parallel the available studies), you code and record the studies' various conditions, such as type of experimental condition, length of the treatment, types of criteria, types of subjects, decade in which the study was done, and, of course, the means of the various experimental and control groups, their standard deviations, and numbers of subjects in each. These data should be reported in the research and should not be a further problem. The standard deviations may require some further development from those originally reported for the statistical tests to obtain a better indication of the true variability in the population, so crucial to determining the true effect size. [For the past 60 to 70 years, seemingly the whole thrust of statistical analyses in psychology and education has been to assuage the great god of statistical significance with larger t's and F's. Thus several major strategies in statistical analyses are all designed to reduce the standard deviation of the natural variability of the samples (which we want for meta-analysis) to a smaller standard deviation (or variance, or the mean square) used as the error term. Some of these statistical analysis strategies are analyses of covariance, restriction in the range of the samples via blocking, and, of course, the use of multivariate treatment analyses where the variance ascribable to each of the several treatments and all of their interactions is removed from the overall variance; and thus that remaining for the mean square (or standard deviation) used for the error term is reduced, increasing the chances of obtaining statistical significance for the main effect or treatment sources of variance.]

More explicitly for those wishing to do a meta-analysis, in order to obtain the natural individual differences indicator (the unreduced standard deviation in a sample) it is necessary to put all the sources of variance removed in an analysis back into the mean square used for the error term! In a standard analysis of variance this is fortunately not difficult. You can simply add all the sums of squares used for the error term and degrees of freedom *not* attributable to the treatment variable under consideration, and add them to the sums of squares, and also do the same for the degrees of freedom for the error term. You can then divide the totaled sums of squares by the new totaled degrees of freedom to obtain a new mean square. The square root of that mean square is the natural standard deviation of that sample of subjects. For analyses of covariance you use only the criterion variable and, in addition to the above, include all the covariance term sums of squares. When these data are not readily available, rather than exclude the study it is sometimes possible to reconstruct, from the statistical analyses given, what the means, standard deviations, and numbers of subjects should be. This usually requires the skills of a rather sophisticated user of statistics and a number of formulas found, among other places, in Glass, McGaw, and Smith (1981, Chapter 5); McGaw and Glass (1980); and Smith and colleagues (1980, Appendix 7).

Once you have obtained the means and standard deviations it is a simple matter to calculate the effect sizes, using the formula given above. This effect size is then entered in the meta-analysis for the particular study for which it is calculated.

The next entries for the studies are the codings for the characteristics of the studies. Did the study use particular types of criteria variables, such as personality tests, achievement tests (and in what subject-matter areas), creativity measures, other cognitive measures, locally developed measures, or standardized measures? Also, the various types of treatment given can be coded within:

General classification, for example, acceleration
    Radical or nonradical
    Early or late in the educational program
    Early entrance into college
Methods of grouping
Length of treatment
Subject matter
Types of subjects
    Highly gifted
    Gifted

Well above average
Male/female
Age of the subjects
Religious affiliation
Ethnic heritage
Country of origin of the study, and so forth

All of these classifications and subsequent coding should have theoretical relevance and, of course, have descriptions available from the research reports. As a strategy, it is better to overclassify into a smaller number of categories rather than use larger groupings. In meta-analysis we can statistically test for differences among the coding classifications and, if there are no differences, combine the groupings. However, the opposite is not easily possible, that is, recoding large groups into smaller coded groups, without going back and rereading all the studies.

Finally, you can code across studies for interesting results. For instance, the results may systematically shift by the decade in which the study was done, by the particular university or investigator, by whether the studies were published or unpublished, by the particular criterion measure used, or by whether the research design was a true or quasi-experiment. These across-studies analyses can be useful in ruling out possible artifacts of a particular situation, allowing more studies to be combined for more definitive results. The great contribution of ruling out the alternative hypothesis of particular research artifacts is to allow the substantive theories developed to be more general, and thus far more powerful, in their explanations.

A more general explanation is the goal of research. When all the available data bearing on a topic are combined and examined for general explanations, relationships, and possible artifacts of methods, conditions, subjects, or criteria, you can offer more general explanations of the results. Also, you can ask more explicit further questions as the result of these comprehensive data examinations and recognize gaps in the literature and data. Meta-analysis is a major paradigm shift in how researchers interpret data, and the results of meta-analysis need to be read and understood by all scholars in the field.

META-ANALYSIS IN GIFTED AND TALENTED EDUCATION

There have been one general summary and at least five meta-analyses of the experimental literature in gifted/talented education. Birch in 1962 and Birch, Tisdall, and Barney in 1964 reported a federally supported

Cooperative Research demonstration project on the efficacy for gifted children of early entrance to school. They noted at the time that further research on early entrance was unnecessary because the results of extensive prior research were so favorable to this educational accommodation for gifted children. The major purpose of the funded demonstration project more than 25 years ago was to publicize this clearly useful accommodation among educators! More accessible now in the literature, however, is the review of 21 early admissions of the gifted to elementary school by Proctor, Black, and Feldhusen (1986). These studies, dating back to 1928 and 1929, are almost unanimous in their support of selective early entrance of gifted children.

For instance, Proctor and colleagues report that in the area of academic achievement, 16 of the 17 studies examining this dimension indicated that the early entrants equaled or surpassed their classmates. In the realm of social/emotional adjustment the majority of the 17 studies investigating this realm generally indicated no significant differences. Of the 7 studies reporting physical ratings in general, there were no significant differences between the early entrants and their peers. In the 4 longitudinal studies reviewed, early-admission children excelled academically, received more honors, were more likely to be admitted to college, had strong positive self-concepts, and participated in a wide range of extracurricular activities.

While this literature review of early admission of gifted children was not a meta-analysis, it can be considered in light of what is known about the results of meta-analysis in general. First, the average sample size of eight of the studies was 39 and ranged from 11 to 89 subjects. These are typical gifted research sample sizes. Second, many of the results reported *no significant differences*. Third, most of the directions of the *no significant difference* results stated are in the direction of being favorable to the gifted students.

Given what is far more apparent from the study of meta-analysis as a research integration method, it is now clear that early admission of carefully selected gifted children is an exceptionally powerful and valuable educational accommodation for these children. From the meta-analysis literature we now know that research with these sample sizes on a study-by-study basis generally is inconclusive, for example, shows statistically *no significant difference* even when the treatment effect is rather large. Next, we know that there are *conflicts* in the literature, that results fluctuate from study to study and can even be negative, even while the overall effect is clearly positive. Thus to obtain such favorable results from the 21 studies is a clear-cut sign that early admission of gifted children is of overwhelming advantage educationally. The tragedy is that nearly 30 years after the point at which Birch felt that no more research needed to be done, the practice of early admission is still not widespread in gifted education.

In this older literature (and even some of the more recent research), a number of the studies *matched* gifted students with their peers or age mates on mental age or IQ. We have known for some 50 years that, given the necessarily imprecise measurements available to us in educational and psychological research, matching of unequal groups of students (as gifted samples often will be) will inevitably lead to regression toward the mean, thus making the research results harder to interpret accurately. [See Asher (1976) for a more thorough discussion of this problem.] The results of these matched samples involving gifted students will often be in a direction detrimental to the gifted students. Thus the research outcomes still favorable to the gifted samples even more strongly suggest that the practice of early admission of selected gifted students is exceptionally advantageous to them.

Rose and Lin (1984), in a meta-analysis of the results of 46 long-term creativity training programs, found that "most of these programs moderately improve verbal creativity and that they have a strong impact on verbal originality" (p. 21). Further, they found that "generally verbal creativity is more affected by these programs than figural creativity" (p. 21) and that "the overall results . . . suggest that training does affect creativity" (p. 22). Rose and Lin noted the problems of the results of prior literature reviews by Parnes and Brunelli (1967), Torrance (1972), and Mansfield, Busse, and Krepelka (1978) in terms of research methodology, test validity, and the construct of creativity, which also had been made by earlier critics. Rose and Lin then noted that, in addition, "reviewers tend to compare the number of significant findings against the number of nonsignificant findings. A major difficulty with this approach lies in the inherent problems of inferential research—that a Type I or Type II [statistical] error was made" (p. 12). They further noted that ordinary statistical analyses do "not tell us how powerful the effect of the treatment was on subjects" (p. 12). In essence, Rose and Lin noted the general problems of research methodology, measurement validity, and statistical analyses inherent in the usual research study by a single-study approach to a literature review and the particular problem of attempting to summarize the results of statistical analyses of a series of single studies on a one-by-one basis.

Kulik and Kulik (1982) summarized 14 studies of gifted students as a part of a meta-analysis of 52 studies of ability groupings. Later, Kulik and Kulik (1984) studied the effects of accelerated instruction on students. Finally, Kulik and Kulik (1987, 1990) studied homogeneous grouping.

In the first meta-analysis, Kulik and Kulik (1982) reported an effect size of .33 with the high-ability secondary students in honors classes. For the 26 studies of elementary and secondary students in the second Kulik and Kulik (1984) study, there were two major findings. First, talented students accelerated into higher grades performed as well as the older, talented students already in those grades. Second, talented accelerates in the subjects in which they were accelerated were about a year ahead of talented, same-age nonaccelerates. In the latest Kulik and Kulik studies (1987, 1991), which were primarily concerned with within-class and between-class homogeneous grouping, they also developed effect sizes by ability levels, especially for talented students. They found that for between-class groupings for talented students placed in special classes, the average effect size from these 25 studies was .33. (It should be noted that the effect size range over all 25 studies was from −.27 to +1.25, which should give pause to anyone attempting to generalize from one or a few studies. The variation of results simply due to sampling variation alone is enormous.) For within-class grouping especially designed for talented students, the average effect size was .62.

AN EXAMPLE OF A META-ANALYSIS

From seeing the results of the meta-analysis studies on ability grouping, acceleration, creativity training, as well as the early-entrance research summary, all showing positive effects for gifted students, our interest was drawn to a meta-analysis of the most common accommodation of instruction for gifted students, enrichment pull-out programs, an accommodation not studied by Kulik and Kulik or Rose and Lin. (I use the plural *our* because most of the actual work in this research project was done by Vicki Vaughn, a graduate student at Purdue in an independent study course that I offered.) We believe that it would also be useful to document—as had the Kuliks, Rose and Lin, Birch, and Proctor and colleagues for other aspects of gifted instruction and educational accommodations—the effect sizes of this widely used educational method.

Our first task was to search the literature for all experimental studies. We wanted experimental studies, because we wanted the value of the cause-and-effect relationships that can be inferred from true and quasi-experiments. An initial visual ERIC search was made using search terms such as *ability grouping, cluster grouping, mentoring, advanced placement classes, enrichment programs, pull-out, revolving door, advanced courses, summer programs,* and *gifted* to see generally what was available within these terms that would yield experimental studies for the gifted with quantified criteria.

Following this trial search a more specific ERIC search was made using such terms as *pull-out, enrichment, three-stage-triad, triad,* and *PACE.* To these results were added ERIC search materials from Reva Jenkins-Friedman (for which we thank her) and a visual search of *Dissertation Abstracts.* Experts in the field (in addition to Jenkins-Friedman) were consulted for any studies they could remember from their experience in the field of gifted education. John Feldhusen and Joseph Renzulli were both helpful.

Next, the references in known studies of pull-out programs and enrichment were reviewed for cues to prior studies. A careful search was made of the resources of the Shared Information Services for Gifted and Talented, a library and curriculum resource center at Purdue University supported by the state of Indiana. We wanted a fairly large number of experimental studies to obtain the universe of reported studies in pull-out enrichment programs. Kulik and Kulik (1982) had 14 studies; Kulik and Kulik (1984) had 85 studies, 40 at the elementary level and 45 at the secondary level; Kulik and Kulik (1987) had 101 reports. Certainly, for probably this most used method of adapting instruction to gifted students, we would find at least as many studies and could use a subset as an example for this chapter to illustrate the relatively simple arithmetical processes used to develop the powerful conclusions about educational programs derived from meta-analyses.

Vaughn pursued many leads. The contributions of her work partially fill an important gap in the literature on gifted programs. However, one of the truly important outcomes of research is finding, not what you carefully spell out in your dissertation and federal research proposals, but what the condition of your particular part of the gifted research world really is like. She was able to find only five experimental studies of pull-out enrichment programs (Aldrich & Mills, 1989; Beckwith, 1982; Carter, 1986; Kolloff, 1983; Nielsen, 1984). Five studies are really not sufficient to illustrate meta-analysis. However, the results forcefully brought to our attention the need to do more experimental research in the most widely used educational method.

However, for educational purposes in how to do a meta-analysis, we went through the calculations. Nielsen (1984) had two groups on which she reported, Grades 7–8 and Grades 3–6. In Grades 7–8 she reported the data in Table 11.1 for her enrichment experiment, using the Cornell Critical Thinking Test as the criterion variable.

The effect size difference between the gains of the experimental and control groups is relatively simple to calculate:

TABLE 11.1   Nielsen's Grades 7-8 Critical Thinking Test Data

Group	n	Pretest X	Pretest SD	Posttest X	Posttest SD
Experimental	16	50.56	4.13	53.63	5.55
Control	6	50.50	4.93	51.00	2.76

(Experimental Posttest − Pretest) − (Control Posttest − Pretest) =
(53.63 − 50.56) − (51.00 − 50.50) = 3.07 − .50 = 2.57

To obtain the combined standard deviation is slightly more complicated, requiring each of the two posttest standard deviations (5.55 and 2.76) to be squared and multiplied by their group size minus 1, before being combined and then divided by the combined group sizes minus 2. Then the square root of that dividend is taken (see Figure 11.1 for calculations). Finally, to obtain the effect size the difference between the means divided by the combined standard deviation is calculated. The effect size is equal to 2.57/5.00 = .51. For Nielsen's Grades 3–6 we used the same process to obtain an effect size of .77.

Kolloff (1983) had already reported the effect sizes in her thesis for both Figural Originality (.26) and Verbal Originality (.42). Now our concern is whether to use both or to combine the two. If we use both, we essentially double the weighting of Kolloff's research in the meta-analysis, so we examined the relationship between these two criterion variables. Kolloff used the Wallach-Kogan Instrument and in her thorough reporting style also reported the correlations between the two variables (Kolloff, 1983, p. 136) as $r = .54$. Earlier she had reported the reliabilities of the variables for all but two of the ten subtest coefficients as exceeding .80. However, Kolloff divided each of the five subsets of the Wallach-Kogan into two parallel forms (to obtain the ten subtests) using a table of random numbers to assign the items in each subset. This essentially reduces the reliability of each subtest and the Spearman-Brown Prophecy Formula can

FIGURE 11.1   Standard deviation calculation for Nielsen's Grades 7 and 8 data

$$(5.55^2 \times 15) = (2.76^2 \times 5) = 462.04 + 38.09 \ = \ 500.18$$
$$500.18 + 20 \ = \ 25.01$$
$$\sqrt{25.01} \ = \ 5.00$$

FIGURE 11.2 Calculation of half-test reliabilities using the Spearman-Brown prophecy formula

$$r_{kk} = \frac{K(r_{ii})}{1 - (K - 1)\,r_{ii}} = \frac{(.50)(.80)}{1 - (.50 - 1)(.80)} = \frac{.40}{1 - (-.50)(.80)}$$

$$= \frac{.40}{1 - .40} = \frac{.40}{.60} = .66$$

easily be used to estimate these half-test reliabilities using a reliability of .80 as an estimate of the starting reliability and $K = .50$ (see Figure 11.2).

Further, there is a marked restriction of range of talent because only students scoring at or above the 85th percentile on the Iowa Test of Basic Skills in reading or mathematics were selected for the initial pool. Then these high-achieving students were rated by their teachers on three of the Renzulli scales, one of which was Creativity Characteristics. In addition, some students achieving at least a grade level above their grade were added to the pool on the basis of a checklist of creative characteristics. These restrictions of range also reduce the reliabilities. Clearly, reliabilities of .66 on each of the originality scales could be an upper estimate for this population. With a correlation of .54 between them, this correlation is approaching the upper limit of what it can be, given the reliabilities; $r_{12} \leq \sqrt{r_{11} \times r_{22}}$, the estimated maximum correlation, would yield $r_{12} \leq \sqrt{.66 \times .66} = .66$. This conclusion is confirmed by the fact that Kolloff did a multivariate analysis of variance of her results and found only a single variable, although she also analyzed five criterion variables as well. Thus we established a rationale for using a single effect size from the Kolloff study.

Next, we wanted to see if the results of Nielsen's two groups, Grades 7–8 and Grades 3–6, differed. Since only two groups were involved, we could do this analysis in either of two ways: (1) in general to see if all the results are homogeneous, with an H test or (2) simply do a chi-square test of possible differences between the means. (Here the results for two groups will be identical. If more than two studies are used, the H test would be done first. If the results are heterogeneous, then additional explorations for differences within the group should be done using the chi-square test.)

For the H test of homogeneity and for the chi-square test, a simple table using the means, d's (effect size), the n of the experimental group, and the n of the control group needs to be developed. Then, four more variables

FIGURE 11.3 *H* test of homogeneity

$$\tilde{n} = \frac{(n_c)(n_e)}{n_c + n_e} \qquad w = \cfrac{1}{\cfrac{1}{\tilde{n}} + \cfrac{d^2}{2(n_c + n_e)}}$$

$$dw = \text{Effect Size} = d \text{ times } w$$

$$d^2w = dw \text{ times } d \qquad H = \Sigma\Sigma\, d^2w - \frac{(\Sigma\Sigma\, dw)^2}{\Sigma\Sigma\, w}$$

---

are readily calculated, $\tilde{n}$, w, dw, and d^2w as shown in Figure 11.3. [H is a chi-square statistic with degrees of freedom equal to the number of studies minus 1. When $n_c + n_e = 22$, the correction for a small n would be .96, not enough to bother with (Hedges & Olkin, 1985, p. 80).] For Nielsen's two groups the data are as shown in Figure 11.4.

An H test of .19 with 1 degree of freedom is not statistically significant. Thus, the effect size results of the two studies are not different, and we can conclude that the two enrichment treatments are equally effective over the elementary and the junior high levels.

Alternatively, to directly test the possible differences between the effect sizes of the two groups (unnecessary here because of the homogeneous results but done here for illustrative purposes), we proceeded with a chi-square test as shown in Figure 11.5. (This result differs from the prior result of .19 only by rounding errors.)

What we have demonstrated is a method to determine more rigorously whether or not results across experiments are the same or different. In this

FIGURE 11.4 Nielsen meta-analysis data preparation and *H* test of homogeneity

---

Grades	n_e	n_c	d	$\tilde{n}$	w	dw	d^2w
7 - 8	16	6	.51	4.36	4.26	2.17	1.11
3 - 6	24	14	.77	8.84	8.27	6.38	4.91

$$H = 6.02 - \frac{(8.55)^2}{12.53} = \frac{73.10}{12.53} = 6.02 - 5.83 = .19$$

FIGURE 11.5   Chi-square test of differences between Nielsen's two groups

$$\text{Chi square (1 df)} = \frac{(\Sigma\, d_1 w_1)^2}{\Sigma\, w_1} + \frac{(\Sigma\, d_2 w_2)^2}{\Sigma\, w_2} - \frac{(\Sigma\Sigma\, d_t w_t)^2}{\Sigma\Sigma\, w_t}$$

$$= \frac{(2.17)^2}{4.26} + \frac{(6.38)^2}{8.27} - \frac{(8.55)^2}{12.53}$$

$$= 1.11 + 4.92 - 5.83$$

$$= .20$$

case we can now declare that Nielsen's pull-out enrichment programs worked as well in the elementary grades as they did in junior high school.

Further, we suggest that the actual arithmetic of the meta-analysis process is relatively straightforward and no more complicated than the usual analyses found in introductory statistics courses. However, we point out that attempting to obtain the means for each group, numbers of subjects in each group, and the overall sample standard deviation (unreduced by other treatment and interaction sums of squares, blocking variables, matching, covariances, etc.) can be a major exercise in reverse statistical analysis if these data are not reported directly. The decisions about which of several subtest criterion variables to choose and the degrees of interrelationship among them as influenced by the reliabilities of the subtest variables, and especially restrictions of range of talent in gifted samples, are also exercises in psychometric analyses. However, the breadth of results and resulting general theory are well worth the effort.

More important to users of research in gifted education is the ability to understand the importance of meta-analyses, which are *the* preferred method of integration of the results of the experimental research in gifted and talented education.

Fortunately Kulik and Kulik, in their continuing integration of the experimental research in homogeneous grouping, have always used level of ability as a coding variable, and they have shown beyond any reasonable doubt that for high levels of talent, when instruction has been adapted to these classes, homogeneous grouping clearly produces major gains in achievement. Their capping study integrating the results of some 101 experiments clearly demonstrate this (Kulik & Kulik, 1987). This is true of elementary and secondary classes, separate full-time classes for the gifted, and within-class groupings of gifted students. Thus a major portion of the work of grouping gifted students for instructional purposes has been done for us. Their prior work (Kulik & Kulik, 1984) also clearly demonstrates that acceleration works. Birch's (1962) and Proctor and colleagues' (1986) summaries demonstrate that early entrance works. Rose and Lin's meta-analysis clearly shows the effectiveness of instruction in gifted samples for creativity.

What remains to be done, certainly, is more experimental work on the effects of pull-out enrichment programs for the gifted and, ultimately, a meta-analysis of these experiments. A start on this meta-analysis—a search of the literature and communications with researchers in gifted education—has been begun by Vaughn (1989). Her initial effort may trigger the memories of those in the field and perhaps lead to the discovery of other experimental studies of enrichment for the gifted, or its variants. More directly, it is hoped that the discovery of this paucity of experiments in this central adaptive procedure for gifted students will encourage more graduate students (and their professors) to do more experimental research in pull-out, enrichment programs for the gifted.

REFERENCES

Aldrich, P. M., & Mills, C. J. (1989). A special program for highly able rural youth in grades five and six. *Gifted Child Quarterly, 33*(1), 11–14.

Asher, J. W. (1976). *Educational research and evaluation methods.* Boston: Little, Brown.

Asher, J. W. (1986). Conducting research with meta-analysis: A new direction for gifted education. *Gifted Child Quarterly, 30,* 7–9.

Beckwith, A. H. (1982). Use of the Ross test as an assessment measure in programs for the gifted and a comparison study of the Ross test to individually administered intelligence tests. *Journal for the Education of the Gifted, 5,* 127–140.

Birch, J. W. (1962). The effectiveness and feasibility of early admission to school for mentally advanced children. (ERIC Document Reproduction Service No. ED 00 1336).

Birch, J. W., Tisdall, W. J., & Barney, W. D. (1964). Early admission of able children to school. *School Life, 47,* 7–8.

Carter, K. R. (1986). A cognitive study to evaluate curriculum for the gifted. *Journal for the Education of the Gifted, 1,* 41–55.

Eysenck, H. J. (1978). An exercise in mega-silliness. *American Psychologist, 33,* 517.

Glass, G. V. (1976). Primary, secondary, and meta-analysis of research. *Educational Researcher, 6,* 3–8.

Glass, G. V., McGaw, B., & Smith, M. L. (1981). *Meta-analysis in social research.* Beverly Hills, CA: Sage.

Hedges, L. (1986). Issues in meta-analysis. In E. S. Rothkopf (Ed.), *Review of Educational Research: Vol. 13* (pp. 353–98). Washington, DC: American Educational Research Association.

Hedges, L., & Olkin, I. (1985). *Statistical methods for meta-analysis.* Orlando, FL: Academic Press.

Hillocks, G. (1986). *Research on written composition.* Urbana, IL: National Conference on Research in English.

Hunter, J. E., Schmidt, F. L., & Jackson, G. B. (1982). *Meta-analysis: Cumulating findings across research.* Beverly Hills, CA: Sage.

Kolloff, M. B. (1983). *The effects of an enrichment program on the self-concepts and creative thinking abilities of gifted and creative elementary students.* Unpublished doctoral dissertation, Purdue University, West Lafayette, IN.

Kulik, C. C., & Kulik, J. A. (1982). Effects of ability grouping on secondary school students: A meta-analysis of evaluation findings. *American Educational Research Journal, 19,* 415–428.

Kulik, C. C., & Kulik, J. A. (1984). Effects of accelerated instruction on students. *Review of Educational Research, 54,* 409–425.

Kulik, J. A., & Kulik, C. C. (1987). Effects of ability grouping on student achievement. *Equity & Excellence, 23*(1–2), 22–30.

Kulik, J. A., & Kulik, C. C. (1991). Ability grouping and gifted students. In N. Colangelo & G. A. Davis (Eds.), *Handbook of Gifted Education.* Boston: Allyn & Bacon.

Lauer, J. M., & Asher, J. W. (1988). Meta analysis. *Composition research: Empirical designs* (pp. 204–220). New York: Oxford.

McGaw, B., & Glass, G. V. (1980). Choice of the metric for effect size in meta-analysis. *American Educational Research Journal, 17,* 325–337.

Mansfield, R. S., Busse, T. V., & Krepelka, E. J. (1978). The effectiveness of creativity training. *Review of Educational Research, 48,* 517–536.

Nielsen, M. E. (1984). *Evaluation of a rural gifted program: Assessment of attitudes, self-concepts, and critical skills of high-ability students in grades 3 through 5.* Unpublished doctoral dissertation, Purdue University, West Lafayette, IN.

Parnes, S. J., & Brunelli, E. A. (1967). The literature of creativity (Part 1). *Journal of Creative Behavior, 1,* 52–109.

Proctor, T. B., Black, K. N., & Feldhusen, J. F. (1986). Early admission of selected children to elementary school: A review of the research literature. *Journal of Educational Research, 80*(2), 70–76.

Rose, L. A., & Lin, H. T. (1984). Meta-analysis of long-term creative programs. *Journal of Creative Behavior, 18*(1), 11–22.

Slavin, R. E. (1986). Best evidence synthesis: An alternative to meta-analytic and traditional reviews. *Educational Researcher, 15,* 5–11.

Slavin, R. E., & Karweit, N. (1984). *Within-class ability grouping and student achievement.* Paper presented at the annual meeting of the American Educational Research Association, New Orleans, LA.

Smith, M. L., Glass, G. V., & Miller, T. I. (1980). *The benefits of psychotherapy.* Baltimore: Johns Hopkins University Press.

Torrance, E. P. (1972). Can we teach children to think creatively? *Journal of Creative Behavior, 6,* 114–143.

Vaughn, V. L. (1989). A meta-analysis of pull-out programs in gifted education. Unpublished research prepared for William Asher, Purdue University, West Lafayette, IN.

Vaughn, V. L., Feldhusen, J. F., & Asher, W. (in press). Meta-analysis and review of research on pull-out programs in gifted education. *Gifted Child Quarterly.*

PART III

PROGRAM EVALUATION

CHAPTER 12

EVALUATION OF GIFTED PROGRAMS

Kyle R. Carter

The trend toward educational accountability has made program evaluation an essential component for all gifted programs. Program coordinators must routinely convince decision makers that their gifted programs
are necessary and make a difference. This is especially true in times of
fiscal recession when school boards are required to trim the budget.

Since gifted and talented programs are sometimes regarded as educational frills by board members, they become targets of budget cutting
(Mitchell, 1988). Those recommending the elimination of gifted programs typically believe the gifted can reach their potential without special help. These beliefs run counter to the Marland Report (1972), which
issued this warning:

> Research has confirmed that many talented children perform far below their
> intellectual potential. We are increasingly being stripped of the comfortable
> notion that a bright mind will make its own way. Intellectual and creative
> talent cannot survive educational neglect and apathy. (p. 9)

In the face of this budget cutting, proponents of gifted education are
often required to demonstrate that gifted children need differentiated
education via gifted programs in order to reach their potential.

Although educational accountability/fiscal responsibility is a com-
pelling reason to promote educational evaluation, there is also a basic
pedagogical reason to advocate routine evaluation of gifted programs.
Coordinators of gifted programs should be concerned with the effectiveness of the educational components that comprise the gifted program:

Portions of Chapter 12 are based on the following articles by Kyle R. Carter: "Evaluation
design: Issues confronting evaluators of gifted programs," *Gifted Child Quarterly*, 30, 88–92;
"Measuring program outcomes: Suggestions to evaluators of gifted programs," *Illinois Council
for the Gifted Journal*, 5, 38–40.

Are the components working as planned? Are all components in place or have some been omitted? Can the components be improved? Implementation of a gifted program requires considerable time, and many corrections and modifications will be necessary before the program runs smoothly and begins to offer experiences that impact student learning. There will be false starts, bugs to work out, ideas that fail and some that succeed. Unless program coordinators routinely monitor the program components and make corrections, the gifted program will lack consistency and direction. Student outcomes, if any, will probably have very little relationship to the goals and objectives that were created in response to a perceived need.

We, as educators, could learn a lesson from industry. For example, managers of manufacturing plants routinely perform a number of evaluation tasks to insure that production is acceptable: they routinely inspect product quality, compare production costs from month to month, count the number of products assembled daily, and monitor the number of days that workers are absent. If any of these measures exceed preestablished standards, steps are taken to correct the problem. Admittedly, the outcomes of gifted programs are more abstract than those in manufacturing; however, the lessons are the same. You must:

1. Know what you are trying to produce
2. Monitor the processes that are used to produce the product
3. Evaluate the product
4. Make corrections if the product does not meet expectations

WHAT IS PROGRAM EVALUATION?

Educational evaluation can take on different forms depending on the questions asked. For example, sponsors of evaluations of gifted programs might ask one or more of the following questions: Who should be served by the program? Is the curriculum consistent with the goals and objectives of gifted education? Do students become more creative as a result of the program? Is the program worth the cost? These questions represent different types of evaluations. Respectively, they are:

1. Needs assessment
2. Process evaluation
3. Outcome evaluation
4. Evaluation of cost-effectiveness

Although each of these evaluations has different goals, they have one characteristic in common. Each seeks to gather information to help people make decisions. This commonality is why Cronbach (1963) defined educational evaluation as the process of collecting information to make decisions about educational programs. Therefore the purpose of any evaluation is to gather information for decision making. The major difference between the various types of evaluations is related to the stage of program development and the philosophy guiding the evaluation. For example, a needs assessment is conducted prior to program implementation to determine the program goals and objectives, while a process evaluation occurs after the program has begun to determine whether the program elements have been implemented as planned.

Evaluations may also differ in terms of the philosophies or motivations behind them. Decision makers may order an evaluation because they want to determine whether an established program should continue to exist, or they may want to monitor a program and use the feedback to improve the program. Scriven (1967) labeled these types of program evaluations as summative and formative. Summative evaluations are characterized by assessment of the outcomes of established programs to determine their overall effectiveness. Presumably, the results of the evaluation are then used to determine whether or not the program will continue to exist. On the other hand, formative evaluations are conducted to monitor new programs. Cronbach (1982) expanded the concept of formative evaluation to include the measurement of program outcomes for the purpose of program improvement. The overriding assumption of Cronbach's conception of formative evaluation is that the program addresses a significant social need and will continue to exist. As Cronbach (1982) points out, "to cut off a program without substituting an alternative is to abandon the commitment to alleviate the social problem in question" (p. 13).

EVALUATION VERSUS RESEARCH

No definition of program evaluation would be complete without indicating the differences between evaluation and research. Popham (1988) distinguishes between evaluation and research on three criteria: focus, generalizability, and philosophy. First, the focus of an evaluation is to gather information that will be helpful in making decisions, whereas researchers use information to draw conclusions about theory. Second, in contrast to researchers, evaluators are not concerned with the generalizability of their results. Evaluators interpret the results as they apply to a specific program, whereas researchers attempt to extend their findings to other phenomena, hoping to discover laws and principles that lead to theory. Finally, in terms of philosophy, evaluations are conducted to determine the worth of some program, whereas research is conducted to discover truth, some higher order of understanding.

As shown by this comparison, evaluations must be viewed differently from the typical research study. Since evaluations are conducted outside the laboratory in the field setting, they must be designed around administrative constraints such as time, money, and logistics. These constraints may restrict the evaluator's ability to manipulate and control variables. Consequently, evaluations in the school setting are not as "tight" as more traditional research studies that occur in the laboratory. However, evaluations are not conducted to establish external validity; that is, the ability to generalize beyond the program setting. Instead, evaluators seek to provide decision makers with information that shows how effective "their" program is in "their" setting.

Evaluation Challenges Unique to Gifted Education

Evaluations of gifted programs are particularly difficult because of factors unique to the gifted. First, the concept of giftedness has many different meanings and interpretations. Second, there is little agreement about the type of program outcomes that should be emphasized and there are very few standardized instruments appropriate to measuring them (Callahan, 1983; Ganopole, 1982). Third, those tests that are available may be subject to the ceiling effect (Stanley, 1976). Fourth, since the best type of evaluation includes a comparison of some kind (Cronbach, 1982), it is often difficult to find an appropriate group to which the performance of gifted children can be compared. Descriptions and recommendations for the first three problems will be described in this section of the chapter. Although the comparison group problem will be described here, approaches for dealing with it will be discussed below in the section on design problems unique to product evaluations.

Conceptions of Giftedness. As Sternberg and Davidson (1986) point out, there are many competing conceptions of giftedness. Included among those most widely known are Renzulli's (1978) three-ring approach, Stanley's (Stanley, Keating, & Fox, 1974) mathematically precocious youth, Sternberg's (1981) componential theory, Gardner's multiple intelligences (1983), and Guilford's structure-of-intellect (SOI) model (1981). Having different conceptions of giftedness does not cause a problem per se for program evaluators. Evaluators can operationalize the concept and develop expected outcomes on the basis of the conception of giftedness that is being served by the program. What is a problem, however, is symbolized by the lack of agreement in the field. Since experts view giftedness differently, we should not be surprised to find the stakeholders (defined as anyone who has an interest in the program) of a program evaluation to have different conceptions of giftedness, as well as different expectations for program outcomes. Lack of consensus about program outcomes may be a common characteristic of all evaluations but is especially true regarding gifted program evaluations, because it is so easy for the stakeholders to have different ideas about who the gifted are and what they should be doing. Even when a single definition such as Renzulli's (1978) has been adopted, individuals may continue to hold to their own beliefs that go counter to the adopted definition. If this occurs, it is very difficult for the evaluator to develop consensus in identifying the evaluation objects and expected outcomes. Therefore, evaluators must make certain that all stakeholders are working from the same frame of reference, have similar expectations, and agree on the nature of the students they are serving.

Program Outcomes. The nature of program outcomes is another characteristic of gifted programs that causes problems for program evaluators. Gifted programs usually have two sets of curricular objectives. The first set reflects the broad program outcomes, for example, increase creativity or promote critical thinking. The second is more narrow and reflects the curriculum; that is, the student will be able to analyze a problem to discover its underlying relationships. Leaders in the field disagree about the importance of specifying specific or broad outcomes for program evaluation.

Gallagher (1979), for example, has encouraged evaluators to focus on broad outcomes rather than specific outcomes for two reasons. First, he believes that we need to spend our energy creating designs to evaluate broad outcomes because the current ones are inadequate. Second, he contends that it has been demonstrated repeatedly that the gifted learn the curriculum. So further evidence of their mastery is unnecessary.

Gallagher is correct in calling for new evaluation designs for investigating broad outcomes. However, it is important to improve evaluation techniques for specific program outcomes because specific program outcomes provide formative evaluation data (Scriven, 1967) that can be used to modify and improve the program. In my opinion, a comprehensive evaluation plan should include designs for continuous assessment of specific outcomes as well as broad outcomes.

Evaluators have typically used two approaches to measure broad program outcomes. The first approach tests program participants and nonparticipants and compares their scores. If the mean of the program group is higher, the evaluator infers the program produced this effect. Since this design lacks control for initial group differences and many other threats to internal validity (see Campbell & Stanley, 1966), the evaluator's conclusion is unjustified.

The other approach employs a pretest/posttest control group design and compares the adjusted posttest scores via analysis of covariance (ANCOVA). Since ANCOVA adjusts initial group differences and the control group handles the other important threats to internal validity (maturation, history, etc.), this design seems to be appropriate for measuring the broad program outcomes. However, studies typically find no significant difference or differences of limited practical value. Why? One probable answer to this question is that broad outcomes such as promoting critical thinking or improving self-concept are manifest over a period of years. Evaluators have failed to recognize this trait and have incorporated inadequate time intervals in their designs.

If evaluators are going to measure broad program outcomes effectively, they will have to adopt repeated measures designs (Borg & Gall, 1983). Students need to be tested or observed over a period of years. Ideally, students should be assessed several times prior to admission and during subsequent years while enrolled. In addition, a comparison group of children not enrolled in the program should be included in the design.

Coleman and Fults (1983) used an approximation of this design to assess the impact of a gifted program on self-concept. Children enrolled in a gifted program were categorized into high-IQ and lower-IQ groups and given the Piers-Harris Self-Concept Scale four times over an 18-month period. The data showed a significant increase of scores for high-IQ students, while scores of lower-IQ students declined slightly. Although this design did not incorporate an average ability comparison group and students were not tested prior to the program, it does illustrate the repeated measures design and how it can be used to provide important data.

If evaluators are to assess specific program outcomes, they will have to develop their own achievement tests because there are few standardized tests designed specifically for assessing gifted curricula (Ganopole, 1982). Tests will have to be specific to the gifted curriculum and of appropriate difficulty. Since test construction is time consuming, the process requires a large commitment by program coordinators and teachers—usually a 2- to 3-year period. Teachers would have to attend seminars on test construction, testing principles, item writing, and item analysis. They would develop curricular objectives (if they do not exist already) and write items to measure those objectives. They would administer these items to gifted students and analyze their performance. Over time, the teachers would develop new items and revise the old ones. All items would be stored in a test item file organized by the curricular objectives. Eventually, teachers would have a sufficient pool of items to construct reliable and valid achievement tests over several curricular areas.

Ceiling Effect. The ceiling effect occurs when a test is too easy for the group taking it. The group as a whole scores at the top of the scale with very little variance, and the ability to discriminate between individuals becomes very difficult. To illustrate, imagine giving a ten-item, single-digit addition test to a group of gifted third graders. Most, if not all, would make a perfect score. From these test results it would be impossible to determine differences in math ability.

The ceiling effect is likely to occur for gifted students if they are given a standardized test that has been designed for their age group. This is due to two factors. First, these tests are usually normed on samples purported to be representative of the normal population. Ideally, the standardization sample is very heterogeneous, that is, there is great variability on the construct being measured. Second, test developers design tests so that the test scores of the standardization sample are normally distributed. This is accomplished by selecting items of appropriate difficulty for the standardization sample. Although item difficulties range from easy to hard, most items are of moderate difficulty because this will produce the greatest variance, improve reliability, and promote a normal distribution.

To illustrate, consider the possible consequences of administering the Ross Test of Higher Cognitive Processes to a group of students intellectually superior to the norm group. As reported by Ross and Ross (1979), their norm group was composed of gifted fourth through sixth graders whose mean IQ was 126.13. Although a separate mean IQ was not reported for the sixth-grade group, their individual mean is probably not significantly higher than that of the total group and could be lower.

What would happen if the Ross test were used to measure program outcomes for a group of sixth graders intellectually superior (individual IQs > 140) to the norm group? In a typical pre/post design the test would be given at the beginning of the year and then again at the end of the year. Since the sixth-grade norm group's mean score on the Ross test (78.49; no standard deviation was reported) was relatively close to a perfect score (105), we might expect a group of gifted children with IQs over 140 to approach the test's ceiling. If these gifted students scored at the top of the scale at the beginning of the year, there is little possibility of gain. What is worse, posttest scores might actually regress toward the mean, implying a loss in ability, which is an artifact of measurement error.

One solution to the ceiling effect is to follow the advice of Stanley (1976) and employ out-of-level testing. You would use a test that was standardized on an age group several years older than the gifted. Although you would be unable to use the norms accompanying the test, evaluators would be able to compare pre- and posttest means for gains. Interpretation, of course, would have to be limited because of the threats to internal validity controlled by the design (see Campbell & Stanley, 1966).

Comparison Groups. Program evaluators often assess a program's worth by comparing the performance of program participants and nonparticipants, usually in an alternative program. It should be obvious that fair evaluations depend on comparison groups being as similar as possible to the program participants on variables that could bias the outcome measures. For example, participants and nonparticipants should be of equivalent age, background, and ability. Following this reasoning, gifted nonparticipants would be the most appropriate comparison group for evaluating program outcomes. This requirement poses a real dilemma for program evaluators. How does one find gifted nonparticipants? Splitting the identified gifted into two groups and withholding the program (i.e., treatment) from one group poses ethical problems, and few parents would consent to this practice. Matching, counterbalanced designs and retrospective pretesting are approaches that have been suggested by a number of authors (Callahan, 1983; Carter, 1986; Payne & Brown, 1982). These approaches will not be discussed in this section, but will be presented in detail in the section below on design problems unique to product evaluations. The important point to remember at this time is that gifted evaluations should include relevant comparison groups. Although identifying a suitable comparison group may be difficult, evaluators have approaches that can eliminate this problem from the evaluation design.

Planning and Conducting an Evaluation

At times, decision makers will have clear objectives for the program evaluation. If this is the case, the evaluation team will be told which program objectives to evaluate. At other times decision makers may have general concerns about program effectiveness without specific expectations. During these situations, they will rely on the evaluation team to clarify their concerns and to identify the objects of the evaluation. When this occurs, the evaluator may solicit input from various stakeholders who have an interest in the program. Examples include parents of gifted students, gifted students, teachers of the gifted, principals, board members, and central administrators. The team may suggest targeting one or more of the program elements: definition, philosophy, program evaluation, identification procedures and criteria, program goals and objectives, student goals and objectives, curriculum, personnel, and budget. However, to identify specific elements within these project components, the evaluation team needs specific input from the stakeholders.

Input from Stakeholders. The use of focus groups is an approach that I have used successfully to determine objects for program evaluation. A focus group consists of 5 to 15 stakeholders who share common backgrounds—parents, teachers, students, and so on. The group is asked to respond to several broad, open-ended questions, such as: What aspects of the program are you most concerned about? Before the one- to two-hour session begins, several groundrules, similar to those for brainstorming, are established. Participants are told to (1) express their opinions freely, (2) refrain from evaluating other members' comments, and (3) minimize editorializing. No solution is expected from the group. Instead, the emphasis is on the production of as many ideas as possible. (The reader will note the difference between brainstorming and focus groups at this point. Brainstorming is normally used to solve a specific problem. Focus groups are intended to find one.) The evaluator's job is to record all ideas, preferably in a manner that is observable to the group, enforce the rules, and keep the group focused on the questions. After meeting with all groups, the evaluator synthesizes the responses by organizing them around each question and forming categories for the responses. As shown in Table 12.1, the analysis is helpful in determining areas of common interest. This information can be shared with the decision makers, who, along with the evaluator, can use the information to select objects of the evaluation.

Since most evaluations are limited in some respect by money, time, or personnel, decision makers usually have to make a choice regarding those program objects that are to be a part of the evaluation and those that must wait. Selecting objects is a collaborative effort between the evaluation team and the decision makers. Priorities are determined in relation to the purpose of the evaluation, as well as time and money constraints.

TABLE 12.1   Results of focus group responses by group

What question about the gifted program would you most like to have answered?	FOCUS GROUPS							
	G_1	G_2	G_3	G_4	G_5	G_6	G_7	G_8
Does it promote elitism?	X	X		X	X	X	X	X
Do students learn at greater levels than if they were in the regular classroom?								X
Is it cost effective?	X			X	X	X	X	X
Is the identification system missing anyone?							X	
Do classroom teachers expect more out of the gifted?		X		X	X	X	X	
Are the teachers properly trained?	X		X		X			X
Does participation in the program cause resentment by non-enrolled peers?	X						X	

G_1=Parents of gifted G_5=Teachers of gifted
G_2=Parents of nongifted G_6=Regular classroom teachers
G_3=Gifted students G_7=Principals
G_4=Nongifted students G_8=School board members

When objects have been selected, the evaluation team selects criteria that are suitable for making judgments about the evaluation objects. These criteria must fit within the overall evaluation framework, as determined during the initial meeting with the decision makers. Specifically, evaluators must choose criteria that are reasonable and practical measures of the evaluation objects.

The selection of criteria will determine the approach the evaluation team will follow. If the criteria are outcome-oriented then the evaluation will be more empirical, using a research design that requires data collection and analysis. Experimental, quasi-experimental (see Campbell & Stanley, 1966), and descriptive designs are all possible methods of this process. If criteria are more process-oriented, the evaluator uses a qualitative approach. For example, existing written documents about evaluation objects could be inspected and evaluated against predetermined standards. This process helps answer questions such as: Are the program goals outdated? Does the program have a clearly defined curriculum?

Stufflebeam (1983) identifies four major tasks involved in planning a program evaluation. These include:

1. Defining the charge
2. Formulating a data collection plan
3. Establishing a management plan
4. Developing a plan for reporting the results

Each of these activities will be discussed below.

Defining the Charge. Evaluators have a number of major tasks during this phase of the evaluation that will call on their political savvy, creativity, and insight. They must be able to identify the stakeholders and decision makers and differentiate between them. Stakeholders are individuals who have an interest in the program and may be able to alter the evaluation through their influence, whereas decision makers have control and power. The ideal situation is that the decision makers and stakeholders have similar expectations for the evaluation. If they do not, the evaluator must be aware of the differences and determine how to handle them (one option is to withdraw from the evaluation).

After identifying the stakeholders and decision makers, the evaluator must determine the objects and purpose of the evaluation. The objects are program components such as definition, identification procedures, program goals and objectives, curriculum, and personnel. Since the nature of the data collection techniques depends on the objects chosen, it is essential that the objects be clearly defined to avoid misunderstandings between the evaluator and decision makers later on. For example, if the identification process is the object of the evaluation, the evaluator could develop a number of different approaches depending on the specific questions related to the object: Does the identification process identify minority students? Are the identified gifted performing successfully in the program? Is the process cost-effective? To avoid costly misunderstandings, the evaluator must be certain that all decision makers are defining the objects the same way as the evaluation team.

The purpose of the evaluation will influence the type of evaluation used and may set the climate for the evaluation. For example, a formative evaluation designed for program improvement sets a very different tone than a summative evaluation to determine whether the program is funded next year. Clarifying the purpose at the outset is fundamental to a successful evaluation. Prudent evaluators will make certain that they have agreement on the evaluation's purpose before proceeding to any further planning, because the purpose is prerequisite to further planning: it affects the evaluation design, determines the political climate, identifies objects, and influences logistical arrangements.

Data Collection Plan. The primary task during this step is to identify the major strategy or strategies used to collect the data. The evaluator will review the charge and operationalize the questions being asked about the objects. For example, if the stakeholders want to assess a program outcome related to problem solving, the evaluator will have to propose specific measures of problem solving that, in turn, will define the problem-solving outcome. Frequently, it is at this point that the evaluator determines the true expectations of the stakeholders and decision makers. When presented with a measure of the outcome, their general expectations often become very clear and specific. It is not uncommon for them to reject the measure(s) being proposed. The evaluator must be patient and continue to present alternatives until the decision makers agree that the proposed instrumentation provides appropriate information for judging the outcome that is under study.

The evaluator must also be prepared to develop measures specific to the local evaluation. As pointed out earlier, there are very few standardized tests, surveys, and so on that were designed specifically for the gifted. When this situation occurs, evaluators must plan extra time to develop and field test the instruments.

Since stakeholders and decision makers hold different personal beliefs and preferences, it would be unreasonable to expect that one set of measurement strategies will be universally accepted across gifted programs even when measuring common outcomes. Some stakeholders may believe that outcomes should be measured by tests, others may prefer observations, some may insist on large-scale studies involving a large sample, whereas others may prefer a case study approach. The evaluator will have to keep these variables in mind when proposing measurement strategies. The type of measurement device is also influenced by other factors, such as cost, time, and logistical support. All of these factors must be considered when developing a data collection plan such as the one shown in Table 12.2.

Management Plan. The management plan includes all the logistical arrangements for the evaluation study. The plan should include times, dates, and responsibilities of key personnel for all activities. Since the overall functioning of the evaluation project depends on the financial support, the management plan should also include a detailed budget.

TABLE 12.2: Sample Data Collection Plan

Research Questions About the Gifted Program

1. Why does gifted program enrollment decline from elementary to high school?
   a. Are dropouts encouaged to continue?
   b. Are new students informed about the program?
   c. Is there an exit interview? What effect does it have?
2. Are dropouts having their educational needs met elsewhere?
3. How does membership in the gifted program impact students' social relationships with peers or teachers?

Overview

Q #	Target Group	Sampling	Methodology	Comments
1-2	Student who dropout after June 1983 and their parents; categorized by level: elementary, middle, etc.	Random sample from each level	Structured interview with both parents and children; parents may be interviewed by phone, students in person	Secure parental permission and inform parents about telephone interview; use interns and parent groups to interview
3	a. PEAK students—all levels	a. Entire population	a. Survey	a. Administer survey/interview (use interns and parents) at school
	b. Parents of PEAK students—all levels	b. Random sample by level	b. Structured interview	b. Keep records of respondents and send follow-up
	c. Classroom teachers—all levels	c. Entire population?	c. Survey	c. Keep records of respondents and send follow-up
	d. Regular students—all levels	d. Random sample by level	d. Survey	d. Administer survey to students at school. Pull out from class?

Question 1: Procedures

1. Compile a list of dropouts since June 1983 for each grade; include address, telephone number, and parents' names
2. Compute descriptive statistics on dropout data
3. Determine if random sampling is needed or if all individuals can be interviewed
4. Conduct random samples
5. Write letter of transmittal/permission to parents
6. Develop interview for parents; field test
7. Train interns to conduct interview
8. Administer interview
9. Collect and code data
10. Develop data file

257

Evaluators will do well to summarize all of these elements into a memorandum of agreement that is signed by the client.

Evaluators will find the program evaluation review technique (PERT) a very useful approach for developing a management plan. As shown in Figure 12.1, key tasks are identified to show their time sequence and relationship to other activities in the evaluation. Analysis of the evaluation via PERT (see Borg & Gall, 1983) allows the evaluator to view the entire evaluation, sometimes an overwhelming task, as a series of

FIGURE 12.1   PERT network detailing the initial elements of an evaluation plan to assess outcomes for a junior high school gifted program

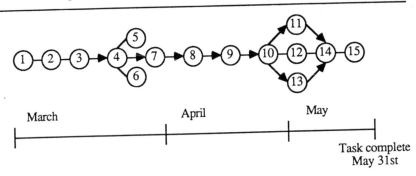

Activity or Procedure

1. Meet with decision makers for input
2. Develop evaluation plan
3. Submit evaluation plan to decision makers for feedback
4. Finalize plan
5. Make logistical arrangements for data gathering, procurement of supplies
6. Develop biographical and educational data form
7. Collect biographical and educational data for the gifted group from school records at target schools
8. Establish data base for subjects
9. Code and enter data into data base
10. Develop and pilot teacher and parent inventories of student independent learning
11. Develop and pilot Student Activity Questionnaire
12. Administer Torrance Tests for Creative Thinking to enriched language classes and gifted classes at target schools
13. Develop and pilot teacher and parent inventories of student leadership performance
14. Submit Torrance test for scoring
15. Develop matrix sampling plan for Watson Glaser Critical Thinking test

smaller tasks that occur in sequence. Use of this approach enables the evaluator to set priorities, make plans, and accomplish tasks in the proper order. In addition, PERT enables the evaluator to identify hidden costs that are a part of the evaluation.

Reporting the Results. The type of report should be determined at the time of the charge. The evaluator must determine whether the decision makers require a written report, oral report, or both. The report should include a description of the charge, the objects of the evaluation, the strategies used to measure them, the results, and recommendations. In addition, most decision makers appreciate an executive summary that focuses on each of these elements. Depending on the wishes of the decision makers, the report may include appendixes of important written documentation that was a part of the evaluation, such as sample instruments, instructions, and letters.

The amount of detail and level of sophistication contained in the report depend on the target audience. Although the evaluator may be able to get some direction by discussing the content with the decision makers, evaluators will have to use their own judgment. The important point to remember is that the decision makers and stakeholders are most interested in the outcome of the evaluation. The results should be easy to find and understand, and recommendations should be clear and useful.

A Model. Evaluators of gifted programs will find the CIPP model by Stufflebeam (1983) to be particularly helpful in planning and conducting program evaluations. This model, shown in Table 12.3, consists of four stages:

1. Context (C)
2. Input (I)
3. Process (P)
4. Product (P)

The labels are descriptive of the functions that occur within each stage. Context refers to the procedures for identifying the target population and program needs. Input involves developing a program plan around the identified needs. Process evaluations check to determine whether the program plan was implemented properly, and product evaluations focus on the intended outcomes that were specified during the input stage.

Stufflebeam's approach describes an ideal model for program development and evaluation. Unfortunately, his approach is different from how most stakeholders view evaluation. Stakeholders often forget that

TABLE 12.3: Four Types of Evaluation

	Context Evaluation	Input Evaluation	Process Evaluation	Product Evaluation
Objective	Define institutional context, identify target population & assess needs; identify opportunities for addressing needs; diagnose problems underlying needs & judge whether proposed objectives are sufficiently responsive to assessed needs	Identify & assess system capabilities, alternative program strategies, procedural designs for implementing the strategies, budgets, & schedules	Identify or predict, in process, defects in the procedural design or its implementation; provide information for the preprogram decisions; record & judge procedural events and activities	Collect descriptions & judgments of outcomes; relate them to objectives & to context, input, & process information; interpret their worth and merit
Method	System analysis, survey, document review, hearings, interviews, diagnostic tests, & the Delphi technique	Inventory & analyze available human & material resources, solution strategies, & procedural designs for relevance, feasibility, & economy; use literature searches, visits to exemplary programs, advocate teams, & pilot trials	Monitor activity's potential procedural barriers & remain alert to unanticipated ones; obtain specified information for program decisions; describe the actual process; continually interact with project staff and observe their activities	Operationally define & measure outcome criteria collect judgments of outcomes form stakeholders; perform both qualitative and quantitative analyses
Relation to decision-making in the change process	Decide upon setting to be served, goals associated with meeting needs or using opportunities, & objectives associated with solving problems (i.e., planning needed changes); provide a basis for judging outcomes	Select resources of support, solution strategies, & procedural design (i.e., for structuring change activities); provide a basis for judging implementation	Implement & refine program design & procedure (i.e., for effecting process control); provide a log of the actual process for later use in interpreting outcomes	Decide whether to continue, terminate, modify, or refocus a change activity; present a clear record of effects (intended & unintended, positive & negative)

Source: Stufflebeam, 1983

evaluators should be involved in needs assessment, program development, and implementation. It has been my experience that most gifted programs develop without a formal analysis of the context or input, and go unmonitored to determine whether the program plan was implemented properly (process evaluation). When decision makers call for evaluation, they usually want to know if the program has been effective. Yet how can an evaluator conduct a fair product evaluation if the program was not developed and implemented around specific needs and plans? A case in point was reported by Carter and Hamilton (1983), who were asked to conduct a product evaluation but found that the program had not been fully developed or implemented—there were no goals or objectives or implementation plan to guide the program. When situations like these arise, it becomes the evaluator's task to work with the decision makers to redefine the evaluation and focus it on the first three stages of Stufflebeam's model.

Space does not permit a detailed description of Stufflebeam's ideas and procedures in this chapter. If you are interested in conducting program evaluations, you would do well to study Stufflebeam's model. It provides detailed procedures and guidelines for conducting evaluations at each of the CIPP stages. In addition, use of the model could lead to the overall improvement of gifted programs because the approach calls for the development of programs in response to real needs, specification of program goals and format, continuous monitoring, and assessment of program outcomes.

DESIGN PROBLEMS UNIQUE TO PRODUCT EVALUATIONS

Issues Confronting Evaluators of Gifted Programs

Two major issues confront evaluators of gifted programs as they design evaluation studies. The first is termed the *comparison group problem* and the second the *control problem*. Each of these situations is discussed below.

The Comparison Group Problem. Before proceeding with the general discussion of this topic, a distinction should be made between comparison and control groups. A control group is a nontreatment group that is formed through random selection, while a comparison group is a nontreatment group that has been selected as an intact group. Since comparison groups are more typical in evaluation designs, this discussion will focus on methods of selecting an appropriate comparison group.

Program outcomes must be judged by comparing the performance of program participants to a meaningful comparison group. Comparison groups should be as similar as possible to the program participants on variables that could bias the outcome measures. For example, participants and nonparticipants should be of equivalent age, background, and ability. Following this reasoning, gifted nonparticipants would be the most appropriate comparison group for evaluating program outcomes. This requirement poses a real dilemma for program evaluators. How do you find gifted nonparticipants? Splitting the identified gifted into two groups and withholding the program (i.e., treatment) from one group poses ethical problems, and few parents would consent to this practice. In a later section several alternatives will be presented that address the ethical and logistical issues of forming comparison groups.

The Control Problem. It is often impossible to determine whether participant outcomes are due to the program or some other variable(s)—a matter of internal validity (Campbell & Stanley, 1966)—unless controls are imposed that, ironically, may create a setting that is atypical of the program. In fact, Snow (1974) argues that true program effects can only be determined when a *representative design* is employed. Snow recommends designs that are representative of the natural environment, because he assumes that experimental manipulation causes the learners to act differently than they would under normal conditions. This situation presents a dilemma for program evaluators. They must seek designs that control extraneous variables but do not disturb the natural setting or violate the school's administrative structure. Based on my experience, there is no such design. That is why evaluators must learn the art of compromise. They must select designs that come closest to meeting the ideal design while accommodating situational constraints and circumstances. Whatever design is chosen, it must enable the evaluator to answer the evaluation questions in the amount of time allotted to the project.

The following sections offer several approaches to handling the comparison group and control problems. I will indicate how others have approached the problem and suggest new alternatives.

Designs and Techniques for the Comparison Group Problem

Matching. Payne and Brown (1982) recognized this problem and described a method for selecting a comparison group from school districts that do not have gifted programs. The aggregate rank similarity method allows the evaluator to rate each district on critical variables and select the district that most closely matches the program's district.

This matching technique provides a viable alternative, but it does present problems. For example, school districts that do not have gifted programs probably have not identified gifted students. It would be up to the evaluator to identify them. In addition, logistics become more formidable since the evaluator now has two school districts to coordinate. Finally, researchers have criticized the matching technique. They argue that matching does not necessarily equate groups. For every set of variables matched, there are many more that are left uncontrolled.

Counterbalanced Designs. Callahan (1983) used the principles of counterbalancing designs to address the control group problem for curriculum evaluation. Her design compared gifted children exposed to a curriculum to gifted children who were not. The comparison was accomplished by dividing the curriculum into units and scheduling a different ordering of curriculum units for a different cluster of classes. Thus, while one cluster received curriculum X, another received curriculum Y. So the cluster exposed to curriculum Y acted as a comparison for the effectiveness of curriculum X, and the cluster exposed to curriculum X served as a comparison for curriculum Y.

Callahan's design is shown in the top half of Table 12.4. Notice that clusters A and B are gifted classes that receive curricular units X and Y at different times during the school year. The evaluation of the curriculum takes place at the end of time 1. (Time 2 is included in the table merely to show that all gifted classes eventually received the curriculum.) In this example, cluster B is the comparison group for curriculum X and cluster A, for curriculum Y. By including several classes within each other, the researcher can also test for the teacher effect.

Although the Callahan design solves one major control group problem, it does not provide a means for judging the significant curricular issue of differentiated education. In my own evaluation studies, I have modified this design to determine whether the curriculum was appropriate for differentiated programming. The lower half of Table 12.4 shows this important addition to Callahan's design. Clusters are composed of classrooms of nongifted students who receive the same curricular units as the gifted classes from teachers of the gifted. Cluster C provides the comparison for cluster A, and cluster D is the relevant comparison for cluster B. This arrangement enables the evaluator to compare the performance of regular classroom students to gifted students on such variables as breadth and depth of achievement and rate of learning. Such comparisons enable

TABLE 12.4: Callahan's Design for Evaluating Gifted Curriculum

Class	Curriculum Unit Evaluation	
	Time 1	Time 2
Cluster A (gifted classes)		
G_1	X	Y
G_2	X	Y
G_3	X	Y
Cluster B (gifted comparison classes)		
G_4	Y	X
G_5	Y	X
G_6	Y	X
Cluster C (nongifted classes)		
R_1	X	Y
R_2	X	Y
R_3	X	Y
Cluster D (nongifted comparison classes)		
R_4	Y	X
R_5	Y	X
R_6	Y	X

X = Experimental curriculum unit
Y = Other curriculum unit

the evaluator to determine if regular classroom students can profit from the gifted curriculum to the same degree as the gifted. (A study illustrating this design is described below in the discussion of nonequivalent control groups in the section on quasi-experimental designs.)

Retrospective Pretesting. At times it is impossible to include a comparison group in the design. This may occur because of logistical constraints or because there is no other comparable group available. Nevertheless, it is still important to compare the program participants' performance to a meaningful standard.

When a comparison group is unavailable, retrospective pretesting provides a means of comparison because the program participants act as their own controls (Payne & Brown, 1982). After receiving instruction, participants are given a test or questionnaire to measure outcomes. Then they are given the same instrument and asked to respond as they would have prior to instruction. These data can then be compared for mean differences. Payne and Brown (1982) report retrospective pretesting has been used most extensively with affective outcomes but has also been used successfully for cognitive outcomes.

Designs for the Control Problem

Program evaluation operates under a different set of constraints from experimental research. Evaluators usually have to employ designs that lack control; rarely do they have the luxury of using true experimental designs. For this reason I will focus on three typical categories of designs used by evaluators: (1) causal-comparative, (2) correlational, and (3) quasi-experimental.

Causal-Comparative Design. Causal-comparative designs may be used to gather data about the effects of programs when manipulation of variables is impossible. In its simplest form the design includes two naturally formed groups: one that has experienced a treatment and one that has not. Note the total lack of control. There is no random selection of subjects or random assignment of treatment. The only control the evaluator can exert is the selection of the comparison group. It should be as equivalent as possible to the treatment group on the variables most likely to bias the outcome measures.

Since the statistics for causal-comparative designs are similar to true experimental designs, there is a tendency to infer causation to explain existing group differences. These causal explanations are inappropriate because the design lacks experimental control over variables. Only relational statements are appropriate, for example, "higher achievement is associated with group A" (relational) as opposed to "the instruction of group A will lead to higher achievement" (causal). Nevertheless, relationships provide meaningful information for program evaluators and may be sufficient, depending on the purpose of an evaluation study.

A study by Tremaine (1979) provides examples of both the advantages and pitfalls of the causal-comparative design. This study compared enrolled and nonenrolled gifted children on a variety of outcome measures, many of which included existing information. Data from school records revealed that enrolled gifted took more advanced classes and had higher grade-point averages (GPAs) than the unenrolled. Additional data were gathered by mailing questionnaires to each group. In comparison to the unenrolled, the enrolled gifted reported engaging in significantly more school activities, were more satisfied with their high school teachers, and indicated a stronger tendency to obtain a college education.

Before you accept the Tremaine study as a model for the causal-comparative approach, I should point out several problems with its methodology. First of all, Tremaine never demonstrated equivalence between the two groups. There is no demographic data reported on important variables such as intelligence, achievement, age, or sex. Second, the response rate to Tremaine's survey was only 35%. This proportion is too low to assume that the nonrespondents could not have altered the results. Finally, Tremaine is much too liberal in suggesting causal inferences between enrollment in the gifted program and the behavior outcomes reported in the study. As pointed out earlier, causal explanations are inappropriate with this design. In spite of these weaknesses, the Tremaine study provides a good example of the causal-comparative methodology that may be useful to the program evaluator.

Correlational Designs. Correlational designs, similar to causal-comparative designs, lack control and reveal relational data. They differ from causal-comparative designs since only one group is studied and data are analyzed via correlational statistics.

Correlational designs seem to be ignored by evaluators who have published in the literature. This may be because correlation is equated with bivariate procedures, which provide limited information. However, correlational statistics include multivariate approaches (e.g., multiple correlation, discriminant analysis, canonical correlation), which can be very powerful approaches for the program evaluator.

To illustrate the approach, consider an evaluation study that I conducted several years ago (Carter, 1985). Officials of a school district wanted to know whether their curriculum met the needs of the creatively gifted to the same degree as the intellectually gifted. This concern was precipitated by several teachers who advocated separating the children into two groups and developing separate teaching strategies for each. This question could be answered best by separating the intellectually and creatively gifted into two groups, controlling extraneous variables, teaching the curriculum, and comparing the groups on outcome measures. Unfortunately, the administration had to reject this approach because of limited resources and time constraints.

My approach was to develop a correlational design around existing information. Although this design cannot establish a causal link between the type of giftedness and success in the curriculum, it will show whether you can predict performance on the basis of the type of giftedness.

After consulting student records, a regression equation such as the following was constructed: $Y = b_1 X_1 + b_2 X_2 + b_3 X_3 + b_4 X_4$ (see Glass & Stanley, 1970), where Y = achievement on teacher-made tests over the curriculum, X_1 = time in program, X_2 = category of gifted, X_3 = grade, and X_4 = sex. Although the district was only interested in the relationship between type of giftedness and achievement, the other independent variables were included to increase precision and to provide alternative explanations of achievement for different student performances. In brief, the results of this analysis showed little support for the teachers' beliefs, that is, the strongest relationship explained only 13% of the variability of achievement.

By employing correlational designs, the evaluator can provide relational information to the school quickly with limited disruption of the school environment and without a comparison group. Since evaluators often find themselves in situations such as this, correlational designs should prove valuable.

Quasi-Experimental Designs. The purpose of outcome evaluations is to establish a causal link between the program and outcome. True experimental control, a requirement for causal inference, is usually not the objective of the evaluator. However, the ability to establish causal links between program and outcomes can be increased when evaluators make observations of program participants before and after the program, as well as by observing the performance of nonparticipants (Posavac & Carey, 1989). Campbell and Stanley (1966) described a number of designs incorporating these principles and labeled them "quasi-experimental." Although these designs do not achieve the control that true experiments do, they control many threats to internal validity and provide important evaluation information. This section will describe two such designs: the time-series design and the nonequivalent control group design.

The key features of a *time-series design* include measuring the performance of a single group of subjects at periodic intervals. The treatment is administered between two of these intervals and then withdrawn. If the treatment produces an effect, it will be indicated by the differences in the measurements before and after the treatment.

A hypothetical example will be used to illustrate the time-series design. The task is to evaluate a curriculum unit on self-worth. As shown in Figure 12.2, children are administered an attitude scale at intervals O_1–O_3 prior to the unit and at intervals O_4–O_6 following the unit. The effectiveness of the unit is based on discrepancies between O_3 and O_4 in relationship to the other points in the time series. If the other points in the time series are ignored, erroneous interpretations will result. For example, time series A shows a shift from O_3 to O_4, but analysis of the entire series shows a trend that started before the treatment and continued after the treatment. The effect is more likely due to threats to internal validity—such as *maturation* or *test sensitization*—and not the treatment. Time series C also shows an effect from O_3 to O_4. However, measures prior to treatment and following treatment demonstrate a similar pattern of fluctuations, suggesting historical events may be responsible for changes, not the treatment. Time series B presents data that are supportive of a treatment effect. Measures prior to the treatment reveal a stable baseline. After the treatment the measures show an increase that is maintained over intervals O_5 and O_6.

The time-series design is particularly useful for evaluating gifted programs when no comparison group is possible. The participants act as their own controls. However, you should use the time-series design with caution. It does not control for history effects that occur at the same time as the treatment. Consider the previous hypothetical example. What if the children were receiving instruction on self-worth through some other medium (television, church, scouts, etc.) at the same time as the self-worth unit? The treatment effect could be due to that instruction. The time series, unable to detect this bias, could still look like pattern B in Figure 12.2. For this reason it is important to gather qualitative data during the treatment to detect any history effect that may be operating.

The *nonequivalent control group design* in its simplest form consists of two intact groups that are tested before and after treatment. The treatment is randomly assigned to one group and the other acts as a control, more properly termed a comparison group since groups were not formed through random selection. The nonequivalence of the two groups is the main weakness of the design. To make meaningful interpretation of treatment effects, evaluators must detect pretreatment group differences through pretesting and comparison of other important variables such as age, ability, and motivation.

This type of analysis is contingent on the results of pretesting. If pretesting shows equivalence on relevant variables, the analysis of the posttest scores is straightforward usually via a *t* test. However, if groups differ on pretesting, or other critical variables, analysis of covariance can be used to make adjustments in the posttest scores to help offset initial differences.

To illustrate, I used a variation of the design to conduct an outcome evaluation of a curriculum on higher-level thinking (Carter, 1986). Six

FIGURE 12.2   An illustrative time-series design

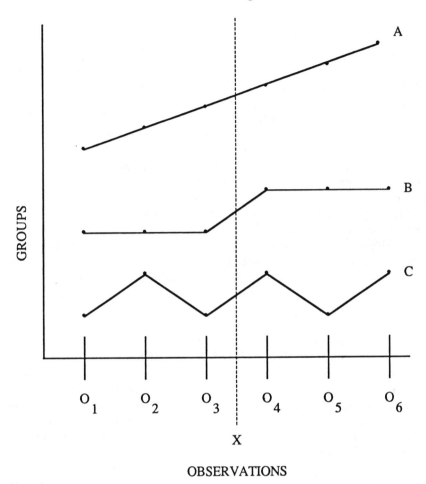

intact third-grade gifted classes from six different schools were randomly assigned to a treatment or comparison condition. In addition, one classroom of normal-ability students was assigned to the treatment condition as a means of measuring the effectiveness of a differentiated curriculum. (This is an example of the design described earlier in the section on counterbalanced designs.) The treatment consisted of an eight-week curriculum (two hours a week) on higher-level thinking, while the gifted comparison groups received a curriculum on independent learning (the Callahan strategy described earlier was employed).

Pretreatment differences between groups were assessed for intelligence, creativity, content knowledge, and demographic background. Mean scores on the Cognitive Abilities Test (CAT) and the Torrance Tests of Creative Thinking (TTCT) were compared. No significant differences (alpha = .05) were found between gifted groups, and, as expected, the gifted groups scored significantly higher than the regular classroom students on both the CAT and TTCT. Additional analyses showed all groups to be of similar age and background, that is, socioeconomic level and sex. In addition, teacher-made pretests revealed no group differences. At the end of the eight weeks all groups were administered a posttest. Gifted groups receiving instruction performed similarly to each other, but scored significantly higher than the gifted comparison groups and the regular classroom students.

Although true experimental control was not established, the school district requesting the evaluation regarded these results as strong evidence supporting the unit on higher-level thinking. This conclusion illustrates that true experimental designs do not have to be used to satisfy sponsors of evaluations.

CONCLUDING REMARKS

Conducting a program evaluation can be a very complex task. The nature of an evaluation depends on the questions raised about a program, the timeframe allotted, the logistical support/barriers, and the evaluation's financial support. Individuals planning evaluations should conduct evaluations fully aware of these constraints and expectations. Although the preceding sections have described the process and elements of program evaluations, the list of do's and dont's below summarizes the key strategic and tactical points made earlier.

Do:

1. Identify the decision maker(s), the individual(s) who will approve the evaluation plan and make judgments about the program.
2. Determine the reason for the evaluation. Meet with the decision maker(s), especially the person who has called for the evaluation, and the primary stakeholders, including the individual in charge of the program and representatives from the staff who run the program.

3. Gather historical information on the program. Has it been evaluated before? Has it been criticized or praised?
4. Limit the scope of the evaluation to a manageable number of research questions.
5. Identify information sources (e.g., tests, questionnaires, observations) that are meaningful evidence to the decision maker.
6. Describe strengths as well as shortcomings of the evaluation design to the decision maker(s).
7. Establish a reasonable timeline that provides enough time to conduct an appropriate evaluation.
8. Identify contact people and agree on protocol, policies, and procedures that will guide the evaluation.
9. Establish a budget capable of supporting the plan.
10. Agree on logistical support that is to be provided by the evaluation team and the program staff.
11. Meet with the program staff to establish rapport. Answer all questions to lower their anxiety.
12. Submit a written evaluation plan to the decision maker(s) for approval.
13. Fit the evaluation into the ongoing instructional program rather than the other way around.
14. Be flexible. Unforeseen circumstances will occur and the plan will probably have to be altered.
15. Communicate all changes, problems, and successes to the decision maker(s).

Don't:

1. Agree to conduct an evaluation on a program to justify a decision that has already been made.
2. Attempt to conduct an evaluation that is beyond your capacity: scope, expertise, time, or funding.
3. Conduct an evaluation without a formally approved evaluation plan.
4. Provide sources of information (data and analyses) beyond the sophistication of the decision maker(s).
5. Forget to determine local policy regarding rights to privacy and confidentiality.
6. Exaggerate the meaning of statistically significant results that have limited practical significance.
7. Forget to provide a face-to-face meeting to discuss written reports.
8. Write a report beyond the needs, interests, and sophistication of the decision maker(s).

9. Agree to expand the evaluation plan without altering the timeline or budget.
10. Forget to acknowledge the assistance, support, or time provided by the program staff.

Program evaluations are essential to developing and maintaining quality educational programs. As a program evaluator, you must strive to elicit and provide information that will lead to appropriate educational decision making. This process is particularly perplexing because many program evaluations are conducted to determine whether a program is responsible for a behavior change (causal effect). By implication, these evaluations should be conducted as tightly controlled true experiments. However, we must remember that educational systems are fragile and must not be altered simply to accommodate elaborate evaluation plans. Student learning and well-being must always take precedence over grand designs that interrupt the educational process. Consequently, evaluations are typically developed out of a compromise between the impulse to create a true experiment, with all of its controls, and the need to fit it into the educational context.

The creativity of the evaluator is often stretched to gather enough relevant information to answer the question posed. Sometimes the information may be contaminated by other factors that are left uncontrolled. When this happens, you must provide multiple sources of evidence to answer each question. If each source, although not perfectly unbiased, provides the same answer to the question, then most reasonable people will accept the answer as valid. Termed the "reasonable person hypothesis" (Callahan, 1983), this maxim is the guiding principle for program evaluators. It allows us to answer causal questions about instructional programs without implementing controls that would destroy them. Since we have to provide multiple forms of evidence for each question, we just have to work harder.

REFERENCES

Borg, W. R., & Gall, M. D. (1983). *Educational research: An introduction* (4th ed.). New York: Longman.

Callahan, C. M. (1983). Issues in evaluating programs for the gifted. *Gifted Child Quarterly, 27,* 33–37.

Campbell, D. T., & Stanley, J. C. (1966). *Experimental and quasi-experimental designs for research.* Chicago: Rand McNally.

Carter, K. R. (1985). *An evaluation of the junior high gifted program.* Greeley,

CO: School District 6. Available from Kyle Carter, Graduate School, University of Northern Colorado, Greeley, CO 80639.

Carter, K. R. (1986). A cognitive outcomes study to evaluate curriculum for the gifted. *Journal for the Education of the Gifted, 10,* 41–55.

Carter, K. R., & Hamilton, W. (1983). *Program evaluation report* (Gifted and talented education, grades 3–5). Greeley, CO: School District 6. Available from Kyle Carter, Graduate School, University of Northern Colorado, Greeley, CO 80639.

Coleman, J. M., & Fults, B. A. (1983). Self-concept and the gifted child. *Roeper Review, 5,* 44–47.

Cronbach, L. J. (1963). Course improvement through evaluation. *Teachers College Record, 64,* 672–683.

Cronbach, L. J. (1982). *Designing evaluations of educational and social programs.* San Francisco: Jossey-Bass.

Gallagher, J. J. (1979). Research needs for the education of the gifted. In J. J. Gallagher, J. C. Gowan, A. H. Passow, & E. P. Torrance (Eds.), *Issues in gifted education* (pp. 79–91). Ventura, CA: Ventura County Superintendent of Schools.

Ganopole, S. J. (1982). Measuring the educational outcomes of gifted programs. *Roeper Review, 5,* 4–7.

Gardner, H. (1983). *Frames of mind: The theory of multiple intelligences.* New York: Basic Books.

Glass, G. V., & Stanley, J. C. (1970). *Statistical methods in education and psychology.* Englewood Cliffs, NJ: Prentice-Hall.

Guilford, J. P. (1981). Three faces of intellect. In W. B. Barbe & J. S. Renzulli (Eds.), *Psychology and education of the gifted* (3rd ed., pp. 87–102). New York: Irvington.

Marland, S. P. (1972). *Education of the gifted and talented* (Vol. 1). Report to the Congress of the United States by the U.S. Commissioner of Education. Washington, DC: U.S. Government Printing Office.

Mitchell, B. M. (1988). The latest national assessment of gifted education. *Roeper Review, 10,* 161–163.

Payne, D. A., & Brown, D. L. (1982). The use and abuse of control groups in program evaluation. *Roeper Review, 5,* 11–14.

Popham, W. J. (1988). *Educational evaluation.* Englewood Cliffs, NJ: Prentice-Hall.

Posavac, E. S., & Carey, R. G. (1989). *Program evaluation: Methods and case studies* (3rd ed.). Englewood Cliffs, NJ: Prentice-Hall.

Renzulli, J. S. (1978). What makes giftedness? Reexamining a definition. *Phi Delta Kappan, 60,* 180–184.

Ross, J. D., & Ross, C. M. (1979). *Ross test of higher cognitive processes: Administration manual.* Novato, CA: Academic Therapy Publications.

Scriven, M. (1967). The methodology of evaluation. In R. W. Tyler, R. M. Gagne, & M. Scriven (Eds.), *Perspectives on curriculum evaluation* (AERA Monograph Series on Curriculum Evaluation, No. 1, pp. 39–83). Chicago: Rand McNally.

Snow, R. E. (1974). Representative and quasi-representative designs for research on teaching. *Review of Educational Research, 44,* 265–291.

Stanley, J. C. (1976). Use of tests to discover talent. In D. C. Keating (Ed.), *Intellectual talent: Research and development* (pp. 3–21). Baltimore: Johns Hopkins University Press.

Stanley, J. C., Keating, D. P., & Fox, L. H. (Eds.). (1974). *Mathematical talent: Discovery, description, and development.* Baltimore: Johns Hopkins University Press.

Sternberg, R. J. (1981). A componential theory of intellectual intelligence. *Gifted Child Quarterly, 25,* 86–93.

Sternberg, R. J., & Davidson, J. E. (1986). *Conceptions of giftedness.* New York: Cambridge University Press.

Stufflebeam, D. (1983). The CIPP model for program evaluation. In G. F. Madaus, M. Scriven, & D. Stufflebeam (Eds.), *Evaluation models: Viewpoints on educational and human services evaluation* (pp. 117–142). Boston: Kluwer-Nijhoff Publishing.

Tremaine, C. D. (1979). Do gifted programs make a difference? *Gifted Child Quarterly, 23,* 500–517.

CHAPTER 13

EVALUATING GIFTED PROGRAMS WITH LOCALLY CONSTRUCTED INSTRUMENTS

M. Elizabeth Nielsen and Nina K. Buchanan

Early in March your district superintendent asks you to report on the effectiveness (or, heaven forbid, ineffectiveness) of the new gifted and talented program you coordinate. You might decide to do one of the following:

- Put everything else *on hold* and begin the evaluation yourself
- Use the funds remaining in the gifted budget to hire an outside evaluator
- Collect available data, write the report, and then begin on next year's evaluation
- Simply explain that it cannot be done on such short notice and ask to be transferred back to a regular classroom

The most sensible choice may be number 3, followed by 1 or 2 depending on the evaluation's importance to the continuation of the program and on the available funding.

Too often teachers and administrators of gifted programs are faced with decisions like the one above because evaluation was not considered an essential component of the program. In fact, prior to the 1970s, evaluation of educational programs was viewed by many researchers as the stepchild of educational research. And yet the basic difference between evaluation and research is only one of *motivation* (Weiss, 1972; Wolf, 1984). Evaluation serves two functions: a proactive function that utilizes findings to assist in ongoing, progammatic decision making and a retroactive function that utilizes findings to demonstrate and maintain program accountability (Stufflebeam et al., 1971). In contrast, the primary function of pure educational research is to establish a knowledge base that is generalizable.

Wolf (1984) suggests that the evaluation of educational programs, units, courses, and instruction focus on five key areas (see Figure 13.1):

1. The initial status of the learners
2. Learner performance after participating in the program
3. Execution or implementation of the program
4. Program costs
5. Supplemental program information

FIGURE 13.1   Key program areas to be evaluated (Wolf, 1984)

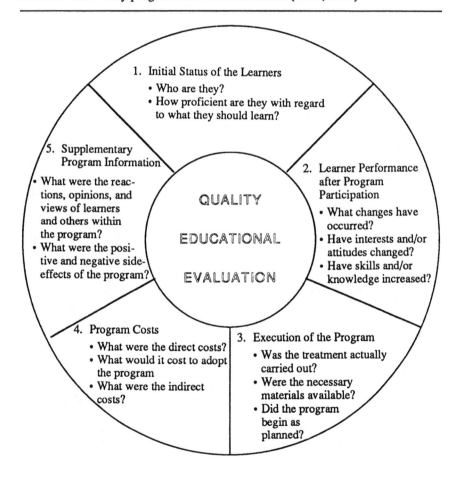

According to this model, an evaluation study is not complete unless it has examined all five areas. Carter (Chapter 12, this volume) provides information related to many of Wolf's key areas. In contrast to Carter's broad perspective, this chapter will focus only on the key area of *supplemental information*. The primary tools for an effective evaluation of supplemental information are informal (nonstandardized) measures such as interviews and questionnaires. The purpose of this chapter is to demystify informal educational measurement so that program evaluators, such as yourself, can approach informal evaluation in a knowledgeable and confident manner.

A RATIONALE FOR NONSTANDARDIZED INSTRUMENTS IN PROGRAM EVALUATION

VanTassel (1980) asserts that "we must carefully construct evaluation designs that are appropriate to the kinds of objectives and activities we are attempting to carry out with students" (p. 112). Most frequently, program success is evaluated through student performance on standardized tests. With this design, standardized (formal) tests are administered to students in the hope that results will show gains directly attributable to program participation. Information obtained from these formal measures provides valuable data for program evaluation. Evaluation based solely on test scores, however, is inadequate and narrowly focused (Renzulli, 1975). To assess program service as well as consumer (student) performance, evaluation should include informal (nonstandardized) as well as formal (standardized) measures.

Advantages of Nonstandardized Evaluation Instruments

We "should be imploring measurement specialists to develop a methodology that reflects the fullness, the complexity, and the importance of their programs" (Stake, 1967, p. 524). Well-constructed informal instruments can assist in capturing that fullness and complexity. They have several major advantages for use in evaluating gifted programs, which are summarized below.

1. *Program-specific information.* The goals and objectives measured by formal (standardized) instruments may be more likely to match those of the regular program rather than those of the gifted program. Locally constructed, informal instruments, on the other hand, may more

consistently reflect the gifted program's specific goals, objectives, and activities.

2. *Process and input as well as outcomes assessment.* Because gifted programs are *special* adaptations to the *regular* program, certain processes such as communication are often critical to gifted program survival. Informal instruments along with reviews of program documents and interviews with key people can be valuable sources of information for evaluating both processes and input within the gifted program (Seeley, 1985; Yarvorsky, 1976).

3. *Multiple sources of input.* Formal measures provide only for student input into the evaluation process. Gifted programs, however, operate within an intercommunicating system of school, home, and community. Informal measures can be designed to solicit input from all who have direct or indirect contact with the program.

4. *Discern student growth.* The gifted are an atypical population. Thus results obtained from national norm-referenced tests may not give an accurate indication of gifted students' growth. For example, a student scoring at the 99th percentile on an achievement test cannot demonstrate academic growth on the measure. Growth in other areas such as self-concept, creativity, and critical thinking is a gradual process, in contrast to the more rapid growth in acquiring facts and information. These gradual changes in beliefs and attitudes are not easily accessible through standardized measures (Gronlund, 1985).

5. *Ease of administration.* Informal questionnaires and surveys are economical and adaptable. If well constructed, they provide direct and reliable assessments of attitudes and eliminate interviewer bias (Kubszyn & Borich, 1987; Oppenheim, 1966).

Some experts criticize gifted educators for their overreliance on attitudinal data in the evaluation process. Others, such as Oppenheim (1966) and Edwards (1957), assert that attitude and self-concept scales can be reliable, valid measures. Since many gifted education programs have goals that are entirely or partially affective in nature (e.g., to increase the students' level of independence, to improve the students' self-concepts), the assessment of attitudes should be an important part of gifted program evaluation. The majority of formal, standardized tests used as a part of program evaluation are selected to assess the cognitive effects of the program. In contrast, program-specific, nonstandardized, informal measures (e.g., questionnaires, interviews, and observations) can serve as effective tools for determining or assessing respondents' beliefs and attitudes about the program and its outcomes.

Additionally, the rapidly growing field of qualitative educational evaluation supports the use of informal measures of program effectiveness (Fetterman, 1989; Patton, 1987). Subjective, qualitative approaches to evaluation can complement and enhance the more objective, rigorous quantitative approaches (Fielding & Fielding, 1986). Furthermore, Campbell and Stanley (1966), Weiss (1972), and the Joint Committee on Educational Evaluation Standards (1981) support the use of multiple approaches and types of measurement instruments within the evaluation process.

MEASURING ATTITUDES

Generally, educational researchers and evaluators are interested in two broad categories of measures: mental ability and personality. While the former includes intelligence and achievement measures, the latter can be visualized as a hierarchy with *personality* as the overarching category followed by values, attitudes, and, finally, beliefs (Oppenheim, 1966). Attitudes are descriptions of how people typically feel about or react to other people, things, or ideas (Kubszyn & Borich, 1987) or how they tend to act or react when confronted with a certain stimulus (Oppenheim, 1966). Interviews and questionnaires are the most frequently used methods of obtaining information about attitudes, feelings, and opinions.

An interview is an information collection technique in which a person (interviewer) talks with another person or group of people. The information collected can be recorded in field notes, structured interview forms, summary reports, or tape recordings. In general, interviews allow respondents to use their own words to communicate their attitudes, opinions, and beliefs.

Questionnaires, in contrast, are self-report survey forms consisting of sets of questions designed to obtain attitudes, opinions, and/or beliefs. Answers to questionnaire items may require free responses (e.g., short answers), forced-choice (e.g., multiple-choice) responses, or a combination of free and forced-choice responses. They frequently are used in large-scale evaluations that seek to obtain the reactions and opinions of participants.

There are advantages and disadvantages to using either interviews, questionnaires, or a combination when evaluating your gifted program (see Table 13.1). Following the guidelines in this chapter, which emphasize questionnaires, can help you avoid many of the problems associated with the use of informal measures of program outcomes. Remember,

TABLE 13.1   Advantages and disadvantages of interviews and questionnaires
in the evaluation of gifted programs

Advantages	Disadvantages
Interviews	
Encourage rich, extensive responses	Can be expensive (e.g., interviewers' fees,
Allow for flexibility	transcribing fees)
Allow for immediate clarification of mis-	Interview process is time consuming
understood questions	Data analysis is time consuming
Allow evaluator to explain in detail the	Require well-trained interviewers
purpose of the interview	Can be strongly influenced by interviewer
Exploit the fact that people are generally	bias
more willing to talk than to write	May generate responses that are influenced
Can be used to obtain data from young	simply by the fact that an interviewer
children, etc.	was asking the questions
Questionnaires	
Less expensive to construct than most	Inappropriate for some populations (e.g.,
instruments	young children, illiterates)
Reasonable/manageable administration	Do not allow for clarification of items
costs (less expensive than interviews)	Do not allow opportunity to probe particu-
Access information from large samples of	lar responses
people simultaneously	Cannot control the order in which respon-
Data can be readily coded and analyzes	dents choose to read and answer items
Eliminate the influence of evaluator bias (a	Cannot control for faking
problem associated with interviews)	Response rates are not always satisfactory

however, that program evaluation should be a comprehensive undertaking that utilizes data from multiple sources and instruments. Questionnaire and interview data should not be used as the sole data for making program decisions.

CONDUCTING PROGRAM EVALUATION
WITH LOCALLY DEVELOPED INSTRUMENTS

As you examine the following ten steps in program evaluation using informal instruments, you will notice many similarities between these steps and the procedures for comprehensive program evaluation as described in Chapter 12. This is as it should be. Using informal evaluation measures is not a quick-and-dirty way to prove the success of a program; rather, it is a variation on the traditional evaluation theme. The remainder of this chapter details each of the ten steps.

1. Determine who is "in charge" of the evaluation.
2. Do some armchair thinking—phase 1 planning.
3. Collect and examine existing attitudinal and other survey/questionnaire instruments.
4. Move back to armchair thinking—phase 2 planning.
5. If necessary, construct your own informal instruments.
6. Pilot test any instruments that you constructed.
7. Revise instruments based on pilot test(s) results.
8. Collect attitudinal data using existing or newly constructed informal instruments.
9. Analyze the data.
10. Report the results, emphasizing the relationship between program outcomes and decisions.

Step 1: Who's in Charge?

This chapter began with a scenario in which you have been asked to conduct an informal evaluation of the gifted program you coordinate. This scenario typifies a major problem related to program evaluation: the lack of prior planning. Decisions about who should conduct a program evaluation should be made in advance and based on collaborative thinking rather than be a last-minute, top-down mandate.

The decision about who should be in charge rests upon the question of credibility (Franklin & Thrasher, 1976). Credibility refers to whether or not the findings and recommendation of a particular evaluator will be accepted by those who will make program decisions. Internal evaluators have knowledge of the program that can give an in-depth perspective to evaluation but that also might make their findings suspect. The findings of external evaluators may appear to be less biased; however, external evaluators do not have in-depth knowledge of the program. The strongest argument in favor of using external evaluators is that their findings may be more credible; the strongest argument for using internal evaluators is that their findings may be more usable.

The Joint Committee on Standards for Educational Evaluation (1981) recommends that evaluation be a team endeavor rather than the task of one individual or a single outside evaluation specialist.

> The Joint Committee rejects the narrow stereotype which pictures evaluations as being conducted by evaluation specialists and used by other educators and by lay citizens. The Committee believes, instead, that educators, psychologists, students, parents, school board members, legislators, and indeed the general public can be legitimately both the producers and the

users of evaluation results. In fact, in the Committee's view, good evaluations ordinarily require the involvement of a team of people drawn from several of these categories. (p. 8)

The selection of evaluator (internal, external, or team) should be made at the conclusion of one school year or, at least, by the beginning of the next school year, so that proper evaluation planning can begin.

Step 2: Armchair Thinking—Phase 1 Planning

You have been selected to lead a team effort to collect data through nonstandardized instruments that will assess whether and to what degree your program is meeting its goals. First, you need to find a quiet place to sit back, put your feet up, and think. Sherlock Holmes's creator termed this *armchair thinking*.

Sometimes, in the excitement or fear of the moment, there is a tendency to jump into the task of evaluation without reflecting on issues central to the process. Decisions made about these issues will influence all remaining aspects of the informal evaluation process. This first phase of armchair thinking includes seven issues that must be considered and resolved prior to any further evaluation action.

Establish the Correct Mindset. The purpose of your informal evaluation is not to prove the success of the gifted program. Rather, it is to collect and analyze enough information to allow you to determine whether the program did or did not have certain effects on the participating gifted students.

Select the Evaluation's Advanced Organizers. Early on, you will need to identify those *issues* that directly relate to your program's effectiveness or ineffectiveness. Stake (1980) has called these "advanced organizers," Renzulli (1975) terms these the "key features," and Rutman and Mowbray (1983) define these as the "key questions." Stake (1980) recommends that these advanced organizers, rather than program objectives or evaluation hypotheses, guide evaluations: "These issues are a structure for the data-gathering plan. The systematic observations to be made, the interviews and tests to be given, if any, should be those that contribute to understanding or resolving the issues identified" (p. 79). An example of a possible advanced organizer for a gifted program's evaluation might be the gifted students' feelings about their giftedness.

Translate the Key Issues into Program Variables. The next step is to clarify the issues to be evaluated by translating them into program-specific variables, such as study skills or creative thinking. *A Handbook of Educational Variables: A Guide to Evaluation* (Nowakowski, Bunda, Working, Bernacki, & Harrington, 1985) can be a valuable resource as you begin to identify these educational variables. This handbook is a quick and convenient guide to multiple sets of variables associated with student learning and services that support learning and a comprehensive, well-organized set of variable-related questions that might be assessed as part of an educational evaluation.

Decide How Much Information to Collect. Often enthusiastic or insecure evaluators attempt to collect more information than is necessary. Too much evaluation information wastes money, creates problems, and may cause the quality of the evaluation to suffer (Rutman & Mowbray, 1983).

Decide the Unit(s) of Analysis for the Evaluation. According to Patton (1987), "the key factor in selecting and making decisions about the appropriate unit of analysis is to decide what unit it is that you want to be able to say something about at the end of the evaluation" (p. 51). Decisions about sampling techniques and specific questionnaires and interview items hinge on the unit(s) that will be studied. If you want to examine the effects of program participation on individual people, then your unit of analysis would be individuals in the program and, according to Patton (1987), data collection would focus on what is happening to individuals in the program. When the program participants have been divided into program-related groups or classes, the unit of analysis would be program groups rather than individuals. If you wish to examine various aspects of the gifted program, then the unit of analysis would be program components. Finally, if there are several different programs that gifted students may select, then the unit of analysis might be entire programs.

Decide Whom to Question. Usually, the participating students will be questioned. Additional possibilities include persons closely associated with the gifted program, such as parents, the program director/coordinator, program teachers, and/or administrators, as well as knowledgeable persons outside the program, such as the regular classroom teachers and school board members. The groups from whom you wish to collect information constitute the evaluation's *population*. However, you may not be able to collect information from every member of that population. If, for reasons of convenience or economy, you select a subgroup from the population to represent that population, you are working with a *sample*. Any number of samples can be drawn from a population (Doyle, 1983). Questions and issues associated with sampling will be addressed below in the sections on pilot testing (step 6) and data collection (step 8).

Determine the Level of Confidentiality. Since your evaluation will involve human subjects, it is essential that you understand the ethical and legal responsibilities associated with the protection of the rights and welfare of the evaluation participants. If you are unfamiliar with this issue, the set of ethical principles developed by the American Psychological Association for psychologists (Committee on Scientific and Professional Ethics and Conduct, 1977) can provide direction and guidance.

Step 3: Investigate Available Instruments

Prior to deciding to create new instruments, you should attempt to locate and examine existing measures. One or more of these may be the best attitudinal measure for your program's informal evaluation.

First, examine the established, often-used formal attitudinal instruments such as the ME Scale (Feldhusen & Kolloff, 1981), the Piers-Harris Children's Self-Concept Scale (Piers & Harris, 1969), or the Intellectual Achievement Responsibility Scale (Crandall, Katkovsky, & Crandall, 1965). There are several texts and sourcebooks that present and evaluate various attitudinal measures: Anderson (1981); Bills (1975); Bonjean, Hill, and McLemore (1967); Borich and Madden (1977); Buros (1972); Gable (1986); Robinson and Shaver (1973); and Shaw and Wright (1967). Using proven attitudinal measures allows you to take advantage of the demonstrated success of those instruments, to compare your program findings to those found by previous users of the instrument, and to add to the body of knowledge about the instruments and outcomes measured.

In addition to established formal measures, you will also want to examine informal (nonstandardized) surveys and questionnaires specifically designed to evaluate gifted programs. These can serve as models (Nasca, 1983; Whitmore, 1984, 1985a, 1985b; Williams, 1979). Sources such as *Successful Programs for the Gifted and Talented* (Juntune, 1986), *Sample Instruments for the Evaluation of Gifted and Talented Programs* (Renzulli, 1979), or *A Guidebook for Evaluating Programs to the Gifted and Talented* (Renzulli, 1975) provide sample questionnaires. Examples of local evaluation forms can be obtained from gifted programs in other school systems and from your state consultant for gifted and talented education.

If you are feeling unprepared to construct your own local instruments, you may be tempted to adopt one of the sample forms and use it, in its entirety, as the sole instrument for your program's evaluation. This instrument might be reliable (that is, yield consistent, stable, dependable information) but may not be valid (does not measure what you intend to measure) for your program. If this is so, you may lose valuable program-specific information or fail to address significant questions. The sample instruments should be used only as resources.

After you have collected, examined, and critiqued a variety of standardized and nonstandardized (local) attitudinal questionnaires, you will need to make some decisions about which, if any, of these instruments might be useful in your program evaluation. If you determine that none of them will adequately measure the attitudes specifically related to your program, then you must consider designing your own program-specific measure.

Step 4: Armchair Thinking—Phase 2 Planning

If you have decided to use only standardized instruments or ones developed by other programs, then you can move directly to the section below in step 8, data collection. If, however, you have decided that you need to construct your own informal instruments, then you are ready to do some more armchair thinking. This time, however, the issues you will consider relate to instrument construction.

Select a Review Panel. This expert or panel of experts in gifted education will review and critique your data collection plan and the various instruments that have been constructed. The use of experts not only provides valuable assistance in the evaluation process but also helps to establish the validity of newly developed informal instruments.

Generate Broad Questions about Program Outcomes. These might include questions such as the following: Did the students think that participation in the gifted program was of benefit to them? What did parents see as the strengths and weaknesses of the gifted program? How should the program be modified? Eventually, these may serve as models for interview questions or may be modified and expanded to become items for questionnaires. Separate lists of questions for the various groups of people who will provide evaluation input, such as students, teachers, parents, and administrators, should be recorded.

Establish the Validity of the Instrument. Validity refers to whether an instrument measures what it is designed to measure. It is the most important attribute of any data collection instrument. The time to consider instrument validity is while you are planning the evaluation, not after meaningless data have been collected.

In general, validity can best be established by minimizing the degree of interview or questionnaire error. This means asking the right questions in the least ambiguous way. The following list summarizes recommendations for increasing the validity of questionnaires and interviews (Best & Kahn, 1986; Franklin & Thrasher, 1976; Joint Committee on Standards for Educational Evaluation, 1981; Nunnally & Durham, 1975; Weiss, 1975):

- Identify each attitude the instrument is to measure.
- List positive and negative examples of each attitude in behavioral terms.
- Write more items to measure each attitude that you plan to have on the final instrument.
- Ask carefully phrased questions in the least ambiguous way.
- Phrase questions so that they do not influence a respondent's answer.
- Define your terms so that all respondents have similar understanding of their meanings.
- Check the instrument against the objectives and content of the program.
- Obtain judgments about the directions, items, and instrument format from teachers and others involved in the program.
- Have a panel of experts critique the items and instrument as a whole to provide estimates of their content validity.
- Have a panel of experts review the instrument to identify any ambiguous items, words, phrases, and/or problems with directions or response format.

Establish the Reliability of the Instrument. As with the issue of validity, the time to consider reliability is when your evaluation is being planned, not during or after it has been completed. Reliability addresses concerns about the suitability of the measurement procedure and about the consistency and stability of the results. Inconsistent, unstable results may originate from a variety of problems: poorly worded interview or questionnaire items, variations in the way the interviews are conducted or the questionnaires are administered, or missing pieces of information. Unreliable results can mislead evaluators, causing them to arrive at biased conclusions about program results. One of the best ways to insure reliability is to pretest (pilot) the measurement instruments (Rutman & Mowbray, 1983).

Methods of estimating reliability involve comparing at least two applications of the same instrument or equivalent instruments and determining the extent to which they agree. The closer the agreement, the greater the reliability. The Joint Committee on Standards for Educational Evaluation (1981) notes that, in many evaluation studies, informal instrument reliability often can only be established in three ways: (1) by carefully and consistently administering the measurement instruments so as to minimize unreliability; (2) by describing the instruments in enough detail for others to form their own opinions about their reliability; and (3) by providing evidence about the instruments' validity as an indirect proof of their reliability.

Step 5: Constructing Informal Evaluation Instruments

You have examined existing instruments and decided to create your own informal attitudinal instrument. Developing questionnaire and interview items is actually a logical, sensible process. As you read the following list of things to do and to avoid in the construction process, you probably will be thinking "I know that!" or "That is so obvious!" And yet, things are never as easy as they seem. "Devising questions, test items, and forms often looks so easy that it comes as a shock to find how many people fail to understand or misinterpret even seemingly simple items" (Weiss, 1972, p. 36). Even the best of evaluators need reminders such as the following list. You might consider copying this list and taping it to your office door during the time you are constructing an instrument. Ideas in the list are based on the works of Best and Kahn (1986), Doyle (1983), Labaw (1980), Oppenheim (1966), Orlich (1978), and Weiss (1972).

Caveats for the Development of Informal Instrument Items:
1. Avoid sex-biased wording within the questionnaire.
2. Avoid jargon or technical (profession-specific) words.
3. Avoid vague words such as *few, any, all,* or *good.*
4. Avoid *loaded* words or phrases—words that are emotionally charged and suggest an automatic feeling of approval or disapproval (e.g., *elitist* or *tracking*). Loaded words cause respondents to react to the word rather than the issue.
5. Avoid biased or *leading* questions—questions that clearly indicate which response is the desirable one. Leading questions are worded so that they are not neutral but rather suggest what the correct response should be (e.g., "Most people consider the activities in gifted classes to be creative; do you agree? Yes/No").
6. Avoid questions that are confusing, use double negatives, or contain

seemingly contradictory words (e.g., "Would you prefer not to have your child attend the gifted program?" or "Are you opposed to not having gifted students attend special classes?")

7. Avoid single items that are really two questions in one (e.g., "Is the gifted program fun and motivating?").

Recommendations for Developing Items and Instruments:

1. Limit questionnaire response length to approximately ten minutes or less. (Check the actual time needed for completion through pilot testing.)
2. State each question/item in 20 words or less.
3. Use simple words rather than complex ones.
4. Use vocabulary and writing style appropriate to respondents. Check the readability level of the final questionnaire.
5. Use descriptive adjectives and adverbs cautiously (e.g., the adverb *frequently* may mean different lengths of time to different people).
6. Include an equal number of favorable and unfavorable statements.
7. Randomly sequence the statements or questions in your rating scales.
8. Define or explain any terms that could be misinterpreted if (e.g., *enrichment*). Even a simple term such as *grade level* might be misinterpreted if the questionnaire is administered near the end of a school year or during the summer.
9. Underline, boldface, or use italics to emphasize words of particular importance.
10. Give a point of reference if you want the respondent to make a comparison. For example, if you want teachers to rate gifted students' level of independence, specify whether you want the respondent to compare the gifted students to regular education children, to other gifted students, to their own performance at the beginning of the year, or to some other group.
11. Critically examine other informal instruments for ideas about construction.
12. Seek help from key program people, colleagues, and gifted evaluation experts to brainstorm and critique questions during this developmental stage.
13. Try out various items on friends and colleagues, even before you officially pilot test the instrument. Revise accordingly.
14. Select a few people from the population of interest to review items before you put them into the pilot questionnaire or interview. Revise accordingly.
15. Write more questions than you will need in the final instrument so that you will have a variety from which to choose.

16. Write the potential questions on separate slips of paper or index cards, or create a flexible computer data base, so that you can arrange and rearrange them as you decide on a final structure.
17. Take into account the way the responses will be tabulated for scoring.

The remainder of this section on instrument construction will help you (1) design specific types of questions, (2) create questionnaire directions, (3) design a portion of the instrument that will collect demographic information, (4) make your questionnaire look attractive, and (5) develop a cover letter.

Figure 13.2 illustrates the various divisions and subdivisions of questions that might be included in interviews and questionnaires. In order to create effective informal evaluation instruments, you willl need a working knowledge of these basic types of questions.

Open-Form Items. Open-form questions typically do not include specific response options; rather, the respondent is free to answer in any manner. According to Labaw (1980), open-form questions are "indispensable to a thorough understanding of complex issues and topics" (p. 132). Also, questions of this type allow respondents to indicate the degree of their feelings on controversial issues or programs. They are of value in collecting in-depth information from a small number of respondents,

FIGURE 13.2   Diagram of question types

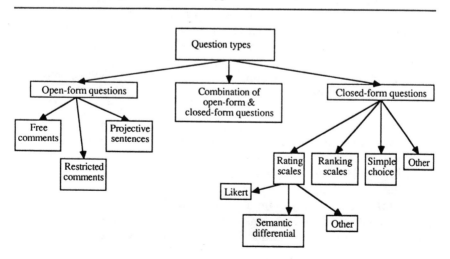

particularly during interviews (Fink & Kosecoff, 1978). There are two major problems, however, with open-form responses: (1) quantifying and tabulating the responses is quite difficult and time-consuming, and (2) open-form questionnaires often have a lower rate of return, since they require more time and effort on the part of the respondents. Therefore, when designing questionnaires, open-form questions should often be avoided, especially if closed-form items can elicit the same information. The most frequent types of open-form items fall into three categories: free comments, restricted comments, and projective sentences.

Free comment items allow the respondent complete freedom to respond to a question or to comment on an issue. For example, "What are your opinions about the gifted program?"

In *restricted comment items* the respondent is free to give an opinion; however, the amount and type of information being sought is indicated within the question. For example, "What do you see as the strengths (if any) of the gifted program; list three." A subtler way to restrict the response on questionnaires is to restrict the number of lines allotted for the answer.

Projective sentence items consist of a number of incomplete sentences or single words, called *stems*, to be completed by the respondent. These items require and measure spontaneity and may vary in ambiguity and subtlety. An example is "Gifted children are . . ."

Combination Items. Items that are combinations of open- and closed-form usually follow a closed-form question or statement with an open-form question or statement. These combination items allow the respondent to comment or elaborate on the response given to the closed-form portion of the question. See part A of Figure 13.3 for an example of a combination question. Orlich (1978) cautions that open comments on questionnaires generally do not add any substantial information to the closed-form items. He notes that those respondents with the most concerns tend to write lengthy comments that can be misleading when the results are interpreted.

Closed-Form Items. Closed-form items provide answer categories for the respondent who is expected to choose the answer category which best represents his or her feelings, beliefs, attitudes, opinions, behaviors, or knowledge of a situation. Responses to closed-form items usually involve: (1) circling a response item (e.g., *Yes* or *No*); (2) ranking specified items; (3) checking an item response; or (4) placing a mark along an answer continuum. When constructing closed-form items, the choices must be exhaustive and mutually exclusive. If it is not feasible to list all

FIGURE 13.3   Sample questionnaire items

A. *Sample Combination Item*
   Did the informational parent meeting in September clearly describe the gifted identification process?
   ____ Yes ____ No ____ Undecided
   Please explain your answer:_____

B. *Sample Closed-Form Item*
   What was the primary reason you placed your child in the gifted program?
   ____ to challenge my child
   ____ because my child's teacher recommended it
   ____ to assure my child's participation in creative activities
   ____ because the gifted teacher has an excellent reputation
   ____ because the regular classroom was not meeting my child's needs
   ____ other (please specify):_____

C. *Sample of a Simple-Choice Item*
   Approximately what percentage of children in your school are gifted? Note: This question does not necessarily refer to the number of students who are attending the gifted program.
   ____ none
   ____ 1-4%
   ____ 5-9%
   ____ 10-14%
   ____ 15-19%
   ____ 20% or more

D. *Sample of a Ranking-Scale Item*
   Listed below are five of the major activities that your gifted class did this year. Place a 5 beside the activity you liked best. Place a 4 beside your next favorite activity. Continue numbering the activities until you have placed a 1 beside the one you liked the least. Even if you liked all activities, please number the choices from most favorite to least favorite.
   ____ Archaeology expedition to Bandelier Monument
   ____ Class play entitled *The Butler Didn't Do It*
   ____ Junior Great Books
   ____ Odyssey of the Mind
   ____ Unit on futures studies—"Changing Our World"

E. *Sample Likert-Scale Item*
   While I was in the gifted program, I developed new skills in solving problems. (Please circle the answer the best describes how you feel.)

5	4	3	2	1
strongly agree	agree	undecided	disagree	strongly disagree

F. *Sample Semantic-Differential Item*

   Gifted Program

pleasant	__:__:__:__:__:__:__	unpleasant
unimportant	__:__:__:__:__:__:__	important
feminine	__:__:__:__:__:__:__	masculine
good	__:__:__:__:__:__:__	bad
active	__:__:__:__:__:__:__	passive
untimely	__:__:__:__:__:__:__	timely

possible choices, always provide space for write-in options (see part B of
Figure 13.3 for an example).

As the Figure 13.2 illustrates, there are different types of closed-form
items. We discuss only those most frequently used in attitudinal and
opinion measures: simple choice items, ranking scales, and rating scales.

Simple choice items are designed to gather basic factual or opinion
information. Yes/No questions and checklists typify these interview or
questionnaire items. Part C of Figure 13.3 is an example of a simple
closed-form item.

Ranking scales are useful in assessing the order of personal preferences. When designing ranking scales, do not ask the respondent to rank
more than ten items (research has shown that rankings beyond ten are
unreliable) (Oppenheim, 1966; Weiss, 1975). An example of a ranking
item that might be used in a gifted program evaluation is provided in part
D of Figure 13.3.

Rating scales are the most widely used instruments for assessing
attitudes and opinions. As with any instrument, rating scales have both
strengths and weaknesses:

> The advantages of the rating and ranking scales are that they are relatively
> inexpensive to construct, they are usually easily understood, and the infor-
> mation they provide readily lends itself to analysis. The disadvantage is that
> they are subject to many types of bias. Some raters are lenient and others are
> not; some base their rating on personal feelings; and sometimes raters are
> asked to make distinctions . . . even when they perceive no differences.
> (Fink & Kosecoff, 1978, p. 27)

A *Likert scale* is a special type of rating scale primarily used for
assessing opinions that can be placed along a continuum (e.g., strongly
agree, agree, undecided, disagree, strongly disagree). Respondents read
the choices and select the one that best matches their feelings from very
positive to very negative. For Likert scale items, the respondent makes
only one choice for each item, as shown in part E of Figure 13.3. There
are three basic decisions that you must make as you create Likert scale
items: (1) what word choices to use, (2) how many choices to include for
each item, and (3) whether to include a neutral position among the
possible choices (Anderson, 1981; Gable, 1986; Oppenheim, 1966; Orlich,
1978; Weller & Romney, 1988).

When constructing Likert items, it is important that the word choices
are mutually exclusive and that the difference between one word and the
next is approximately equal. Also, the word choices should express definite favorableness or unfavorableness to a particular point of view. With

very young children, a series of faces may be the best way to present the Likert choices; for example, a smiling face would indicate a positive response, a face with a straight mouth the neutral response, and a frowning face a negative response.

The number of favorable and unfavorable choices for an item should be approximately equal. For example, in a five-choice (point) Likert scale, word choices would be defined as follows: a *very positive* response, a *positive* response, a *neutral* response, a *negative* response, and a *very negative* response. A three-item selection, on the other hand, would contain one *positive* response, one *neutral* response, and one *negative* response.

Many evaluation and research texts present lists of Likert word choices; for example, Orlich (1978) lists 16 sets of word choices that frequently appear in questionnaires. You also will find ideas for choices on sample instruments you collect and examine. In his instrument development text, Gable (1986) presents a chart of the five most frequently occurring categories of Likert items and numerous actual word sets for each category. These are summarized in Figure 13.4.

Traditionally, Likert scales have seven choices; however, "there is no magic number of steps and the choice of seven-point scales by many researchers is probably due as much to custom as any other reason; seven

FIGURE 13.4 Likert-scale categories and word sets within the categories

Agreement.....................	(from strongly agree to strongly disagree)
	(from completely agree to completely disagree)
Quality.........................	(from very good to very poor)
	(from extremely poor to excellent)
Frequency.....................	(from very frequently to never)
	(from always to never)
	(from a great deal to never)
Likelihood.....................	(from definitely to very probably not)
	(from to a great extent to not at all)
	(from almost always true to almost never true)
	(from true of myself to not at all true of myself)
Importance....................	(from very important to unimportant)

Adapted from Gable (1986), pp. 42–43.

is not the number of choice because of human memory and processing limitations as some have suggested" (Weller & Romney, 1988, p. 41). Ideally, you will determine the number of choices by analyzing your audience. For example, young children may not be as capable of making fine distinctions as are adults.

To have a neutral position or not to have, that often is the question. It traditionally is more acceptable to include a neutral or undecided choice for your Likert items. However, many researchers argue for the exclusion of such midpoints. For example, Doyle (1983, p. 115) comments:

> Although such midpoints are very common, there is good reason not to use them. First, rating scales are already prone to central-tendency error and neutral midpoints seem to draw ratings toward the middle of the scale and thus to exacerbate the error. In addition, it is probably rare that raters are truly neutral, and a neutral midpoint may simply encourage lazy, superficial evaluation. More desirable than the scale above may be a scale without a neutral midpoint but with finer gradations between the central points:

Strongly Agree	Moderately Agree	Slightly Agree	Slightly Disagree	Moderately Disagree	Strongly Disagree

When the neutral position is excluded, the respondent is forced to *take a stand* on the question. We recommend having a neutral midpoint only when the person(s) being questioned may not have enough information to respond accurately otherwise. This means that children who actually participated in the gifted program and teachers who taught in the gifted program are not given the neutral option, while parents might be given that choice.

Semantic differential scales, developed by Osgood, Suci, and Tannenbaum (1957), consist of a series of bipolar rating scales. Extreme ends of the rating scale are defined by opposite adjectives. A concept, person, or object appears above the scale. The respondent is asked to indicate his or her feelings about the concept by placing an X somewhere along the continuum indicated by each pair of adjectives. Typically the scale has 7 equal-interval points, but 3- and 5-point scales are also used.

Visually, the scales appear as follows: (1) there is a centrally positioned *target concept* (e.g., gifted education), object (e.g., the gifted program), person (e.g., gifted children), or issue (e.g., acceleration); (2) there are a series of 7-point rating scales that serve as continua; and (3) paired, bipolar (opposite) adjectives are placed at each end of the different rating scale continua (e.g., hot/cold, good/bad). Part F of Figure 13.3 is an example of a typical semantic differential scale.

Selecting the appropriate adjectives for semantic differential scales can be a problem. They must: (1) be extreme positions; (2) represent factual aspects (e.g., fast/slow) or perceptions (e.g., good/bad); and (3) be evaluative in nature (Anderson, 1981).

Osgood, Suci, and Tannenbaum (1957) developed 20 rating scales that can be widely applied. Additionally, Jenkins, Russell, and Suci (1958) established norms on these 20 scales (see Figure 13.5). You may wish to refer to their sets of words as you develop semantic differential scales. If you develop your own sets, be aware that most adjectives on semantic differential scales are of three types: evaluative adjectives (e.g., happy/sad), potency adjectives (e.g., rugged/delicate), or activity adjectives (e.g., fast/slow) (Gable, 1986).

Once a set of adjectives has been chosen, the words should be placed at either the beginning or end of the scale through random selection. This random placement method is used so that respondents do not expect all positive responses to be on the left and all negative on the right.

Directions for Completing Questionnaires. After you have developed items, you will need to write two types of directions that will become part of the questionnaire: global and item-specific. The *global directions* should help the respondent understand the focus (purpose) of the questionnaire. Three global directions should be included at the beginning of opinion or attitudinal questionnaires: (1) that the instrument is not a test, (2) that there are no *right* or *wrong* responses, and (3) that they should respond in the way that best matches their actual feelings or beliefs.

FIGURE 13.5 Suggested semantic differential scale adjectives

cruel/kind	curved/straight	active/passive	masculine/feminine
untimely/timely	savory/tasteless	wise/foolish	unsuccessful/successful
hard/soft	angular/rounded	weak/strong	important/unimportant
good/bad	calm/excitable	new/old	colorless/colorful
slow/fast	false/true	beautiful/ugly	usual/unusual

Adapted from Osgood et al. (1957).

Item-specific directions usually explain how to respond to an item or set of items (e.g., "Circle the response that best expresses your feelings"). Anderson (1981) notes that the directions for Likert scales and semantic differential scales are quite specific and often are followed by a sample item to illustrate how response should be made (see Figure 13.6 for sample directions).

FIGURE 13.6   Sample directions for Likert and semantic differential scales

---

Likert Scale Directions:

The sentences below ask you to tell how you feel about _____ . You are to tell how you feel about each statement by circling one of the five choices that follow the sentence. Here is a practice sentence:

The activities we do in the gifted class are too difficult.

Strongly Agree   Agree   Can't Decide   Disagree   Strongly Disagree

Which of the five choices best tells how you feel about the statement: strongly agree, or agree, or can't decide, or disagree, or strongly disagree? Circle your choice. Please work carefully and quickly. Do not spend a long time on any one sentence. Please respond to every sentence. Circle only one response to each sentence.

Semantic Differential Scale Directions:

The purpose of this scale is to find out how students feel about _____ . Since different students have different feelings, please respond on the basis of your own feelings. Here is how to use the scales:

   Read the different adjectives at each end of the line. Place a check mark in the space that best describes your feelings about _____ . Your feelings may be very closely related to one end of the scale or the other; may quite closely relate to one end or the other; may slightly relate to one end or the other; or may be neutral.

There are three rules to remember when responding to the scales:

1. The check marks should be placed in the middle of the spaces (between the colons), not on the boundaries (colons).

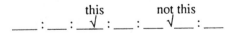

2. Check every set of adjectives.
3. Use only one check mark for each set of adjectives.

Demographic Information. Demographic information often helps you interpret questionnaire or interview results. For example, it might be important to know whether the views of teachers certified in gifted education differ from those without certification. The issue of confidentiality/anonymity is closely related to the collection of demographic data. If you promised anonymity, then you cannot ask for demographic data that would identify the respondent; for example, you should not ask what current grade-level is taught if there is only one teacher at each grade level among those questioned.

The nonexhaustive list in Figure 13.7 may be useful in deciding which demographic data to collect. Obviously the type of demographic information sought will depend on the response group; that is, student data will differ from teacher data and so on. Remember, if the data will not be used in the analysis, do not ask for it.

Designing a User-Friendly Format. After you have constructed the questionnaire items, developed both global and item-specific directions, and decided what demographic data to collect, you are ready to create the best layout or format for the questionnaire. This process is similar to putting jigsaw pieces together to create the *best* picture. Below are a series of helpful hints to assist you in this process.

1. Make the questionnaire attractive, not like a federal tax form. Remember, the *white spaces* as well as the print are important for overall appearance. (Oppenheim, 1966)
2. Do not overlook seemingly small decisions, such as the type and color of paper used.
3. Remember, the respondent is doing you a favor in filling out the instrument. The questionnaire should require as little effort on the part of the respondent as possible.

FIGURE 13.7   Possible demographic data

Age	Educational level or highest degree held
Gender	Number of years taught
Grade level	Socioeconomic or income level
Ethnicity	Occupation
Number of years in gifted program	Certified in gifted education
Number of children in the family	Grade level/subject taught

4. In general, minimize the amount of writing required. Except in special cases, use open-form questions sparingly. If you use open-form questions, request only a limited number of responses. For example, "Please list three strengths of the gifted program."
5. Remember, using different types of questions (open-form, closed-form, and a combination of these) and types of scales (Likert, semantic differential) on the same questionnaire can be valuable for two reasons. It takes advantage of the desirable qualities of the different types, and it makes the questionnaire more interesting to the respondents.
6. Decide whether you will cluster items that are similar in type (all rating scale items) or items that relate to similar topics (all items related to teaching methods). There is no consensus among instrument developers as to which approach is best; thus your decision should be based on knowledge of the population and on pilot test results.
7. Decide whether the demographic items will appear at the beginning or the end of the questionnaire. Again, there is not consensus among instrument developers as to which approach is best; thus your decision should be based on knowledge of the population and on pilot test results.
8. If there are sensitive areas that will be explored by your instrument, arrange items so the respondent begins with nonthreatening items and gradually moves toward the more sensitive items. (Orlich, 1978)

Letter of Introduction. When questionnaires are administered by mail rather than in person, a letter of introduction is essential. Even if you are a fine letter writer, the content and style recommendations in Table 13.2 may be helpful. Notice that the last four content recommendations should also be placed on the questionnaire.

Step 6: Is It Going to Work?

Now that you have constructed the questionnaire, you are ready to pretest (pilot test) to see if it effectively collects the data you are seeking. A *pilot test* constitutes a ministudy to establish the validity and reliability of the instrument by answering a series of vital questions about the newly constructed instrument:

1. Is the wording clear?
2. Are the overall directions and the various item-specific directions clear?

TABLE 13.2   Letters of introduction content and style recommendations

Content Recommendations	Style Recommendations
Explain the purpose	Be polite and courteous—use "please" and "Would you mind?"
Tell why the questionnaire is important	
Explain how the data will be used	Do not talk down to or over the heads of the respondents
Tell respondents how they were selected	
Explain whether the responses will be kept confidential or anonymous	Maintain a balance between being too casual and too sophisticated
State the deadline for returning the questionnaire (should also appear on the questionnaire)	Avoid slang, colloquialisms, and educational jargon
	Avoid abbreviations
Include explicit directions for completing the questionnaire (should also appear on the questionnaire)	Proofread for spelling, grammar, and typing errors
Tell how to return the completed questionnaire, including the address, telephone number, and contact person (should also appear on the questionnaire)	Use quality stationery, preferably with letterhead
	Date the letter
	Sign the letter personally
State which institution is sponsoring the questionnaire (should also appear on the questionnaire)	

3. Are the procedures for administering the instrument clear, and can they be consistently followed?
4. Is the format clear and attractive?
5. Is the questioning sequence effective?
6. Does the letter of introduction clearly define the purpose of the questionnaire?
7. Is the length of time necessary to complete the questionnaire acceptable?
8. Is the instrument appropriate for the specific group with whom it will be used, not too technical, or complex, or simplistic?

Just as there are steps that direct program evaluation, there also are steps that should guide pilot testing.

Step 1. Conduct informal critiques of individual questionnaire items as they are being prepared.
Step 2. After the questionnaire has been developed, have one or more key persons associated with the program critique the instrument.
Step 3. Revise based on the reviewers' input.

Step 4. Repeat step 2 using one or more experts in gifted education and program evaluation. According to Fink and Kosecoff (1978), these experts should have experience and familiarity with gifted programs and their various components, psychometric skills, and knowledge of data collection using informal measures.

Step 5. Revise as needed on the basis of reviewer's input.

Step 6. Administer the revised questionnaire to a sample from the target population. During the pilot test, however, respondents should be given additional space and encouraged to comment about individual items and any aspect of the questionnaire, cover letter, or administration procedures.

Step 7. If there are enough pretest subjects, you may calculate an estimate of reliability and investigate the relationships between responses on different items. (McMillan & Schumacher, 1984)

In step 6 of the pilot test, the issue of sampling must be considered. Whenever possible, the same sampling plan proposed for the actual evaluation should serve as the model for selecting a minisample for the pilot test. Ideally, the sample will reflect those characteristics that represent your target population (e.g., ability, gender, school type).

Wolf (1984) describes a method of sampling called *chunk sampling*, administering the pilot instrument to some fraction of the population that was selected primarily on the basis of availability or for the purpose of economy. Although open to serious criticism, this method "will sometimes suffice for pilot studies, when one is interested in testing out instruments and data collection procedures, but it should not be used as the basis for drawing substantive conclusions about a population" (p. 152).

Sometimes complete, extensive pilot testing is not possible; however, it is your responsibility to conduct as thorough a pilot test as is feasible given the constraints of time and money. While the size of the pretest sample should be more than 20 subjects, it is better to have even 10 subjects than not to conduct a pilot test at all (Weiss, 1975). Whatever the size of the sample or the type of sampling procedure used, it is important to remember that those who participate in the pilot test should not be included in any subsequent evaluation activities, since they will be familiar with the instruments.

Step 7: Back to The Drawing Board—Are Revisions Necessary?

After you have conducted a pilot test of the instrument and administration procedures, you will need to decide whether or not to revise the instrument. If revisions are extensive, it may be necessary to test the revised version.

Step 8: Using the Informal Instruments—Collecting the Data

The actual administration of your instrument should follow as closely as possible the traditional guidelines for the administration of any standardized instrument.

Questionnaires can be administered to individuals or groups either in person or by mail. The advantage of direct contact administration is that the purpose can be clearly explained, items can be clarified, and the response rate will be high. When questionnaires are directly administered to groups of respondents, the environment should be structured so that copying, talking, and other problems that may contaminate the results are avoided. When administered by mail, the following sequence should be followed (Weiss, 1972).

Prior to mailing:
Directly contact the questionnaire recipients through a telephone call, visit, or an announcement letter to let them know the questionnaire is coming. (optional)

At the time of mailing:
1. Accompany the questionnaire with a personally typed letter on letterhead.
2. Include a stamped return envelope.
3. Include a token reward for completing and returning the questionnaire, such as a bookmark or coupon. (optional)

After mailing:
1. Send a reminder letter or postcard to all nonrespondents after the first week.
2. If the return rate remains low, send another questionnaire with a new cover letter emphasizing the importance of the respondent's participation.
3. If the return rate remains low, consider sending additional reminders and perhaps even a third questionnaire. (optional)
4. If the rate is still too low, implement last-ditch efforts such as telephone calls, personal visits, or even telegrams. (optional)

Efforts to increase the number of returned questionnaires should continue until you reach a satisfactory rate of return. Babbie (1973) suggests that a response rate of 50% is adequate, 60% good, and 70% excellent. The acceptable rate for your evaluation, however, may vary.

Generally, a traditional approach to sampling in an evaluation study may be unnecessary and, perhaps, even inappropriate (Wolf, 1984). Obviously, it is better to have data from all members of a group than from a part of that group. Where data is collected from all students in the gifted program, these students are considered to represent the population of all gifted students who will eventually be served. Evaluation inferences are then based on this assumption. According to Wolf, this is a reasonable approach as long as there is no substantial change in the population from year to year.

The qualitative methodology of *purposeful sampling* is another appropriate approach. Purposeful sampling is based on the belief that well-chosen, information-rich cases can provide you with a great deal of information about important issues related to a program. It requires that you develop and articulate a careful rationale for the selection of particular cases (samples). Also, you will need to provide information about possible distortions in the data due to the sample. According to Patton (1987), there are no guidelines for determining the size of purposeful samples. The sample should be large enough to be credible given the purpose of the evaluation, but small enough to permit adequate depth and detail for each case or unit in the sample. Patton's (1987) *How to Use Qualitative Methods in Evaluation* and other qualitative research methodology texts, such as the series from Sage Publishers (Van Maanen, 1985), can provide details about purposeful sampling methodology.

Step 9: What to Do with All That Data—Data Analysis

As noted earlier, *open-form items* are difficult to analyze and report. In some cases, you will organize and translate the information by using a predetermined coding system (Doyle, 1983; Orlich, 1978). First, anticipate the types of responses most likely to be received and develop categories for those likely answers. Obviously, this type of analysis is time consuming and may be problematic.

The tabulation and scoring of most *closed-form items*, on the other hand, is straightforward: tally the responses and then calculate means, frequencies, percentages, and other descriptive statistics. The scoring of Likert and semantic differential scales is slightly more complicated.

Likert scales can be scored in three ways: (1) simply calculate and report the frequencies and percentages for each item/question; (2) combine the outer choices in either direction (e.g., strongly agree + agree;

strongly disagree + disagree) and then report frequencies and percentages; or (3) assign a numerical value to each choice on the scale (e.g., strongly agree = 5, agree = 4, undecided = 3, disagree = 2, strongly disagree = 1) and then multiply the total number of Likert items by 5 to determine the highest score that the most favorable response could receive, by 4 for the next most favorable, and so on. For example, if there were ten Likert items on the scale, the highest score for most favorable would be 50 (10 × 5). Lastly, calculate each respondent's total Likert scores and determine if it indicates a positive attitude (is above the neutral total) or a negative attitude (below the neutral total). For convenience, Likert choices should be coded so the highest points are assigned to the most positive (favorable) statement and the lowest points to the most negative (unfavorable) statement.

Semantic differential items can be scored by assigning points to the various positions along the scale. On a 7-point scale, +3 would be assigned to the position nearest the positive adjective response and −3 to the position nearest the negative adjective. Tally responses for each adjective pair. Calculate and chart mean scores for each item (see Figure 13.8).

Guidelines for Analyzing Informal Evaluation Data. The Joint Committee on Standards for Educational Evaluation (1981) and other evaluators (Best & Kahn, 1986; Brinkerhoff, Brethower, Hluchyj, & Nowakowski, 1983; Oppenheim, 1966; Weiss, 1972; Wolf, 1984) have made

FIGURE 13.8 Sample semantic differential item score and report of results

	+3	+2	+1	0	−1	−2	−3	
Strong	___ :	___ :	___ :	___ :	___ :	___ :	___	Weak

The typical gifted student is:

Strong	_x_ : _o_ : __ : __ : __ : __ : __	Weak	x = average response gifted program parents
Bright	xo : __ : __ : __ : __ : __	Dull	
Good	__ : __ : _o_ : _x_ : __ : __ : __	Bad	o = average response of gifted program teachers
Kind	__ : _x_ : _o_ : __ : __ : __ : __	Cruel	
Good	_x_ : _o_ : __ : __ : __ : __ : __	Bad	

recommendations for analyzing quantitative and qualitative evaluation data. These are summarized below.

- Don't expect dramatic results in either a positive or in a negative direction when analyzing attitudinal and opinion data.
- Look for both positive and negative unanticipated outcomes.
- Use analysis methods that are practical and affordable.
- Remember that not all items need statistical analysis.
- Use analytical methods that are appropriate for your audience.
- Do not use complex statistical techniques just to impress; often the analyses may be more effective using simple techniques such as graphs, frequency distributions, and scatterplots.
- Do not overemphasize rigor at the expense of relevance, or vice versa.
- Do not spend so much time emphasizing the unique features of your program that you ignore or overlook its generalizable features.
- Remember that not all evaluations need to be comparative experimental studies.
- Remember that qualitative and quantitative data complement one another.

Statistical Analyses of Informal Evaluation Data. Analysis should be designed to allow you to compare, contrast, and arrive at conclusions about the various units of analysis whether the units are individuals, small groups, various program parts or components, or even the program as a whole. "Descriptive statistics are among the most useful analysis techniques in evaluations because they are inherently meaningful and easily understood. They are the units of more complex and less intuitive statistical procedures." (Fink & Kosecoff, 1983, p. 48). Generally, they include: (1) central tendency (mode, median, mean); (2) variability or dispersion (standard deviation and range); (3) frequency distributions (the number of responses to each alternative); and (4) comparison of individual and group scores (percentile ranks). In qualitative evaluation methods, descriptive statistics are used to organize narrative information from interviews or responses to open-ended questions into summaries that highlight patterns and features.

When the evaluation includes data from different groups, inferential statistics can be used. These include, but are not limited to: correlation, regression, analysis of variance, and chi-square (see Chapters 3 and 4, this volume, for details). Comparison analyses can be made in several ways (Kerlinger, 1973; Wolf, 1984). Data obtained from interviews can be compared to questionnaire data to determine where the information is mutually parallel, supportive, or conflicting. You might also want to compare information from different groups (parents, students, teachers, administrators). This approach addresses questions such as: Do parents' opinions of the program parallel or differ from the opinions of students and, if so, in what ways? The third approach is rarely utilized by program evaluators, yet it has the potential to yield valuable formative as well as summative program information. With this approach, you gather interview or questionnaire data at three or more points in time. Data might first be collected just before implementation of the program; this data would reflect respondents' expectations related to the new program. Next, data would be collected at one or more predetermined times while the program is in progress. The final collection time would occur at the conclusion of the program or program year. Data from these periodic evaluations could then be compared and contrasted to identify patterns and to track changes in attitudes and opinions over time.

Which is the "best" methodology? Brinkerhoff and colleagues (1983) suggest the following:

> Overall there seems to be more support among evaluators for a more eclectic approach to evaluation methodology. Such an approach seeks to find the best method or set of methods for meeting a particular evaluation purpose, rather than assume that one method is best for all purposes. (p. xviii)

Step 10: Putting It in Writing—The Outcome Report

When all the data have been collected and analyzed, you are ready to write a report. The final informal evaluation report should enable those associated with the gifted program to make fully informed decisions about program effectiveness or ineffectiveness as demonstrated by the attitudinal data from interviews and questionnaires. In order for that to occur, your writing should be straightforward, audience-appropriate, and jargon-free. It should include an interpretation of the data, concrete examples from the questionnaires and interviews, and visual displays of data. At a minimum, the report should include the following:

- Explanation of how your informal measurement data can help the persons receiving the report make programming decisions.
- Description of how each instrument and/or set of interview questions was developed and used, including decisions made during your armchair thinking sessions.
- Reprints of the questionnaire and/or interview questions.
- Description of how you established the validity and reliability of the

measures, which might include reviews by a panel of experts and pilot testing.
- Description of those persons interviewed and/or given the questionnaires.
- Description of how and when the interviews were conducted and/or questionnaires administered.
- Description of how the measures were scored and responses tabulated.
- Description of the methods you used to analyze the data.
- Written and visual summaries of the data.
- Your interpretation of how the results answer key questions or address key issues.
- An analysis of the program's strengths and weaknesses based on the informal measurement data.
- Recommendations when appropriate and/or requested.
- Discussion of any limitations of the evaluation.
- Any reasonable extrapolations that might be made from your findings.

Outcome Decisions. Since evaluation is an action-oriented activity whose purpose is to facilitate decision making, this discussion of the final report would be incomplete without briefly examining the types of decisions that might result from your evaluation study. According to Weiss (1972), there are six potential outcome decisions associated with evaluation studies:

1. To continue or discontinue the program
2. To improve its practices and procedures
3. To add or drop specific program strategies and techniques
4. To institute similar programs elsewhere
5. To allocate resources among competing programs
6. To accept or reject a program approach or theory (pp. 16–17)

However, even within these decisions, the range of possible actions is considerable. Wolf (1984) concludes that "modification in content, organization, and time allocations could occur, as well as decisions about additions, deletions, and revisions in instructional materials, learning activities, and criteria for staff selection" (p. 6).

Generalizations from the Results. Finally, you will need to address the issue of generalizability. Since the primary purpose of evaluation is to allow educators to make programmatic decisions, this issue is often neglected or overlooked completely. However, evaluations can produce information and findings that may have an impact beyond the immediate program. Cronbach (1980) believes program evaluations should achieve a balance between broad, generic investigations and in-depth, program-specific studies. This balance would permit evaluators to make reasonable *extrapolations*, "logical, thoughtful, and problem-oriented" speculations about applying the results of one evaluation to other evaluations (Patton, 1987, p. 168).

SUMMARY

This chapter provides a rationale and process for using informal (nonstandardized) instruments to evaluate your gifted program. We have included specific information about how to design and use attitudinal measures such as questionnaires and interviews. The guidelines, recommendations, and examples presented are designed to dispel myths concerning the difficulties or inadvisability of developing informal, program-specific outcome measures. Even though the number and quality of standardized instruments is steadily increasing, there will be a continuing need to supplement information from these with well-constructed locally developed measures.

Informal program evaluation need not be a mystery. You, like a modern Sherlock Holmes, must acquire basic information, such as that offered in this volume, and then analyze this information during armchair-thinking sessions. The decisions made during these sessions, combined with general guidelines for instrument construction, allow you to proceed in a logical, step-by-step manner. After the overall evaluation is designed, questionnaires and interviews are formulated, pilot tested, revised, and administered to supplement other sources of program information. Data are analyzed, reports written, and program decisions made. No mystery exists—just knowledge, thought, logic, and an element of creativity.

The keys to a successful program evaluation are: (1) the thoughtful integration of the evaluation as an essential component of the total gifted program, equal in importance to the identification system, the administration, or the curriculum and (2) the allocation of necessary time and resources to complete the task.

REFERENCES

Anderson, L. W. (1981). *Assessing affective characteristics in the schools.* Boston: Allyn & Bacon.

Babbie, E. R. (1973). *Survey research methods.* Belmont, CA: Wadsworth.

Best, J. W., & Kahn, J. V. (1986). *Research in education* (5th ed.). Englewood Cliffs, NJ: Prentice-Hall.

Bills, R. (1975). *A system for assessing affectivity.* Tuscaloosa: University of Alabama Press.

Bonjean, C., Hill, R., & McLemore, S. (1967). *Sociological measurement.* San Francisco: Chandler.

Borich, G. D., & Madden, S. K. (1977). *Evaluating classroom instruction: A sourcebook of instruments.* Reading, MA: Addison-Wesley.

Brinkerhoff, R. O., Brethower, D. M., Hluchyj, T., & Nowakowski, J. R. (1983). *Program evaluation: A practitioner's guide for trainers and educators.* Boston: Kluwer-Nijhoff Publishing.

Buros, O. K. (1972). *The seventh mental measurement yearbook.* Highland Park, NJ: Gryphon Press.

Campbell, D. T., & Stanley, J. C. (1966). *Experimental and quasi-experimental designs for research.* Chicago: Rand McNally.

Committee on Scientific and Professional Ethics and Conduct. (1977). Ethical standards of psychologists. *APA Monitor, 8,* 22–23.

Crandall, V. D., Katkovsky, W., & Crandall, V. J. (1965). Children's beliefs in their own control of reinforcement in intellectual academic situations. *Child Development, 36,* 91–109.

Cronbach, L. J. (1963). Course improvement through evaluation. *Teachers College Record, 64,* 672–83.

Cronbach, L. J. (1980). *Toward reform of program evaluation.* San Francisco: Jossey-Bass.

Doyle, K. O. (1983). *Evaluating teaching.* Lexington, MA: Heath.

Edwards, A. (1957). *Techniques of attitude scale construction.* New York: Appleton-Century-Crofts.

Feldhusen, J. F., & Kolloff, M. B. (1981). ME: A self-concept scale for gifted students. *Perceptual and Motor Skills, 53,* 319–323.

Fetterman, D. (1989). *Qualitative approaches to evaluation in education: The silent scientific revolution.* New York: Praeger.

Fielding, N. G., & Fielding, J. L. (1986). *Linking data.* Newbury Park, CA: Sage.

Fink, A., & Kosecoff, J. (1978). *An evaluation primer.* Washington, DC: Capitol Publications.

Franklin, J. L., & Thrasher, J. H. (1976). *An introduction to program evaluation.* New York: Wiley.

Gable, R. K. (1986). *Instrument development in the affective domain.* Boston: Kluwer-Nijhoff Publishing.

Gronlund, N. E. (1985). *Measurement and evaluation in teaching* (5th ed.). New York: Macmillan.

Jenkins, J. J., Russell, W. A., & Suci, J. (1958). An atlas of semantic profiles for 360 words. *American Journal of Psychology, 71,* 688–699.

Joint Committee on Standards for Educational Evaluation. (1981). *Standards for evaluations of educational programs, projects, and materials.* New York: McGraw-Hill.

Juntune, J. (Ed.). (1986). *Successful programs for the gifted and talented* (2nd ed.). St. Paul, MN: National Association for Gifted Children.

Kerlinger, F. N. (1973). *Foundations of behavioral research* (2nd ed.). New York: Holt, Rinehart & Winston.

Kubszyn, T., & Borich, G. (1987). *Educational testing and measurement: Classroom application and practice.* Glenview, IL: Scott, Foresman.

Labaw, P. J. (1980). *Advanced questionnaire design.* Cambridge, MA: Abt.

McMillan, J. H., & Schumacher, S. (1984). *Research in education: A conceptual introduction.* Boston: Little, Brown.

Nasca, D. (1983). *Evaluating gifted programs: Formative evaluation.* East Aurora, NY: DOK Publishers.

Nowakowski, J., Bunda, M. A., Working, R., Bernacki, G., & Harrington, P. (1985). *A handbook of educational variables: A guide to evaluation.* Boston: Kluwer-Nijhoff Publishing.

Nunnally, J. C., & Durham, R. L. (1975). Validity, reliability, and special problems of measurement in evaluation research. In E. L. Struening & M. Guttentag (Eds.), *Handbook of education research* (Vol. 1) (pp. 289–352). Beverly Hills, CA: Sage.

Oppenheim, A. N. (1966). *Questionnaire design and attitude measurement.* New York: Basic Books.

Orlich, D. C. (1978). *Designing sensible surveys.* Pleasantville, NY: Redgrave.

Osgood, C. E., Suci, G. J., & Tannenbaum, P. H. (1957). *The measurement of meaning.* Urbana: University of Illinois Press.

Patton, M. Q. (1987). *How to use qualitative methods in evaluation.* Newbury Park, CA: Sage.

Piers, E. V., & Harris, D. B. (1969). *The Piers-Harris children's self-concept scale.* Nashville, TN: Counselor Recordings & Tests.

Renzulli, J. S. (1975). *A guidebook for evaluating programs for the gifted and talented.* Ventura, CA: National/State Leadership Training Institute.

Renzulli, J. S. (Ed.). (1979). *Sample instruments for the evaluation of programs for the gifted and talented.* Storrs, CT: Bureau of Educational Research.

Robinson, J. P., & Shaver, P. R. (1973). *Measures of social psychological attitudes.* Ann Arbor, MI: Survey Research Center.

Rutman, L., & Mowbray, G. (1983). *Understanding program evaluation.* Newbury Park, CA: Sage.

Seeley, K. (1985). Evaluating programs for gifted learners. In J. F. Feldhusen (Ed.), *Towards excellence in gifted education* (pp. 163–176). Denver, CO: Love.

Shaw, M., & Wright, J. (1967). *Scales for the measurement of attitudes.* New York: McGraw-Hill.

Stake, R. (1967). The countenance of educational evaluation. *Teachers College Record, 68,* 523–540.

Stake, R. (1980). Program evaluation, particularly responsive evaluation. In W. B. Dockrell & D. Hamilton (Eds.), *Rethinking educational research* (pp. 72–87). London: Hodder & Stoughton.

Stufflebeam, D. L., Foley, W. J., Gephart, W. J., Guba, E. G., Hammond, R. L., Merriman, H. O., & Provus, M. M. (1971). *Educational evaluation and decision-making.* Itasca, IL: Peacock.

Van Maanen, J. (Ed.). (1985). *Qualitative research methods series.* Newbury Park, CA: Sage.

VanTassel, J. (1980). Evaluation of gifted programs. In J. B. Jordan & J. A. Grossi (Eds.), *An administrator's handbook on designing programs for the gifted and talented* (pp. 110–128). Reston, VA: ERIC Clearinghouse on Handicapped and Gifted Children.

Weiss, C. H. (1972). *Evaluation research: Methods for assessing program effectiveness.* Englewood Cliffs, NJ: Prentice-Hall.

Weiss, C. H. (1975). Interviewing in evaluation research. In E. L. Struening & M. Guttentag (Eds.), *Handbook of education research* (Vol. 1) (pp. 355–395). Beverly Hills, CA: Sage.

Weller, S. C., & Romney, A. K. (1988). *Systematic data collection.* Newbury Park, CA: Sage.

Whitmore, J. R. (1984). *Evaluating educational programs for intellectually gifted students (EEPIGS).* East Aurora, NY: DOK Publishers.

Whitmore, J. R. (1985a). *A Teacher Attitude Inventory (TAI): Identifying teacher position in relation to educational issues and decisions.* East Aurora, NY: DOK Publishers.

Whitmore, J. R. (1985b). *Thinking About My School (TAMS).* East Aurora, NY: DOK Publishers.

Williams, E. F. (1979). *Performance levels of a school program survey.* East Aurora, NY: DOK Publishers.

Wolf, R. M. (1984). *Evaluation in education: Foundations for competency assessment and program review* (2nd ed.). New York: Praeger.

Yarvorsky, D. K. (1976). *Discrepancy evaluation: A practitioner's guide.* Charlottesville, VA: University of Virginia Evaluation Research Center.

CHAPTER 14

TESTS IN PERSPECTIVE: THE ROLE AND SELECTION OF STANDARDIZED INSTRUMENTS IN THE EVALUATION OF PROGRAMS FOR THE GIFTED

Ann Robinson

Faced with the prospect of evaluating a program, educators intone "you get what you measure." Tests are powerful. They can drive program goals and instructional opportunities; they can increase program credibility or undermine it. In the education of the gifted, standardized tests have played a major role in identification, instructional adaptation, and program evaluation. In a comprehensive assessment of the knowledge base in the education of the gifted, Shore, Cornell, Robinson and Ward (in press) found the use of tests to be one of the most enduring practices.

In the area of program evaluation, the literature on the gifted is leavened with cautions about overreliance on standardized tests in the evaluation of these programs (Callahan, 1983; Reis, 1984). Student product assessments, program-specific questionnaires, classroom observations, and archival records are all offered as alternatives (Callahan, 1983; Reis, 1984; Rimm, 1982). The most frequent objections to the use of tests in evaluating programs include (1) the tenuous relationship between standardized, grade-level achievement batteries and the goals of specialized programs for the gifted and (2) the measurement limitations of ceiling effects and restricted range.

The problem can be conceptualized as the perceived inability of standardized tests to *capture* the extent and diversity of the complex outcomes of programs for gifted students and the need to provide data for decisions about program effectiveness in a credible and efficient way.

Is there a role for standardized instruments in the evaluation of gifted programs? If so, what kinds of standardized instruments exist?

How are appropriate instruments selected? Where can information about standardized instruments be found? What special issues affect instruments used in the evaluations of programs for the gifted? This chapter is organized to address each of these questions in turn.

THE ROLE OF STANDARDIZED TESTS

First, what is the role of standardized tests in the evaluation of gifted programs? Standardized instruments are those which have been field tested with appropriate norm groups and whose directions for administration have been written completely enough to minimize differences among testers and testing sessions. In addition, a technically sound score or scale system has been developed and relevant norms or criteria have been established to provide performance comparisons.

Some years ago, Renzulli and Ward (1969) and Renzulli (1975) developed a road map, or flow chart, for evaluating gifted programs according to key features of their DESEG model. In the larger context of a comprehensive program evaluation, they depict graphically that tests are only one of many sources of information (see Figure 14.1). However, despite cautions, test information is as powerful in the evaluation of gifted programs as it is in the identification of students for them.

Are there some rules of thumb for using test information as wisely as possible? Yes. In part, the appropriate use of standardized tests depends on the kind of evaluation being undertaken. Specifically, if the focus of the evaluation is to determine the effectiveness of the program in terms of student outcomes, a standardized test is far more important than if the purpose of the evaluation is to assess the level of implementation of the program.

A program evaluation may be judged along several dimensions:

1. Credibility
2. Relevance
3. Timeliness
4. Usefulness

If measures are used in the evaluation of a gifted program and are not considered credible, the evaluation has been uselessly conducted. The credibility of instruments is more sensitive in a summative evaluation than in a formative one.

Specifically, if the evaluator is to produce a statement about the effectiveness of a program and if the evaluation information is intended

FIGURE 14.1 Overview of the Key Features Evaluation system

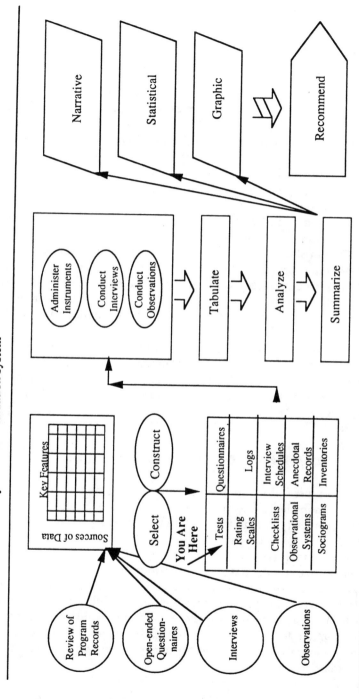

Adapted from J. S. Renzulli (1975), *A guidebook for evaluating programs for the gifted and talented.* Printed with permission from the National/State Leadership Training Institute on the Gifted and Talented (N/S—LTI—G/T), Office of the Superintendent, Ventura County Schools, Ventura, CA.

primarily for decision makers outside the program (summative evaluation), then the use of credible outcome measures is a primary concern. It may be that for these tough audiences, only test data will do. Standardized tests carry considerable weight with several evaluation audiences, for example, with administrators, school board members, and program funding agencies, particularly those at the federal level. If the persons who make up the evaluation audience believe that only the *hard data* of tests will convince them of the worth of the program, then including a standardized test appropriate to the goals and objectives of the program is advisable.

In contrast, if the purpose of the evaluation is to produce interim information for persons working in the program (formative evaluation), then standardized test data are considerably less important. These persons, who have a more intimate view of the program, may not need the technical rigor of standardized test scores or may need to sample student test information informally rather than examine it comprehensively. Particularly in the early stages of program development and formative evaluation, other kinds of measures, such as on-site observations and questionnaires, provide richer and more useful information to personnel.

In summary, standardized tests do have a role in the evaluation of gifted programs. They can provide high-quality, credible information to decision makers. However, as with all measurement issues, the professional who seeks to use these instruments should be mindful of the advantages and disadvantages of using standardized tests in the evaluation of gifted programs.

ADVANTAGES OF STANDARDIZED TESTS

The first and most self-evident advantage of using standardized tests in gifted program evaluation is to save time and money. Instrument development is technically demanding and literally doubles the time, possibly the calendar, for the evaluation.

Second, standardized tests with existing reliability and validity data are persuasive to decision makers and funding agencies. There is comfort in incorporating instruments with a *history* of prior use. They have been subjected to professional review and their applicability to field settings examined. Using an *outside instrument* may add an aura of objectivity, somewhat similar to the use of an outside evaluator. In addition, the increasing popularity of student performance evaluations encourages the use of standardized instruments.

A third advantage of standardized instruments is that the performance of students in the program being evaluated can be compared to other groups of students not being served, to norms, or to criterion-referenced benchmarks. These kinds of comparisons greatly increase the credibility of the information, particularly in summative evaluation.

LIMITATIONS OF STANDARDIZED TESTS

The greatest limitation of standardized instruments in the evaluation of gifted programs is the same as it is for all evaluations—a lack of congruence between the goals of the program or curriculum and the content or skills assessed by the instruments. A number of professionals have stated that the mismatch between program and instruments is especially severe in special programs for the gifted (Archambault, 1984; Callahan, 1983; Ganopole, 1982; Renzulli, 1975). Specifically, gifted programs often stress independent study and investigation or other process skills that are unlikely to be included or assessed in traditional achievement tests. Similarly, the availability of standardized tests that emphasize higher-order thinking and problem solving is limited (Baron, 1987; Quellmalz, 1985). With restricted choices, the difficulty in finding an already existing standardized instrument becomes more problematic.

Secondly, standardized tests, particularly those that are batteries or specialized achievement tests, may have ceiling problems for gifted students. In other words, a test normed on a heterogeneous sample may have too few items of sufficient difficulty to challenge the brightest students. Essentially, students are prevented from demonstrating what they know. In the case of norm-referenced tests, comparisons between groups of students when ceilings have occurred may mask real differences in performance. In the case of criterion-referenced tests, the specified criterion behaviors may not be complex or varied enough to reflect all the possible student gains due to the program. Further discussion of the problems associated with and suggestions for estimating ceiling effects are included below in the section on checking for ceiling effects.

KINDS OF STANDARDIZED INSTRUMENTS

Although the evaluation of a gifted program is dependent on its particular features, an inspection of program evaluations indexed in the Educational Resources Information Center (ERIC) bibliography indicates that four general kinds of instruments appear most often in gifted program evaluations (Jenkins-Friedman, Murphy, & Robinson, 1987). These areas are:

1. Critical thinking
2. Creative thinking
3. Specialized content achievement
4. Self-concept or self-esteem

Although self-concept instruments are not generally considered *tests*, they are included in this review because of their prevalence in evaluations of gifted programs and because issues of technical adequacy are as relevant to self-concept instruments as to achievement measures.

In a study of professional and parental judgments of the relative importance of various program objectives, Hickey (1988) found that the three most often cited are:

1. To provide a learning environment that will permit and encourage the capable student to develop his or her individual potential while interacting with intellectual peers.
2. To establish a climate that values and enhances intellectual ability, talent, creativity, and decision making.
3. To encourage the development of and provide opportunities for using higher-level thinking skills (analysis, synthesis, evaluation)

By examining the goals for programs for the gifted listed above, one can see the correspondence between goals and outcome measures related to the four areas into which the tests have been categorized. For example, critical thinking tests may be used to establish the effectiveness of a program in meeting goal 3.

The compendium of frequently used measures outlined in Table 14.1 is organized to provide basic descriptive information about each instrument. The compendium is not an exhaustive review; it is a sampling of some of the more frequently used measures. Neither should the compendium be considered an endorsement of the instrument. Where possible, citations for a review of the technical adequacy of the instrument are included. In addition, procedures for reviewing and selecting standardized tests are outlined below. The combination of published technical measurement reviews and a procedure for evaluating the specimen sets of instruments maximizes the chances for selecting the most appropriate instruments for evaluating gifted progrms.

LOOKING FURTHER FOR STANDARDIZED INSTRUMENTS

Several sources exist for locating standardized tests. Widely available reference books such as *Tests* (Sweetland & Keyser, 1984, 1986), *Tests in*

Print III (Mitchell, 1983), and the *Mental Measurements Yearbooks*, of which the ninth edition (Mitchell, 1985) is most current, are found in the reference sections of academic and large public libraries.

The Educational Testing Service (ETS) maintains a set of test bibliographies compiled by subject area, age, type of test, or specific population. The bibliographies are a part of the ETS Test Collection Service and may be ordered for a fee.

A third source of information is the published literature on evaluations of programs for the gifted. Such reports are scattered throughout professional journals and the ERIC computer data base. An annotated bibliography on programs effectiveness from these sources is available through the Council for Exceptional Children (Jenkins-Friedman et al., 1987).

PROCEDURES FOR SELECTING STANDARDIZED TESTS

Although it is more efficient to rely on published technical reviews, several of the instruments included in the compendium have not been reviewed by the *Mental Measurements Yearbooks* or *Test Critiques*. In addition, published reviews of new instruments, particularly those specially designed for use with gifted populations, may not appear in the literature quickly enough to be useful for program evaluators. Therefore, reviewing often falls to the prospective user. The following procedure from Salvia and Ysseldyke (1988) has been adapted to include information specific to the review of standardized instruments for gifted program evaluation (Robinson & Briggs, 1988). In addition to procedures for reviewing the technical adequacy of standardized instruments, this section also describes a method for determining how well a test fits a program, recommendations for selecting an out-of-level test, and procedures for determining ceiling effects. The seven-step procedure for reviewing the technical adequacy of standardized tests suggested by Salvia and Ysseldyke (1988) is discussed below.

REVIEWING FOR TECHNICAL ADEQUACY

Step 1: Secure Materials

Salvia and Ysseldyke (1988) suggest that the first step, securing a specimen set and manuals, is not as easy as it sounds. A specimen set generally provides the student booklet, answer key, and administration manual,

Text continues on p. 322

Table 14.1 Measures Used in Gifted Program Evaluation

Measure	Publisher	Grade (Age)	Types of Scores	Time	Reviews
1. Critical Thinking and Reasoning Tests					
Arlin Test of Formal Reasoning (Arlin, 1984)	Slosson Educational Publications 140 Pine St. East Aurora, NY 14052	6-12 (11-19 yrs.) Adult	Total (concrete, high concrete, transitional, low formal, high formal); 8 subtests: compensation, probability, correlations, combinatorial reasoning proportional reasoning, conservation, mechanical equilibrium, coordination of systems	45 min.	Fakouri, 1985
Cornell Critical Thinking Tests (2 levels, no alternates) (Ennis & Millman, 1985)	Midwest Publications P.O. Box 448 Pacific Grove, CA 93950	4-12 (level X) 13+ (level Z)	Total score; subtests include induction, deduction, observation, credibility, assumptions	50 min.	Michael, Devaney, & Michael, 1980
Developing Cognitive Abilities Test (alternate forms) (Beggs et al., 1980)	American Testronics 8600 W. Bryn Mawr Suite 910 N. Chicago, IL 60631	2-12	Total score and 3 subtest scores: verbal, quantitative, and spatial ability	50-60 min.	Fox, 1985 Karnes & Lee, 1984
Ennis-Weir Critical Thinking Test (Ennis & Weir, 1985)	Midwest Publications P.O. Box 448 Pacific Grove, CA 93950	7-college	Total score	60 min.	None available
Ross Test of Higher Cognitive Processes (Ross & Ross, 1976)	Academic Therapy Publications 20 Commercial Blvd. Novato, CA 94947-6191	4-6	Raw scores, percentile ranks; 8 subtests: analogies, deductive reasoning, missing premises, abstract relations, sequential synthesis, questioning strategies, analysis of relevant information, analysis of attributes		Bracken, 1985

318

Test	Publisher	Age	Scores	Time	Reviews
SEA (Synthesis, Evaluation, Analysis) Test (alternate forms) (Callahan, Covert, & Aylesworth, n.d.)	Bureau of Educational Research 275 Ruffner Hall Curry School of Education University of Virginia 405 Emmett St. Charlottesville, VA 22903	5-8 (gifted)	Raw, normalized scores, both objective and open-ended items, 5 general areas, including setting up experiments	Parts I & II, 20 min. each Part III, 30 min.	None available
Watson-Glaser Critical Thinking Appraisal (alternate forms) (Watson & Glaser, 1980)	The Psychological Corp. 555 Academic Court San Antonio, TX 78204	9+	Percentile rank for total score; 5 subtests: inferences, recognition of assumptions, deduction, interpretation, evaluation of arguments	40 min. or untimed	Woehlke, 1985

2. Creative Thinking Tests

Test	Publisher	Age	Scores	Time	Reviews
Creative Reasoning Test (2 levels, A & B; alternate form for B) (Doolittle, 1989)	Midwest Publications P.O. Box 448 Pacific Grove, CA 93950	Presecondary (level A) Secondary and college (level B)	t-scores and percentile rank for total score	30 min.	None available
Creativity Assessment Packet (Williams, 1986)	DOK Publishers P.O. Box 605 East Aurora, NY 14052		3 separate tests: Divergent Thinking (DT), Divergent Feeling (DF), & Williams Scale (WS); DT provides fluency, flexibility, originality, elaboration, and titles raw scores; DF provides subtest sores in curiosity, imagination, complexity, and risk-taking; WS is a parent or teacher rating scale	DT, 20-25 min. DF, 20-30 min. WS (not provided)	Fekken, 1985
Thinking Creatively in Action and Movement (Torrance, 1981)	Scholastic Testing Service 480 Meyer Rd. Bensonville, IL 60106	3-8 yrs.	Raw scores reported for fluency, originality, and imagination	15 min.	Renzulli, 1985 Rust, 1985

Table 14.1 *continued*

Measure	Publisher	Grade (Age)	Types of Scores	Time	Reviews
Torrance Tests of Creative Thinking (verbal & figural forms) (Torrance, 1966)	Scholastic Testing Service 480 Meyer Rd. Bensonville, IL 60106	K–grad school	Raw scores provided for fluency, flexibility, originality, and elaboration; scoring services provide comparative information	45 min. each (verbal & figural)	Chase, 1985 Treffinger, 1985
3. Specialized Content Achievement Tests					
Cooperative Mathematics Test (COOP) (alternate forms, 9 levels)	CTB/McGraw-Hill Del Monte Research Pk. 2500 Garden Rd. Monterey, CA 93940	7-9 8-9 high school college	Raw scores and percentiles (national norms and urban norms); tests include arithmetic, structure of the number systems, algebra I & II, geometry, trigonometry, algebra III, analytic geometry, & calculus	40 min. each (geom. & calc.: 2 40-min. sect. each)	Travers, 1972 Caldwell, 1972
Mathematics Applied to Novel Situations (MANS) (2 forms, 5 levels) (Herbert, 1984)	CEMREL c/o Martin Herbert 7227 Colgate St. Louis, MO 63130	2-6 (gifted)	Total & subtest raw scores, percentiles; subtests include computations, estimation, mental arithmetic, number presentation, relations and number problems, elucidation, word problems; special topics in certain levels include algebra, geometry, logic, organization of data, probability	30-60 min. (depends on grade level)	None available
Sequential Tests of Educational Progress (STEP)	CTB/McGraw-Hill Del Monte Research Pk. 2500 Garden Rd. Monterey, CA 93940	Preschool-12	Raw scores, national percentile rank, national stanines, local percentile rank, local stanines	40 min.	Floden, 1985

4. Self-Concept Instruments

Instrument	Source	Age	Content	Time	Reference
Barber Scales of Self-Regard (Barber & Peatling, 1977)	Union College Character Research Press 202 State St. Schenectady, NY 12305	2-5 yrs.	7 scales completed by teacher	Unavailable	Bartos, 1985
Behavioral, Academic Self-Esteem (Coopersmith & Gilberts, 1982)	Consulting Psychologists Press 577 College Ave. P.O. Box 60070 Palo Alto, CA 94306	Preschool-6	Teacher observation; global score	Unavailable	Sullivan & Guglielmo, 1985
Self-Perception Profile for Children (Harter, 1982)	University of Denver Dept. of Psychology Denver, CO 94306 Attn: Susan Harter HD09613	3-9	Four subscales: cognitive, social, physical, general	30 min.	None available
Piers-Harris Children's Self-Concept Scales (Piers, 1969)	Western Psychological Services 12031 Wilshire Blvd. Los Angeles, CA 90025	9-16 yrs.	Global score	15-20 min.	Cosden, 1984
Sears Self-Concept Inventory (Sears, 1966)	Not available	9-12 yrs.	9 subscales: physical ability, attractive appearance, social relations, convergent mental abilities, social virtues, divergent mental abilities, work habits, happy qualities, school subjects	Not timed	None available
Self-Esteem Inventory (SEI) (forms A & B) (Coopersmith, 1981)	Consulting Psychologists Press 577 College Ave. P.O. Box 60070 Palo Alto, CA 94306	9-15 yrs.		25 min. (Form A) 10 min. (Form B)	Adair, 1984

but the complete technical manual is not always included. It may have to be ordered separately. Test publishers differ in the listing and marketing of the various test components, so securing everything needed for a technical review may be a lengthy process. For example, the Raven Progressive Matrices, a nonverbal reasoning measure sometimes used in identification, is packaged so that the *Examination Kit* does not contain the North American norms. To examine the instrument thoroughly, you would also need to purchase the *Research Supplement Number 3*, which contains them.

Step 2: Organize Topics to Be Reviewed

Label separate sheets of paper for each topic to be considered:

1. Background and purposes
2. Behavior sampled
3. Scores
4. Norms
5. Reliability
6. Validity

Salvia and Ysseldyke (1988) suggest this procedure because manuals are organized differently and do not always index information so it can be located easily.

Step 3: Check for Test Relevance

To be most efficient, begin with behaviors sampled by the instrument. Jot down any lists of subtest titles found in the manual on a sheet labeled "behaviors sampled." The manual may list only the general behaviors, for example, critical thinking. However, a more thorough manual will list components or describe behaviors more completely to give a better picture of what is assessed by the instrument. For example, the manual for the Ennis-Weir Critical Thinking Test breaks down the construct of critical thinking into more specific behaviors, such as seeing reasons and assumptions, stating one's point, and seeing other possibilities.

These kinds of descriptions are useful to you because they provide information about the match between the goals of the program to be evaluated and the outcome behaviors sampled by the instrument. If few behaviors sampled by the instrument are considered important by the evaluator, then the review of this instrument can be quickly terminated to save time. There is no need to review the reliability data or validity sections if behaviors are not what will interest the audience for the evaluation. Another quick check for instrument appropriateness is obviously to scan the actual instrument items. If they do not look like content, skills, or other outcomes considered important in the program, the instrument is a poor match with program goals. Eliminate it as a possible choice. If the instrument is relevant to the program goals and objectives, then briefly jot down the behaviors sampled on the appropriate labeled sheet.

Step 4: Examine the Norms

In deciding to review a test, you should already have done a quick check to determine if the instrument is appropriate for the ages of the students. In the case of achievement tests, the decision whether to use out-of-level testing should be taken into account now. If it is necessary to test out of level in order to ameliorate the problems of ceiling, then the test should provide a range of levels at minimum one to two years above the oldest grade level to be evaluated. If the test does not *cover* the necessary age or grade ranges, eliminate it as a possible choice. Recall that the age and grade levels reported in the manual may not be an exact match if out-of-level testing is being considered. For example, a science problem-solving measure developed for heterogeneous students in grades 4–6 should not be eliminated automatically as a possible choice for the evaluation of a special science program for grades 3–4. If out-of-level testing is a possibility, then the test should be retained for review. If the instrument is appropriate for the ages or grade levels of the students in the program being evaluated, then proceed to examine the other characteristics of the norm groups. These should be presented numerically. The total number of students should be categorized by age or grade, by gender, and by ethnicity. Geographic distributions are also important. If the norm groups are small (and this is the case for some instruments normed only on a gifted sample), then information on the urban, suburban, or rural school attendance is also important. In addition, you may find that explicit reference is made to inclusion of identified gifted students in the sample. A heterogeneous sample would be expected to include gifted students, but some instruments, such as the Cornell Critical Thinking Test, explicitly state that identified gifted students are in the sample.

Salvia and Ysseldyke (1988) encourage you to look for an explicit comparison of the characteristics of the norm group with the most recent census conducted prior to the publication of the instrument. Further, they recommend a 5 percent correspondence between the sample and the population. In other words, if the most recent census indicates that 17% of the school-age population is African-American and the norm sample for the test is 14% African-American, the differences are not alarming. If, on the other hand, the census reported that 36% of the U.S. population lives in the Northeast and only 2% of the norm sample was drawn from this area, then you may be more wary of the technical adequacy of the norm sample.

Step 5: Determine the Types of Scores

The kinds of scores reported as a result of testing become quite important for the purpose of program evaluation. Salvia and Ysseldyke (1988) point out that the information about scores may be located in several places in the manual, but the most efficient location is the norm table. There you can locate subtest or total scores and will be able to find raw scores and derived scores if they are available. Well-labeled tables provide a raw score, standard score, and percentile ranks. The availability of a raw or easily interpretable standard score is a key issue for program evaluations that include statistical comparisons between groups of students. "Easily interpretable" here is defined as providing the means and standard deviations of the raw and/or standard score distributions. Instruments that report only percentile ranks are not useful for program evaluations employing inferential statistics, because comparative calculations become very difficult to make with these kinds of scores. If the evaluation design requires a test of differences between students served and not served, then an instrument that does not report raw or standard scores or provide a conversion table should be discarded as a choice.

Step 6: Evaluate the Reliability

According to Salvia and Ysseldyke (1988), reviewers should demand numbers. Verbal descriptions of an instrument's reliability are not enough to be convincing. The most technically sophisticated manuals will report reliability coefficients for each subtest score or for each age or grade level. Reviewers should determine what scores are to be interpreted and make note of those reliabilities. Some tests, for example, the Math Applied to Novel Situations (MANS), recommend the use of total scores only, even though subtests exist. Other tests, such as the Developing Cognitive Abilities Test (DCAT), are designed to provide interpretable subtest scores.

In addition, the technical manual should identify the kind of reliability coefficients reported. Both test/retest and item generalizations (internal consistency) are appropriate. For open-ended responses, interrater reliabilities should be reported. For example, the Synthesis, Evaluation and Analysis Test (SEA) contains both objective and open-ended items. The SEA Test manual reports test/retest, internal consistency, and inter-rater reliabilities.

Once appropriate reliability coefficients are located in the manual, you must judge them for adequacy. If given a choice among equally attractive tests, the choice is clearly the test with the highest reliability coefficient. However, the purpose for which the test is being used also affects judgments about its reliability. Salvia and Ysseldyke (1988) recommend that group tests like those used in program evaluations should have reliabilities of .60 or above. In contrast, tests used to make decisions about an individual student should be much higher, .80 for screening and .90 if used for placing children in a special program. Aylesworth (1984) cautions that the reliability coefficients reported in manuals are generally calculated on samples of heterogeneous students. Because of the possibility of ceiling effects and inappropriate norms, the reliability of the instrument will be somewhat lower for a sample of gifted students.

Step 7: Judge Test Validity

Determining a test's validity is an equivocal business. You must consider a number of factors and examine several different parts of the technical manual and promotional material.

The adequacy of the norms and reliability data contributes to a test's validity. However, the key issue at this point in the review process is to determine if the test tests the domain it purports to test. Salvia and Ysseldyke (1988) point out that some manuals address *content validity* in the section of the test manual on the development of the test. Here, the authors may give a rationale for their instrument because other tests on the market fail to tap the important domains. By examining their claims, you are able to get a "feel" for the content validity of the test.

Other kinds of validity data may also appear in the manual. Although it would be less common among tests used for program evaluation than tests used in the identification procedure, a manual might report the effectiveness of the test in terms of how well it predicted performance in school or adult life. This will be identified as *predictive validity* in the manual. In addition, tests with a research base will include studies of the relationship between the test under review and another test that has wider acceptance as a valid measure of the domain.

However, in the final analysis, the crucial factor in assessing the validity of a test for program evaluation is whether or not it measures any of the program goals. For example, in the manual of the SEA Test, the authors explicitly caution that using the SEA Test is inappropriate for gifted programs that do not have critical thinking as one of their goals.

Although it is possible to discard tests that have little relevance to the problem by browsing informally, selecting one test over another when both appear to be likely choices requires more thorough examination. Morris, Fitz-Gibbon, and Lindheim (1987) report a procedure developed by the Center for the Study of Evaluation for estimating the match between program goals and test items. The procedure, attributed to Walker and colleagues (1979), guides you in constructing quantitative indices for the proportion of items on a standardized instrument that are relevant to the program. These indices include:

1. The proportion of the program objectives covered by the test
2. The number of items per objective, and an overall index of the test-program match
3. The grand average

You can refer to Morris, Fitz-Gibbon, and Lindheim (1987) for a step-by-step explanation for calculating such indexes. Thus the final question you ask in deciding to use a test for evaluating a gifted program is whether or not it matches the goals of the program. If it does not, no matter how well it meets the other standards for adequacy—norms, reliability—eliminate it as a possible choice. Select another test and begin the review process again.

CHECKING FOR CEILING EFFECTS

Because many standardized instruments, particularly achievement batteries, are constructed for grade-level performance, ceiling effects are a problem for gifted students. Using an out-of-level test—in this case, another test or a higher level of the same test—may be necessary in order to allow possible gains to be detectable. In evaluations of gifted programs, it is advisable to check previous assessments or to pilot the test with a group of students to determine if ceiling effects are operating. Ceiling effects can be detected in two ways.

First, check the shape of the distribution of scores by graphing them. If the distribution for a norm-referenced test is negatively skewed (to the left)—that is, many scores are clustered in the high range—ceiling effects may be operating.

To check further, determine the average raw score for a previous sample or for the pilot groups of gifted students. Archambault (1984) suggests that ceiling effects are likely if the average score of the groups is greater than three-fourths of the maximum possible score.

For example, the Ross Test of Higher Cognitive Processes has 105 items, each worth 1 raw score point, for a total maximum possible score of 105. If the average score of the pilot group exceeds 78, ceiling effects are a problem for the evaluation. Although ceiling effects are possible on any standardized instrument, they are a particular problem for grade-level achievement tests or other tests of academic content. Specifically, if subject-matter acceleration is a major component of the program being evaluated, using grade-level achievement tests is doubly suspect because of possible ceiling effects and a possibly poor match between test content and program goals.

SPECIAL CONCERNS IN EVALUATING PROGRAMS FOR THE GIFTED

Two areas of concern in evaluating programs for the gifted are related to measurement issues. These are the problems associated with cultural bias and complex outcomes.

The issue of *cultural bias* haunts all educational endeavors involving standardized tests. The evaluation of gifted programs is no exception. When selecting a test, you should ferret out information on cultural bias. Research studies of ethnic and cultural differences are one source of information. Technical reviews generally address issues of cultural bias, particularly if the test is biased. However, explicit information on bias may not be available. In such cases, return to information in the technical manual. If the norm sample included members of ethnic and cultural groups in relation to their numbers in the population at large, bias is less likely.

A second issue involves *complex outcomes*. The goals of gifted programs involve higher-order thinking, independent study skills, and other sophisticated behaviors. Standardized tests, particularly those with a multiple-choice format, have been criticized for being too low level to evaluate these complex outcomes. The call for standardized measures that better assess higher-order thinking has begun to appear in general education (Beyer, 1987; Cohen, 1988; Quellmalz, 1985) as well as in the education of the gifted. Consequently, additional, innovative measures relevant to the goals of gifted programs are likely to be developed, thus increasing the repertoire of standardized instruments at your disposal. By selecting item content and formats that encourage interpretation rather than memory and by increasing the use of free response items, standardized tests will be able to assess complex outcomes more credibly.

A related issue is that educational programs for gifted students may be highly individualized. For example, programs for the gifted that are based on the use of individualized educational plans may not be able to articulate common objectives. Thus the use of standardized group tests relevant to preselected goals may not be appropriate for all students in the program. In such cases, the evaluation should include other measures, such as product assessment.

SUMMARY

In conclusion, standardized tests can play a role in the evaluation of programs for the gifted. In particular, when decision makers demand information for summative purposes, the use of standardized tests lends credibility to the evaluation. When the goals of the program include critical or creative thinking, standardized tests may provide useful information. And finally, in programs for the gifted that include subject-matter acceleration, standardized tests of specialized content document high-level achievement. Tests do have a valuable role to play in the evaluation of programs for the gifted. If selected on the basis of technical adequacy—which includes a lack of cultural bias and attention to complex outcomes—and, above all, with relevance to program goals, standardized instruments can inform both formative and summative evaluations of specialized programs for the gifted.

REFERENCES

Adair, F. L. (1984). [Review of *Self-Esteem Inventory*]. *Test Critiques, 1*, 226–232.

Archambault, F. X. (1984). Measurement and evaluation concerns in evaluating programs for the gifted. *Journal for the Education of the Gifted, 7*, 12–25.

Arlin, P. K. (1984). *Arlin Test of Formal Reasoning*. East Aurora, NY: Slosson Educational Publications.

Aylesworth, M. (1984). Guidelines for selecting instruments in evaluating programs for the gifted. *Journal for the Education of the Gifted, 7*, 38–44.

Barber, L. W., & Peatling, J. H. (1977). *A manual for the Barber Scale of Self-Regard—Preschool Form*. Schenectady, NY: Character Research Press.

Baron, J. B. (1987). Evaluating thinking skills in the classroom. In R. J. Sternberg & J. B. Baron (Eds.), *Teaching thinking skills: Theory and practice* (pp. 221–247). New York: Freeman.

Bartos, R. B. (1985). [Review of *Barber Scales of Self-Regard*]. *Test Critiques, 4*, 48–57.

Beggs, D., Mouw, J., Cawley, J., Wick, J., Smith, J. Cherkes, M., Fitzmaurice, A.,

& Cawley, L. (1980). *Developing Cognitive Abilities Test*. Glenview, IL: Scott, Foresman.

Beyer, B. K. (1987). *Practical strategies for the teaching of thinking*. Boston: MA: Allyn & Bacon.

Bracken, B. A. (1985). [Review of *Ross Test of Higher Cognitive Processes*]. *Ninth Mental Measurements Yearbook, 2*, 1298–1299.

Buros, O. K. (1982). *Eighth mental measurements yearbook*. Highland Park, NJ: College Board Publications.

Caldwell, J. R. (1972). [Review of *Cooperative Mathematics Tests: Algebra III*]. *Seventh Mental Measurements Yearbook, 2*, 896–897.

Callahan, C. (1983). Issues in evaluating programs for the gifted. *Gifted Child Quarterly, 27*, 3–7.

Callahan, C., Covert, R., Aylesworth, M., & Vanco, P. (n.d.). *SEA (Synthesis, Evaluation, Analysis) Test*. Charlottesville, VA: Bureau of Educational Research, University of Virginia.

Chase, C. I. (1985). [Review of the *Torrance Tests of Creative Thinking, Verbal and Figural Forms*]. *Ninth Mental Measurements Yearbook, 2*, 1630–1632.

Cohen, M. (1988). *Restructuring the education system: Agenda for the 1990's*. Washington, DC: Center for Policy Research National Governor's Association.

Coopersmith, S. (1981). *Manual for the Self-Esteem Inventories*. Palo Alto, CA: Consulting Psychologists Press.

Cosden, M. (1984). [Review of *Piers-Harris Children's Self-Concept Scale*]. *Test Critiques, 1*, 511–521.

Ennis, R. H., & Millman, J. (1985). *Cornell Critical Thinking Test, Levels X and Z*. Pacific Grove, CA: Midwest Publications.

Ennis, R. H., & Weir, E. (1985). *Ennis-Weir Critical Thinking Essay Test*. Pacific Grove, CA: Midwest Publications.

Fakouri, M. E. (1985). [Review of *Arlin Test of Formal Reasoning*]. *Test Critiques, 2*, 40–44.

Fekken, G. C. (1985). [Review of *Creativity Assessment Packet*]. *Test Critiques, 2*, 211–215.

Floden, R. E. (1985). [Review of *Sequential Tests of Educational Progress*]. *Ninth Mental Measurements Yearbook, 2*, 1363–1364.

Fox, L. H. (1985). [Review of *Developing Cognitive Abilities Test*]. *Ninth Mental Measurements Yearbook, 1*, 460–461.

Ganopole, S. J. (1982). Measuring the educational outcomes of gifted programs. *Roeper Review, 5*, 4–7.

Herbert, M. (1984). *Mathematics Applied to Novel Situations*. St. Louis, MO: CEMREL.

Hickey, G. (1988). Goals for gifted programs: Perceptions of interested groups. *Gifted Child Quarterly, 32*, 231–233.

Jenkins-Friedman, R., Murphy, D., & Robinson, A. (1987). *The effectiveness of programs for the gifted*. Reston, VA: Council for Exceptional Children.

Karnes, F. A., & Lee, L. (1984). Cognitive abilities of gifted students as measured by the Developing Cognitive Abilities Test. *Journal for the Education of the Gifted, 7,* 170–177.

Michael, J. J., Devaney, R. L., & Michael, W. B. (1980). The factorial validity of the Cornell Critical Thinking Test for a junior high school sample. *Educational and Psychological Measurement, 40,* 437–450.

Mitchell, J. V., Jr. (Ed.). (1983). *Tests in Print III.* Lincoln: University of Nebraska Press.

Mitchell, J. V., Jr. (Ed.). (1985). *Mental measurements yearbook* (9th ed.). Highland Park, NJ: Gryphon.

Morris, L. L., Fitzl-Gibbon, C. T., & Lindheim, C. (1987). *How to measure performance and use tests.* Newbury Park, CA: Sage.

Quellmalz, E. S. (1985). Needed: Better methods for testing higher-order thinking skills. *Educational Leadership, 43*(2), 29–35.

Reis, S. M. (1984). Avoiding the testing trap: Using alternative assessment instruments to evaluate programs for the gifted. *Journal for the Education of the Gifted, 7,* 45–59.

Renzulli, J. S. (1975). *A guidebook for evaluating programs for the gifted and talented.* Ventura, CA: National/State Leadership Training Institute on the Gifted and Talented.

Renzulli, J. S. (1985). [Review of *Thinking Creatively in Action and Movement*]. *Ninth Mental Measurements Yearbook, 2,* 1619–1620.

Renzulli, J. S., & Ward, V. S. (1969). *Diagnostic and Evaluative Scales for Differential Education for the Gifted.* Storrs: University of Connecticut.

Rimm, S. (1982). Evaluation of gifted programs—Easy as ABC. *Roeper Review, 5,* 8–11.

Robinson, A., & Briggs, K. (1988, November). *Evaluation sampler.* Paper presented at the Annual Convention of the National Association of Gifted Children, Orlando, FL.

Ross, J. D., & Ross, C. M. (1976). *Ross Test of Higher Cognitive Processes.* Novato, CA: Academic Therapy Publications.

Rust, J. O. (1985). [Review of *Thinking Creatively in Action and Movement*]. *Ninth Mental Measurements Yearbook, 2,* 1621.

Salvia, J., & Ysseldyke, J. E. (1988). *Assessment in special and remedial education* (4th ed.). Boston: Houghton Mifflin.

Sears, P. S. (1966). *Memorandum with respect to the use of the Sears Self-Concept Inventory.* (Available from Dr. Pauline S. Sears, 1770 Bay Laurel Drive, Menlo Park, CA 94025)

Shore, B. M., Cornell, D. G., Robinson, A., & Ward, V. S. (in press). *Recommended practices in gifted education: A critical analysis.* New York: Teachers College Press.

Sullivan, A. P., & Guglielmo, R. (1985). [Review of *Behavioral Academic Self-Esteem*]. *Test Critiques, 3,* 35–42.

Sweetland, R. C., & Keyser, D. J. (1984). *Tests supplement: A comprehensive reference for assessments in psychology, education, and business.* Kansas City, MO: Test Corporation of America.

Sweetland, R. C., & Keyser, D. J. (1986). *Tests: A comprehensive reference for assessments in psychology, education, and business.* Kansas City, MO: Test Corporation of America.

Torrance, E. P. (1966). *Torrance Tests of Creative Thinking, Verbal and Figural Forms.* Bensonville, IL: Scholastic Testing Service.

Torrance, E. P. (1981). *Thinking Creatively in Action and Movement.* Bensonville, IL: Scholastic Testing Service.

Travers, K. J. (1972). [Review of *Cooperative Mathematics Tests: Algebra I and II*]. *Seventh Mental Measurements Yearbook, 2,* 894–895.

Treffinger, D. J. (1985). [Review of the *Torrance Tests of Creative Thinking, Verbal and Figural Forms*]. *Ninth Mental Measurements Yearbook, 2,* 1632–1634.

Walker, C. B., Dotseth, M., Hunter, R., Smith, K., Kampe, L., Strickland, G., Neafsey, S., Garvey, V., Bastone, M., Weinberger, E., John, K., & Smith, L. L. (1979). *Criterion-referenced test handbook.* (ERIC Document Reproduction Service No. ED 186 457)

Watson, G., & Glaser, E. M. (1980). *Watson-Glaser Critical Thinking Appraisal.* San Antonio, TX: Psychological Corporation.

Weiss, P., & Gallagher, J. J. (1982). *Report on education of gifted: Vol. 2: Program effectiveness education of gifted and talented students: A review.* Report for the Advisory Panel, U.S. Office of Gifted and Talented, Washington, DC.

Williams, F. (1986). *Creativity Assessment Packet.* East Aurora, NY: DOK Publishers.

Woehlke, P. L. (1985). [Review of *Watson-Glaser Critical Thinking Appraisal*]. *Test Critiques, 3,* 682–685.

ABOUT THE CONTRIBUTORS

Susan R. Amidon is an Assistant Professor at Lamar University in Beaumont, Texas. She has been a teacher and coordinator in gifted programs and has authored articles in gifted education.

J. William Asher is a Professor of Education and Psychological Sciences at Purdue University. He received the Best Research Paper award in 1986 from the National Association of Gifted Children. In addition, he is the author of two texts on research and education.

Nina K. Buchanan is an Assistant Professor of Education and Consultant to the Center for Native Hawaiian Gifted and Talented Children at the University of Hawaii, Hilo. She has designed, taught, and coordinated gifted programs and courses in gifted education in Montana, Indiana, California, and Hawaii.

Kyle R. Carter is a Professor of Educational Research, Dean of the Graduate School, and President of the Research Corporation at the University of Northern Colorado. His recent research is in gifted program evaluation, but he has also published articles on cognitive development of gifted children and classroom learning.

Pamela R. Clinkenbeard is presently an Associate Research Scientist in the Department of Psychology at Yale University and is also affiliated with the National Center on the Gifted and Talented. She coordinated the graduate program in gifted education at the University of Georgia and was Assistant Director for Educational Programs at the Duke University Talent Identification Program.

John F. Feldhusen, a nationally recognized leader in gifted education, is a Professor of Education and Psychological Sciences and the Director of the Gifted Education Resource Institute at Purdue University. He has written numerous articles and edited books on issues related to gifted education.

Reva C. Friedman (Jenkins) is an Associate Professor of Educational Psychology and Research and the Director of Graduate Studies for Educators of Gifted, Talented, and Creative Students at the University of Kansas. Her teaching and research interests include the creative process and affective issues impacting gifted students' adjustment.

Ronald H. Heck is an Associate Professor of Education at the University of Hawaii, Manoa. His research interests include organizations, policy making, and the evaluation of student learning.

MARILYNN KULIEKE is currently the Director of Research and Testing for Township High School District 214 in Arlington Heights, Illinois. Previously she was an evaluation specialist at the Center for Talent Development at Northwestern University, working on evaluation of gifted programs and conducting research on families of gifted students and personality characteristics of gifted adolescents.

SARA LUNDSTEEN is a Professor of Education at North Texas State University and Creative Studies Institute who specializes in early childhood and reading. She has written numerous books and articles that focus on language arts but include a variety of topics such as creativity.

SIDNEY M. MOON is completing her doctorate in gifted education and beginning a postdoctoral appointment in the family therapy program at Purdue University. She has taught and coordinated gifted programs as well as conducted qualitative studies of gifted students. Her research interests include qualitative research design, program development and evaluation, talent development, gifted family systems, and change processes.

DOUGLAS L. MURPHY is the Assistant Director for Research, Beach Center on Families and Disability at the University of Kansas. He was a classroom teacher and adjunct faculty member in educational measurement. His research interests include cognitive approaches to affective issues such as self-concept, perfectionism, and coping.

M. ELIZABETH NIELSEN is an Associate Professor in Special Education and Assistant Dean for Research for the College of Education at the University of New Mexico. She formerly taught and coordinated gifted programs and currently directs a Jacob Javits research grant to identify and provide programs for handicapped gifted students.

PAULA OLSZEWSKI-KUBILIUS is the Director of the Center for Talent Development, Northwestern University, where she directs the Midwest Talent Search program as well as a variety of educational programs for gifted students. She is actively engaged in research in areas such as intensive accelerated educational programs and social support structures for talent development.

FRANCES S. O'TUEL is an Associate Professor, Department of Education Psychology, University of South Carolina. She has authored one measurement and evaluation text and numerous articles about the cognitive development of gifted and average students.

MICHAEL C. PYRYT is a faculty member at the University of Calgary at the Centre for Gifted Education. He conducts research and teaches courses on gifted children, tests and measurement, and personality development.

ANN ROBINSON is an Associate Professor in the Center for Research on Teaching and Learning at the University of Arkansas at Little Rock. She has taught in classroom and gifted program settings, authored numerous articles on gifted programs, and currently directs a federally funded research project to identify and serve economically disadvantaged gifted students in the middle school.

RENA SUBOTNIK is Coordinator of Gifted Education at Hunter College in New York. She is currently conducting research in sex differences in mathematical achievement and continuing her earlier longitudinal study of Westinghouse Talent contest winners.

R. H. SWASSING is an Associate Professor at Ohio State University and author of a text on teaching gifted children and adolescents. In addition, he is the Coordinator of programs and Director of the Ohio State University Summer Institute for gifted students and Assistant Director of the Martin Essex School for the Gifted.

INDEX

Ability grouping, 232–233
Acceptance finding, 15, 21–23, 29
Achenbach, T. M., 105
Across-studies analyses, 230
Action plans, 15, 21–23
Adair, F. L., 321
Ahtola, O., 203
Aldrich, P. M., 234
American Educational Research
    Association Special Interest Group on
    the Intellectually Talented, 11
American Psychological Association
    (APA), 40, 42
    Publication Manual of, 34–35, 37, 42
Amick, D., 203
Amidon, Susan R., 137–156
Analysis of covariance (ANCOVA)
    and coding studies for meta-analysis,
        228–229
    in experimental research, 54
    in inferential statistics, 89
    MANOVA as alternative to, 207
    in program evaluation, 250
Analysis of variance (ANOVA), 92
    and coding studies for meta-analysis,
        229
    in comparing two or more means, 87–89
    factorial, 88
    in longitudinal research, 110–111
    MANOVA as alternative to, 207–208
    multivariate techniques as extensions of,
        203
    prediction methods as alternatives to,
        184–187, 198
    repeated measures, 88–89
Anderson, L. W., 284, 292, 295–296
Anderson, T. H., 153
Angleberger, N. W., 145, 150
Anthony, J. B., 10
Anthony, M. M., 10
Applied Imagination (Osborn), 15

Archambault, F. X., 315, 326–327
Arlin, P. K., 318
Ary, D., 53, 58, 61, 70–71, 73, 76–78, 81,
    84, 87
Asher, H., 212–213
Asher, J. William, 37–39, 159, 173–174,
    220–241
Association, measures of, 79–83
Aylesworth, M., 318, 325

Babbie, E. R., 301–302
Baer, D. M., 137, 142, 147, 152, 154
Baird, L. L., 181, 196
Baker, J. E., 137, 153
Baldwin, A., 202
Baldwin, L. J., 164
Ballering, L. D., 13
Baltes, P. B., 105
Barbe, W. B., 10
Barber, L. W., 321
Barlow, D. H., 137, 139–141, 145
Barney, W. D., 230–231
Baron, J. B., 315
Bartos, R. B., 321
Baselines, 141–148, 152
Bass, J. E., 21
Becker, B. J., 206, 216
Beckwith, A. H., 234
Beggs, D., 318
Benbow, C. P., 65, 96, 212
Benefits of Psychotherapy, The (Smith,
    Glass, & Miller), 225
Bentler, P., 216
Bernacki, G., 283
Berquist, C. C., 105
Best, J. W., 41, 286–287, 303–304
Best-evidence studies, 34, 226
Beyer, B. K., 153, 327
Bijou, S. W., 138–140
Biklen, S. K., 117, 119, 159–160, 162, 170
Bills, R., 284

337

Birch, J. W., 230-233, 239
Biserial correlation coefficients, 81-82
Bish, C. E., 10
Bivariate relationships, 79
Black, K. N., 43, 231, 233, 239
Blalock, P., 212
Bloom, B. S., 97, 145, 158, 161, 196
Bloom, M., 137
Bogdan, R. C., 117-119, 159-160, 162, 170
Bonjean, C., 284
Borg, W. R., 35-39, 41-43, 45, 48, 105,
    160-162, 173, 250, 258-259
Borich, G. D., 278-279, 284
Bounds, W. G., Jr., 60-61, 87
Bracken, B. A., 318
Bradley, R. H., 192-193
Bramble, W. J., 196
Bransky, P. S., 197-198
Brethower, D. M., 303-305
Briggs, K., 317
Brinkerhoff, R. O., 303-305
Brooks, W. D., 203
Brown, D. L., 252, 262, 264-265
Brown, S. D., 145-147, 150
Brunelli, E. A., 232
Buchanan, Nina K., 1-32, 111, 134, 161,
    275-310
Bunda, M. A., 283
Burks, B. S., 157, 160, 171
Buros, O. K., 110, 284
Burstein, L., 202
Busse, T. V., 232

Caldwell, J. R., 320
California Psychological Inventory (CPI),
    205, 207-208
Callahan, C. M., 47, 188, 248, 252, 263-264,
    270, 272, 311, 315, 319
Campbell, D. T., 56, 60, 100, 105, 142, 144,
    159, 163, 173, 250, 252, 254, 262, 267,
    279
Campbell, J., 137
Campbell, M., 161
Canonical analysis
    in determining relationship among
        indices of college performance and
        demographic variables, 210-211
    limitations of, 211-212
    in MANOVA, 209-212
Carey, R. G., 267

Carter, Kyle R., 1-2, 234, 245-274, 277
Case study research, 157-176
    clinical, 160-161
    construct validity of, 172-173
    data analysis in, 169-170
    data collection in, 168-169
    definition of, 158-160
    designs for, 163-165
    developmental, 161
    dissemination phase of, 170-172
    external validity of, 174
    in future, 175-176
    goals of, 159
    historical bias against, 158-159
    holistic designs for, 163
    implementation phase of, 168-170
    internal validity of, 173-174
    observational, 161-162
    one-shot, 159
    planning phase of, 166-168
    protocols for, 168
    reliability of, 174
    situation analysis, 162
    steps in conduct of, 165-172
    task analysis, 162-163
    types of, 160-163
    validity issues in, 172-174
Cattell, R. B., 205
Causal-comparative design, 265-266
Ceiling effects, 251-252, 326-327
Center for Native Hawaiian Gifted and
    Talented Children (Nā Pua No'eau),
    2-3
Center for the Study of Evaluation, 326
Central tendencies, measures of, 74-77
Chains of evidence, 168
Changing-criterion designs, 147
Chase, C. I., 320
Chi-square tests, 89-90
    in meta-analysis of enrichment pull-out
        programs, 236, 238
Choosing Elites (Klitgaard), 198
Chwalek, A. R., 33, 35, 43, 45-46, 48
Classical composers, using path analysis to
    predict eminence of, 213-215
Clinical case studies, 160-161
Clinkenbeard, Pamela R., 33-50
Closed-form items, 290-295
    sample of, 291
    scoring of, 302

Cognitive Abilities Test (CAT), 270
Cohen, J., 203, 209
Cohen, L., 34
Cohen, M., 327
Cohen, P. R., 203, 209
Cohort difference effect, 98
Coleman, J. M., 250
College performance indices, relationships to demographic variables, 210–211
Combination questions, 290–291
Combination reviews, 34
Committee on Scientific and Professional Ethics and Conduct, 284
Commonwealth Fund of New York City, 96
Comparison group problem
  in designing product evaluations, 261–265
  designs and techniques for, 262–265
  matching techniques and, 262–263
  retrospective pretesting for, 264–265
Context, input, process, product (CIPP) model, 259–261
Context evaluation, 259–261
Contingency coefficients, 80–82
Control group problem
  causal-comparative design for, 265–266
  correlational designs for, 266–267
  counterbalanced designs for, 263–264
  in designing product evaluations, 262–270
  nonequivalent control group design for, 268–270
  quasi-experimental designs for, 267–270
  time-series design for, 267–269
Convey, J. J., 33, 35, 43, 45–46, 48
Cook, T. D., 60, 100, 105, 159–160, 163, 173
Cooley, W. W., 211
Coomer, A., 157
Cooper, H. M., 34, 37, 47
Cooper, J. O., 138–143, 147, 149–150, 152
Coopersmith, S., 321
Cormier, W. H., 60–61, 87
Cornell, D. G., 12, 311
Cornell Critical Thinking Test, 234–235, 323
Correlations
  coefficients, 79–83
  control group problems and, 266–267

multiple, 83, 183–184
in prediction methods, 182–184
Cosden, M., 321
Council for Exceptional Children, Talented and Gifted (CEC-TAG), 11, 317
Courtright, R. D., 10
Covert, R., 319
Cox, C. M., 160
Cox, D. J., 28
Cramond, B., 13
Crandall, V. D., 284
Crandall, V. J., 284
Creative problem solving, 9–30
  acceptance finding in, 15, 21–23, 29
  and building background in gifted education, 9–15, 29–30
  and considering multiple perspectives, 13–15, 29–30
  ethnographic research and, 125
  example of, 23–29
  fact finding in, 15–18, 23–25
  idea finding in, 15, 20, 24, 28
  and identifying works in progress, 11–13
  problem finding in, 15, 18–20, 24–28
  solution finding in, 15, 20–21, 28–29
Cronbach, L. J., 247–248, 307
Cross-sectional designs, 107–109
Cullinan, D., 12
Cultural bias, 327–328
Curriculum evaluations
  counterbalanced designs to address control group problem for, 263–264
  nonequivalent control group design in, 268–270

Darlington, R. B., 209–211, 215
Data
  in case study research, 168–170
  demographic, 297
  description analysis of. *See* Descriptive statistics
  establishing dimensional characteristics of, 204–207
  in ethnographic research, 120, 124–128, 132–133
  exploring structural characteristics of, 207–212
  inferential analysis of. *See* Inferential statistics

Data (*continued*)

• methods for organization and analysis
of, 69–92

multimodal, eclectic approaches to
collection of, 168–169

in program evaluations, 256–257,
301–305

quantitative analysis of, 69–70

in single-subject research, 149–152, 154

Davidson, J. E., 212, 248

Delisle, J. R., 10

Denton, C., 195

Denzin, N. K., 119–120

Descriptive statistics, 70–83, 92

in analysis of informal evaluation data,
304

contingency coefficients in, 80–82

frequency distributions in, 74–75, 150

indices of location within distributions
in, 78–79

interval scales in, 73

measurement scales in, 71–74

measures of association in, 79–83

measures of central tendency in, 74–77

measures of variability in, 77–78

multiple correlation or multiple
regression in, 83

nominal scales in, 71

ordinal scales in, 71–73

partial correlation coefficients in, 82–83

Pearson product-moment correlation in,
80

percentile ranks in, 78

quartile deviations in, 77–78

ratio scales in, 73–74

Spearman rho coefficient in, 80

summary of, 83

variance and standard deviation in, 78

z-scores in, 78–79

Detterman, D., 151, 153

Dettmer, P., 19

Devaney, R. L., 318

Developing Cognitive Abilities Test
(DCAT), 184, 324

Developmental case studies, 161

Difference-oriented methods, 191–192

Dillon, D. R., 159

Discriminant analysis, 208–209

Dissertation Abstracts International, 11, 39,
227, 234

Doyle, K. O., 284, 287, 294, 302

Durham, R. L., 286

Dyche, B., 51–52, 54–55, 57–58, 60

Early entrance to school, meta-analysis on,
231–232

Ebel, R. L., 10

Ebmeier, H., 51–52, 54–55, 57–58, 60

Educational Resources Information Center
(ERIC), 39–40, 227, 233–234, 315, 317

Educational Testing Service (ETS), 317

Edwards, A., 278

Effect sizes, meta-analysis and, 222–224

Einstein, Albert, 30

Embedded designs, 163–164

Encyclopedia of Educational Research,
10–11

Ennis, R. H., 318, 322

Enrichment pull-out programs, meta-
analysis on, 233–239

Ericsson, K. A., 151, 153

Erikson, F., 175–176

Error variance, minimization of, 56

Ethnographic research, 114–135

access, entry, and rapport in, 118–119

case study research compared with, 162

data analysis in, 132–133

data collection and management in, 120,
124–128

examples of observation in, 122–124

field note management in, 128–132

in gifted education, 114–116, 134

measurement instruments in, 126–127

nature of reality in, 115–116

nonreactive, 122

products of, 133–134

project selection in, 116–118

quantitative research compared with,
114–116

question formulation in, 119–120

reactive, 120–122

sampling, exceptions, and transferability
of contexts in, 115

setting and time frame in, 115

steps in, 116–134

Experimental research, 51–67

ANCOVA in, 54

applications of, 62–64

case study research compared with, 159

characteristics of, 53

common problems related to, 64–66
ex post facto design for, 61–62
factorial design for, 59–60
generalizability and, 65–66
introduction to, 51–62
maxmincon principle in, 54–56
nonexperimental designs for, 60–62
pretest-posttest control group design for, 57–58
pretest-posttest multigroup design for, 58
purpose of, 52
quasi-experimental design for, 60–61
random assignment in, 56–57
Solomon four-group design for, 58–59
and use of standardized tests, 64–65
Exploratory research, prediction methods for, 197–198
Ex post facto research, 61–62
Eysenck, H. J., 224–225

Fact finding, 15–18, 23–25
Factor analysis, 204–207
Factorial design, 59–60
Fakouri, M. E., 318
Fekken, G. C., 319
Feldhusen, John F., 1–5, 43, 161, 165, 167, 231, 233–234, 239, 284
Feldman, D. H., 158, 161, 196–198
Feldman, R. D., 196
Ferguson, G., 203
Fetterman, D., 279
Fichter, G., 137
Fielding, J. L., 279
Fielding, N. G., 279
Field note management, 128–132
Fine, M. J., 61
Fink, A., 290, 292, 300, 304
Fischer, J., 137
Fiscus, E. D., 47
Fisher, R. A., 137
Fitz-Gibbon, C. T., 326
Flack, J. D., 157
Flay, B., 202
Fliegler, L. A., 10
Floden, R. E., 320
Flower, L., 162–163
Formative evaluations, 247, 255
Foster, W., 137, 159–160, 162, 175
Fox, L. H., 248, 318

Franklin, J. L., 281, 286
Free comment items, 290
Frequency distributions, 74–75, 150
Friedman (Jenkins), Reva C. *See* Jenkins-Friedman, Reva C.
Friedman Two-Way Analysis of Variance, 89
Fults, B. A., 250

Gable, R. K., 284, 292–293, 295
Gage, N. L., 45
Gall, M. D., 35–39, 41–43, 45, 48, 105, 160–162, 173, 250, 258–259
Gallagher, J. J., 10–11, 249
Ganopole, S. J., 248, 250, 315
Gardner, H., 2, 197, 248
Gary, A. L., 137
Gephart, W. J., 18
Gifted Child Quarterly, 1, 3, 11–12, 40, 47
"Gifted Persons" (Renzulli & Delisle), 10
Glaser, B. G., 158, 174
Glaser, E. M., 319
Glasman, N., 213–214
Glass, G. V., 220, 225, 229, 267
Glover, J., 137
Goertzel, M. G., 160, 196
Goertzel, V., 160, 196
Goetz, E. M., 137
Goetz, J. P., 114, 124, 159, 162, 166, 168, 170, 173–174
Goldberg, M. L., 10
Goldsmith, L. T., 158, 161
Good, C. V., 16
Goodnow, J. J., 97
Gowan, J. C., 10
Graham, D. L., 105
Green, K., 137
Greenberg, L. S., 123, 162
Gronlund, N. E., 278
Gross, M., 134, 157
Grossberg, I. W., 12
Guba, E. G., 115, 117, 159, 169, 171
Guglielmo, R., 321
Guidebook for Evaluating Programs for the Gifted and Talented, A (Renzulli), 284, 313
Guilford, J. P., 2, 206, 248

Hackett, G., 212, 214
Hall, M., 51–52, 54–55, 57–58, 60

Hamilton, W., 261
Handbook of Educational Variables
  (Nowakowski et al.), 283
Harrington, P., 283
Harris, C. W., 10
Harris, D. B., 284
Harris, J. J., 203
Hartman, R. K., 188
Hayes, J. R., 162-163
Hayslip, M., 10-11
Heath, S. B., 117, 120, 123, 128, 133, 135
Heck, Ronald H., 201-219
Hedges, L., 220, 222, 237
Henson, F. O., 137
Herbert, M., 320
Heron, T. E., 138-141, 143, 149-150
Hersen, M., 137, 139-141, 145
Heward, W. L., 138-141, 143, 149-150
Hickey, G., 316
Hill, R., 284
Hillocks, G., 222
Histograms, 74
Hluchyj, T., 303-305
Hocevar, D., 206
Hollinger, C. L., 43
Hollingworth, L. S., 157
Horner, R. D., 147
Horowitz, F. D., 197
How to Use Qualitative Methods in
  Evaluation (Patton), 302
Huck, S. W., 60-61, 87
Hunter, J. E., 220

Idea finding, 15, 20, 24, 28
Idea webbing, 43-44
Independent variables, 141
Inferential statistics, 70, 83-92
  in analysis of informal evaluation data,
    304
  comparing means of two samples in,
    85-87
  comparing proportions in, 89-90
  comparing two or more means in, 87-89
  levels of significance in, 85
  Mann-Whitney U test in, 86
  median tests in, 86
  population parameters in, 84-85
  sign tests in, 86-87
  t tests in, 85-86, 92
  Wilcoxin matched pair test in, 87, 92

Informal instruments. *See* Questionnaires
  and interviews
Ingle, R. B., 18
Input evaluation, 259-261
Instrument development
  gathering evidence of criterion-related
    validity for, 194-196
  refining theories for, 194
  using prediction methods for, 193-196
Integrative Research Review, The
  (Cooper), 37
Integrative reviews, 34
Intellectual Achievement Responsibility
  Scale, 284
Interobservation agreement, 152, 154
Interval scales, 73
Interviews. *See* Questionnaires and
  interviews
Iowa Test of Basic Skills, 236

Jackson, G. B., 220
Jacobs, L. C., 53, 58, 61, 70-71, 73, 76-78,
  81, 84, 87
Jenkins, J. J., 295
Jenkins-Friedman, Reva C., 12, 19-20,
  179-200, 202, 234, 315-317
Jensen, D. W., 157, 160, 171
Johnston, J. M., 139, 152
Joint Committee on Standards for
  Educational Evaluation, 279, 281-282,
  286-287, 303-304
Jones, B. F., 153
Jones, E. D., 47
Joreskog, K. G., 111, 206, 215
Joyce, B., 34, 45
Juntune, J., 284

Kahn, J. V., 286-287, 303-304
Karnes, F. A., 318
Karweit, N., 226
Katkovsky, W., 284
Keating, D. P., 248
Kellogg, R., 97
Kelly, K. W., 161, 165, 167
Kennedy, D. M., 134
Keppel, G., 191
Kerlinger, F. N., 9, 18-19, 54-56, 163, 173,
  203, 211, 304
Keyser, D. J., 316-317
Kidder, L., 173

Kim, J. O., 205
Kitano, M. K., 135
Klitgaard, R. E., 198
Knapp, T. R., 209
Koch, A., 13
Koepke, D., 202
Kolloff, M. B., 12, 234–235, 284
Kosecoff, J., 290, 292, 300, 304
Kramer, L. R., 135
Krasney, N., 42
Krathwohl, D. R., 46
Krepelka, E. J., 232
Kruskal-Wallis test, 88, 92
Kubszyn, T., 278–279
Kulieke, Marilynn J., 42, 69–92
Kulik, C. C., 232–234, 238–239
Kulik, J. A., 232–234, 238–239

Labaw, P. J., 287, 289
Larkin, J. H., 151, 153
Larsen, T., 202, 206, 216
Laubenfels, J., 10
Lauer, J. M., 159, 220
LeCompte, M. D., 114, 124, 159, 162, 166, 168, 170, 173–174
Lee, L., 318
Lefcourt, H. M., 28
Light, R. J., 35, 37
Likert scales
  categories and word sets for, 293
  description of, 292–294
  sample questionnaire directions for, 296
  sample questionnaire items using, 291
  scoring of, 302–303
Lin, H. T., 232–233, 239
Lincoln, Y. S., 115, 159, 169, 171
Lindheim, C., 326
Literature reviews, 33–49
  analyzing literature for, 42–44
  collecting literature for, 40–41
  construction of, 37–48
  contextualizing literature for, 46–47
  defining of, 34–37
  evaluating literature for, 41–42
  finding literature for, 38–40
  general advice on, 37–38
  helpfulness of, 35–36
  idea webbing for, 43–44
  recommended abstracts and indices for, 39–40
  recommended resources for, 38–40
  special concerns arising in, 36–37
  synthesizing literature for, 44–46
  what they are, 34–35
  what they are not, 35
  writing of, 47–48
Lockhead, J., 151, 153
Lohnes, P. R., 211
Lomax, R. G., 111
Long, J. S., 205–206
Long, T. J., 33, 35, 43, 45–46, 48
Longitudinal/developmental research, 95–112
  advantages of, 98–99
  amount and/or pattern of change in, 97
  antecedent events and later behaviors in, 97–98
  appropriateness of, 97–98
  compensatory equalization and, 103
  cross-sectional designs for, 107–109
  design issues in, 104–109
  and diffusion or imitation of treatment, 102–103
  and direction of causal influence, 102
  disadvantages of, 99–100
  early behavior and later behavior in, 97
  external validity of, 103–104
  gifted and, 95–96
  historical influences on, 100
  instrumentation and, 101
  internal validity of, 100–103
  maturational influences on, 100–101
  measurement problems in, 99–100
  methodology of, 104–111
  mortality and, 102
  objectivity in, 110
  preserving developmental information in, 97
  reliability in, 110
  resentful demoralization and, 103
  sampling in, 109
  selection and, 102
  statistical analysis in, 110–111
  statistical regression and, 101–102
  summary of major principles of, 111–112
  time-series designs for, 105–108
  validity issues in, 100–104, 110
Long-term creativity training programs, 232
Lowenfeld, V., 97

Lowery, J., 57, 59
Ludwig, G., 12
Lundsteen, Sara W., 114–136
Lutz, F. W., 134
Lutz, S. B., 134

McDermott, J., 151, 153
McGaw, B., 229
McGill, A. M., 210–211, 216
McLemore, S., 284
McMillan, J. H., 73, 300
Madden, S. K., 284
Maddux, C. D., 21
Magargee, E., 207
Maker, C. J., 157
Management plans, 256–259
Manion, L., 34
Mann-Whitney *U* test, 86
Mansfield, R. S., 232
Marcoulides, G., 202, 206, 213–214, 216
Marland, S. P., 1, 179, 245
Martin, C. E., 13
Mason, E. J., 196
Math Applied to Novel Situations
    (MANS), 324
Maxmincon principle
    controlling extraneous variance in, 55–56
    in experimental research, 54–56
    maximizing variance in, 55
    minimizing error variance in, 56
Maxwell, S. E., 208
Mayer, G. R., 147–148
Means
    and coding studies for meta-analysis,
        228–229
    in measuring central tendencies, 74–77
    of two or more samples compared,
        87–89
    of two samples compared, 85–87
Medians
    in measuring central tendencies, 74–77
    testing of, 86
Mental Measurements Yearbook (Mitchell),
    317
Merriam, S. B., 159
Merrill, M., 2
Meta-analysis, 220–239
    on ability grouping, 232–233
    advantages of, 220, 222–224
    coding studies for, 228–230

defining problems in, 227
disadvantages of, 224–226
on early entrance into school,
    231–232
effect sizes and, 222–224
on enrichment pull-out programs,
    233–239
examining studies for, 227–228
in gifted and talented education,
    230–233
locating studies for, 227
on long-term creativity training
    programs, 232
performance of, 226–230
problems in, 220–221
purpose of, 220
as research integration method, 231
review articles and, 34
theory building with, 222–226
Type I errors and, 232
Type II errors and, 221–223, 225,
    232
Methodological reviews, 34
Michael, J. J., 318
Michael, W. B., 19, 21, 318
Mill, J. S., 53
Miller, T. I., 225, 229
Millman, J., 318
Mills, C. J., 234
Mitchell, B. M., 245
Mitchell, J. V., Jr., 316–317
Mitzel, H., 10
Modes, 74–75
Monroe, W. S., 10
Montour, K., 160
Moon, Sidney M., 157–178
Morris, L. L., 326
Mowbray, G., 282–283, 286
Mueller, C., 205
Multidimensional-Multiattributional
    Causality Scale, 28
Multi-element designs, 147–149
Multiple-baseline designs, 145–147
Multiple-case study designs, 164–165
Multivariate analysis of variance
    (MANOVA), 207–212
    canonical analysis in, 209–212
    discriminant analysis in, 208–209
    example of, 208–209
    major assumptions of, 208

Multivariate techniques, 1, 201–216
and coding studies for meta-analysis,
228
determining appropriateness of, 215
as extension of univariate analysis,
203–204
factor analysis in, 204–207
and nature of giftedness, 202–203
path analysis in, 212–215
summary of, 216
uses of, 201–203
Murphy, Douglas L., 12, 19–20, 179–200,
315–317
Myers, R. E., 49

Narrative reviews, 34, 45
Nasca, D., 284
National Association for Gifted Children
(NAGC), 3, 11
Naturalistic Inquiry (Lincoln & Guba), 169
Nature's Gambit (Feldman), 196
Nero, D., 96
Nesselroade, J. R., 105
Newell, A., 162
Newland, T. E., 10
Nielsen, M. Elizabeth, 9–32, 234–238,
275–310
Noll, V. H., 10
Noonan, N., 10–11
Norms, 323–324
Norris, D. E., 10–11
Nowakowski, J. R., 283, 303–305
Nunnally, J. C., 286

O'Brien, D. E., 148, 150
O'Brien, M., 197
Observation
case studies based on, 161–162
in ethnographic research, 122–124
in single-subject research, 150, 152, 154
Oden, M. H., 160–161
Olkin, I., 222, 237
Olszewski-Kubilius, Paula M., 42, 51–92, 196
One-shot case studies, 159
Open-form questions, 289–290, 302
Oppenheim, A. N., 278–279, 287, 292, 297,
303–304
Orlich, D. C., 287, 290, 292–293, 298, 302
Osborn, A., 15
Osgood, C. E., 294–295

Otis-Lennon Ability Index, 51–52
O'Tuel, Frances S., 95–113, 206
Out-of-level testing, 252

Parke, B. W., 60–61
Parnes, S. J., 15, 30, 232
Partial correlation coefficients, 82–83
Path analysis, 212–215
Patton, M. Q., 160, 279, 283, 302, 307
Payne, D. A., 252, 262, 264–265
Pearson correlation coefficient, 182
Pearson product-moment correlation, 80
Peatling, J. H., 321
Pedhazur, E. J., 203, 211
Pennypacker, H. S., 139, 152
Percentile ranks, 78
Piaget, J., 97
Piers, E. V., 284, 321
Piers-Harris Children's Self-Concept Scale,
250, 284
Piery, F. P., 162
Pillemer, D. B., 35, 37
Pilot tests, for questionnaires, 298–300
Pitner, N., 206
Point-biserial correlation coefficients,
81–82
Popham, W. J., 182, 247
Posavac, E. S., 267
Postlethwaite, K., 195
Prediction methods, 179–199
advantages of, 189–190
as alternative to ANOVA design,
184–187, 198
application of, 184–187, 198
in applied settings, 187–196
correlations in, 182–184
deductiveness of, 181, 198
disadvantages of, 190–191
for exploratory research, 197–198
flexibility and, 180–181, 198
for instrument development, 193–196
key terms used in, 181–184
multiple correlations in, 183–184
for program evaluation, 191–193
quantitative research and, 180–181, 199
in research, 196–198
for selection and placement, 187–191
for theory testing, 196–198
time sensitivity of, 181, 198
value of, 199

Pretest-posttest control group design, 57–58
Pretest-posttest multigroup design, 58
Problem finding, 15, 18–20, 24–28
Problem statements
  in creative problem solving, 15, 18–20, 27–28
  in meta-analysis, 227
Process evaluation, 259–261
Proctor, T. B., 43, 231, 233, 239
Prodigy theory, 197
Program evaluation and review technique (PERT), 37, 258–259
Program evaluations, 245–328. *See also* Questionnaires and interviews; Standardized tests
  advice on, 270–272
  for appropriate educational decision making, 272
  and challenges unique to gifted education, 248–252
  CIPP model of, 259–261
  comparison group problem in, 261–265
  comparison groups in, 252
  and conceptions of giftedness, 248–249
  control problem in, 262–270
  counterbalanced designs for, 263–264
  creativity in, 272
  data analysis in, 302–305
  data collection in, 256–257, 301–302
  defining charge in, 255–256
  and design problems unique to product evaluations, 261–270
  and educational accountability/fiscal responsibility, 245, 270
  of enrichment pull-out programs, 233–239
  formative, 247, 255
  input from stakeholders in, 253–255
  investigating available instruments for, 284–285
  management plans in, 256–259
  matching techniques in, 262–263
  meaning of, 246–247
  with meta-analysis, 232
  multivariate techniques for, 202
  outcome decisions for, 306
  overview of key features of system for, 313
  planning and conducting of, 252–261, 280–302

proactive function of, 275
  problems of difference-oriented methods in, 191–192
  program outcomes and, 249–251
  purpose of, 247
  qualitative methods in, 192, 302
  regression discontinuity for, 192–193
  reporting results of, 259, 305–307
  research vs., 247–261, 275
  retroactive function of, 275
  retrospective pretesting for, 264–265
  summative, 247, 255
  using prediction methods for, 191–193
Projective sentence items, 290
Public Law 95-561, 202
Purposeful sampling, 124, 302
Pyryt, Michael C., 1, 201–219

Qualitative methods and research
  in analysis of informal evaluation data, 304
  case study research compared with, 160, 162
  in program evaluation, 192, 302
Quantitative analysis
  ethnographic research compared with, 114–116
  introduction to, 69–70
  prediction methods and, 180–181, 199
Quartile deviations, 77–78
Quasi-experimental designs, 60–61
  for control group problem, 267–270
Quellmalz, E. S., 315, 327
Questionnaires and interviews
  administration of, 301–302
  advantages and disadvantages of, 277–280
  closed-form items for, 290–295
  combination items for, 290–291
  conduct of, 280–302
  construction of, 287–298
  deciding on amount of information to collect with, 283
  deciding on analysis units for, 283
  deciding on whom to question in, 283–284
  demographic information for interpretation of, 297
  designing user-friendly formats for, 297–298

determining level of confidentiality for, 284

determining who is in charge of, 284

development of, 287-292, 295-298

directions for completion of, 295-296

establishing correct mindset for, 282

establishing reliability of, 286-287

establishing validity of, 286

evaluation reports based on, 305-307

generalizability of, 306-307

generating broad questions about program outcomes for, 285

guidelines for evaluating data from, 303-304

item-specific directions for, 296

key focus areas of, 276-277

letters of introduction for, 298-299

after mailing, 301

measuring attitudes with, 279-280, 284-285, 290-292

open-form questions for, 289-290, 302

pilot testing of, 298-300

prior to mailing, 301

program evaluations with, 275-307

rationale for, 277-279

recommendations for, 288-289

revisions for, 300-301

sample of, 291

selecting advanced organizers for, 282

selecting review panels for, 285

statistical analysis of data from, 304-305

at time of mailing, 301

translating key issues into variables for, 283

Ranking-scale items, 291-292

Raven Progressive Matrices, 322

Rawl, R. K., 206

Razavieh, A., 53, 58, 61, 70-71, 73, 76-78, 81, 84, 87

Reese, H. W., 105

Regression coefficients, 182-183

Regression discontinuity, 192-193

Reichardt, C. S., 160

Reis, S. M., 47, 311

Renzulli, Joseph S., 10, 188, 202, 212, 234, 236, 247, 249, 277, 282, 284, 312-313, 315, 319

Restricted comment items, 290

Reversal designs, 144-145

Review of Educational Research (RER), 39, 44

Review of Research on Education (RRE), 39, 44

Revised Children's Manifest Anxiety Scale, 206

Reynolds, C. R., 206

Rice, L. N., 123, 162

Rimm, S., 311

Risley, T., 142, 152, 154

Robinson, Ann, 47, 192-193, 311-331

Robinson, J. P., 284

Robinson, S. E., 207, 209, 216

Rogers, K. B., 40

Romney, A. K., 292, 294

Rose, L. A., 232-233, 239

Rosenberg, M., 119, 122, 124-125

Rosenthal, R., 196

Rosnow, R. L., 196

Ross, C. M., 251, 318, 327

Ross, J. D., 251, 318, 327

Ross Test of Higher Cognitive Processes, 54, 58, 251-252, 327

Analysis of Irrelevant and Relevant Information subtest of, 188-189

Rulon, P. J., 203

Russell, W. A., 295

Rust, J. O., 319

Rutman, L., 282-283, 286

Safran, J. D., 123, 162

Sage Publishers, 302

Salvia, J., 317-325

Sample Instruments for the Evaluation of Gifted and Talented Programs (Renzulli), 284

Sauernman, D. A., 19, 21

Scheiber, L. M., 21

Schmidt, F. L., 220

Scholastic Aptitude Test, 203-204

Scholwinski, E., 206

Schumacher, S., 73, 300

Science and Human Behavior (Skinner), 140

Scientific manipulation, 139-140

Scriven, M., 247, 249

Sears, P. S., 321

Seeley, K., 278

Selection and placement, using prediction methods for, 187-191

Self-concept instruments, 316
Self-reporting, 151-152
Semantic differential scales
  appropriate adjectives for, 295
  description of, 294-295
  sample questionnaire directions for, 296
  sample questionnaire items using, 291
  scoring of, 303
Shaver, P. R., 284
Shaw, M., 284
Shigaki, I., 96
Shore, B. M., 311
Sidman, M., 18, 139-140
Significance, levels of, 85
Sign tests, 86-87
Silver, P., 207-209
Silverman, F. H., 80
Simon, D. P., 151, 153
Simon, H. A., 151, 153, 162
Simonton, D. K., 213-216
Simple-choice items, 291-292
Single-case study designs, 164
Single-subject research, 137-154
  basic designs for, 140-149, 154
  changing-criterion designs for, 147
  criteria used in judgment of, 141-142
  emphasis of, 154
  future possibilities for, 153-154
  interobservation agreement for, 152, 154
  measurement and reporting in, 149-152,
    154
  multi-element designs for, 147-149
  multiple-baseline designs for, 145-147
  observational systems for, 150
  principles of, 138-140
  self-reporting for, 151-152
  tactics of, 139-140
  terminology used in, 141
  units of measurement in, 150-151
  withdrawal and reversal designs for,
    144-145
Sirotnik, K. A., 182, 202
Situational analysis case studies, 162
Skinner, B. F., 139-140
Slavin, R. E., 34, 39-40, 44-46, 225-226
Smilansky, M., 96
Smith, L. H., 188
Smith, M. L., 225, 229
Smith,Winberry, C., 208

Snow, R. E., 262
Social Science Citation Index (SSCI),
  39-40
Solomon, R. L., 58-59
Solomon four-group design, 58-59
Solution finding, 15, 20-21, 28-29
Sorbom, D., 111, 206
Sosniak, L. A., 97
Southern, W. T., 47
Spaeth, J., 212, 215
Spearman-Brown Prophecy Formula,
  235-236
Spearman rho coefficient, 80
Speck, A. M., 135
Sprenkle, D. H., 159
Stainback, S., 118, 132
Stainback, W., 118, 132
Stake, R. E., 159, 171, 277, 282
Standard deviations, 78
  and coding studies for meta-analysis,
    228-229
  in meta-analysis of enrichment pull-out
    programs, 235
Standardized tests. *See also specific tests*
  advantages of, 314-315
  cautions about overreliance on, 311
  ceiling effect and, 251-252, 326-327
  checking relevance of, 322-323
  compendium of frequently used, 316,
    318-321
  complex outcomes and, 327-328
  cultural bias in, 327-328
  determining types of scores resulting
    from, 324
  evaluating reliability of, 324-325
  examining norms for, 323-324
  in experimental research, 64-65
  judging validity of, 325-326
  kinds of, 315-316
  limitations of, 315
  objections to use of, 311
  organizing topics to be reviewed by,
    322
  persuasiveness of, 314
  procedures for selection of, 317-326
  in program evaluations, 250-252,
    277-278, 284-285, 311-328
  reviewing technical adequacy of,
    317-326

securing materials for, 317–322
sources of, 316–317
special concerns in, 327–328
as time and money savers, 314
Stanley, Julian C., 56, 65, 96, 142, 144, 173, 210–212, 216, 248, 250, 252, 254, 262, 267, 279
Stanley, T. D., 192–193
Stephens, T. M., 10
Sternberg, R. J., 2, 18, 40–41, 46–48, 151, 153, 197, 212, 248
Stone, M. H., 110
Strauss, A. L., 132, 158, 174
Strauss, S. M., 65–66
Structure-of-Intellect Learning Abilities Test (SOI-LA), 206
Stufflebeam, D. L., 255, 259–261, 275
Subotnik, Rena F., 51–68
subproblems, 19–20, 27–28
Successful Programs for the Gifted and Talented (Juntune), 284
Suci, G. J., 294–295
Suci, J., 295
Sugden, V. M., 16
Sullivan, A. P., 321
Sulzer-Azaroff, B., 147–148
Summative evaluations, 247, 255
Summing Up: The Science of Reviewing Research (Light & Pillemer), 37
Swanson, H. L., 1–2
Swassing, R. H., 137–156
Sweetland, R. C., 316–317
Synthesis, Evaluation and Analysis Test (SEA), 325–326

Tannenbaum, A. J., 164
Tannenbaum, P. H., 294–295
Task analysis case studies, 162–163
Tatsuoka, M. M., 207–209
Taylor, P., 51–52, 54–55, 57–58, 60
Taylor, S., 118
Terman, L. M., 1–2, 96, 112, 157–158, 160–161, 171–172
Test Critiques, 317
Tests (Sweetland & Keyser), 316–317
Tests in Print (Mitchell), 316–317
Theoretical reviews, 34
Theories
componential, 18, 207

grounded, 158
meta-analysis in building of, 222–226
prediction methods in testing of, 196–198
refining of, 194
Thompson, B., 209, 211
Thrasher, J. H., 281, 286
Three-ring approach, 248
Three-term contingencies, 138
Time-series designs, 105–108
control problem and, 267–269
Tisdall, W. J., 230–231
Tollefson, N., 12, 19–20, 61
Tomlinson-Keasey, C., 208
Torrance, E. P., 49, 202–203, 212, 232, 319–320
Torrance Tests of Creative Thinking (TTCT), 57–58, 151, 202, 270
Transient observers, 123
Travers, K. J., 320
Travers, R. M. W., 39, 42
Treffinger, D. J., 320
Tremaine, C. D., 265–266
Trials to criterion, 150–151
Triangulation, 120
t tests, 85–86

Van Dalen, D. B., 13, 16, 21
Van Maanen, J., 302
Van Tassel-Baska, J. L., 47, 161, 196, 277
Variables
demographic, 210–211
dependent, 141
endogenous and exogenous, 212–214
error, 56
in single-subject research, 141, 143, 145
translating key issues into, 283
Variance. *See also* Analysis of covariance; Analysis of variance; Multivariate analysis of variance
error, 56
extraneous, 55–56
Friedman Two-Way Analysis of, 89
maximization of, 55
measures of, 77–78
standard deviations and, 78
Variation ratios, 77
Vaughn, Vicki L., 233–234, 239

VonBaeyer, C. L., 28
Vote counting, 45

Wagner, R. K., 41, 46
Walberg, H. J., 203, 209–211
Walker, C. B., 326
Wallach-Kogan Instrument, 235
Ward, M., 206
Ward, V. S., 311–312
Ware, E. E., 28
Watson, G., 319
Webb, W. B., 16–17
Wechsler, D., 2
Weinberg, S. L., 209–211
Weiner, N. C., 207, 209, 216
Weir, E., 318, 322
Weiss, C. H., 275, 286–287, 292, 300–301,
    303–304, 306
Weller, S. C., 292, 294
Whimby, A., 151, 153
White, A. J., 188
Whitmore, J. R., 157, 284
Wiersma, W., 34, 37, 39, 41
Wilcoxin matched pair test, 87, 92
Wildt, A., 203
Wilks's lambda ratio, 207

Willer, J., 137
Williams, E. F., 284
Williams, F., 319
Winston, A. S., 137, 153
Wisnyai, S. A., 153
Withdrawal designs, 144–145
Witty, P., 10, 157
Woehlke, P. L., 319
Wohlwill, J. F., 97–98
Wolcott, H., 117, 119–120
Wolf, M. M., 142, 152, 154
Wolf, R. M., 275–277, 300, 302–304, 306
Wolf, W., 96
Wolfle, L., 111
Wooster, J., 202
Working, R., 283
Works in progress, identification of,
    11–13
Wright, B. D., 110
Wright, J., 284

Yarvorsky, D. K., 278
Yin, R. K., 157, 159–160, 162–164, 168–174
Ysseldyke, J. E., 317–325

Z-scores, 78–79